D0896802

Also by Robert J Mueller

Fields of War: Fifty Key Battlefields in France and Belgium
Fields of War: Battle of Normandy
The Bulge Battlefields
American Doughboys in the First World War
Pearl Harbor: A Day of Infamy

OPERATION MARKET-GARDEN:
AIRBORNE INVASION
OF THE
NETHERLANDS

A FIELDS OF WAR VISITOR'S GUIDE TO HISTORIC SITES

ROBERT J MUELLER

Robert J Mueller

French Battlefields
Arlington Heights

French Battlefields
PO Box 4808
Buffalo Grove, Illinois 60089-4808
Fax: 1-224-735-3478
Email: contact@frenchbattlefields.com
Web address: http://www.frenchbattlefields.com

Copyright 2021 by Robert J Mueller
All rights reserved
Cover design by Vince Martinez
First Edition
Manufactured in the United States
Library of Congress Control Number: 2020922442
ISBN-13: 978-0-9823677-8-0
Unless otherwise indicated, all photographs and illustrations are the property of the author. No part of this book may be reproduced or transmitted without the written permission of the publisher.

Cover photographs:
Main image: The Parachute Memorial to the 82nd Airborne Division stands on the edge of Drop Zone 'O' in Overasselt.
Time line:
– British paratroopers with Sten sub-machine guns move through a shell-damaged house in Oosterbeek. (IWM – BU1121)
– The Airborne Memorial in Oosterbeek with the figure of Liberty topping the column.
– Cromwell tanks of Guard's Armoured Division drive along 'Hell's Highway' towards Nijmegen on 20 September 1944. (IWM – B 10131)
Spine: A section of the base of the Liberation Memorial in Eindhoven depicting the invading German Army.
Rear cover: John Frost Bridge, Arnhem

Abbreviations used for photographs:
NARA: National Archives and Records Administration, College Park, Maryland
IWM: Imperial War Museum, Lambeth Road, London
Bundesarchiv: German Federal Archives, Koblenz, Rhineland-Palatinate, Germany

Dedicated to:
Ted, Roger, Art, Al, Madeleine, and Judy

In Peace, sons bury their fathers

In War, fathers bury their sons

-Herodotus

Introduction ix
Chapter One
    Operation Market-Garden Summary 1
Chapter Two
    Guards Armoured Division 14
        Battle of Hechtel 14
        Capture of JOE's Bridge 16
        Eindhoven 34
        Side Trip: Netherlands American Cemetery 36
        Side trip: Stirling Heavy Bomber Crash Site 38
        Side Trip: 'Clay Pigeon' and 'Piccadilly Filly' Crash Site 38
        Side Trip: Mierlo War Cemetery and Mierlo-Hout Memorial 41
        Side Trip: Ysselsteyn (IJsselsteyn) German War Cemetery 42
        Side Trip: Battle of Overloon 43
Chapter Three
    American 101st Airborne Division 'Screaming Eagles' 48
        Son Bridge and Entry into Eindhoven 51
        Battle for the Best Bridge 63
        Capture of Sint-Oedenrode 70
        Capture of Veghel 75
        Defense of Hell's Highway 77
        Battle of Heeswijk-Dinther 79
        Battle of Schijndel 79
        Battle of Veghel 82
        Battle of the Sand Dunes 85
        Battle of Koevering 86
        Side Trip: Sint-Michielsgestel 100
        Side Trip: Vught Concentration Camp 101
        Side Trip: Peel–Raamstelling Bunker Line 102
Chapter Four
    American 82nd Airborne Division 'All-American' 105
        Capture of the Grave and Heumen Bridges 107
        Battle for the Nijmegen Bridges 114
        Nijmegen 133
        Battle of Groesbeek Heights 153
        Side Trip: Jonkerbos War Cemetery 175
Chapter Five
    British 43rd (Wessex) Infantry Division 'Yellow Devils' 176

Chapter Six

British 1st Airborne Division 'Red Devils': The Landings   186

    1st Airlanding Brigade and 1st Parachute Brigade   188

    4th Parachute Brigade   197

    Arnhem   200

    Third Lift Disaster   217

Chapter Seven

British 1st Airborne Division: Battle for the Arnhem Bridge   220

    Relief Force Stymied   220

    Defense of the Arnhem Bridge   228

Chapter Eight

British 1st Airborne Division: Oosterbeek Cauldron   248

    Oosterbeek   255

Chapter Nine

South Bank of the Nederrijn   276

    Polish 1st Independent Parachute Brigade   276

    101st Airborne Division   279

    Battle of Opheusden   280

    Side Trip: Grebbeberg War Cemetery   293

    Side Trip: German Surrender Site   294

    Side Trip: Loenen Field of Honor   295

Chapter Ten

Recriminations   296

Appendices

    Appendix A: Postwar activities of the senior commanders   303

    Appendix B: Comparison of Military Ranks   306

    Appendix C: Glossary of German Military Terms and Abbreviations   307

    Appendix D: Order of Battle   311

Index   327

Introduction

Operation Market-Garden constituted a major effort by American and British forces to bring the Second World War to a rapid close. It was a high-risk attempt to breach German western defenses and occupy the main armaments manufacturing areas of the Ruhr industrial basin thereby robbing Germany of the capability to continue the war. The effort receives considerably less public attention than the brilliant D-Day Invasion in Normandy or the heroic stand of American troops during the later Battle of the Bulge in eastern Belgium – perhaps because it ended in defeat. The main objective of the entire effort was not obtained and ended instead with an ignominious withdrawal after suffering catastrophic casualties.

The entire effort displays Allied disdain of a retreating and fractured enemy that arrogant Allied commanders believed to have been beaten. A delay of one week in continuing the Allied advance into Holland allowed German commanders to regroup and create fighting commands from practically nothing. Instead of victory over a defeated enemy, competent staffs and experienced commanders frequently leading undermanned, ill-equipped, and poorly trained rear echelon troops withstood attack by the best troops in the Allied armies.

Nevertheless, the various confrontations during Market-Garden present courageous efforts by lightly armed paratroopers literally surrounded amongst the enemy resisting enemy armored attacks with hand fired weapons. Similarly, German soldiers with little or no military experience resisted advancing British armored columns.

The daylight crossing of the Waal River in Nijmegen by American paratroopers against massed artillery, machine gun and riflemen has justly entered American military legend as the bravest assault since Pickett's ill-fated charge at Gettysburg.

British paratroopers are rightly proud of the courageous defense of the captured end of the Arnhem bridge and the Oosterbeek perimeter against eventually overwhelming forces. However, that defeat also presents how interservice rivalry and poor leadership doomed the best British airborne division to defeat at a terrible cost.

The Dutch have a great appreciation for history and an enduring respect for the young men who traveled across a channel or an ocean to fight and possibly die for their liberation. American and British visitors are still welcomed and thanked for their sacrifices to liberate their country from oppressive Nazi occupation. No grand edifice commemorates these events, but numerous tributes mark the major engagements, individual small unit actions, and downed aircraft. Annual remembrances at war cemeteries engage younger generations to give thanks to those who sacrificed everything.

Touring Battlefields

A highway route labeled 'The Corridor' follows the old highway used by British XXX Corps for their assault on Arnhem and many maps still so label these highways to maintain the historical significance of the roads. The tour follows 'The Corridor' where practical, but congested urban areas are generally avoided and diversions to specific sites are offered as options. This methodology requires a geographic orientation of events rather than chronological one.

Sections of the 1944 Corridor, labeled 'Hell's Highway' by the American paratroopers who fought between Eindhoven and Nijmegen, have been upgraded to limited access motorway standards and are now Autoroute A50. Similarly, much of the road between Nijmegen and Arnhem is now Autoroute A325.

An officially designated Liberation Route follows the course of the Allied advance during the liberation of Europe. The route starts in Normandy and continues via Nijmegen and Arnhem in the direction of Berlin. Liberation Route signed boulders identify points of interest or describe historical events throughout the region. The attached information panels carry only generalized information, but cell phone transmitted audio segments at selected locations recall the impressive experiences of one or more of the participants and can be obtained via the displayed QR code. Many Liberation Route sites are included in the battlefield tours. For the location of all the Liberation Route markers, see www.liberationroute.com.

Local citizens retain a deep respect to the men who liberated their country despite the accompanying devastating destruction. They are generally very tolerant of visitors, but, as always, they expect respect for their private property. An awareness of pedestrian, bicycle, and vehicular traffic will create a safer environment for visitor and resident.

Visiting Historic Sites

The book has been written with the intent of touring battlefields by automobile. Public transportation to battlefields is seldom a viable option. The book is constructed to facilitate viewing locations of individual interest while permitting skipping locations of lesser interest. Every battlefield site mentioned in the text is located by its GPS co-ordinates, permitting the visitor to construct their own tour route as desired. The use of a global positioning system navigator is highly recommended even when utilizing the suggested tour route. For those unable or unwilling to provide their own transportation, tour companies offer a reasonable alternative.

After a summary of the entire eight-day operation, separate chapters are devoted to the major British and American units involved. Each chapter begins with a divisional battle summary stating divisional and regimental objectives, introducing commanders, and a broad description of the outcome. Finally, at selected battlefield sites, the actions of individuals or small units are related. For reference, the first mention of any military unit of any size or importance to the outcome includes the unit commander's name in parentheses. As in previous works, burial locations or the post-war careers of selected individuals are given in footnotes rather than the text to reduce interruptions to the narrative.

Since many actions were essentially concurrent, descriptions of events are not in strict chronological order to eliminate driving back and forth over the same territory, which can, however, lead to some confusion regarding the sequence of events. For that reason, events are frequently introduced by stating their time and date.

Military units, ranks and time

The spelling of British unit names have been maintained; thus, for example, British 'Guards Armoured Division' appears in the text. Military ranks are displayed as appropriate to the country. The American rank of lieutenant colonel becomes the British lieutenant-colonel. German SS ranks are generally unfamiliar to English readers and literally awkward, therefore we have adopted the convention of noted authors Robert Kershaw and Michael Reynolds by substituted their American / British equivalent for improved readability. See Appendix B for a table of comparative ranks.

Commonly used foreign language military terms are not in italic font as is custom to aid readability. The more unusual terms are defined in footnotes at their first appearance. German military terms can be complex compound words; therefore, for brevity, their German abbreviations are frequently used. For example, Fallschirmjäger Regiment becomes FJR. A reference table of such terms is in Appendix C.

Unit names are presented as they were used at the time. Thus, the second company in a battalion would appear as Company B in the American Army, B Company in the British Army, and #2 Kompanie in the German Wehrmacht. German is used in their unit names such as II Bataillon for 2nd Battalion.

Twenty-four-hour military time is in use in Europe; therefore, operational hours in this book are so presented. Few museums are handicap accessible; those that so advertise are indicated. The hours of operation contained herein are believed to be accurate at the time of printing, but museum hours are notoriously subject to change. If access to a certain site is of paramount importance, it is best to contact it in advance.

American visitors must also accommodate the use of the metric system as it is the measure used on local road signs and maps.

Maps

Battlefield maps can contribute significantly to understanding troop positions, movements, and terrain features. Therefore, they are generously utilized. Because of the nature of mobile warfare, the indicated position of a military unit on battlefield maps is approximated for ease of viewing and does not necessarily indicate its location at any particular time. Unit size and function is indicated by the unit symbol; names and commanders are identified when practical. See Appendix D Order of Battle for unit structures and relationships between sub-units. For simplicity of presentation, units not engaged in Operation MARKET-GARDEN are usually omitted. A key to battlefield map symbols appears at the end of this introduction.

Maps show modern roadways for reference; but they should never be considered a substitute for current highway road maps. Each year roadways are improved or re-routed and intersections reconstructed. Therefore, up-to-date road maps or GPS locators are a necessity. Local area cycling maps are detailed and provide better resolution than road maps and can generally be obtained from area tourist offices

Tourist offices for selected locales are included in the tour route and are identified by their blue and white 'VVV' symbol. Hours are noted in the text but can vary by season.

Military Cemeteries

In the contingencies of warfare, numerous bodies were hastily buried in fields or local community cemeteries. Each participant country strives to locate and transfer battlefield remains to their respective military cemeteries, but additional remains are still occasionally discovered. Numerous community cemeteries still contain the graves of soldiers and airmen who, for a variety of reasons, have been left where originally buried. These graves are treated with great respect.

Access to military cemeteries is controlled by the respective country's regulations. Most are handicap accessible. British, Dutch, and German military cemeteries allow unrestricted access except for those located within military camps. American military cemetery hours are restricted from 09:00 to 17:00. An American representative is always on duty to assist relatives to locate graves of family members.

Major combatant countries provide websites to identify cemetery locations and at least a partial listing of identified burials within each cemetery. Those websites are:

American Battle Monuments Commission: https://www.abmc.gov/

Commonwealth War Graves Commission: https://www.cwgc.org/

Slachtofferregister Oorlogsgravenstichting (Dutch Victims Register War Graves Foundation): https://oorlogsgravenstichting.nl/

Volksbund Deutsche Kriegsgräberfürsorge (German War Graves Commission): https://www.volksbund.de/

Slowly walking through these cemeteries presents the horrific cost of warfare. Commonwealth gravestones are noted for listing the ages at which these young men died robbing them of a full lifetime of experiences. German cemeteries are noted for the large percentage of grave markers inscribed 'Unbekannt' or unidentified detailing the forlorn and forgotten remains never reunited with loved ones. Reading the differing states of origin on the gravestones in American cemeteries demonstrates how men fought to liberate someone else's country and gives proof to America's motto 'E Pluribus Unum' — Out of Many, One. No other evidence of the strength of the United States need be found.

The Holocaust

Religious tolerance was an important motive for the separation of the Netherlands from Spanish rule in the 16th century. Acceptance of religious freedom attracted religiously oppressed Jews who migrated to the newly independent state. The rise of Nazism in Germany added German-Jewish refugees to this influx in the 1930s. By 1939, 140,000 Dutch Jews lived in the country largely centered around Amsterdam. By war's end, fully seventy percent of the country's Jewish population had died in the Holocaust.

In 1997 German artist Gunter Demnig placed the first *Stolpersteine* – literally tripping stones – in Berlin's Kreuzberg district to identify the last known address of an individual victim of the Holocaust. The concept has spread to many major European cities. The concrete stones measure 10 centimeters by 10 centimeters and bear a brass plate with the name, dates of birth and death, and place of death, thus giving each victim a private memorial. Demnig believed that 'A human being is forgotten only when his or her name is forgotten.' Look for these stones embedded in the walkways of old districts of many Dutch cities.

Language

Anglicizing names and locations makes reading history books easier but makes finding the actual locations on the ground or on maps more difficult. Thus, this book utilizes Dutch spellings. Knowledge of a few Dutch words assists in identifying map references:

begraafplaats – cemetery	oorlog – war
bevrijding – liberation	oosten – east
bos – forest	oude – old
dorp – village	pad – path
brug – bridge	plein – square
dijk – dike	Rijn – Rhine
gebouw – building	sluis – lock (canal)
geld – money	stads – city
grote – great	stichting – foundation or institute
heide – heath	straat – street
het – the	veld – field
hout – wood	weg – road
huis – house	westen – west
kanaal – channel or canal	woud – forest
kerk – church	ziekenhuis – hospital
laan – lane	zuiden – south
noord – north	

Footnotes

Some may wonder why large numbers of footnotes detail names and burials of soldiers. These records convey the message that we must remember them – the men who fought tyranny and died to liberate someone else's country. These young men have no future. We can only wonder what they would have accomplished if they had lived. We can also wonder what future those of us who followed them would have had if they had not done what they did. While the last members of this generation pass on, their exploits and sacrifices provide examples of selflessness and dedication to duty to those who follow.

Many German soldiers realized that the war was lost but felt the need to defend their homeland from invasion. A similar recording of their latter actions is frequently difficult. Unit reports were lost in the bombings of Berlin, their identifies purposely hidden or obscured to hide membership in the SS, or their fate plainly never recorded in the chaos of a losing war.

Map key:

Roads:

≡ ≡ ≡	Autoroute
———————	National
———————	Major Highway
———————	Minor Road
———————	Street
———————	Foot Path
┼┼┼┼┼┼┼┼┼	Railroad
— — — — —	National Border

City

Town

Forest

River

Stream

Canal

Custom Map Symbols:

⌐ᵥ	Antitank Gun	●→	Machine Gun
↘	Artillery	⇉	Overlook
⋈	Bridge	⊂⊃	Tank or SP gun
▬	Blockhouse / Bunker	⊂ ⊂ ⊂	The Corridor
⊓⊓⊓⊓	Defense or Roadblock		Troop Movements:
DZ	Drop Zone	→	American
▐	Farm / Buildings	← -	German
		⋙	Westwall

Military Symbols

Unit Size (infantry example):

⊠ (·)	Squad	⊠ (x)	Brigade
⊠ (···)	Platoon	⊠ (x x)	Division
⊠ (ı)	Company	⊠ (x x x)	Corps
⊠ (ıı)	Battalion	⊠ (x x x x)	Army
⊠ (ııı)	Regiment	⊠ (x x x x x)	Army Group

Sub-Unit
Size

Unit Indentification: Sub ⊠ Unit
Unit

Commander

Unit Type:

⊠	Airborne Infantry	E	Engineering
⊡	Airborne Artillery	⊠	Glider Infantry
⊘	Armored (Panzer)	⊠	Infantry
⊿	Reconnaissance	⋈	Signals
·	Artillery	⊛	Tank Destroyer
⊠ (shaded)	German (infantry example)		

Chapter One
Operation Market-Garden Summary

Allied Military Situation

In the Fall of 1944, the charging Allied armies drove thousands of German soldiers, German civilians, and Nazi sympathizers of various nationalities eastward from France and Belgium. On 4 September 1944, Antwerp fell to British Second Army (General Sir Miles Dempsey),[1] but the second largest port in Europe was unable to resolve the Allies' supply problems because the port was at the inland end of the 85-kilometer-long Schelde estuary, which was interdicted by German artillery on both banks.

The rout reached its climax on 5 September as vehicles of all types — motorized, animal drawn, or hand pushed — strove for safety north toward the Dutch city of Arnhem and beyond. The sound of explosions rumbled from military camps as German engineers blew up ammunition dumps, fuel storage tanks, aircraft runways, and hangers. The German military had virtually no forces capable of stopping the Allies as units disintegrated and soldiers abandoned their posts, equipment, and, in some cases, even their uniforms.

On 5 September the exhausted and inadequately supplied Allied armies paused while commanders debated the next course of action – the broad front versus single thrust discussion that pitted both British Field Marshal Bernard Montgomery and American Lieutenant General George Patton Jr, who each argued to command the single thrust, against Supreme Allied Commander General Dwight Eisenhower, who, for the sake of Allied unity, demanded a broad front approach. However, the supply situation would not permit a broad-based advance. On the other hand, a delay could allow regrouping of German forces and a stiffening of their defense.

Fresh Allied troops in the form of three airborne divisions sat in England. The newly formed First Allied Airborne Army commanded by American Lieutenant General Lewis Brereton[2] held some of the best trained and most experienced troops in Europe. The past several weeks had seen planned airborne missions repeatedly cancelled when rapidly advancing ground troops captured the airborne objectives. The limited range of airborne transport aircraft dictated their use in a northern sector of occupied Europe with the Netherlands providing a prime target.

Montgomery pressed hard to utilize the available supplies and the fresh airborne troops for a single thrust to the dense German armaments manufacturing district of the Ruhr. However, Netherland's numerous river systems, connecting canals, and low-lying recovered seabed known as polder could be difficult ground

---

1   General Sir Miles C Dempsey had fought in France during the First World War as a junior officer. During the Second World War, he commanded a brigade in France in 1940, a corps during the invasion of Sicily, and the British Second Army during the Normandy invasion.

2   Lieutenant General Lewis Hyde Brereton was an early military aviator who commanded the 12th Aero Squadron in the First World War. His efforts in the Second World War started in the Far East Air Force in the Philippine Islands. He commanded the Middle East Air Force, and later the Ninth Air Force. In August 1944, Brereton was chosen by Eisenhower to command the First Allied Airborne Army.

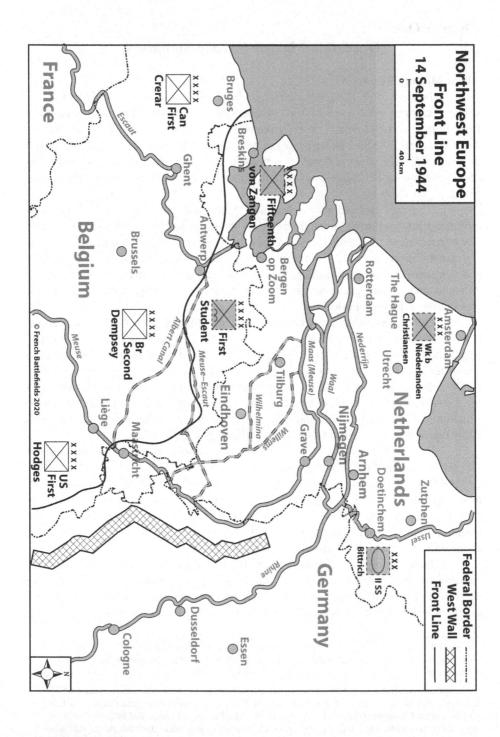

that offered the Germans excellent defensive opportunities. General Dempsey openly questioned the operation in conversations with Montgomery.

There was little doubt in the minds of American senior commanders that Montgomery wanted the honor, for himself and his country, of being the first to enter Berlin and claim victory over the vanquished enemy. Montgomery's original assault plan, Operation COMET, was cancelled only hours before take-off because of the hardening of German defenses and the inadequate size of the attacking force.

On 10 September, Eisenhower flew to Brussels to discuss plans with Montgomery. The Supreme Allied commander appreciated the advantages of outflanking the 640-kilometer-long German defense barrier known as the West Wall[3] nicknamed the Siegfried Line by the Allies and the possibility of encircling the Ruhr. In addition, two days earlier V-2 rockets had fallen on London from bases in the Netherlands less than 24 hours after Winston Churchill had declared London safe from German air attack. The prime minister put top priority on eliminating those launch sites. Eisenhower approved an enlarged version of COMET which added two American airborne divisions to Montgomery's plan and redistributed fuel supplies in favor of Montgomery's 21st Army Group.

'MARKET' became the code name given to the airborne drop of three-and-one-half divisions to seize bridges over several canals and the Maas, Waal, and Nederrijn (Lower Rhine) Rivers, the last natural barriers to the North German Plain, terrain suitable for armored and mechanized maneuver all the way to Berlin. Brereton appointed Lieutenant-General Sir Frederick Browning[4] as deputy and commander of the British I Airborne Corps.

In detail, the US 101st Airborne Division (Major General Maxwell Taylor)[5] was to capture two major canal crossings at Son and Veghel and four small bridges over the Dommel River in Eindhoven. The US 82nd Airborne Division (Brigadier General James Gavin)[6] was to support the ground advance by securing the Groesbeek Heights and capturing highway bridges over two major rivers, the Maas at Grave

---

3   West Wall: a defensive network of 3,000 pillboxes, mine fields, and machine-gun emplacements that ran along the western border of Germany. Originally built in the 1930s opposite the French Maginot Line, it was largely abandoned and stripped of weapons after the German victory of 1940. With the approach of the Allied Armies in 1944, Germany initiated a crash program to reconstitute the defenses. Its defensive possibilities figured highly in Allied military planning.

4   Some historians speculate that the dashing, elegant Lieutenant-General Sir Frederick Arthur Montague 'Boy' Browning, a qualified glider pilot, hero in the First World War, and husband of the famous novelist Daphne du Maurier, demanded this separate command over the more experienced Lieutenant General Matthew Ridgway, commander of the American XVIII Airborne Corps, because Browning did not want to see the war end without his having participated with a significant command.

5   Major General Maxwell Davenport Taylor served in engineering, artillery, and diplomatic roles before transferring to airborne forces. He led a secret mission behind German lines to Rome to open discussions with Italian leaders to end the war in Italy. Taylor was assigned command of the 101st Airborne Division in May 1944.

6   At age 37, Major General James Maurice Gavin was the youngest divisional commander in the US Army during the Second World War and the only American general officer to make four combat jumps having parachuted into Sicily, Italy, Normandy, and the Netherlands. Impressed with the German airborne assault on Fort Eben-Emael in 1940, Gavin volunteered for the new United States Parachute School in 1941, then wrote the book on how to utilize airborne troops.

and the Waal at Nijmegen. His objectives also included several smaller bridges over the Maas–Waal Canal. Finally, the British 1st Airborne Division (Major-General Robert Urquhart),[7] with the 1st Polish Independent Airborne Brigade (Major-General Stanislaw Sosabowski)[8] attached, was to secure the road, railway, and pontoon bridges over the Nederrijn at Arnhem. In total, the airborne forces would land 20,190 men by parachute and 13,781 men, 1,927 vehicles, and 568 artillery pieces carried by more than 2,500 gliders in the greatest air armada ever assembled.

Without heavy artillery or tanks, the lightly armed airborne forces would be highly vulnerable to German countermeasures. The code name 'GARDEN' referred to the ground attack by British XXX Corps (Lieutenant-General Brian Horrocks)[9] led by his Guards Armoured Division (Major-General Allan Adair)[10] to supply desperately needed combat firepower necessary to hold any airborne successes. The Guards would be supported by the 50th Northumbrian and 43rd (Wessex) Infantry Division, 8th Armoured Brigade, and the Dutch Prinses Irene Brigade. Adair's mission was a 120-kilometer (75-mile) dash from an earlier established bridgehead across the Meuse–Escaut Canal in French nomenclature or Maas–Schelde in Flemish now named Bocholt–Herentals, to the ultimate objective of the bridge over the Lower Rhine river at Arnhem consolidating Allied positions along the way. The route required the use of a narrow highway that became known as 'The Corridor.' The concept perceived the operation as a preliminary to cut-off all enemy forces in the western Netherlands. Thus, Operation MARKET-GARDEN was born.

Only Montgomery's closest staff had any hint of the bold decision to execute the MARKET-GARDEN plan until 10 September, barely one week before it was to commence. Because of the short planning period before the launch of MARKET-GARDEN preparation time and briefings were shorter than normal. The airborne units were thrown into the monumental task of coordinating the preparation and transport of men, vehicles, guns, and equipment necessary to support divisions dropped well behind enemy lines. The transport requirements were so huge that complete units could not be delivered to their respective combat areas at one time. Thus, the schedule required three separate lifts, each including parachute drops and glider landings. The entire plan gambled on speed, boldness, and surprise. The aggressive plan was not without

---

7   Major-General Robert Elliott 'Roy' Urquhart served in India during the early years of the Second World War. Posted to North Africa, he held staff positions during the invasions of Sicily and Italy. Strictly an infantry officer, Urquhart had never commanded an airborne unit before given command of the 1st Airborne Division in January 1944. In fact, he was prone to air sickness.

8   Major-General Stanislaw Sosabowski was drafted into the Austro-Hungarian Army before the First World War. He was awarded medals for bravery fighting against the Russians. He ably led his regiment in engagements against the invading German Army in September 1939, then escaped a PoW camp to join the Polish Resistance and later Polish forces in France before evacuating to Great Britain.

9   Lieutenant-General Brian Gwynne Horrocks was noted for his ability to relate to the rank and file soldiers. He was out of command for fourteen months after being strafed by a German fighter in 1943. He assumed command of XXX Corps in August 1944 and distinguished himself in command of the advance across France and Belgium.

10   Major-General Allan Henry Adair, 6th Baronet, served as a junior officer in the trenches of France and Belgium during the First World War and received two Military Crosses for gallantry. He remained in units that eventually became the Guards Division and commanded that unit since 1942.

its critics. While most unit commanders proceeded to carry out their orders, General Sosabowski was the only unit commander to officially express the impossibility of achieving the assigned objectives, although privately General Gavin also expressed disbelief in Urquhart's plans to his staff.

The size of the support forces was incredible. Over nine thousand engineering troops were assigned to provide bridging capability over the numerous waterways. Leopoldsburg swelled with over twenty thousand vehicles awaiting the call to advance. To resolve contingencies breakdown gangs roamed the vehicular column. Traffic control depended upon wireless and telephone communications that were unknown. No unit was permitted to put more than five vehicles on the road without explicit permission from General Horrocks' headquarters staff.

On 12 September, the British I Airborne Corps intelligence chief, Major Brian Urquhart — no relation to Major-General Robert Urquhart — received vague reports from Dutch Resistance that battered panzer formations were in the Netherlands to rest and refit possibly in the vicinity of Arnhem. Three days later, Major Urquhart, identified the 9th and 10th SS Panzer Divisions near the Arnhem area. Enigma decrypts of German radio signals indicated the same but, due to the secrecy surrounding the source, that information was not shared with subsidiary commands. All the warnings went unheeded. When Major Brian Urquhart brought the reports to Browning's attention, Major Urquhart was relieved from duty as suffering from overstress.[11]

Field Marshal Montgomery was unusually hands-off during Operation MARKET-GARDEN, especially considering it was his concept. He was deeply involved with important discussions taking place during the Second Quebec Conference which decided the zones of occupation in postwar Germany and Lend Lease aid to Britain.

On 14 September, a Dutch underground leader, Christiaan Lindemans,[12] was sent to Eindhoven to advise resistance groups of the planned Allied attack. Lindemans,

---

11   Sir Brian Urquhart joined the Army upon the start of the war. He transferred to the Airborne Division, but suffered serious injuries during a training drop. Upon recovery, he served in North Africa and the Mediterranean. After the war, Urquhart was instrumental in creating the United Nations peacekeeping forces eventually becoming Deputy Secretary General of the United Nations. Urquhart turned 100 years old in February 2019.

12   Christiaan Lindemans was a Dutch SOE agent operating under the nickname 'King Kong' because of his lumbering gait, which was the result of a previous serious motorcycle accident. Lindemans gained credibility early in the war by killing twenty-seven Germans during guerrilla warfare around Antwerp. Captured by the Germans he was later released and established escape routes for downed airmen through occupied Europe to Spain and Portugal. His contact with local Communist resistance groups led to him becoming a Soviet agent. In February 1944, the Gestapo arrested his younger brother for assisting escapes and Lindemans agreed to become a German agent in return for his brother's release.
In October 1944, Lindemans was exposed by a captured Abwehr agent and arrested by British intelligence and shortly later transferred to Dutch custody. In April 1946, his wife was observed visiting the Soviet Embassy in Rotterdam. In exchange for his wife's safety, Lindemans offered information on a Soviet organization with ties to senior civilians in France, Germany, and the Netherlands. Sentenced to death by the Dutch government, he committed suicide in prison in July 1946. Rumors of his escape to South America persisted, although his body was exhumed in 1986 and positively identified through his motorcycle accident injuries.
Lindemans' role, if any, in revealing GARDEN plans to the Germans remains controversial. American records on Lindemans are still classified.

however, was a Soviet double agent working both sides. He divulged the rough outline of GARDEN compromising the ground attack up The Corridor. German reconnaissance activity previously observed on 11 September identified the vehicular buildup around Leopoldsburg reinforcing the intelligence. Fortunately, he had not been informed about MARKET.

By 15 September, news of German armored units in the Arnhem area had reached SHAEF's[13] intelligence chief, British Major-General Kenneth Strong. He informed Lieutenant General Walter Bedell Smith, General Eisenhower's chief of staff. Although the whereabouts of the two panzer divisions had been confirmed, there was uncertainty as to their strengths. Both units had suffered huge losses in men and equipment during the pursuit across France. Later that day, Smith flew to Montgomery's headquarters near Brussels with the reports. Montgomery ridiculed the idea of a threat. At the same time, photo reconnaissance evaluated in England revealed the presence of obsolete PzKpfw III and still-formidable PzKpfw IV tanks practically on the edges of the designated drop zones at Arnhem.

German Military Situation

The early September pause in the Allied advance allowed German commanders to regroup their shattered armies. German Generalfeldmarschall Gerd von Rundstedt, commander of OB West,[14] ordered Fifteenth Army (General der Infanterie Gustav-Adolf von Zangen) to man the channel ports at Boulogne-sur-Mer, Calais, and Dunkerque and to evacuate his remaining troops by sea to the island of Walcheren. Von Zangen marched across that island and crossed the narrow South Beveland peninsula to regain the mainland north of Antwerp. Dempsey's failure to occupy the base of the Beveland Isthmus allowed the German Fifteenth Army to evacuate 65,000 men and 225 guns and represents one of the greatest tactical mistakes of the war.

Generaloberst Kurt Student[15] started to reform German defenses along the 120-kilometer-long German front line from the North Sea to Maastricht. The newly created First Fallschirmjäger Army established a defensive line on the north banks of the Albert Canal, scene of the German Army's spectacular 1940 capture of the Dutch fortress at Eben-Emael. Student's Fallschirmjäger Regiments (FJR) were highly regarded, but they were shells of their former names, filled with barely trained new recruits. Other units held old men swept from hospitals and convalescent centers.

The 719th Infantry Division (Generalleutnant Karl Sievers), a fortress division of poorly trained old men, headed for positions north of Antwerp. Generalleutnant Kurt Chill's 85th Division had suffered heavy losses in France but swept up retreating

---

13   SHAEF: Supreme Headquarters Allied Expeditionary Force was the headquarters of the commander of Allied forces in north west Europe, General Dwight Eisenhower.

14   *Oberbefehlshaber* (Supreme Commander) *West* or OB West was the office of the commander of all German Armed Forces on the Western Front.

15   Generaloberst Kurt Student began his military career as a German Army pilot in the First World War. Student was responsible for establishing the airborne infantry after transferring to the Luftwaffe in 1934 and he commanded that force for most of the Second World War. He personally led airborne troops during the 1940 invasion of the Netherlands and directed the invasion of Crete in 1941 earning a Knight's Cross of the Iron Cross with Oak Leaves.

stragglers from other units to refill its rosters. His staff officers forced troops retreating from France into ad hoc formations at collection points established at major river crossings.

Territory north of the Waal River held *Wehrmacht-befehlshaber in den Niederlande* (Army Forces in the Netherlands), a collection of rear area formations of little combat value commanded by General der Flieger Friedrich Christiansen.[16]

Newly appointed Generalfeldmarschall Walter Model,[17] the third commander of Army Group B in the past two months, ordered that all retreating troops were to immediately report to the nearest command post. He feared that Allied forces entering the Netherlands could outflank the German West Wall which terminated at Kleve on the Dutch-German border. If so, the Ruhr, the great industrial heartland of Germany's military machine, would be exposed and an armored drive across the North German Plain would lead directly to Berlin.

Model created temporary fighting units which were composed of mixed, various-arms units from training units, previously non-combat naval troops escaping from Atlantic Wall installations overrun by the Allies, Luftwaffe ground troops from overrun airfields, partially trained replacement units, so-called 'kranken' troops who suffered wounds or illnesses that would otherwise exempt them from frontline duty, NCO training schools, and Dutch National Socialist groups which supported the Nazi occupation.

The 9th and 10th SS Panzer Divisions were rebuilding around their remaining experienced officers and NCOs after their defeat in Normandy. They trained and acclimated new recruits, received recovered wounded back into their units, repaired weapons and equipment, and received new equipment in camps around Arnhem and Zutphen

The two divisions were grouped into II SS Corps (SS-Lieutenant General Wilhelm Bittrich)[18] and underwent training specifically to counter airborne landings. Much of the salvaged equipment of the 9th SS Panzer Division *Hohenstaufen* (SS-Lieutenant Colonel Walter Harzer) had been turned over to the 10th SS Panzer

---

16   General der Flieger Friedrich Christiansen was a First World War flying ace credited with thirteen victories for which he was awarded the Pour le Mérite. After the war, he was arrested for ordering a raid on the Dutch village of Putten in retaliation for the death of a German officer at the hands of the Dutch Resistance. For that war crime, he was sentenced to twelve years imprisonment, but served only three.

17   Blunt and frequently tactless Generalfeldmarschall Otto Moritz Walter Model was known as 'Hitler's fireman' for his ability to rapidly assess and reformulate German defensive positions in a crisis. An advocate of combined arms training and the frequent use of special battle groups known as kampfgruppe (plural: kampfgruppen), Model frequently rescued deteriorating situations on the Eastern Front. Lacking the military stature of much of the German General Staff, he was looked down upon by fellow officers, but was well liked by Adolf Hitler.

18   SS-Lieutenant General Wilhelm Bittrich was an infantry officer in the First World War before transferring to the Fliegertruppe as a fighter pilot. Bittrich was a Waffen-SS general during the Second World War serving in famous units such as 1st SS Panzer Division Leibstandarte SS Adolf Hitler during the invasion of Poland and 2nd SS Panzer-Division 'Das Reich' in the Soviet Union. He later commanded the 9th SS Panzer Division on the Eastern Front and later in France, the Netherlands, and Ardennes Offensive as commander of the II SS Panzerkorps.

Division *Frundsberg* (SS-Colonel Heinz Harmel) to more rapidly reestablish at least one of the two divisions.

Terrain

Waterways played a major role in the battle in this region of the Netherlands. Drainage ditches checker-boarded nearly every field, although little water was in the ditches at this time of year. Broad, swiftly flowing rivers cut across the battlefield in generally east – west orientation, necessitating the capture of long bridges for any north-south movement. Roadways, elevated to assure proper drainage into roadside ditches, prohibited vehicular movement into adjacent fields. The clay soil was heavily cultivated, but often damp and slick making off-road travel for wheeled or even tracked vehicles nearly impossible. The terrain presented only small, scattered woods, except in the Arnhem area where large forested tracts are present. September rainfall is frequent, accompanied by days of cloudy or foggy weather making air operations undependable.

Battle Summary

Sunday, 17 September 1944 was a sunny and warm autumn day under brilliant blue skies. That afternoon, 435 British and 983 American aircraft inflicted a preliminary bombardment upon German flak positions, ammunition depots, and barracks around and in Arnhem. Fighters strafed the Ede-Arnhem railroad line.

Shortly after 10:00 transport planes took off from airfields across England. Three three-plane 'V' formations established nine-plane 'Vs'. Five such formations constituted a serial of 45 aircraft. Pathfinders, who were designated to mark the drop and landing zones with brightly colored panels, preceded the main drop by thirty minutes.

The 1,545 transport planes and 478 gliders escorted by 1,131 fighters formed a flowing mass 16 kilometers wide and 150 kilometers long. The serials began to receive German antiaircraft fire upon crossing the Dutch coast, but small groups of enemy fighters were easily driven-off by Allied fighter escorts. The Dutch terrain below the air armada displayed German efforts to flood much of the countryside.

Parachute drops were from an altitude of 500 feet at 120 miles per hour. These characteristics presented a trade-off between avoiding small-arms and antiaircraft fire against a safe minimum altitude for parachute deployment. Although the daylight combat jump exposed the airborne divisions to ground fire, the risk was accepted to establish the tighter drop and accelerated re-organization of units once on the ground.

Around 13:00, Dutch civilians and German military were at first mystified by the low whisper of the approaching aircraft that slowly intensified into a pulsating roar. Bittrich, in the II SS Panzer Corps headquarters in Doetinchem, received a situation report from the Luftwaffe communications network at 13:30 and immediately put his two panzer divisions on alert. Headquarters staff correctly identified the Allied objectives as bridges at Nijmegen and Arnhem. At 13:50 the first reports arrived at LXXXVIII Corps headquarters which described between 500 and 2,000 paratroopers and thirty gliders landing at Groesbeek and Mook near Nijmegen five minutes earlier.

German anti-airborne doctrine held that troops must drive into the teeth of the

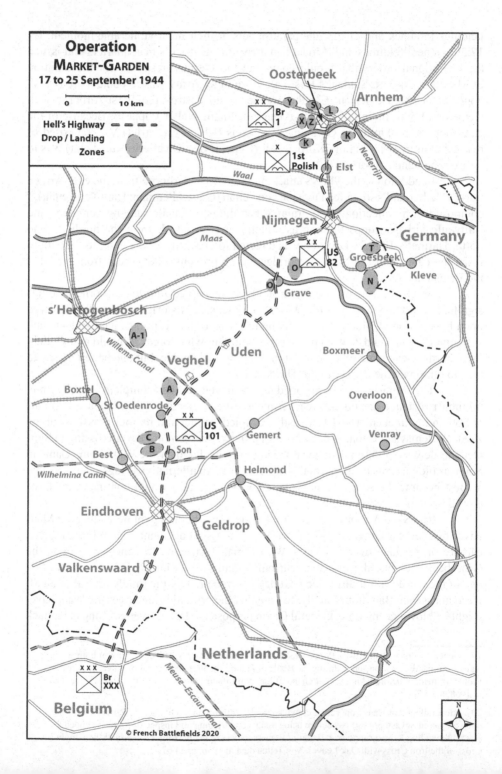

Operation
MARKET-GARDEN
17 to 25 September 1944

0   10 km

Hell's Highway
Drop / Landing
Zones

Oosterbeek

Arnhem

Y S L
Br 1
X, Z

K   K

1st Polish   Elst

Waal

Nederrijn

Nijmegen

Maas

Germany

US 82   Groesbeek
O
Grave   N   Kleve

s'Hertogenbosch

A-1

Willems Canal   Veghel   Uden   Boxmeer

Boxtel   A

St Oedenrode

US 101   Overloon

C   Gemert   Venray
Best   B   Son

Wilhelmina Canal   Helmond

Eindhoven   Geldrop

Valkenswaard

Netherlands

Br XXX

Meuse-Escaut Canal

Belgium

© French Battlefields 2020

N

landings to attack and disrupt the paratroopers at their most vulnerable moment. By 17:30, Generalfeldmarschall Model had arrived at Bittrich's headquarters and issued the operational orders that would command the German response for the duration of MARKET-GARDEN. Student's First Fallschirmjäger Army was to contain the British opposite the Meuse–Escaut Canal bridgehead and destroy the 101st Airborne with elements of 59th Infantry Division (Generalleutnant Walter Poppe)[19]. Because of the paratroopers' proximity to Germany, Wehrkreis (Military District) VI, composed of rear echelon troops – mainly Korps Feldt (General der Kavallerie Kurt Feldt) was to destroy the 82nd Airborne.

In addition to the 9th SS attacking the British Airborne from the east, Armed Forces Netherland's so-called Division von Tettau (Generalleutnant Hans von Tettau),[20] composed of a collection of SS training battalions, a naval manning company, and Luftwaffe airbase troops fighting as infantry, was to attack from the northeast and north. Harmel's 10th SS Division was directed to cross the Rhine and move south to resist the capture of the Nijmegen bridge and to prevent relief forces from reaching the British at Arnhem.

At OB West, von Rundstedt gradually accepted that the airborne landings signified an offensive to turn the West Wall defenses. His original disbelief centered upon his opinion of Montgomery who he felt was 'overly cautious, habit-ridden, and systematic.' Von Rundstedt spent the night grabbing what forces he could and sending them north. Weakening other areas of the front was a gamble, but one he felt he had to take to eliminate the danger to the Third Reich.

The American airborne landings achieved almost complete surprise, met minimal resistance, and quickly reached most of their objectives with notable exceptions at Son and Nijmegen. The 101st easily occupied Veghel and its four crossings of the Zuid–Willemsvaart Canal and Aa River. Similarly, the Dommel River crossing in Sint-Oedenrode was captured. However, the highway bridge over the Wilhelmina Canal in Son was blown up as the paratroopers approached. An alternative bridge over the canal at Best became the scene of intensive woodland fighting which continued for three days despite this bridge also being detonated.

The 82nd Airborne easily swept aside a small contingent defending the Maas River bridge near Grave. A more intense, day-long engagement resulted in the intact capture of a bridge over the Maas–Waal Canal. Instructed to concentrate upon the Groesbeek Heights, the division sent only small patrols into Nijmegen on the first day of the battle. A full thrust the next day was repelled by the timely arrival of an SS Reconnaissance Battalion. Finally, fearing that the critical bridge over the Waal River might be blown at any time, General Gavin proposed a daring river crossing and attack

---

19   Generalleutnant Walter Fritz Poppe was a career German infantry officer serving in both world wars. Commanding various units during the Battle of France, the French occupation force, the Eastern Front, Normandy, before taking up command of the 59th Infantry Division in July 1944. Poppe died in 1968, aged 76.

20   Generalleutnant Hans von Tettau commanded the 24th Infantry Division in Russia where that unit conquered Sevastopol fortress before being assigned to training and inspector roles. He ended the war commanding Korpsgruppe von Tettau in Pomerania where his performance earned the Knight's Cross of the Iron Cross with Oak Leaves. Von Tettau died in 1956, aged 67.

to capture both approaches to the bridge at the same time. In one of the most dramatic actions of the war, a battalion of paratroopers rowed flimsy collapsible boats across the swiftly flowing river in broad daylight, secured the opposite bank, and eliminated enemy troops guarding the northern end of the bridge. On 20 September 1944, the tanks of British XXX Corps rolled across the Nijmegen bridge.

British 1st Airborne Division at Arnhem quickly found itself in trouble. The landing zones were near German encampments and the enemy response was amazingly swift. One of the three battalions dispatched to capture the river bridge, did occupy the northern approaches but German troops held the southern end. Surrounded and without additional forces or supplies, a four-day struggle began first for control of the bridge and then for survival as the paratroopers were surrounded and slowly eliminated in some of the fiercest fighting of the war.

On the ground, British vehicles, confined to one main highway, quickly crossed the Dutch border but were repeatedly halted by well-placed German guns. With each delay, the armored advance fell more behind schedule. By the end of 17 September, they had failed to reach the Eindhoven objective, the Son bridge had been blown, and no bridges over the Waal or Rhine had been taken although paratroopers had driven close to both objectives. German strength was building as units were rerouted to the scene.

Delayed by ground fog in England, the second air lift on 18 September did not arrive until 14:00. It was as massive as the previous day's air armada. The number of planes was staggering: 1,336 C-47s, 340 troop carriers, 1,205 gliders, and 252 B-24 'Liberator' bombers all protected by 867 fighters. The lift brought 6,674 airborne troops and badly needed artillery pieces.

Reinforced by the new troops, British paratroopers attempted an assault to strengthen their hold on the Arnhem bridge. Blocked by German armor and caught in a savage crossfire, the new battalions were all but destroyed in the streets of western Arnhem and withdrew to form a perimeter defense around divisional headquarters in the Arnhem suburb of Oosterbeek. They awaited arrival of the Polish 1st Independent Airborne Brigade by air or the British ground forces by land before launching a renewed attack for the bridge. Neither ever arrived.

Bad weather in England delayed the Third and Fourth Lifts. After they were finally dropped on the south side of the Nederrijn, the Poles had no effective means to cross the river to the British perimeter on the north side.

By 20 September, Model felt that he had accumulated sufficient forces to launch his counteroffensive against MARKET-GARDEN. To strangle the forces in Arnhem, he aimed attacks against The Corridor at Son, Veghel, and Nijmegen. Each German effort, although beaten back, delayed the progress of the British Guards Armoured Division toward Arnhem while the paratroopers in Arnhem and Oosterbeek were slowly ground down.

With all hope of relief from the ground gone and an inability to transport the Polish airborne troops across the river, on 25 September General Urquhart received the order to leave his wounded to the Germans and to execute a fighting withdrawal to the Polish positions south of the river. That night in darkness and a driving rainstorm, paratroopers slowly abandoned their positions and moved to the riverbank where

Canadian and British engineers manned boats and transported the survivors to safety. Operation MARKET-GARDEN was over.

Casualties

The consequences of the operation were catastrophic for British Airborne troops. Seldom mentioned are the casualties suffered during the subsequent months defending the exposed salient that the operation created.

Allied killed, wounded or missing, including PoWs, by unit were British 1st Airborne Division: 7,077; US 82nd Airborne Division: 1,432; US 101st Airborne Division: 2,118; British XXX Corps: 1,480; glider pilots: 730; RAF aircrew: 294; American aircrew 424; and Polish Brigade: 203. British casualties, including the attached Polish, totaled 9,784. American losses totaled 3,974. Although their efforts to extend the flanks of the Corridor are little discussed in this volume, British VIII and XII Corps suffered another 3,874 killed, wounded, or missing.

British PoWs from the bridge battle and the Oosterbeek perimeter were transported to PoW camps in Germany. The wounded were treated humanely at German hospitals and, once recovered, were also sent to German PoW camps.

German casualties are difficult to determine. Estimates of those killed vary wildly in keeping with the nature of the temporary formations engaged in the battle and range from 3,300 to 9,000.

The civilian population also suffered. While those liberated by the Allied armies joyfully celebrated, those that remained under Nazi rule, especially in Arnhem, suffered deprivation during forced evacuation and food shortages.

Analysis

Operation MARKET-GARDEN was not a single battle but a series of engagements between forces of differing sizes, capabilities, and decidedly unequal strengths. German troops were mostly inexperienced, partially trained infantry, but frequently led by experienced NCOs under highly proficient commanders. In some instances, they were not infantry troops at all, but naval and Luftwaffe troops, who, generally, were mostly useless and quick to surrender. The increasing availability of heavy armor weapons as units were rerouted from other duties became the determining factor at Arnhem. The rapid German response was a result of efficient, professional staffs and successful implementation of the concept of forming and dissolving kampfgruppe. The German command structure and well-functioning communications system outperformed the Allied equivalents.

Allied airborne troops, whether parachute or glider delivered, were some of the best, most-experienced combat veterans in the entire European Theater of Operations. However, for the most part they could not equal the German superiority in heavy weapons until the arrival of XXX Corps. The inability of the unit to apply its overwhelming armored force against the enemy provides the Germans an opportunity for victory.

Aftermath

After the failure of Market-Garden, a fierce battle raged in which the Germans tried to reoccupy 'The Island', territory between the Waal and Nederrijn Rivers. The front eventually stabilized along the line of the Linge River. Despite occasional patrols in force, the area remained occupied until April 1945.

The two American airborne divisions remained in the Netherlands under command of XXX Corps for six more weeks and suffered an additional 3,594 casualties — more than they suffered during MARKET-GARDEN while they repulsed German efforts to re-occupy the Island or secure breathing room along the Dutch-German border.

After the battle the Germans ordered a complete evacuation of Arnhem forcing 123,000 civilians to leave without provision for where they were to go or how they were to be fed. It was the beginning of the 'hunger winter' for the people of the Netherlands. Perhaps as many as 25,000 died of starvation. The German occupation forces systematically looted the ruins and sent the goods to bombed German cities.

On 7 October the RAF dropped bombs and crashed the Arnhem Bridge into the Rhine. Arnhem was not liberated until almost the end of the war when the British 49th Infantry Division under Canadian command arrived on 14 April 1945.

Chapter Two
Guards Armoured Division
The Guards Armoured Division was created in June 1941 by converting battalions of the Grenadier Guards, Coldstream Guards, Scots Guards, Welsh Guards, and Irish Guards Regiments to armored or motorized units and adding the Household Cavalry Reconnaissance Battalion. The unit landed in Normandy on 13 June and participated in much of the heavy fighting around Caen including Operation GOODWOOD. In early September the Guards liberated Brussels.

After being repulsed in his efforts to establish a bridgehead across the Albert Canal north of Antwerp, Lieutenant-General Horrocks turned his attention 64 kilometers east to successfully cross the canal at Beringen. Unknown to Horrocks, Generalleutnant Kurt Chill, an experienced infantry commander, recognized the tactical importance of the Albert Canal to the entire German defense in the Netherlands, disregarded orders to withdraw his depleted 85th Infantry Division to Germany and instead added his kampfgruppe to the Albert Canal defenses. Chill established reception centers at bridge crossing sites manned by his officers and NCOs to intercept thousands of retreating troops. The disparate soldiers from numerous parent organizations were folded into his division's positions. Generalleutnant Karl Sievers' 719th Infantry Division established positions on Chill's right flank covering the Albert Canal from Antwerp to the junction with the Meuse–Escaut Canal. General von Zangen's 15th Army escapees strengthened defenses throughout the Netherlands. Fighting for the next seven days took place on the terrain between the two major canals – Albert and Meuse–Escaut – where the British faced the first serious resistance since the Falaise Gap in Normandy.

Battle of Hechtel
7 to 12 September 1944
The town of Hechtel was on the front line between 7 to 12 September 1944. FJR 20 (Major Franz Grassmel) was moving through Hechtel toward the Albert Canal on 7 September when a Welsh Guards Group of the Guards Armoured Division approached the town from the south. The Welsh Guards intended to continue to the Groote Barrier bridge across the Meuse–Escaut Canal when they encountered Grassmel's fallschirmjäger troops and were driven back with the loss of three Cromwell tanks.

On 9 September, after two failed British attempts to clear the town, matters deteriorated with the arrival from the north of II Bataillon (Hauptmann Willi Müller) of the Ausbildungs und Ersatz (Training and Replacement abbreviated AuE) troops from the Hermann Göring Regiment.

After three days of determined combat, often from building to building, the British 11th Armoured Division launched an assault from the south while the Irish, Grenadier, and Coldstream Guards units fought across difficult terrain from the west. The two German units were now trapped in the center of Hechtel. At 10:00 on 11 September, British infantry attacked from the southwest while five M10 tank destroyers and four 17-pounders kept the German troops sheltering in foxholes or cellars. By mid-afternoon, German casualties were high and Müller was wounded, but

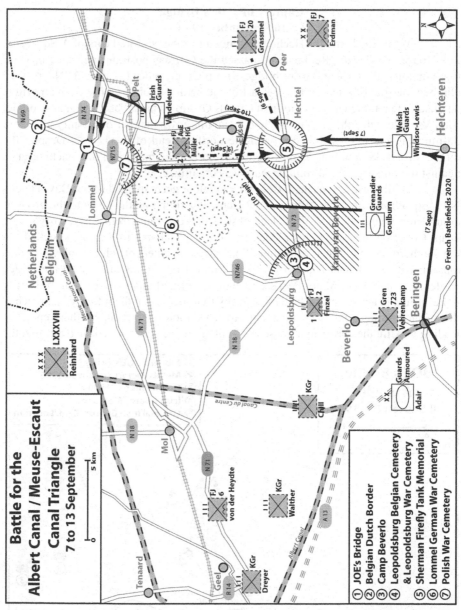

Battle for the
Albert Canal / Meuse-Escaut
Canal Triangle
7 to 13 September

① JOE's Bridge
② Belgian Dutch Border
③ Camp Beverlo
④ Leopoldsburg Belgian Cemetery
　 & Leopoldsburg War Cemetery
⑤ Sherman Firefly Tank Memorial
⑥ Lommel German War Cemetery
⑦ Polish War Cemetery

the British attack had been withstood. The morning of 12 September marked the end of German resistance. At 08:15 a 45-minute artillery barrage leveled what was left of the blazing town. British infantry followed on the heels of the artillery fire and occupied the central crossroads by noon. At 14:00 the final German stronghold surrendered.

　　Müller's troops and I Bataillon, FJR 20 were wiped out, although Major Grassmel escaped to the east with the unit's II Bataillon leaving a total of 150 dead, 220 wounded, and 500 prisoners.

Capture of JOE's Bridge
10 September 1944

While the battle for Hechtel continued to rage, armored cars of A Squadron, 2nd Household Cavalry Regiment by-passed the German positions and sped forward to reconnoiter the Groote Barrier bridge. Troop Commander Lieutenant JN Creswell climbed the roof of a metals factory east of the bridge to observe the German bridge defenses. He returned to report to Irish Guards Group commander Lieutenant-Colonel John Vandeleur that the bridge was held by an unknown number of infantry and three 88-mm flak guns concentrated around the northern end of the bridge. Despite the threats of the 88-mm guns against lightly armored Shermans and the machine guns against the infantry, a bold *coup de main* was organized.

While dusk approached, Colonel Vandeleur accompanied Major David Peel's No 1 Squadron with infantry from No 2 Company riding on the tanks to the grounds around the metals factory. Vandeleur observed the assault from the factory's slag heap. Covering fire from tanks hidden in the industrial area to the east knocked out the southern 88 and ignited its ammunition carrier. Lieutenant John Stanley-Clarke's platoon with Lieutenant Duncan Lampard's tank troop following rushed the bridge while the remainder of Major Peel's eleven tanks applied suppressive fire. A red Verey light flashed in an arc across the darkened sky to indicate that the infantry had reached the bridge and signaling the parked tanks to cease their fire onto its northern end. The leading tank hit the corner of a house and stalled; the second tank crashed through the

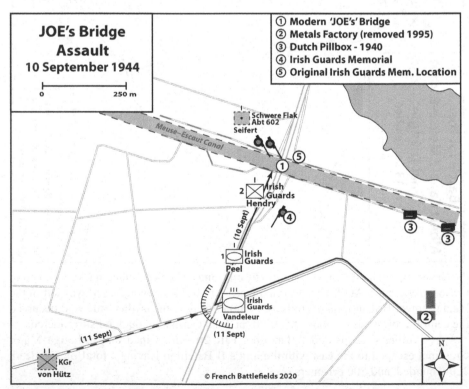

JOE's Bridge
Assault
10 September 1944

0   250 m

① Modern 'JOE's' Bridge
② Metals Factory (removed 1995)
③ Dutch Pillbox - 1940
④ Irish Guards Memorial
⑤ Original Irish Guards Mem. Location

Meuse–Escaut Canal

Schwere Flak
Abt 602
Seifert

2 ⊠ Irish Guards
Hendry

1 ◻ Irish Guards
Peel

III
⊠ Irish Guards
Vandeleur

⊠ KGr
von Hütz

(11 Sept)   (11 Sept)

© French Battlefields 2020

flaming debris of a burning half-track to capture the northern end of the bridge. The other two Shermans followed and dispersed the crews of the two remaining antiaircraft guns.[1] Royal Engineers removed demolition charges. From that moment, the bridge was named JOE's Bridge after the Irish Guards infantry commander, Lieutenant-Colonel John Ormsby Evelyn 'JOE' Vandeleur.

When German units south of the Meuse–Escaut Canal were threatened with encirclement by the Irish Guards' advance northward, LXXXVIII Corps commander, General der Infanterie Hans Reinhard ordered a nighttime evacuation to the north forming a new defensive line along that canal. General Allan Adair's Guards Armoured Division now faced FJR von Hoffmann (Oberst Helmut von Hoffmann)[2] along the Hechtel-to-Valkenswaard Road. This German unit had formed only three weeks earlier as a training unit with two battalions and an antitank company with eight 75-mm cannon. Most of its officers had no combat experience and the men had been gathered from non-combat ground units that had supported Luftwaffe airfields. In contrast, the Guards had landed in Normandy at the end of June to participate in Operation GOODWOOD near Caen. The division was reorganized later into battle groups teaming infantry battalions with armored units.[3] The Guards joined XXX Corps in August for the chase across France and liberated Brussels on 3 September.

On 15 or 16 September, I Bataillon (Major Helmut Kerutt), FJR 18 formed a reserve in depth against the British forces around JOE's Bridge. Companies established well-camouflaged positions in woods on either side of the Valkenswaard Road. Thirty men from Major Kerutt's headquarters platoon armed with panzerfausts[4] and machine guns formed a second tank ambush from foxholes 2.5 kilometers behind the battalion's line. Kerutt's Panzerjäger Kompanie commanded Hauptmann Brockes positioned nine Russian-made 76.2 -mm PaK[5] guns along the right and left shoulders of the roadway yet farther north, although the unit's lack of prime movers denied safer positions deep in the woods. Six hundred men of the experienced, but much reduced in fighting capability, FJR 6 (Oberstleutnant Friedrich Freiherr von der Heydte)[6] held ground northwest of the Neerpelt bridgehead.

---

1   Major David A Peel, aged 33 from Neatishead, Norfolk, was awarded the Military Cross for this action. He was killed the next day during a failed German counterattack. He is buried in Leopoldsburg War Cemetery in Plot VI, Row C, Grave 3.

2   Oberst Helmuth von Hoffmann was briefly the commandant of Eindhoven before commanding FJR 9 during the Battle of the Bulge.

3   British military terminology can be quite confusing. On 2 September the Guards Armoured Division reorganized into four combat groups each composed of one tank battalion and one infantry battalion. The Irish Guards Group, for example, held its 2nd (Armoured) Battalion and its 3rd (Infantry) Battalion. Lieutenant-Colonel Giles Vandeleur commanded the armored battalion while his cousin Lieutenant-Colonel John Vandeleur commanded the infantry battalion and the Irish Guards Group.

4   Panzerfaust: literally 'tank fist'; a single-shot, hand-held German antitank rocket launcher.

5   PaK: German abbreviation for *Panzerabwehrkanone* or antitank cannon

6   Oberstleutnant Friedrich-August Freiherr von der Heydte studied law and philosophy before rejoining the Wehrmacht in 1936. He was an infantry staff officer in the 1940 invasion of France. After transferring to the parachute force, he led an airborne force in Crete and in North Africa. He defended Normandy in 1944 as commander of FJR 6 and personally led his troops against the 101st Airborne Division during the Battle of Carentan.

Battle

On 17 September at precisely 14:00, 350 British guns open a twenty-minute barrage against predetermined targets that sounded like an overhead express train to the soldiers below who were awaiting the order to advance. The barrage extended 1,000 meters on either side of the road to Valkenswaard, avoiding the road itself to not damage the route of advance. Tons of explosives created gales of dust and shrapnel in the dense forests while German soldiers sheltered in foxholes hoping to survive. Brockes Panzerjäger Kompanie was destroyed not having fired one shell. Brockes was killed instantly when a mortar round hit his command post sited in a house beside the Valkenswaard road.

General Horrocks watched the huge airborne formations bomb German positions along the highway from the roof of a large metals factory on the south bank of the canal since demolished. The leading squadron of Irish Guards tanks moved toward to the start line. Behind them, two more squadrons sat nose to tail lining the narrow roadway.

At 14:35 the squeaking tank tracks of the Irish Guards Group announced the armored attack when Captain Michael 'Mick' O'Cock signaled the leading tanks of No 3 Squadron to move forward from the bridgehead with Lieutenant Keith Heathcote in the leading vehicle. Tank Squadrons No 1 and No 2 carrying infantry Companies No 1 and No 4 respectively followed with Company No 2 in trucks bringing up the rear. A squadron of the Household Cavalry Regiment in scout cars, 2nd Battalion Devonshire Regiment and tanks of the 15th/19th Hussars[7] followed. Each vehicle displayed yellow streamers to identify it to the Typhoon fighter-bombers above.

The tanks followed a rolling barrage advancing 180 meters per minute so closely as to be blinded in the billowing smoke and dust. All went well for the first ten minutes. Kerutt's I Bataillon crouched in its foxholes as the leading tank slowly approached their ambush 1.4 kilometers north of the Belgian-Dutch border. From a range of five to ten meters, the panzerfausts could hardly miss and the tanks could not escape off road onto the sandy bog that lined both sides of the highway. The Germans first struck against the rear of Squadron 3 and the head of Squadron 1. Within minutes, nine burning or disabled tanks were scattered over almost one kilometer of roadway. Many of the tankers never saw what hit them, but desperately escaped their burning vehicles into roadside ditches to avoid a flaming death. One of the disabled tanks was that of Lieutenant Lampard, the conqueror of JOE's Bridge, who was wounded in the action. The entire column halted.

Purple smoke shells identified possible enemy gun positions to rocket-firing Typhoons from 83 Group, RAF Second Tactical Air Force. During the next hour 230 sorties neutralized the enemy guns. With the Typhoons firing only meters ahead, British Infantrymen jumped from trailing tanks and began the grim business of rooting

---

7   The 15th/19th Hussars were formed by the amalgamation of two First World War cavalry regiments in 1922. It was the divisional armored reconnaissance unit for the 3rd Infantry Division during the Battle of France. In 1944 it reentered Normandy in the same function for the 11th Armoured Division held three squadrons of twenty tanks each, a reconnaissance squadron of the Royal Dragoons, and one artillery battery of the 86th Field Regiment. The regiment was temporarily attached to the 101st Airborne Division from 19 to 21 September.

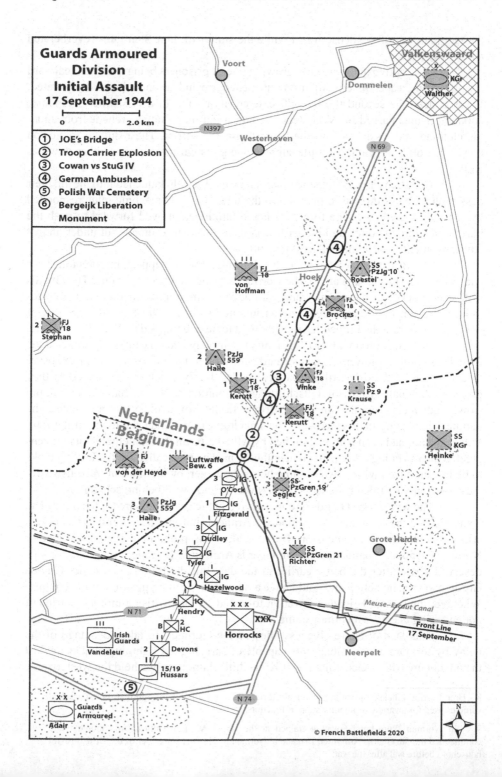

Guards Armoured Division Initial Assault 17 September 1944

0   2.0 km

① JOE's Bridge
② Troop Carrier Explosion
③ Cowan vs StuG IV
④ German Ambushes
⑤ Polish War Cemetery
⑥ Bergeijk Liberation Monument

Valkenswaard
KGr Walther

Voort
Dommelen

N397
Westerhoven
N 69

FJ 18 von Hoffman
Hoek
SS PzJg 10 Roestel

④
④
FJ 18 Brockes

2 FJ 18 Stephan

2 PzJg 559 Haile

1 FJ 18 Kerutt
③
FJ 18 Vinke
2 SS Pz 9 Krause
④
T FJ 18 Kerutt

Netherlands
Belgium

②
⑥

SS KGr Heinke

1 FJ 6 von der Heyde
Luftwaffe Bew. 6

3 IG O'Cock
3 SS PzGren 19 Segler

3 PzJg 559 Haile
1 IG Fitzgerald

3 IG Dudley

2 IG Tyler
2 SS PzGren 21 Richter

Grote Heide

4 IG Hazelwood
①

2 IG Hendry
B 2 HC

xxx Horrocks

Meuse–Escaut Canal

N 71
Front Line 17 September

Irish Guards Vandeleur
2 Devons

Neerpelt

15/19 Hussars
⑤
N 74

Guards Armoured Adair

© French Battlefields 2020

N

the Germans out of the dense forest while the stutter of their Sten guns reverberated among the trees.

One captive in the steadily growing line of prisoners being marched rearward attempted an escape. Several infantrymen opened fire and, as one witness dryly stated, 'he was dead the second the thought entered his mind.' In a less timely response, another prisoner passed Joe Vandeleur's scout car before pulling a grenade from under his clothing and tossing it into the nearest infantry carrier. The resultant explosion blew a leg off a sergeant. Multiple submachine guns cut that enemy soldier down as well.

Two Bren carriers[8] hit land mines and were literally launched into the air, their passengers' bodies thrown in pieces into the trees. Guards' machine guns responded by spraying the edges of the forest. Armored bulldozers moved forward to push the burnt hulks into the ditch and the Irish Guards movement resumed, but under almost constant attack as an admonishment to caution.

The British gained the upper hand through the air support, but precious time had been lost. The passage along The Corridor was not to be an easy one. The Guards staff was shocked at the number and variety of German units encountered. Besides fallschirmjäger, they discovered veteran infantry from the 9th and 10th SS Panzer Divisions and from the Fifteenth Army, thought to be still trapped on Walcheren Island.

No 2 Squadron with No 4 (Infantry) Company aboard cautiously traveled the final 1.5 kilometers toward Valkenswaard across open terrain wary of their exposure to enemy fire. A British artillery battery shelled likely points of resistance as they progressed. Small groups of fallschirmjäger mounted forays to harass the column slowly advancing up the highway. Bright flashes of explosions punctuated the darkness indicating their successes. The squadron did not enter the town until 19:30. Valkenswaard had been heavily bombed by Allied aircraft, but nonetheless its citizens greeted the liberating army with great enthusiasm. The plan called for the leading tanks to be in Eindhoven within two to three hours; however, by nightfall in Valkenswaard, they were only half that distance. GARDEN was already well behind schedule.

The whole Irish Guards Group laagered in the central square for the night. The delay chaffed those anxious to continue to Arnhem, but in a decision that has drawn criticism nighttime movement on The Corridor was prohibited. Perhaps Brigadier Norman Gwatkin,[9] commander of 5th Guards Armoured Brigade, thought the troops deserved a rest after the battle earlier in the day, but the trailing Grenadier Guards Group had seen no action and could have assumed the leading position in the column. Whatever the reason, Brigadier Gwatkin followed official British armored doctrine of not engaging enemy with armor in the dark.

This lack of aggressiveness allowed the Germans to take advantage of the delay by forming new combat units capable of carrying out lightning attacks against the advancing Allies. Generalleutnant Kurt Chill's kampfgruppe held the western side

8   Bren Carrier: officially a British Universal Carrier, describes a family of lightly armored, tracked vehicles used for a variety of infantry support functions.

9   Sir Norman Wilmshurst Gwatkin trained at the Royal Military College in Sandhurst and commanded the 5th Guards Armoured Brigade in Normandy. He was a member of the British Royal household before and after the war.

of the slowly developing 'Corridor' while remnants of Kampfgruppe (KGr) Walther[10] (Luftwaffe Oberst Erich Walther), attempting to restructure into a fighting force, held the eastern side. Von der Heydte seethed over the German command's decision defining the Valkenswaard road as the unit boundary between his unit and KGr Heinke (SS-Major Heinrich Heinke). In his mind the decision was an organizational disaster. Unit boundaries were always less well defended and in this case the defense fell to four independent commanders from three different services, namely Luftwaffe, Fallschirmjäger, and SS.

When the main body moved the next morning, another German blocking position again stopped forward progress. Two 88-mm guns covered approaches to a small bridge over the Tongelreep north of Aalst. Two attempts to find an alternative route to the east were defeated by Dutch terrain and German guns. An attempt to the northwest met with more success and eventually contacted the 101st Airborne Division in northern Eindhoven.

Meanwhile, after an all-day engagement, antitank guns covering the Tongelreep bridge were abandoned. At 19:00 the first tank rolled into Eindhoven amid wild civilian celebrations. GARDEN, however, was now eighteen hours behind schedule. The Irish Guards Group lost sixty men in the breakout battle.

At the same time, Bittrich and Model argued over the detonation of the bridges at Nijmegen and Arnhem. Model refused Bittrich's rationale to blow the bridges feeling that they would be necessary for a successful German counterattack.

Battlefield Tour

The battlefield tour starts south of the Meuse–Escaut canal where several military cemeteries in the Belgian military camp hold the dead of the battle, continues to the crossing of the Meuse–Escaut Canal, the Dutch border, and along The Corridor into Eindhoven.

> The tour begins at the train station in the center of Leopoldsburg. (51.117705, 5.258142)

Leopoldsburg was liberated on 12 September 1944 by the Belgian Piron Brigade (Bevet Lieutenant-Colonel Jean-Baptiste Piron)[11] under command of the British 8th Armoured Brigade. By 16 September, the town was bursting with troops,

---

10 KGr Walther, although only existing for one month and composed of a continuously varying array of subunits, played a major role in MARKET-GARDEN.
Oberst Erich Walther was an experienced parachute commander leading a battalion in the invasion of Norway, the assault upon Rotterdam, the invasion of Crete, the defense of Cassino and Anzio, Italy. He also fought on the Leningrad Front in the Soviet Union.
Walther ended the war as a generalmajor fighting the Red Army in East Prussia where he was captured and sentenced to 25 years imprisonment. He died after three years in Soviet Special Camp 2 which occupied the grounds of the former Buchenwald German Concentration Camp.

11 The Belgian Piron Brigade was formed in England from escaped Belgian soldiers and consisted of motorized infantry, an armored squadron, artillery battery, and support units. The brigade landed in Arromanches, France on 8 August 1944 and was attached to various British Army divisions during subsequent engagements.

supplies, bridging equipment, and over 20,000 vehicles of all types in preparation for the advance north.

A **Sherman M4A4 'Firefly' tank** mounting a British 17-pounder gun stands outside the Leopoldsburg train station. The turret mounts a Browning machine gun in addition to the standard hull M1919A4 machine gun. The tank's side bears the Guards Armoured Division insignia.

The **Cinema Splendid** held the XXX Corps briefing by General Horrocks on 16 September. Horrocks stood before an enormous hand-drawn map of the Netherlands and began his presentation with, 'This is a tale that you will tell your grandchildren and mighty bored they will be.' He followed with a casual and upbeat description of the operational plan that included phrases 'no stop, no pause' and 'keep going like hell'. He expected the first tanks to be in Eindhoven within two or three hours; to be in Arnhem in sixty hours. The assembled unit commanders greeted the effort with enthusiasm and few questions.

Leopoldsburg

0   250 m

①   Beverlo Museum
②   Leopoldsburg Belgian Cemetery
③   Leopoldsburg War Cemetery
④   Sherman Tank
⑤   Flemish SS Memorial Obelisk
⑥   Museum K-Block and Oscar Kapel

© French Battlefields 2020

The cinema, across Nicolaylaan from the rail station, was gutted by fire in 1979, torn down, and replaced by a row of bleak cafés and bars. A small plaque on the front wall identifies the location. Ironically the barrel of the Sherman tanks points in their general direction.

> Proceed south, turn right at the first opportunity, cross the rail line that bisects the town, then immediately right again and follow IJzerlei for 500 m to a small park on the right. (51.120268, 5.256229)

On 6 September 1944, members of a Flemish SS unit, possibly drunk, exited a bar and collected forty-nine local citizens that they disliked. After herding the group to a then remote location, the SS executed the group; the bodies falling into a water-filled ditch. Twenty-two died but seventeen survived when bodies fell on top of them shielding them from the fusillade. A **memorial obelisk** identifies the location and a row of white crosses lines the ditch into which the innocent fell.

> Visitation to the museums and cemeteries within Camp Beverlo is allowed without permit; however, restricted zones must be avoided and sporadic closures for military events can be expected.
> The Camp Beverlo military museum is on highway N73 900 m east of the Leopoldsburg train station. (51.118228, 5.267136)

Kamp van Beverlo
Hechtelsesteenweg 9, 3970 Leopoldsburg
Tel: +32 (0)11 34.48.04
Email: museumkvb@belgacom.net
Web: http://www.3970leopoldsburg.be/site/museum-of-camp-beverlo/?lang=en
Camp Beverlo was established in 1835 shortly after Belgium achieved its independence from the Netherlands. Barren heath, adjacent to the town of Leopoldsburg, was chosen for its proximity to the Dutch border, abundance of underground water, and low cost. The Germans utilized the camp during both world wars for training several German Kriegsmarine units. The camp was heavily bombed in May 1944 by British forces, but the so-called K-Block was spared because it housed political prisoners.

Today, the camp remains as the largest garrison in Belgium and retains two rather old and ramshackle military museums, The Beverlo Museum and Museum K-Block.

The former military hospital, constructed in 1850 and considered one of the most modern facilities of its day, houses the Beverlo Museum. Old photographs, scale models, and documents record the history of the camp and its hospital and highlight events of local interest. A First World War film is interesting in that it presents rare action footage. The future of this museum is in doubt. Efforts to construct a new museum dedicated to British XXX Corps are underway, but no firm schedule has been developed.

> The K-Block is 1.8 km southwest of the Camp Beverlo Museum. (51.108766, 5.256523)

Museum K-Block and Oscar Kapel (MKOK)
Buskelstraat 131, 3970 Leopoldsburg
Tel: +32 (0)4 76 47 40 92
Web: http://www.museum-mkok-leopoldsburg.be/
A volunteer non-profit organization has been granted access to the grounds, but its continued existence is in doubt. Contact the museum before planning a visit.

Although originated in 1848, the cavalry camp experienced its greatest expansion in 1913 eventually reaching 53 blocks, 34 stables and associated out buildings. The German Army occupied the camp in 1914 and used it as a test ground for their deadly chlorine gas before its first use during the Second Battle of Ypres in 1915. Mechanization of Belgian armed forces in 1936 reduced the camp's importance. Postwar reductions of defense expenditures threatened the camp's existence until a local volunteer worked to save the camp.

The MKOK presents a few of the remaining blocks of K section of the cavalry camp, hence Museum K-Block name, and the wooden chapel of its once commanding officer whose first name was Oscar. The museum display of military vehicles and historical materials complements the Camp Beverlo Museum's photographs and documents. Re-enactment camps occur several times per year although the schedule is spotty.

> Belgian and British military cemeteries are located on the southeast outskirts of Leopoldsburg along Koning Leopold II-laan. (51.112544, 5.265596)

Leopoldsburg Belgian Cemetery
Koning Leopold II-laan 3, 3970 Leopoldsburg, Belgium
Open 24 hours

The cemetery grounds originally held graves of German troops who had died in the camp's military hospital. After the war, these bodies were re-interred in the Lommel German War Cemetery. Currently the laurel hedge lined cemetery holds 826 burials from the First World War, of which 408 are Russians, and 418 Belgian and Russian soldiers, deportees, and political prisoners from the Second World War behind the chapel. The wooden shelter in front holds the register and visitor's book. A red crushed stone avenue leads to a white chapel dedicated to unknown prisoners of war. A second chapel to the east commemorates unidentified political prisoners of both world wars. Rows of crosses at the rear of the cemetery are in remembrance of Belgian Resistance members who were executed nearby during the German occupation. Their remains have since been removed to other locations.

> The British cemetery is 200 m to the east. (51.112773, 5.268417)

Leopoldsburg War Cemetery
Koning Leopold II-laan 3, 3970 Leopoldsburg, Belgium
Web: https://www.cwgc.org/find-a-cemetery/cemetery/2009300/leopoldsburg-war-cemetery/
     The first thirty-five burials originated from engagements in or near the town in May 1940. The cemetery now holds 800 burials from the Leopoldsburg military hospital or from isolated graves sites in the region predominantly of downed air crews. The nationalities of the soldiers and airmen are representative of the British Army of 1944 and include Canadian, Australian, Polish, South African, Dutch, and New Zealanders.
     Two brick pillars flank the entrance gate which accesses the grass avenue dividing the almost perfectly rectangular burial grounds into eight plots facing shelters on either end. The Cross of Sacrifice is center rear from the entrance gate.
     The cemetery holds the graves of two recipients of the Victoria Cross. Corporal John Harper aged 28 in Plot V, Row B, Grave 15 successfully led his infantry section against a strongly defended German canal dike in September 1944. Major Edwin Swales aged 29 in Plot VIII, Row C, Grave 5, was a bombardier whose aircraft was seriously damaged by enemy night fighters over Germany in February 1945. Captain Swales successfully commanded the aircraft to its target and brought the plane back to friendly territory before ordering the crew to bale out. As the last crew member jumped, the unstable craft became uncontrollable and plunged to earth carrying Major Swales to his death.

Continue east for 8 kilometers into Hechtel and stop at the almost hidden small park on highway N73 380 meters west of the center of the town (51.125852, 5.362362)

     To commemorate the Battle of Hechtel, which cost the lives of 62 British soldiers, 35 civilians, and 124 German troops, a **Sherman M4A2** tank is accessible along a flag-lined walkway behind buildings across from the Total gas station. Plaques mounted upon the base identify soldiers killed in the battle by unit and the civilians including twenty-two civilians executed by German paratroopers after false accusations of being partisans.

A German Military Cemetery is 5.6 km south of Lommel with its access road signed in Dutch and German from highway N746. Parking is limited. (51.190262, 5.305177)

Lommel German War Cemetery (Duitse Militaire Begraafplaats)
Dodenveldstraat 30, 3920 Lommel
Web: https://www.volksbund.de/kriegsgraeberstaette/lommel.html
     The cemetery originated in 1946 as a temporary American cemetery before being ceded to the Germans and the transfer of German remains from a temporary cemetery at Henri-Chapelle and other sites. The cemetery is the largest German military cemetery in Western Europe outside of Germany holding 39,111 graves, each under an aggregate stone cross bearing one plaque on either side that identify the

dead. Most of the burials are from the Second World War although 542 bodies were transferred from a First World War cemetery. Over 6,000 of the bodies have never been identified and 1,200 have been classified as child soldiers because of their age. The deaths occurred in any of the six large engagements that occurred during the 1940 invasion or during the late 1944-45 battles near the German border.

The cemetery holds approximately 90 Latvians who were impressed into the German Army to fight the Soviets. Escaped or captured by Western Allies toward the end of the war, they became British PoWs who eventually died in the hospital in Ostend where they were initially buried in the Ostend German Military Cemetery. In August 1946 they were reburied in Lommel.

The cemetery also holds the bodies of three members of Colonel Otto Skorzeny's Operation GREIF who donned American uniforms and created chaos behind American lines during the opening days of the German Ardennes Offensive (or the Battle of the Bulge tas it is known to Americans. The three were captured by American forces and executed as spies on 23 December 1944.[12]

The entrance shelter holds the register and visitors' book. The mosaic lined walls of the crypt focus sunlight upon a prone stone figure of a German soldier on the floor. The crypt is topped by a stone calvary flanked by grieving figures of black basalt. From the entrance, the seemingly endless rows of crosses disappear in the distance under a canopy of 5,000 pine, oak, maple, and birch trees. The enormity of the grave plots is almost incomprehensible. The central plots are noted for their purple heather border plants.

The Polish Cemetery is 4.9 km east of Lommel on highway N715 south of the intersection with highway N712. Park on the opposite side of the street. The location is near the starting point for the opening engagements of Operation MARKET-GARDEN. (51.216562, 5.363188)

Polish War Cemetery Lommel
Luikersteenweg 3, Lommel 3920, Belgium
Web: http://www.polishwargraves.nl/lom/lmm.htm#engels
The cemetery was created in 1946 on the initiative of the British government for Polish soldiers who fell during the liberation of Belgium. Remains of 257 soldiers were exhumed from various parts of the country and reburied here in four uniform plots.

The cemetery is situated in a wooded area and is entered through simple iron gate. The four plots of white stone crosses are arranged on each side of a central, gravel court. Once inside the gateway, the Polish sacrifice is commemorated by a marble sculpture of a woman with a laurel wreath bearing a plaque in Polish, Dutch and French declaring:

---

12   The three were Gunther Billing, aged 21, Manfred Permass, aged 23, and Wilhelm Schmidt, aged 18. The three, members of FJR 12, targeted a bridge over the Meuse River behind the front lines while wearing American uniforms. They were apprehended on 17 December after failing to give the proper password. The trio were executed by firing squad six days later. In total, seventeen Operation GREIF members were captured, tried, and executed

A thousand-year-old Poland had its sons fallen on this ground.

In the rear a huge metal cross is mounted upon on a wall constructed of various stone materials with each indicating a Polish battlefield during the two World Wars – Ieper, Gent, Stekene, Roeselare, Merksplas and others mark the battle trail of those who lie in the cemetery. Unit plaques single out the 1st Polish Armored Division and Squadrons 302, 308 and 317 of the twelve such units that comprised the Polish Air Force in Great Britain in which over 17,000 Poles served line the plinth bottom.

On the morning of 1 January 1945, the Luftwaffe launched its last major air attack of the war in an effort to regain some level of air superiority over the Ardennes Offensive battlefields. Although almost 400 Allied planes were destroyed or damaged, most of them on the ground, the German losses of over 200 irreplaceable pilots doomed the Luftwaffe for the remainder of the war. Flight Lieutenant Tadeusz Powierz, aged 30, from 317 Squadron, RAF responded to the air attack and was able to get his Spitfire airborne only to be shot down. He crashed south of Ghent, Belgium suffering severe head injuries that caused his death. He is buried in Plot I, Row C, Grave 12.

Continue north 2.7 km on highway N715. As the highway starts to rise to the bridge structure, a slip road (Vaartstraat) on the right leads to a parking area for a Barrier-park Lommel. Proceed to the memorial on foot. (51.238140, 5.378678)

The Irish Guards tanks crossed the canal on a Class 40 Bailey bridge, which the division engineers had built a few meters to the west of **JOE's Bridge**. Sint-Lucasstraat west of the highway led to a pre-war turning bridge which had been blown by the Belgian Army in 1940 but still descends to the canal's banks.

The **Irish Guards Memorial** once stood under the trees along the canal on the north side of the bridge. Recent construction required the upright stone slab memorial to be relocated to a new park on the south side of the canal. The original polished granite plaque is now encased in a stone frame. The text identifies the bridge and the events of 10 September. The memorial currently occupies the position of one German 88-mm gun. The other two guns were on the opposite bank just west of the bridge.

Liberation Route Marker #100 stands nearby, and its audio recording describes the JOE's Bridge action.

Proceed 3.3 km north of JOE's Bridge and stop at the monument on the right. Highway N715 in Belgium joins highway N74 shortly before the Belgian / Dutch border, then becomes highway N69 in the Netherlands. (51.267, 5.3964998)

On 17 September, a Royal Artillery officer hid in the attic of a Dutch customs house on the left side of the road. He and a signalman directed the opening barrage, which struck approximately 150 meters north of the memorial. Three days later the Royal Dutch Prinses Irene Brigade occupied this border crossing becoming the first Dutch military unit to reenter its country.

The **Bergeijk Gate of Liberation Monument** on the Belgian – Dutch border is sandwiched between two fast food establishments on the right side of the road immediately after crossing the border. The striking multi-colored granite stone bears the Bergeijk coats of arms and the insignia of the Household Cavalry Regiment and the Dutch Prinses Irene Brigade.[13]

Liberation Route Marker #101 stands to the right. 'The Ambush' audio relates how four civilians greeted the 11 September reconnaissance only to fall under suspicion and interrogation later by German troops. Despite their release, the four were fired upon killing two and wounding two. The audio also recalls the ambush six days later by KGr Walther in the forests ahead creating the first of numerous delays that would doom those at Arnhem.

> The mixed deciduous and pine forests on both sides of slightly raised highway N69 held ambush sites 1.4 km north of border and again 3.3 km north of border. Unfortunately, the busy road offers no opportunity to stop.
> A farm track on the left 1.9 km north of the border accesses the Odiliahoeve Farm. (51.283035, 5.406763)

Lance-Sergeant George Cowan commanded a Sherman 'Firefly' which mounted the powerful British 17-pounder gun instead of the less potent American 75-mm. Cowan entered these open fields to bypass the blockage ahead and noticed a Sturmgeschütz from Panzerjäger Abt 559 sheltering near a farm building. He knocked it out with one shot and placed a captured German soldier on his tank who, threatened with execution, pointed out targets for Cowan, who destroyed three additional German Sturmgeschütz. The loss of the self-propelled guns forced von der Heydte's fallschirmjägers away from the road opening the route for those following.

> Exit the forest and make a brief stop at the parking slip on the left or slightly farther ahead at a minor dirt road of Achterste Brug on the right. (51.285032, 5.407988)

The major issue of terrain can be reviewed from this early location of British XXX Corps' advance. Clear, open fields to the west demonstrate the scant protection offered to vehicles traveling on the highway. The slight elevation of the highway above that flat ground presented the enemy with easy profiles of target vehicles against the sky background. The dense forests that the highway has just passed through provided excellent ambush sites for camouflaged enemy soldiers utilizing short range weapons such as panzerfausts. In all, a terrible place to start a campaign.

> Pass through the Hoek roundabout 2.7 km ahead and stop 200 m farther at the monument on the right across Oude Dorpsstraat from the Family Suykerbuyck Creperie. (51.308723, 5.423841)

---

13   The Prinses Irene Brigade was formed of Dutch citizens who escaped to England in 1940 augmented by volunteers of Dutch ancestry from numerous other countries. The brigade landed in Normandy in August 1944 to serve under the First Canadian Army and became involved in fighting at locations in France and particularly the Netherlands.

By 17:00, the British tank column approached the Hoek roundabout 5 kilometers south of Valkenswaard. SS-Captain Franz Roestel of the SS 10th Panzer Division's Panzerjäger[14] Bataillon had positioned eight Jagdpanzer IVs[15] and towed antitank guns in the flanking woods facing open fields to the south. His armor occasionally emerged from the dense vegetation to strike the British spearhead on the roadway. However, after an uncertain number were destroyed by Typhoons or British antitank guns, the survivors pushed off to the east.

Earlier, on 11 September, the 2nd Household Cavalry Regiment became the first Allied unit to enter the Netherlands when two armored cars led by Lieutenant Rupert Buchanan-Jardine[16] performed a reconnaissance to reconnoiter the Dommel River bridge near Valkenswaard to determine its ability to carry the weight of British tanks. Four scouts in two Daimler reconnaissance vehicles raced at full speed past German troops, who were so amazed they failed to respond. While one car remained at what was then café Rustoord, Lance-Corporal Henry Brook proceeded forward to find a German PzKpfw IV stopped on the bridge. The corporal therefore knew the bridge was strong enough and drove back to this café to report to Buchanan-Jardine.

The tall stone with a spiral engraving stands as a **Liberation Monument** commemorating the exploits of the 2nd Household Cavalry during its reconnaissance mission to the bridge. **Liberation Route Marker #104** at the intersection commemorates 'A beer for the liberation.' The British commander of the 11 September reconnaissance mission was invited into the café by the innkeeper's daughter to celebrate liberation. Buchanan-Jardine accepted the invitation but warned the civilians that their celebration was premature.

Continue 400 m to the cemetery on the left at mile marker 46.8. Parking can be found on both sides of the road. (51.311982, 5.425729)

The **Valkenswaard War Cemetery** lies in a pine forest and contains the graves of 220 British soldiers including six unidentified Irish Guards and two airmen who fell in fighting around Valkenswaard during September 1944. The cemetery's simple design places the Cross of Sacrifice in the right side. A descriptive map titled 'The liberation of Belgium and the Netherlands and the Advance into Germany, September 1944 – May 1945' displays the movements of the British Army during the final nine months of the war.

One of the burials is that of Lance Corporal Joseph Seaton of the Welch Regiment who was killed 22 September on a bridge near Casteren over the Groote Beerze river. The 29-year-old left a widow and two sons, aged five and three. Joseph

---

14 Panzerjäger: ant-tank branch of the Wehrmacht which fielded anti-tank armor also called panzerjäger.

15   Jagdpanzer IV: one of several variations of tank destroyer based upon the Panzer IV tank chassis without a turret but armed with a 75-mm PaK gun and an MG 34 machine gun.

16   Lieutenant, later-Major Sir Rupert Buchanan-Jardine, 4th Baronet was immediately awarded a Military Cross for his daring exploit. He left the army in 1949 to attend to the estate that he would later inherit. Buchanan-Jardine died in 2010, aged 87.

came from East London and worked on the railway before the war. Upon our last visit, his grave in Plot I, Row F, Grave 4 was adorned with a bouquet of red carnations bearing a note 'To Granddad Joe ...'

> Continue 3.2 km and pass over the Dommel River bridge aware that it is impossible to safely stop on or near the structure. (51.338919, 5.443711)

The Dommel River is lazy little stream that formed a moderate tank barrier due to its six-to-eight-feet width and two-to-three-foot-high banks. The leading troops of No 3 Squadron reached the undefended bridge at 17:30 only to find the wreckage of Brockes Russian guns. Although the narrow, two-lane bridge was only a temporary structure but strong enough to support the weight of the tanks, it quickly became a choke point for two-way traffic. The Irish Guards spent two hours crossing the bridge while reshuffling the column to put the 2nd Squadron in the lead. A Bailey bridge was built later alongside to accommodate vehicles in both directions.

The **Valkenswaard Dommel Bridge** bears a small brass plaque labeling it 'Victorie Brug.' The bicycle path appears as if it was the original old highway, which in this area is four-to-five feet above the surrounding pastures.

> Enter Valkenwaard Markt on Eindhovenseweg (N69) and proceed to the marker in the pedestrian walk on the right. (51.350494, 5.459231)

VVV De Groote Heide (Valkenswaard Tourist Office)
Markt 19, 5554 CA Valkenswaard
Tel: +31 (0)40 201 5115
Email: info@vvv-valkenswaard.nl
Web: https://www.vvvdegrooteheide.nl/nl/valkenswaard
Open daily from 10:00 to 17:00.

Valkenswaard was the first town to be liberated on the main line of the British advance into the Netherlands. The town had suffered death and destruction from Allied bombardments and air attacks.

The evening of 17 September found this central square jammed with British tanks, trucks, armored cars, ambulances, and even a captured German tank. The congestion was flanked by officers and NCOs getting their respective command groups in long columns on both sides of the square.

Liberation Route Marker #105 'A Fatal Delay' audio analyses various causes for the British XXX Corps' stopping for the night in Valkenswaard. Was it rest for the troops after the first day's intense battle, or was nighttime advance too risky? Or perhaps the fiercer than expected German resistance and their ability to rapidly form new combat units greatly outstripped British organizational inflexibility. Whatever the reason, the delay proved fatal to troops in Arnhem.

> The 'Bunker' is found on the northwestern edge of Valkenswaard on Nieuwe Waal-reseweg. (51.364468, 5.445178)

The Bunker 'Birkenhof'
Nieuwe Waalreseweg 189, Valkenswaard
Tel: +31 (0)40 285 3085

In the early years of the war *Forschungsstelle (*interception station) Langeveld stood in Noordwijk on the coast north of The Hague. Due to the construction of the Atlantikwall and potential risk of invasion or bombardment, the station was relocated in 1943 to a camouflaged bunker in Valkenswaard. The Abwehr or German military intelligence service station transmitted radio communications to the German U-boat fleet and intercepted Allied radio traffic and radar signals. The results and analysis were then retransmitted to Berlin. This site played a part in the 'double-cross' intelligence operation known as *Englandspiel*.[17]

This red-roofed, red brick structure appears to be a residence, however closer examination reveals that behind the glass windowpanes and brick walls lays a concrete fortification. The four-room, east-west wing of the L-shaped structure holds the bunker complex. The north-south wing housed living quarters and as such was not concreted.

Now, the building is a Bed and Breakfast with meeting rooms. Plans are being developed to establish a small museum describing the function of the building, but no definite schedule has been issued. A guardhouse stands at the entrance to the park where postal deliveries utilize the original military observation slit.

Continue north on highway N69 for 4.9 km to the intersection with Kon Julianalaan on the southern limits of Aalst. (51.392904, 5.475022)

By the morning of 18 September, additional German blocking positions had formed south and north of Aalst. Ground fog forced postponement of the planned 06:30 departure from Valkenswaard to 09:30. No sense of urgency appeared evident even though the column was already well behind schedule. The armored scout cars of Lieutenant David Tabor's No 3 Troop of B Squadron (Major FEB Wignall), 2nd Household Cavalry Regiment with No 3 Squadron, Irish Guards tanks trailing began to move along the one-tank-wide road north from Valkenswaard toward Eindhoven.

Major Kerutt had split survivors of Regiment von Hoffmann, an antiaircraft platoon manning a 20-mm cannon and eleven 75-mm antitank guns between blocking positions at the southern edge of Aalst and near the Tongelreep bridge north of the city.

When Lieutenant Tabor's armored cars approached Aalst, he spotted a StuG III on the edge of a crossroads. After further delay, the Irish Guards Sherman tanks came forward – again led by Lance-Sergeant Cowan's Firefly. Cowan put five rounds onto the enemy SP-gun only to find that it had been abandoned because of a broken

---

17   *Englandspiel*: formally known as Operation NORDPOL (North Pole) was a German counterintelligence operation of the Abwehr. Captured Allied radio operators parachuted into the Netherlands by the British Special Operations Executive were forced to continue radio communications with their spy masters in England resulting in the interception of Allied information, supplies, and additional agents. The Dutch network was penetrated in early 1942 and the Germans continued to successfully run their counterintelligence operation until April 1944 when the Germans revealed their deception after a lack of new agents. Approximately sixty Allied agents were identified and most were later executed.

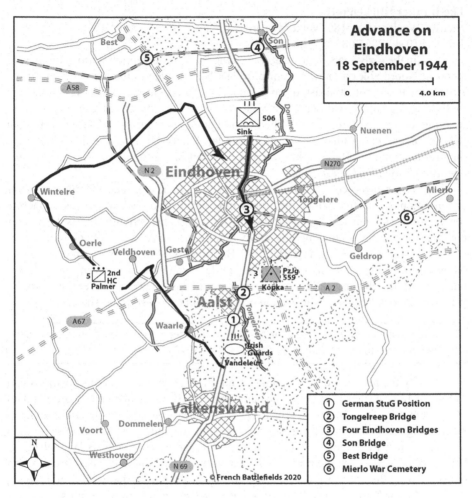

Advance on Eindhoven
18 September 1944

0   4.0 km

① German StuG Position
② Tongelreep Bridge
③ Four Eindhoven Bridges
④ Son Bridge
⑤ Best Bridge
⑥ Mierlo War Cemetery

© French Battlefields 2020

track. The scout cars then charged into the town.[18]

Aalst has grown considerably since 1944 when the intersection of the main highway and Kon Julianalaan crossing street was rural. The self-propelled gun hit by Cowan's Firefly was at the northwest corner of the intersection. Nothing remains to mark the site.

Earlier that morning, armored cars from C Squadron (Major Peter Herbert) set out at 06:30 undeterred by the fog and pushed northeast from Valkenswaard to provide flank protection and to find a possible alternative route into Eindhoven. Surviving Jagdpanzer IVs from Captain Roestel's unit guarded the route from Valkenswaard to Leende and, supplemented by infantry-borne panzerfausts, ambushed the armored cars in forests west of Leende. Finally, a collapsed bridge across the Tongelreep in

---

18 Sergeant George 'Bertie' Cowan was Mentioned in Dispatches and awarded a Silver Star by the American government for gallantry in destroying two enemy half-tracks and a self-propelled (SP) antitank gun during his unit's advance into Beringen on 5-6 September 1944.

Zeelberg ended the attempt.

Upon the first report of enemy armor before Aalst, Major Wignall ordered troops to the east and west to search for a by-pass. The troop to the east, like Major Herbert's Squadron had experienced farther south, was trapped by impassible water obstacles. No. 5 Troop, under the command of Lieutenant Michael Palmer, was more successful despite crossing numerous waterways over creaky wooden bridges which could not bear a tank's weight. After a detour to the northwest, Palmer contacted the 101st Airborne Division at Woensel in northern Eindhoven around half past twelve. Palmer radioed his headquarters with the vaguely coded message, 'Stable boys have contacted our feathered friends.'

Continue north on highway N69; after 950 m bear right onto the frontage road and continue for 500 m to the bridge. (51.400715, 5.479836)

British tanks again halted at a small bridge over the Tongelreep where they encountered two 88-mm flak guns positioned 200 meters ahead supported by infantry in nearby houses. Coming under fire, the two leading scout cars beat a hasty retreat behind a shield of smoke. Troops jumped from the decks of the tanks to engage the enemy. The leading tank tried to edge down the roadway, only to fall to one gun positioned to fire directly down the road. Joe Vandeleur asked headquarters for air support from the Typhoons that had performed so admirably the day before; however, fog had closed airfields in southern England and France even though the tank column stopped under a clear blue sky. He instead called down heavy artillery upon enemy positions, but resistance continued while Vandeleur fumed.

After receiving reports that the 101st Airborne was in Eindhoven to its rear, Kerutt[19] withdrew to the northeast and the route into Eindhoven was finally open, but it was not until 17:00 when Lieutenant Tabor discovered that the enemy had escaped. Unable to deploy their tanks off the road, the British could not utilize their numerical superiority thus allowing two 88-mm guns and a few determined infantry troops to cost XXX Corps seven more hours.

The **Tongelreep**, like many such waterways in the Netherlands, presents a mere trickle of water in a narrow but deep ditch. The passage in not difficult for troops, but the steep drop prohibits crossing for vehicles, thus the necessity to capture the bridge. The bridge, what there is of it can be viewed from the frontage road bordering the postwar, high speed highway. The German guns stood approximately where the current A2 motorway crosses highway N69. The underpass has been named the **Prinses Irene Brigade viaduct** in commemoration of the Dutch unit's passage along this road into Eindhoven on the night of 20/21 September.

Proceed 3.4 km into Eindhoven along Aalsterweg to Sint Joriskerk. (51.429921, 5.487374)

A church had stood near this site since approximately 1400. In 1885 a neo-

---

19 Helmut Kerutt was awarded the Knight's Cross in October 1944 for his leadership. He survived the war and died in 2000, aged 84.

Gothic replacement was built 150 meters west of the original chapel; whose site is now occupied by a residential apartment building. British armor entered Eindhoven at 19:00 and joined American paratroopers at **Sint Joriskerk** amid joyous citizens celebrating their liberation while, unfortunately, choking the streets and delaying the passage of vehicles.

Liberation Route Marker #109 sits in the small park across Stratumsedijk. 'A Paratrooper in Eindhoven' audio relates the jubilant liberation of Eindhoven through the recollections of a fictional American paratrooper. He tells of the celebration of the inhabitants and their taunting of the captured former occupiers. The audio ends with a citizen stating, 'You only know what freedom means if you lose it.' (51.429436, 5.486041)

Eindhoven

VVV Eindhoven
Stationsplein 17, 5611 AC Eindhoven, Netherlands
Tel: +31 (0)40 297 9115
E-mail: info@thisiseindhoven.nl
Web: https://www.thisiseindhoven.com/en
Open daily from 10:00 to 17:00.

Eindhoven was home of the giant Philips electrical combine founded in 1891 by a cousin of Karl Marx. The sprawling facility originally manufactured light bulbs and electric razors, but in wartime the facility specialized in vacuum tubes, radios and X-ray equipment most of which were exported to Germany for military use.

In 1942 the RAF bombed the Philips factory in the center of Eindhoven targeting the vacuum tube plants that supported German radar equipment. Approximately 130 civilians died in the raid and the main shopping district was flattened. Allied bombers returned on 16 September 1944 as a preliminary to the launch of MARKET-GARDEN.

The Eindhoven liberation celebration was short-lived, however. The next day shortly after nightfall, seventy-eight German aircraft, unhampered by the lack of Allied antiaircraft guns in the city, dropped flares to illuminate the city center and the great Philips manufacturing facility followed by bombs. Exploding ammunition trucks detonated vehicles carrying gasoline. The fire spread to nearby buildings whose walls collapsed into the streets and overwhelmed local firefighting capability. Over 200 buildings were completely gutted and 9,000 damaged. Civilian deaths totaled 227 with over 1,000 injured. The destruction of British supplies and the blockage of passage through the city resulted in shortages of combat supplies for the armored spearhead.

Eindhoven holds numerous memorials scattered around the city to those killed in air raids, during the liberation, those deported and who died in concentration camps, women who suffered deprivation, resistance fighters, and those missing without determination of their fate.

Large swaths of repeatedly bombed Eindhoven have been rebuilt and modernized, but traffic and limited parking make touring the city's central commercial districts problematic. A new ring road has been added. Much of the 1944 road system has been altered as a result, lessening the interest in military sites and objectives. However, for those interested and willing, the following Eindhoven tour reviews those locations. Eindhoven also provides a convenient location from which to visit related sites in the Netherlands. See the several side trips described at the end of this chapter.

The Stadthuis underground parking garage on the eastern side of Eindhoven Stadt-shuisplein offers a central location to explore central Eindhoven on foot. (51.435847, 5.480529)
The city memorial stands in the western corner of the Stadtshuisplein. (51.435493, 5.479789)

The **Eindhoven liberation memorial** forms a series of stone friezes around the base of a platform memorializing the inhabitants of the city who were killed during the war. One such embossing shows German soldiers marching in formation passed a Dutch civilian holding the torch of freedom. Atop the stone platform, three male bronze figures represent the citizen, the soldier, and the freedom fighter. It is expressive while remaining understated. The text states:

> Those who stand here
> Remember their death
> Their sacrifice great
> Before you go.

Polished stone tablets on the inside of the surrounding wall list the names of all the residents of the municipality who died during the war. A torch holder displays an eternal flame that unites Eindhoven with Bayeux, France as the first cities in each country to be liberated.

Proceed to Wal immediately west of the memorial and continue south 180 m. (51.434302, 5.481050)

Liberation Route Marker #108 'A Tragic Mistake' audio relates that the liberation of Eindhoven also took its toll on the city's citizens noting in particular a resistance fighter was killed by friendly fire. Adri Luijkx, a 26-year-old grocery store assistant armed with a confiscated German rifle, was looking for Germans hiding in a house. Although wearing a white armband identifying himself as a member of the Partizanen Actie Nederland (PAN – the local resistance organization), Luijkx was shot in error by an American paratrooper when he smashed a window with the rifle.

The marker stands outside the Van Abbe Museum of Modern and Contemporary Art along a bank of the Dommel River at one of the four Eindhoven bridges secured by the 101st Airborne Division.

Return to the garage entrance and continue north passed Sint-Catharinakerk into the pedestrian zone where stores, bars, and restaurants offer refreshments and goods. Continue north to the intersection of Kerkstraat and Rechtestraat. (51.437515, 5.479381)

On the side wall of a building now housing a Taco Bell restaurant, a bronze tablet remembers the **19 September German bombing of Eindhoven**. The tablet presents the grim visages of the citizens and German twin-engine bombers.

> Continue east on Kerkstraat one block and turn north on Jan Lieshoutstraat and follow into the Markt. (51.439477, 5.478002)

The Marktstraat is the center of Eindhoven's lively open market filled with outdoor dining opportunities, street vendors, and shops. A plaque on the front of the building currently housing a KFC restaurant displays two bronze panels joined by torch flames. The left plaque celebrates the 50 years since liberation; the right plaque celebrates **US 101st Airborne Division General Maxwell Taylor** and **British XXX Corps General Brian Horrocks**. The stone plaque around the corner describes the history of the building as first an investment bank, school, telegraph office, and now fast food restaurant.

> The Philips manufacturing complex northwest of the city's center is undergoing a renaissance as a technology park. Although parking is difficult, spaces can sometimes be available along Glaslaan to the south and west. The memorial stands along PSV-laan. (51.444912, 5.462091)

A long narrow wall bears the copper-patina figure of a reclining cloth-draped corpse forming a **Memorial to the Fallen.** The marble slabs that form the wall are inscribed with the names of Philips employees who died during a strike in May 1943 called to protest Jewish co-workers being transported for slave labor, those who died in Allied and German bombings of the city, or the many killed in other actions during the war.

> Continue 1.0 km southeast on PSV-laan, which becomes Mathildelaan. The memorial is inside the gates of the Inntel Hotels Art Eindhoven. (51.440962, 5.474350)

A memorial to the **Dutch civilians** killed in the Allied Operation OYSTER stands inside the gates of the Arthotel. On 6 December 1942, ninety-four RAF Ventura, Boston, and Mosquito bombers delivered six tons of bombs on the Philips factories to prevent the company from providing vacuum tubes and infrared and radio technology to the German war effort. Although the one-time daylight raid was considered a great success by the British despite the loss of sixteen aircraft, 135 Dutch civilians were killed. The metal memorial resembles a partially open oyster shell which holds the bombed and burned ruins of a factory complex.

Side Trip: Netherlands American Cemetery
The only Second World War American military cemetery in the country is in extreme southeast Netherlands near Maastricht. The grounds hold the remains of many of the American MARKET-GARDEN dead. Its location recommends that it be visited before the start of the battlefield tours.

> The American military cemetery is 76 km southeast of Leopoldsburg and 126 km

east of Brussels. (50.817772, 5.803316)

Netherlands American Cemetery
Amerikaanse Begraafplaats 1, 6269 NA Margraten, Netherlands
Tel: +31 (0)43 458 1208
Web: https://www.abmc.gov/cemeteries-memorials/europe/netherlands-american-cemetery
Open daily from 09:00 to 17:00. Closed Christmas Day and New Year's Day.

The US 30th Infantry Division liberated the cemetery site on 13 September 1944. The first burials began in early November of that year comprised of the dead from MARKET-GARDEN, fighting in Germany, and air operations over European soil.

The cemetery's tall memorial tower can be seen during the approach to the site. A Court of Honor leads to the tower and a statue of 'Mourning Women,' representing those who have suffered from warfare, three doves, and a new branch rising from a war-destroyed tree. The court is framed in Tablets of the Missing bearing the names of 1,722 soldiers and airmen who have no known grave.

The burial area is divided into sixteen plots that gently slope up to a flagstaff at the rear of the cemetery. In all, the plots hold 8,291 dead, of whom 106 have not been identified and whose gravestones are inscribed, 'Here rests in honored glory A Comrade in Arms known but to God.' The cemetery holds forty pairs of brothers, four women, and six soldiers who received the Medal of Honor.[20] Medal of Honor recipient Lieutenant Colonel Robert Cole (see Chapter Three) is buried in Plot B, Row 15, Grave 27 and Silver Star recipient Major Oliver Horton (see Side Trip: Battle of Opheusden) in Plot G, Row 1, Grave 11. The last burial was in 1994.

Since 1945, local Dutch citizens have participated in the 'Adopt a Grave' program, wherein they lay flowers on the assigned serviceperson's grave and research their life to honor their sacrifice. Membership in this civilian organization is considered a great honor and adopted graves have been transferred within family members as adopters have died.

A bi-annual event known as The Faces of Margraten displays collected photographs of the soldiers on their grave during Dutch Memorial Day – in effect bringing visitors face-to-face with almost 6,000 of their liberators. The most recent tribute was in May 2020.

The photographs of over 28,000 American service personnel buried in the Netherlands, Belgium, and Luxembourg can be viewed on the Fields of Honor database.
Fields of Honor Foundation
Stekkenberg 20 b, 6561 XJ Groesbeek, Netherlands
Email: info@fieldsofhonor-database.com
Web: https://www.fieldsofhonor-database.com/index.php/en/.

---

20   Besides Robert Cole, Margraten also holds the graves of Medal of Honor recipients Pfc Willy F James, Private George J Peters, Staff Sergeant George Peterson, Pfc Walter C Wetzel, and 1st Lieutenant Walter J Will.

Side trip: Stirling Heavy Bomber Crash Site

Leave Valkenswaard south on Maastrichterweg which becomes N748 upon cross-
ing the Dutch-Belgian border; continue toward Achel turning onto Achel Statie in
Rodenrijk then following Rodendijk. Turn right onto Witteberg into the forest.
Total distance: 13 km south of Valkenswaard. (51.260404, 5.463656)

Numerous memorials dot the Dutch and Belgian countryside commemorating
aircrews that fell to German fighter aircraft or ground flak while flying bombing
missions against German cities. At approximately 01:35 on 22 June 1943 the four-
engine British Stirling heavy bomber EF-366 of 7 Squadron was shot down and crashed
near Achel. The Stirling belonged to a group of aircraft that guided the bombers of
the Royal Air Force to their targets, which that night was Krefeld, Germany. Two
German Bf 110 night fighters discovered the bomber by its shadow against the search
lights. Seriously hit, the pilot, 21-year-old Australian Flying Officer Robert Bruce
Meiklejohn, ordered the crew to abandon the aircraft at an altitude of 10,000 feet before
it entered a steep, spinning dive. The plane still carried its bomb load and was aimed
to crash into the center of Achel with what would have been disastrous consequences.
Meiklejohn and his navigator Flying Officer Charles Redwood from New Zealand
remained at the controls and succeeded in raising the nose of the aircraft to avoid the
village falling instead into the nearby forest killing both Meiklejohn and Redwood.[21]
The five remaining crew members were captured. Two, badly injured, were treated
in a military hospital and remained PoWs for the remainder of the war. Three crew
members escaped the area only to be captured later in Paris while attempting to reach
a neutral country.

A few weeks later, German Hauptmann Siegfried Wandam, the fighter
pilot who had shot down the Stirling, was himself shot down over the village of
Hoepertingen, Belgium.[22]

A brick chapel at the edge of the forest, constructed in 1987 by local citizens,
replaced a prior chapel and commemorates Meiklejohn and Redwood's sacrifice. A
memorial plaque attached to the exterior wall identifies the two men and describes the
mission upon which they died. The chapel's small interior is attractive and is noted for
its wooden barrel ceiling.

Side Trip: 'Clay Pigeon' and 'Piccadilly Filly' Crash Site

In western Het Bosch, 22 km west of Valkenswaard along the road from Bladel to
Netersel a triangular wood holds a memorial identified by a brown sign indicating
'Oorlogsmonument.' (51.388282, 5.211732) Parking is possible along Het Bosch
85 m to the south.

On 17 September, the planes, 'Clay Pigeon' and 'Piccadilly Filly,' were flying

---

21   Flying Officer Robert Bruce Meiklejohn and Flying Officer Charles Redwood are buried in the
British military graveyard of Heverlee near Leuven, Belgium.

22   Hauptmann Siegfried Wandam and his radio operator Sergeant Schöpke are buried in the
Lommel German War Cemetery.

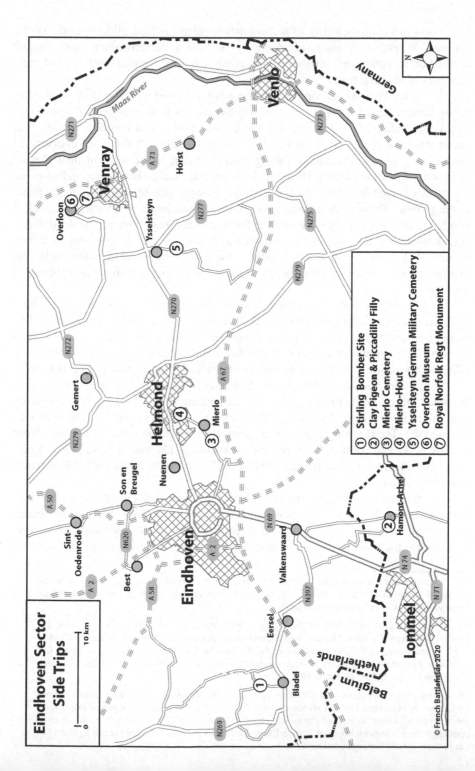

Eindhoven Sector Side Trips

① Stirling Bomber Site
② Clay Pigeon & Piccadilly Filly
③ Mierlo Cemetery
④ Mierlo-Hout
⑤ Ysselsteyn German Military Cemetery
⑥ Overloon Museum
⑦ Royal Norfolk Regt Monument

© French Battlefields 2020

low before dropping their stick of parachutists or releasing their glider over the Dutch countryside when they were shot down by German antiaircraft guns. Both aircraft crashed on a nearby farm owned by the Spliethof family. Several civilians and crew members died in the crash.

'Clay Pigeon,' carrying eighteen paratroopers and a crew of four from 82nd Troop Carrier Squadron, was intent upon delivering its human cargo. A cannon shell struck the middle of the fuselage, cut the control cables, and ignited a roaring fire. Paratroopers of the 101st Airborne Division rushed through the open doorway to escape, only to have the flames trailing from the plane ignite some of their chutes. Six paratroopers were killed. The pilot, 1st Lieutenant Guido Brassesco, and co-pilot, Lieutenant Joseph Andrews, blocked from the door because by flames, rode the plane to the ground. The aircraft plowed through trees, underbrush, and farmer's fences at two hundred miles per hour. Despite the flaming crash, both men survived; Andrews was thrown from the plane by the impact and Brassesco was dragged out by Dutch farmers.[23] The four crewmen were handed to the Dutch underground. Although briefly overrun by retreating Germans, they were saved when the British advance liberated the area.

'Piccadilly Filly' from 83rd Troop Carrier Squadron, was towing a glider when its number 2 engine was hit by flak. The aircraft continued on course for a few seconds before starting a slow climb and right turn to release the glider. The C-47 then made a slight turn with the wing pointing down and dived into the ground. The crash killed all four crew members, three children from the Spliethof family, and JJ Kok.[24]

A third C-47 #42-108884 from 86th Troop Carrier Squadron also crashed in the area that day while towing a glider to the landing zone. The aircraft's right wing was struck several times by enemy flak followed by a flak grenade on the right side of the plane. The resulting explosion engulfed the cockpit in flames. The plane dived straight down and crashed. Four crew members died.[25] The lone survivor, Crew Chief Sergeant Bela Benko, spent the next ten days hiding from the Nazis until able to return to friendly lines.

Sheltered among the well-spaced trees in a well-maintained plot, a path from the roadside passes between benches to a **brick-framed stone** bearing the names of seventeen civilians killed including three members of the Spliethof family who died during the period 1940 - 49, three Dutch soldiers from earlier in the war, and

---

23   Lieutenant Brassesco suffered two broken legs. Lieutenant Andrews recovered consciousness uninjured. The other crew members, radio operator Tech/Sergeant Barry Tinkcom and crew chief Staff Sergeant Joseph Curreri, parachuted to safety.

24   Pilot 1st Lieutenant Charles Gilmore, aged 29 from Wauwatosa, Wisconsin, co-pilot 2nd Lieutenant Robert Van Horn Thomas, aged 28, and radio operator Staff Sergeant William F Golden, aged 26, are buried in Section E, Site 13 in the Zachary Taylor National Cemetery in Louisville, Kentucky. Engineer Corporal Guy L Difalco, aged 27, is buried in Netherlands American Cemetery, Margraten in Plot A, Row 14, Grave 19.

25   Commander Lieutenant Colonel Ralph Lehr, aged 29, is buried in his native Blaine County, Oklahoma; pilot Captain Phillip Uhlenbrock, aged 23 from St Louis, Missouri is buried in his home town; co-pilot Lieutenant Edward Peterson Jr, aged 29 from Belle Vernon, Pennsylvania, and radio operator Sergeant James Rice, aged 26 from Evanston, Illinois are also buried in Section E, Site 13 of the Zachary Taylor National Cemetery.

fourteen identified and two unknown soldiers killed in crashed aircraft. The Memorial recognizes the perils endured by aircrew during their low-level flights over enemy territory.

Side Trip: Mierlo War Cemetery and Mierlo-Hout Memorial

Leave the Eindhoven outer ring road named Piuslaan to the southeast on Geldrop-seweg, into Geldrop. Leave Geldrop on Mierloseweg, which again becomes Gel-dropseweg, to the cemetery on the left.
Total distance: 11 km east of Eindhoven. (51.435272, 5.591624)

Mierlo War Cemetery
Web: https://www.cwgc.org/find-a-cemetery/cemetery/2006700/mierlo-war-cemetery/

The cemetery, in a wooded section outside of town, was created in spring 1945 for those who died during fighting for the Scheldt Estuary and around the Maas River. The grave plots are found in a dense oak forest that surrounds the cemetery. The simple layout displays the Cross of Sacrifice front and center, a shelter to the rear and four large plots on each side. This accumulation cemetery created after the battle holds 657 known and seven unidentified all from the UK but for five Australians[26] and four Canadians. One Dutch soldier, 20-year-old Gerardus Marinus Stönner, from the Prinses Irene Brigade, who died 22 October 1944 fighting around Tilburg, Netherlands, is also included.

Follow Geldropseweg northeast which changes names several times for 5 km to-ward Helmond. Turn right immediately before the rail line in Het Hout. (51.468736, 5.635219)

Helmond was liberated by a flanking operation during which a fierce battle on 22 September centered upon the rail line in Mierlo-Hout. Second Lieutenant John Bruce Millar, 2nd Lancers, 3rd Royal Tank Regiment, was part of a troop of three Sherman tanks assigned to outflank a German strongpoint at the rail crossing. He passed through some gardens and stood upright to direct his troops when wounded in the head by panzerfaust fragments. Millar jumped from his tank but was killed by a sniper's bullet.

At the same time, Private James Ion, 3rd Battalion, Monmouthshire Regiment, was mortally wounded by machine-gun fire from a German position on the opposite side of the tracks. Private Philip Davies attempted to rescue his comrade but was himself killed in the effort. All three young men were temporarily buried under

---

26   The five Australians were from the Royal Australian Air Force and all died on 3 February 1945 when their Avro Lancaster heavy bomber from 100 Squadron, Bomber Command was shot down over the Ruhr, Germany. Flight Lieutenant Robin Ordell aged 24, Pilot Officer Ian Osborne aged 20, Warrant Officer John Gordon Killen aged 24, and Flight Sergeant Keith Reynolds aged 21 were all from New South Wales. Flight Sergeant Raymond McKaskill aged 19 was from Victoria. Crew member British Sergeant Charles Scurr aged 24 was from Durham, England. Tail gunner Flight Sergeant James Harper spent the rest of the war in a German hospital recovering from his injuries.

wooden crosses along Slegersstraat behind Sint-Luciakerk 350 meters to the south and west where an information panel describes the deaths of the young men. (51.466886, 5.632272)[27]

A small park on the corner of the intersection in the Helmond suburb of **Mierlo-Hout** holds an unusually elaborate liberation memorial. Erected in September 2011, it demonstrates the ongoing effort by local Dutch to entrench their gratitude to the liberators of 1944. The rust-colored steel wall commemorates the four named British soldiers who died during the fight for the town on 22 September and the eleven citizens who died during the war with all their names and photographs on the left panel. The right side represents a barn door bearing a drawing of Dutch Red Cross member Francien Hermans-Coolen attempting to save Millar. Five war time photographs adorn the central panel.

Side Trip: Ysselsteyn (IJsselsteyn) German War Cemetery

From Mierlo-Hout Liberation Memorial: Proceed north across the rail line, then turn east onto highway N270 and follow for 15 km. Exit onto highway N277 and follow south into Ysselsteyn.
From Eindhoven: east on highway N270; after 30 km exit onto highway N277 and follow south into Ysselsteyn.
From Ysselsteyn: Proceed south through the town onto Timmermannseweg and follow 2.5 km to the cemetery access road on the left.
Total distance: 36 km east of Eindhoven. (51.469039, 5.892093)

Ysselsteyn (IJsselsteyn) German Military Cemetery
Timmermannsweg 75, 5813 AM Ysselsteyn, Netherlands
Web: https://www.volksbund.de/kriegsgraeberstaette/ysselsteyn.html

German soldiers buried in cemeteries across the Netherlands including most of the German casualties of Operation MARKET-GARDEN, those killed during the retreat from Belgium, and the Rhineland battles were disinterred after the war and reburied in this somber accumulation cemetery. The burials now total 31,598 in 116 grave plots making Ysselsteyn the second most numerous German military burial site outside of Germany and, unusual for a German military cemetery, almost all of the dead are in individual graves marked with a gray granite cross that identifies two head-to-head burials. The tree-lined central path terminates at the far end with a large cross. To the left of the entrance, 85 graves are centered around a stone catafalque. These First World War victims were originally buried in Maastricht and other communities but were transferred here during the accumulation process.

The cemetery holds the remains of German ace pilot Oberleutnant Karl-Heinz Willius, aged 24, who shot down his first enemy plane in August 1940 when he faced a Spitfire over Ramsgate, England. He scored his 50th and last victory in a Focke-Wulf 190 by shooting down a B-24 bomber over the Netherlands in April 1944.

---

27   Second Lieutenant John Bruce Millar, aged 20 from Norwich, is buried in the Mierlo War Cemetery in Plot VI, Row A, Grave 11. Private Philip Davies, aged 19, and Private James Ion, aged 20, are buried in adjacent graves. Also killed was Corporal Selwyn Kettle, aged 21, Monmouthshire Regiment. He is buried in the Mierlo War Cemetery Plot 5, Row F, Grave 9.

Upon attempting to regain altitude immediately afterwards, he was shot down by an American P-47 fighter. Because his aircraft crashed into the soft Dutch polder, it was not recovered until 1967 when his remains were then reburied in Ysselsteyn.

Liberation Route Marker #203, which stands near the white gateway at the end of a rhododendron lined path, speaks to the reconciliation efforts of Lodewijk Johannes Timmermans who worked at the cemetery for twenty-eight years. Timmermans was a Dutch soldier in 1940 who later assisted prisoners and Jews to escape into Belgium. After liberation, he commanded a small section of a Dutch bomb disposal unit when he was injured in an explosion. While in a hospital, he befriended a German soldier and dedicated his life to reconciliation of the two nations. He became manager of the German cemetery in Ysselsteyn.[28]

Side Trip: Battle of Overloon
30 September to 18 October 1944

> The Overloon Museum and Liberty Park are on the eastern edge of town. The tour begins at the local war cemetery, which is nearby.
> Total distance to museum: 44 km east of Eindhoven; 17 km northeast of Ysselsteyn German Military Cemetery

Although this engagement was not part of Operation MARKET-GARDEN, the museum's excellent exhibits offer an opportunity to visualize the form of combat that marked this area. A visit is highly recommended.

Battle

After Operation MARKET-GARDEN, the narrow corridor between Eindhoven and Arnhem gradually widened with the advance of British VIII Corps on the east side of the salient and XII Corps on the west. Generaloberst Student's Fallschirmjägers and the Panzer Brigade 107 held a bridgehead on the west banks of the Maas River from which to threaten the salient near the city of Venlo. The position was protected on the west by the swampy Peel marshes forcing the Allied attack to proceed from the north through Overloon and Venray.

On 30 September, after four days of exchanging artillery fire with the enemy, the American 7th Armored Division (Major General Lindsay Silvester)[29] launched Operation AINTREE. For nine days American Sherman tanks tried to breach the German defenses, but time and again they were stopped by German mines, artillery, Nebelwerfer rockets, and Panther tanks. On 8 October, the Americans were relieved by

---

28 Lodewijk Timmermans died in 1995 and, as he wished, his ashes were spread across the Ysselsteyn Cemetery.

29 Major General Lindsay Silvester, who had been awarded the Distinguished Service Cross and a Silver Star for actions in France during the First World War, was relieved of his command – a controversial action instigated by Field Marshal Montgomery in response to German success against the British-American boundary at the Peel Marshes in October 1944. General Omar Bradley conceded to Montgomery and relieved Silvester. After the war, Silvester asked for an inquiry, which supported Bradley's action on the grounds of commander's discretion. Silvester died in 1963, aged 73, and is buried in Arlington National Cemetery, Arlington, Virginia Section 11.

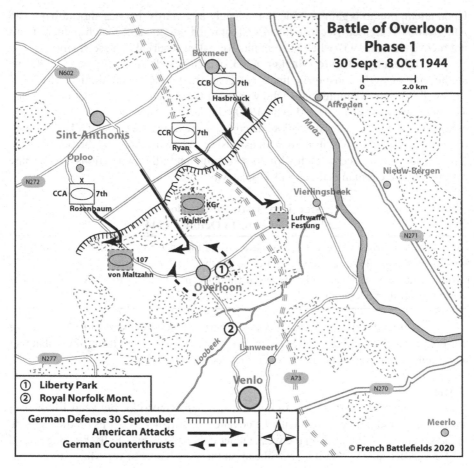

the British 11th Armoured Division (Major-General George Roberts) and the British 3rd Infantry Division (Major-General Lashmer Whistler).

A new attack was scheduled for 11 October, but heavy rainfall forced a one-day postponement. The rainfall changed the terrain into mud limiting the mobility of British tanks and leaving the difficult task of breaking the German resistance to the infantry and artillery.

Nevertheless, on 12 October at 11:00, heavy artillery firing at least 40,000 shells and air strikes pounded German positions for ninety minutes. At 12:30, the tanks of No 2 Squadron, Coldstream Guards moved in line along a narrow lane under constant shelling by German Nebelwerfers. Orders sent the tanks off the lane, through hedges, and onto open ground. Proceeding in a V-formation, the Churchill tank 'Jackal' led. The tank to the left of Jackal was hit, but the formation continued. Moments later Jackal struck a Riegel mine 43[30] that lifted the armored vehicle into the air. Driver Guardsman Robert Dare bailed with his clothes burning. Noticing that his

---

30   Riegel mine 43: a long, thin, bar-shaped antitank mine which held 4 Kg (8.8 pounds) of TNT and was triggered by any one of several fuses.

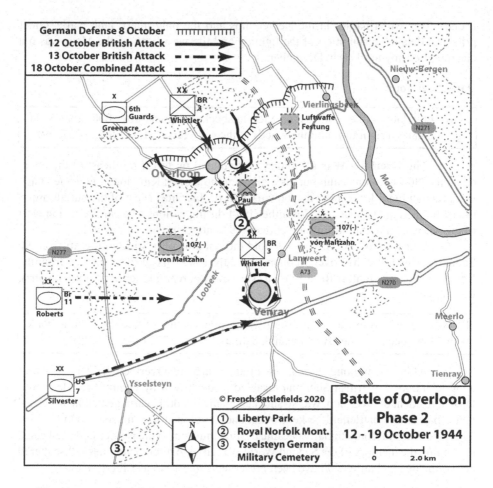

Battle of Overloon
Phase 2
12 - 19 October 1944

① Liberty Park
② Royal Norfolk Mont.
③ Ysselsteyn German
Military Cemetery

© French Battlefields 2020

co-driver's escape hatch was still closed, Dare returned to the burning tank, opened the hatch, and pushed Lance Corporal Jonathan Lambert out. Dare heard the screams of turretmen Guardsman Robert Silman and Gordon Wright, but he could not help them. Dare went back again to rescue the tank commander Sergeant Garner (or Captain Richard Mc Dougal – the records and personal recollections are in conflict as to who was in command), whose hands were on fire. Despite being in a minefield, the three were borne on a tank to the first aid post. Three more tanks suffered similar fates.[31]

The British advance fought from house to house at the cost of huge losses. During the afternoon of 14 October, the last German stronghold in the village church fell, but Overloon was in ruins.

Aftermath

The fighting around Overloon resulted in approximately 2,500 dead, making

---

31   Robert Dare returned to his job as a police officer after the war. Jonathan Lambert, despite losing both legs, worked as an inspector at the General Electric Company and lived to age 74. The fate of the tank commander, who had suffered a large chest wound, is unrecorded.

it one of the worst battles in the Netherlands and the only major tank battle. Other priorities delayed resumption of the fighting and the west bank of the Maas was not cleared of enemy until early December.

Battlefield Tour

Leave Overloon to the northeast on Vierlingsbeekseweg and after 800 m a CWGC sign indicates a right turn into the woods to the cemetery. (51.573967, 5.957559)

The **Overloon War Cemetery**, surrounded by forest northeast of the town, contains 280 Commonwealth burials – all from the United Kingdom – and one Dutch war grave in four plots centered upon the Cross of Sacrifice. Most of the burials are of men who died in October and November 1944 during actions to clear the region west of the Maas in preparation for the February 1945 attack on the Rhineland.

Plot III, Row A, Graves 1-6 hold the remains of a Stirling aircraft from 90 Squadron which was lost over German on 4 July 1943. Six of the crewmen from the Royal Air Force Volunteer Reserve died. The seventh, rear gunner Sergeant IH Norris, was captured.

Proceed on Museumlaan to a large parking area at the 14-hectare Liberty Park, which now occupies the Overloon tank battlefield. (51.570146, 5.953088)

After the fighting ended, the grounds around Overloon held twenty-four American and two British Sherman disabled or destroyed by enemy fire. Harry van Daal, a resident of Overloon, was so shocked by the resulting carnage that he proposed that a part of the battlefield be kept intact and developed as a museum. On 25 May 1946, the War Museum officially became the first museum in the Netherlands dedicated to keeping the memory of the Second World War alive. Armored vehicles left scattered across the deadly battlefield have been preserved since 1946 as Liberty Park.

Overloon War Museum (Oorlogsmuseum Overloon)
Museumpark, 5825 AM Overloon
Web: https://www.oorlogsmuseum.nl/en/home/
Open daily Monday through Friday from 10:00 to 17:00; Saturday and Sunday from 11:00 to 17:00. Closed specified holidays; see website for details. All descriptions are in four languages. Admission fees are high but include all the various buildings. Handicap accessible.

The complex houses the National War and Remembrance Museum of the Netherlands and the Marshal Museum, a hall dedicated to the American Secretary of State responsible for the postwar Marshall Plan to rebuild Europe.

The museum's list of displayed armor is impressive with Churchill, Cromwell, Crusader, Panther, Sherman, and even Russian T34 tanks. Dutch life under German occupation is described including Dutch concentration camps, Dutch resistance, and Dutch SS. An airplane hangar-sized main museum is filled with heavy equipment, including the Churchill tank 'Jackal,' whose action is described above in quasi-natural surroundings that portray events from the war. Spitfire, B-25 'Mitchell' aircraft, and a V-1 flying bomb are also on display. The collections continue into post-WW II equipment with wreckers and amphibious trucks. The displays present a mind-boggling array of equipment and each display is realistically executed. Be sure to push the red buttons that turn on the sound effects. This is a spectacular museum and an absolute must see.

The Museumplein or promenade before the entrance to Liberty Park holds several reminders of the nearby battles. Foremost a Sherman Tank named '**Able Abe**' is a repaired and repainted Sherman M4A1 of another name replacing the partially destroyed 'Able Abe' from the 1944 battle. (51.570538, 5.952859)

The **7th Armored Division Memorial** commemorates America's participation in the battle. The monument's stele, topped with an American helmet, bears the text, 'October 1944 in memory of the soldiers of the US 7th Armored Division who gave their lives during the liberation of Overloon.' (51.570470, 5.952985)

A second, smaller stele stands in the forest west of Overloon commemorating the discovery in 1977 of the remains of American soldiers, George Renda, aged 24 from Pennsylvania and Aloysius Gonsowski, aged 26 from Erie County, New York both from the 48th Infantry Battalion, 7th Armored Division. Both men were killed on 5 October 1944 during the fighting for Overloon. (51.563803, 5.920689)

Liberation Route Marker #117 stands on the promenade outside the museum and describes the battle. 'The Battle of Overloon' audio relates the two-week-long fighting in the quagmire created by days of rain and artillery bombardment. At the end the village was 90% destroyed and 452 Americans, 1,426 British, and 600 Germans had perished. (51.570346, 5.953075)

Leave Overloon south on Venraijseweg to the monument on the right immediately before the Loobeek crossing. (51.550822, 5.966244)

KGr Goltzsch (Oberst Rudolf Goltzsch), consisting of remnants of 344th Infantry Division and Panzer Brigade 107, re-grouped in the woods between Overloon and Venray. The British slowly gained ground around the flooded Loobeek under harsh weather conditions. Finally, a bridge was erected over the mined creek bed, but tanks immediately got stuck in mud on its approaches. British troops attempted to cross the creek against murderous machine gun fire turning the water red with their blood. In the evening of 16 October, their efforts finally succeeded. Three days later, Venray was also taken after heavy house-to-house fighting that ended the great battle.

A short, brick-framed, four-sided, pyramid bears plaques to the **1st Battalion, Royal Norfolk Regiment** which forced a crossing of Loobeek creek at this point. The monument is topped by a miniature soldier and is dedicated to 'all British, Allied, and Dutch soldiers who died for liberty.'

Chapter Three
American 101st Airborne Division 'Screaming Eagles'

The 101st Division was originally organized as an infantry division in November 1918 only days before the Armistice and was quickly demobilized. The unit reappeared in 1921 headquartered in Milwaukee, Wisconsin and adopted the 'Screaming Eagle' nickname from the bald eagle mascot of the 8th Wisconsin Volunteer Infantry Regiment during the American Civil War. Reconstituted as an airborne division in 1942, the unit's first action was in Operation OVERLORD dropping into Normandy, France shortly after midnight on 6 June 1944.

The 101st Airborne Division's mission in MARKET-GARDEN was to secure important crossings over water obstacles along a 22-kilometer corridor from central Eindhoven through Son[1], Sint-Oedenrode and on to Veghel[2] and Uden. General Browning's plan called for parachute drops at scattered locations along The Corridor. General Taylor protested having experienced the difficulties of dispersed drops in Normandy. He likened his assignment to the defense of the western railroad lines against Indian raids during the period following the American Civil War. The objective was to keep The Corridor open, not to capture territory or kill enemy. However, General Taylor could not permit strong enemy forces to accumulate for an attack to cut the vital highway either. The solution was to exercise strong patrols to disrupt enemy troop concentrations. The need for these actions explains some of the rapid engagements / disengagements of his troops during this period. For example, Colonel Howard Johnson of the 501st Parachute Infantry Regiment (PIR) seized Eerde then relinquished it, then captured it again. This dilemma also explains Taylor's decision that the initial glider lift prioritized jeeps over artillery — stressing maneuverability over firepower. Besides, British tanks were to arrive within hours of the drops, and they would provide the necessary firepower.

After crossing the English Channel, the division's planes turned north along the seacoast to cross the front lines near the Belgian-Dutch border, where they first encountered German flak.

The 501st PIR had two landing zones south and west of Veghel where it was to secure four bridges. The 2nd and 3rd Battalions with two platoons of 326th Airborne Engineers jumped into Drop Zone (DZ) 'A' south of the city in what is now an industrialized area to secure road and rail bridges over the Zuid–Willemsvaart Canal. The 1st Battalion targeted DZ 'A1' northwest of Veghel to facilitate capture of the rail and road bridges over the Aa River.

Colonel Johnson's 2nd and 3rd Battalions began their unopposed descent onto DZ 'A' at 13:06 in an action as well executed as any training exercise. Events were different for 1st Battalion as it headed for DZ 'A1'. The forty planes carrying six hundred paratroopers were the leading contingent of the entire air armada. The pathfinder aircraft designated to identify and mark the drop zone was shot down by antiaircraft fire as it crossed the Belgian coast. The following pilots and navigators

---

1   In 1944 and in early literature, the town name was spelled Zon. It has now been jurisdictionally combined with a neighboring community to become Son en Breugel.

2   US Army maps and older references use the town's old spelling as 'Vechel'

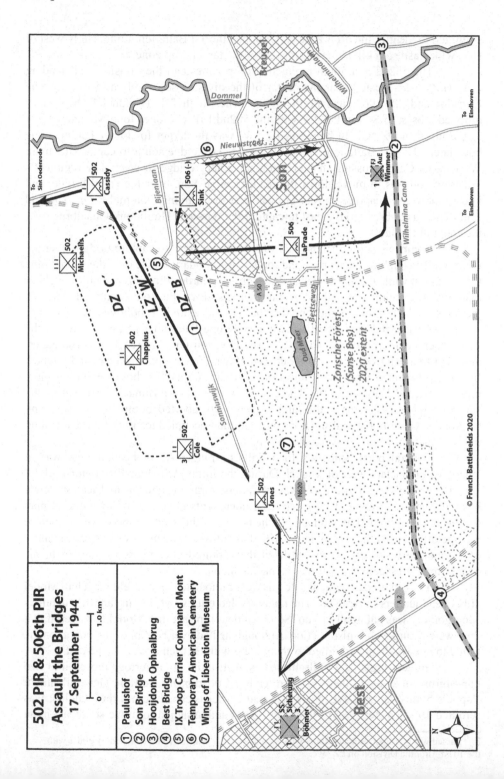

502 PIR & 506th PIR
Assault the Bridges
17 September 1944

① Paulushof
② Son Bridge
③ Hooijdonk Ophaalbrug
④ Best Bridge
⑤ IX Troop Carrier Command Mont
⑥ Temporary American Cemetery
⑦ Wings of Liberation Museum

struggled to identify the drop zone and dropped the 1st Battalion immediately west of Heeswijk Castle 5.5 kilometers northwest of the target drop zone.

The 502nd and 506th regimental drop zones and the division staff landing zone (LZ) were located near the center of the division sector, slightly west of The Corridor and 2.5 kilometers north of Son. The 506th PIR (Colonel Robert Sink) dropped closest to Son in DZ 'B' with the 502nd PIR (Colonel John Michaelis) just to the north in DZ 'C'. In between, LZ 'W' was the target for glider landings one hour later.[3] The 1st Battalion, 506th PIR was to strike due south to capture the main Wilhelmina Canal crossing in Son and a subsidiary bridge to west. The regiment's 3rd Battalion was to move down the road, through Son, over the canal bridge, and into Eindhoven to capture its four bridges over the winding Dommel River. The 2nd Battalion was to break to the east to capture the one-lane Hooijdonk Ohaalbrug over the canal in Breugel.

Companies of the 502nd PIR were to move north to capture bridges over the Dommel River in Sint-Oedenrode and south to a secondary bridge over the Wilhelmina Canal at Best while the remainder of the regiment guarded the drop zone for the glider landings. The regiment was the division reserve and was the connecting link between the 501st to the north in Veghel and the 506th to the south in Eindhoven.

Despite flak and small arms fire, only one Pathfinder plane and two of the 424 parachute aircraft of the 101st Airborne Division failed to reach the drop zones, although fourteen troop carrier aircraft went down after the paratroopers had jumped. In total, 6,684 men made the jump timed within one half an hour beginning three minutes after H-Hour at 13:03. The gliders were not so fortunate. Nineteen of the seventy gliders never made the landing zone. Six aborted before reaching enemy territory, seven suffered malfunctions over German occupied territory before reaching the landing zones, and six were shot down.

Generaloberst Student's First Fallschirmjäger Army headquarters was at Vught 18 kilometers west of Veghel. During the initial Allied air lift, a Horsa glider from Browning's I Airborne Corps was hit by antiaircraft fire and crashed near Student's headquarters. German soldiers discovered documents detailing the operational plan for the 101st Airborne Division among the bodies of the dead troopers. Almost before the operation began the enemy knew Allied intentions. Student, a veteran commander of German airborne operations, utilized the captured documents to implement his countermeasures using what forces he had available.

The captured document's details were radioed to Generalfeldmarschall Model at his headquarters in Arnhem. The plans spelled out everything in fantastic detail as Montgomery was habitually to do. So much detail in fact that Model considered that they were a purposeful misdirection. Although he had every detail of the operation, he failed to believe them and failed to share them with Bittrich or von Rundstedt.

Student organized Fallschirmjäger AuE units in 's-Hertogenbosch into two kampfgruppen and sent them to interdict The Corridor. In addition, Generalleutnent Poppe's 59th Infantry Division, which had earlier escaped across the Schelde, was rerouted 19 kilometers from Tilburg to Boxtel and assigned to move southeast in an

---

3   Famed war correspondent and future television newscaster Walter Cronkite landed by glider with the 101st Airborne Division on LZ 'W'.

attack upon Best and Son. Its leading units began to arrive in Best during the late afternoon of 17 September.

On Monday, 18 September the Second Lift of aircraft towing 450 Waco gliders delivered 2,579 troops of 327th Glider Infantry Regiment (GIR) and 151 jeeps and other equipment. The cost was fifty-four dead and twenty-three injured, many from ground-based, small-arms fire that easily penetrated the fabric skins of the gliders.

The Third Lift on Tuesday, 19 September left England with 386 Waco gliders carrying artillery and antitank weapons. Bad weather over the English Channel and over continental Europe forced the fighters and one half of the troop carriers to turn back. Planes at lower altitudes were particularly exposed to German flak and small-arms fire. Enemy action, weather, or equipment issues caused 132 tugs to turn back or release prematurely. Despite the difficulties, Taylor's 101st received 1,300 additional troops and, more importantly, 40 artillery pieces.

Son Bridge and Entry into Eindhoven
17 to 18 September 1944

Battle

Elements of the 1st Battalion (Major James LaPrade)[4], 506th PIR assembled rapidly into fifteen-man groups at the southern edge of DZ 'B' and made for the Son bridge through the Zonsche Forest. Time was of the essence; the bridge had to be captured intact. When the battalion passed behind the buildings of the Zonsche sanatorium, it encountered fire from two 88-mm guns positioned along the canal. Meanwhile, the 2nd Battalion moved through the village down the main street slightly delayed by a third 88-mm gun. The resistance was overcome, but a company from the I Bataillon (Hauptmann Johann Wimmer), Fallschirmjäger-Panzer AuE Regiment Hermann Göring blew the bridge in Son at about 16:00 just as the two groups of paratroopers converged on the northern approach.

That Sunday evening, engineers fabricated a makeshift footbridge permitting a slow crossing of the canal. The 506th spent the night of 17 September near Bokt, 2.0 kilometers south of Son.

Colonel Sink's instructions for the next morning were to make top speed for the city's bridges even if that meant by-passing small German units. Companies H and I led the march into Eindhoven astride the roadway with only one platoon and some engineers remaining at the Son bridge. Reports indicating a strong enemy concentration in the city were false and the column pushed aside small groups of infantry despite support by a few field guns of the German Flak Regiment 53. Troops of the 101st Airborne entered the city early on Monday, 18 September to find the inhabitants jubilant at their liberation and all of the bridges in the city center intact. The citizens greeted the Americans with wild dancing crowds, orange bunting and ribbons, and offerings of apples and gin.

4　West Point graduate, Lieutenant Colonel James LaPrade, aged 30 from Kenedy, Texas, was killed in Noville, Belgium on 19 December 1944 during the Battle of the Bulge. He is buried in the United States Military Academy Post Cemetery, West Point, New York. His brother, Marine Lieutenant Robert M LaPrade was killed on Guadalcanal after being twice wounded eliminating an enemy machine-gun nest. He was awarded the Navy Cross and is buried in Kenedy, Texas.

That night, British engineers arrived at Son and by early morning on 19 September they had constructed a Bailey bridge across the canal.

On 19 September, Panther tanks of the newly arrived Panzer Brigade 107 (Major Berndt-Joachim Freiherr von Maltzahn) attacked along the Wilhelmina Canal from the east. Bazookas and a single antitank gun beat back the assault. A repeat effort the next day was again repulsed.

Battlefield Tour

The 101st Airborne Division drop zone has been bisected by the new A50 Autoroute. The open fields directly south of DZ 'B' have been developed into a community called De Gentiaan. Thus, following the 1st Battalion's route to the canal is impossible. The tour starts at Paulushof Farm then continues with a review of efforts to capture and hold the Son bridge and entry into the northern, mostly residential, districts of Eindhoven.

Leave Eindhoven northwest along Tilburgseweg to achieve Autoroute A2. Take exit 28 'Best' and continue northwest on Oude Rijksweg. Cross over the Autoroute at the first traffic circle to access Sonseweg eastbound. Turn left onto Molenheideweg which becomes Sonniuswijk and travels along the southern edge of the 101st Division's drop zones. Briefly stop at the entrance drive to Paulushof to view the drop zones to the north. (51.526466, 5.461657)

Sonniuswijk is an attractive, tree-lined way through farms of cash crops, nursery stock, and livestock feed that runs along the southern edge of DZ 'B' north of Sonse Bos. On 17 September Paulushof made an excellent reference for pilots because the farm's name could be seen in large letters on its roof. Now a massage therapy center **Paulushof** has lined its approach road with small parachute sculptures in recognition of the role it played in 1944.

Liberation Route Marker #113, located near the farm building, presents 'Liberation from the Air' audio relating the story of a 15-year-old boy from Paulushof witnessing the death of his friend by American bullets during the pre-drop aerial bombardment. He also witnesses the American paratrooper arrival and the men, supplies, vehicles, and chocolate that they brought.

Continue east for 900 m on Sonniuswijk to the memorial on the left. (51.530187, 5.472542)

The 53rd Troop Carrier Wing flew 424 C-47 aircraft in the First Lift of 101st Division paratroopers to the drop zones around Son and Veghel. Seventeen of the aircraft were destroyed by enemy fire or other incidents and ninety-eight others received various levels of damage resulting in twenty-six dead and fifteen wounded airmen. At least three pilots are noted to have stayed at the controls of their burning aircraft to deliver the paratroopers before crashing.[5] The planes brought 4,634 men to

5   The three men were: Major Daniel Elam, aged 28 from Agnes, Texas, buried in Fort Worth, Texas and 1st Lieutenant Robert S Stoddart Jr, aged 22, buried in Englewood, New Jersey. First Lieutenant

DZ 'B' and 'C' with the remaining 2,050 dropping at DZ 'A' and 'A1'. The drops were tightly clustered greatly facilitating the paratroopers' assembly.

Later in the day, seventy planes arrived towing Waco gliders containing jeeps, equipment trailers, and 311 airborne troops from signal, reconnaissance, quartermaster, and medical sections. One glider inexplicably crashed over Belgium killing the seven men aboard. Six planes were shot down.

Fighter-bombers were effective in eliminating enemy positions in the open drop fields, but less so in the surrounding wooded areas. Intense flak came from Best and other installations along the Wilhelmina Canal.

A granite plaque mounted upon a yellow brick plinth commemorates the men of the **IX Troop Carrier Command**[6] who flew the transports during the operation. Separate plaques in each side of the plinth bear the rough images of a Douglas C-47 Skytrain 'Dakota' transport and a CG-4A Waco glider.

> Cross the Autoroute onto Bijenlaan. At the T-junction turn right and proceed 350 m to the memorial on the left. (51.527494, 5.490790)

A troop of four PzKpfw IIIs and IVs of the Fallschirmjäger-Panzer AuE Bataillon 'Hermann Göring' was stationed on the Wolfswinkel farm 300 meters to the north. Colonel Sink spotted the vehicles as his aircraft approached the drop zone and he was concerned regarding their impact upon the lightly armed paratroopers. He need not have worried. American P-51 fighter-bombers providing aerial protection to the drop zone also spotted the enemy armor and knocked out three tanks before Sink hit the ground. The fourth tank fled north along the highway.

American dead from the fighting around Son were brought to a temporary American cemetery in a field 800 meters from this intersection behind the Waterhoef Farm. German PoWs began construction of the cemetery on 19 September 1944 when they dug the first graves in a turnip field under guard of American soldiers. The grounds eventually held 411 American, 48 British, and 1 Canadian servicemen. In addition, several hundred German troops were buried at the rear of the cemetery.

British casualties were moved to other cemeteries in 1947. In 1948, the United States government began its repatriation program and sixty percent of the US servicemen were returned to the United States in accordance with the wishes of their next of kin. The balance was reinterned in Netherlands American Cemetery in Margraten. Use of the grounds ended on 30 May 1949 and the fields returned to their current use as pasture.

A granite plinth identifies the access road to the **Temporary American Cemetery**. The monument was placed on 8 December 2006 by private initiative. The inscription, in Dutch and English, concludes with 'This is where the soldiers rested who paid the ultimate price for our freedom. Remember them all.' The hanging wooden

---

John Gurecki crash-landed near Paulushof farm but escaped the wreckage before witnessing his C-47 explode.

6   The IX Troop Carrier Command was formed in 1943 by consolidation of all tactical air support units in Britain into the Ninth Air Force. The command consisted of three troop carrier wings, further divided into fourteen troop carrier groups plus one Pathfinder group.

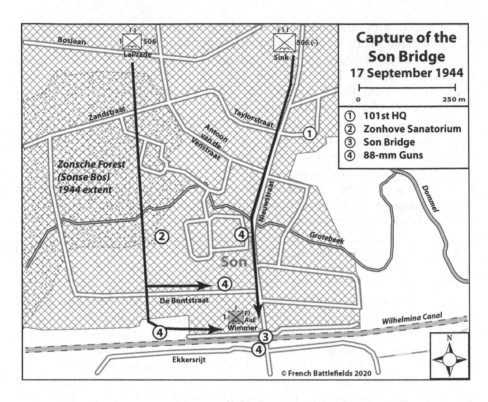

Capture of the Son Bridge
17 September 1944

0 ——————————— 250 m

① 101st HQ
② Zonhove Sanatorium
③ Son Bridge
④ 88-mm Guns

© French Battlefields 2020

sign is a replica of that from the 1940s. It was placed in September 2019.

Continue south on Rooijseweg which becomes Nieuwstraat and turn right immediately after crossing a small bridge over Grotebeek. Turn again right into the small parking area in front of the Disability Home. Continue by foot west past the small residences toward the large sanatorium structure to find a small park under the trees along its north wall. (51.507670, 5.488517)

Major LaPrade had his 1st Battalion off the drop zone in forty-five minutes. He moved directly south through Son Forest toward the Wilhelmina Canal keeping to the woods well west of the main highway in order to avoid potential resistance in the town. When the men of leading Company A (Captain Melvin Davis) entered the Sonse Bos, they spread out in battle formation. Suddenly booming explosions from 81-mm mortars and 88-mm antiaircraft guns tore the trees apart sending bark, branches, and shell fragments into the air. Men fell to the ground seeking shelter, wounded, or dead. There was no adequate protection from tree bursts.

When he approached the rear of the sanatorium, Captain Davis fell bleeding from multiple wounds from the continuing tree-bursts. A medic furiously applied bandages until also hit by a shell explosion that further wounded Davis. The medic ignored his own wounds and resumed tending to Davis who encouraged him, , 'You better hurry up, medic. They're gaining on you.'[7]

Instinctively, the paratroopers charged the presumed source of the shells. Their only defense was to attack a battery of three of Wimmer's 88-mm flak guns sited near the canal two kilometers ahead. Paratroopers reached the edge of a forest clearing and charged madly into the orange flash of the cannons' muzzle blasts to overpower the gun crews – capturing some and killing most.

During the next four months, the nuns, friars, and army medics at **Sanatorium Zonhove** treated over 2,600 wounded soldiers. A monument dedicated to **Company A, 506th PIR** stands in the tree shrouded garden of the former Zonhove sanatorium. The beautiful upright stone bearing the 'Screaming Eagle' emblazoned upon an American flag was erected to commemorate the five troopers killed and eight wounded by German fire in the Sonse Bos behind the buildings. A nearby bridge across the silently flowing waters of the Grotebeek presents an idyllic scene in contrast to the fury of a September afternoon in 1944.

Return to Nieuwstraat and continue south. Stop in front of Sint Emiliusschool on the right. (51.507282, 5.491863)

Meanwhile, 2nd Battalion, with Colonel Sink trailing behind in his jeep, also left the drop zone for Son. The column was halted by fire from an 88-mm gun sighted to fire directly down Nieuwstraat near a bend in the roadway. The 2nd Battalion Headquarters bazooka section closed to within 50 meters of the enemy gun before Private Thomas Lindsey fired and his rocket hit near the elevating mechanism disabling the gun. Six survivors of the gun crew broke for the canal but were killed by machine-gun fire from Sergeant John Rice.

Companies D and E continued clearing the town taking casualties from rifle and machine-gun fire from a house on the opposite side of the canal

---

Continue south 180 m on Nieuwstraat to the canal bridge. (51.505481, 5.492312) A Liberation Route marker stands on the northwest corner of the intersection. (51.505644, 5.492106)

All three of the 2nd Battalion's rifle companies were within 50 meters of the bridge when, suddenly, explosives blew the bridge showering the nearest paratroopers with debris. Moments later, Major LaPrade, 2nd Lieutenant Millford Weller, and Sergeant Donald Dunning swam the canal to establish a bridgehead on the south bank. Several squads ferried across in a rowboat and the combined force silenced the bridge

---

7   The wounded medic saved Captain Davis' life. Davis remained in the US Army until medically discharged with the rank of major. He died in 1967 at age 52 and is buried in Fort Sam Houston National Cemetery, San Antonio, Texas.
The medic is believed to have been Pfc Derek J Saint, known as Doc Saint to the men. Derek Saint was born in England and emigrated to the United States with his family when he was eight years old. Saint had dropped into Normandy and also participated in the Battle of the Bulge. Although rendered unconscious in Son, he refused evacuation and continued to care for the wounded earning a Bronze Star and Purple Heart. Derek Saint of Long Island, New York died in 2010, aged 88. He is buried in Bloomfield, New Jersey.

defenders in a house on the southwest corner of the far side of the canal by a barrage of machine-gun, mortar, and bazooka fire. The fourth German gun remained unmanned on the opposite bank of the canal; its barrel pointed skyward in its antiaircraft role. Reconnaissance confirmed that the two smaller bridges—in Houtens to the west and Hooijdonk Ophaal to the east—had been blown several days earlier. Within 90 minutes Company C, 326th Airborne Engineers spanned the canal with commandeered black-market lumber found in a nearby shed by using the undamaged central pier as a support. Although only one person at a time could cross the shaky footbridge, before midnight the entire regiment was south of the canal and had established a bridgehead centered upon Bokt.

British tanks reached Son at 21:00 the next day and during the night of 18/19 September, British engineers worked to build a 40-ton Bailey bridge over the canal. It was finished early on Tuesday morning and, at 06:45, tanks and other heavy equipment were able to cross the canal. Finally, already thirty-six hours behind schedule, XXX Corps moved toward Nijmegen hoping that the Waal bridge was still standing.

Liberation Route Marker #114 presents 'The Bridge or Your Life' audio in which an American paratrooper, Don, recollects the men lost in the forest and the storming of the German guns followed by the assault and destruction of the Son Bridge.

The Wilhelmina Canal is very wide at this point making it an effective block to any armored advance. The original **Son Bridge** over the Wilhelmina Canal was a swing bridge that rotated upon a massive earthen central pier. The blown bridge was replaced in 1983 with a modern lift bridge high enough to permit larger canal barges and boats and without the central pier. The houses directly to the southwest of the bridge remain from 1944. The **flower garden and flag poles** on the corner were established in 1994 to commemorate the 50th anniversary of the community's liberation as stated on the stone plaque in the garden. (51.504926, 5.492186)

The one-lane secondary **Houtensebrug** to the west still supports foot and bicycle traffic, but it is completely overshadowed by the A50 Autoroute bridge a few meters to its east.

Proceed across the bridge and immediately turn east on Kanaaldijk Zuid. Stop after the first curve to the south. (51.504813, 5.496557)

Von Rundstedt ordered von Maltzahn's fully armored and motorized Panzer Brigade 107[8] rerouted from Aachen where it had just completed a refit, to cut off the head of the British column by attacking through Son to Sint-Oedenrode. The combat group moved forward with two Panther companies carrying the additional paratroopers of 1st Bataillon, FJR 21 as infantry reinforcement. At 17:15 on 19 September, six Panther tanks advanced from the east along the tow path on the south side of the canal against the recently erected Bailey bridge.

Machine-gun bullets from the Panthers' MG 34s rattled the buildings before airborne troops returned small arms fire upon the German infantry. A British artillery

---

8   Panzer Brigade 107 was the strongest German armored unit on the battlefield. It fielded a Panzer battalion with thirty-six Panther tanks, eleven StuG IVs, a full strength Panzergrenadier Bataillon with 116 armored cars and eight 120-mm mortars, and a motorized Pionier Kompanie.

ammunition truck crossing the Bailey bridge was hit and the resulting explosion destroyed the central span blocking German armor from traversing the canal. The second shot hit the bridge causing some damage. The third round hit another British truck to the south and the fourth took the steeple off the Son church, an obvious artillery observation point. The fifth shell killed 2nd Lieutenant James Diel, who exposed himself to charge the tank while carrying an explosive charge.[9]

General Taylor personally led American paratroopers against the Panthers applying small-arms fire to separate the German armor from its protective infantry. Now it was the enemy's turn to suffer from the limited roadways and boggy ground which prohibited a massed armored attack. German troops got only as close as the curve where Driehoek turns south. A glider-borne 57-mm antitank gun arrived towed into position by General Taylor's jeep and its first round hit the leading Panther penetrating the hull above the road wheels and disabling its hydraulics. Bazooka fire took out a second Panther and the remainder withdrew to the tree line a kilometer to the east. Without armor support the German infantry was fought to a standstill and also withdrew.

Von Maltzahn returned the next morning. Amid the morning mist an American jeep patrol stumbled upon approaching German soldiers and executed a tire screeching retreat under enemy fire. While American outposts were overwhelmed, one platoon of Company C (Captain Walter Miller), 327th GIR (Colonel Joseph Harper) held a line south of the canal. Again, with limited maneuverability, the Panthers were stopped by antitank guns of the 81st Airborne Antiaircraft Battalion (Lieutenant Colonel XB Cox). German infantry continued to push forward, but the arrival of the entire 1st Battalion Headquarters troops, including the company clerks, swung the balance. Finally, ten Cromwell tanks and a British battery of 25-pounder self-propelled artillery quickly dispatched four Panthers. Von Maltzahn again ordered a withdrawal leaving the ground littered with German dead.

At 11:45, the Americans cleared the area between the highway and the Dommel River with a sweep by the 327th GIR's Company A on the river side and Company C on the highway side. Three tanks trailed to overcome strongpoints. The movement continued to Bokt capturing 185 enemy troops. Finally, trucks resumed their progress up The Corridor after a five-hour delay.

Continue south toward Eindhoven on Eindhovenseweg (N265). Take the third exit from the large roundabout in Bokt onto Anconalaan; right onto Florencelaan and follow onto De Stoutheuvel which becomes Tarwelaan. Follow 1.5 km until a right turn onto Suikerpeerstraat. Take the first exit onto Airbornelaan and continue 450 m to the park on the right at the intersection with John F Kennedylaan. (51.476386, 5.489678) The suggested route is not the most straightforward to the destination, but roughly follows the path of the 506th PIR's entry into Eindhoven through this substantially rebuilt district of Eindhoven.

---

9   Second Lieutenant Diel, aged 22 from Newton, Illinois, had received a battlefield commission in Normandy. He is buried in Netherlands American Cemetery, Margraten, Netherlands in Plot L, Row 15, Grave 8.

On the morning of 18 September, the advancing 506th PIR entered Eindhoven along Mercuriuslaan which is 300 meters to the east. This intersection, however, presents a wooden sign bearing a dramatic '**Screaming Eagle**' and proclaims the liberation of the city on 18 September 1944 by the 101st Airborne Division and the British Second Army in a beautifully landscaped park dedicated to the 101st Airborne.

An inscribed stone bears a stylized map of the Eindhoven / Son river crossing and a bronze plaque which describes the action:

> [Eindhoven] was the first Dutch city to be liberated by the 101st Airborne Division. The 506th Parachute Infantry Regiment and other units of the division entered Eindhoven and linked up with the British Second Army on the 18th of September 1944. This action successfully completed the initial phase of the division's mission – the seizure of The Corridor and the opening of the highway from Eindhoven to Veghel. This memorial plaque is placed in honor of those 'Screaming Eagles' who gave their lives in this campaign and as a token of esteem and friendship for the people of the Netherlands.

A plaque on the ground lists twenty-two names of American troops who died in the Eindhoven fighting. Benches to the rear are dedicated to the 506th PIR.

Continue west on Airbornelaan. After 350 m, turn left onto Bethlehemlaan and continue 460 m to the marker on the left near Onze-Lieve-Vrouw van Lourdeskerk. (51.472243, 5.483655)

No major battles took place in Eindhoven, but the few German defenders did not relinquish the city without a fight. **Liberation Route Marker #110** 'Snipers and guns' audio relates American paratroopers encountering snipers deployed along Vlokhovenseweg and in the **Vlokhoven Tower**, the church's blunt, square tower. The sniper wounded platoon leader Lieutenant Bill Brewer and then killed Captain John Kiley, the battalion operations officer. A bazooka round destroyed the tower and silenced the sniper.[10] Brewer continued to lead his platoon forward to encounter and eliminate the two 88-mm guns on Woenselsestraat.

It was never determined if the sniper that killed Captain Kiley was, in fact, in the church tower, the current unrepaired condition of the church tower indicate that a bazooka rocket was never fired at the tower. Regardless, the tower remains as it did in 1944 and close inspection reveals bullet damage to the brickwork around its upper windows. The 506th PIR established its first regimental headquarters code-named 'Kidnap' in the adjacent former school building.

Proceed south into the Woensel-Zuid district to Sint-Petruskerk near the intersection of Pastoriestraat and Kloosterdreef. The route of attack against the German guns can be followed north on Kloosterdreef, west on Runstraat, north on Frankrijkstraat which becomes Tonnaerstraat after it crosses Europalaan. This intersection has been

---

10   Captain John W Kiley of New York is buried in Netherlands American Cemetery, Margraten, Netherlands in Plot E, Row 6, Grave 26. His death has been erroneously reported as have taken place at the Woensel church which in more than 1.5 kilometers farther south.

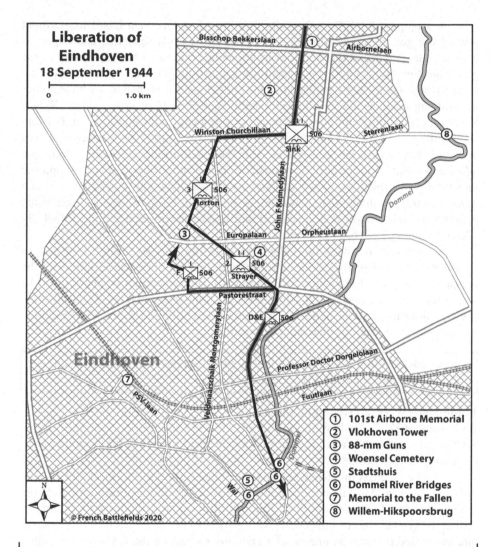

Liberation of Eindhoven
18 September 1944

0 ——— 1.0 km

① 101st Airborne Memorial
② Vlokhoven Tower
③ 88-mm Guns
④ Woensel Cemetery
⑤ Stadtshuis
⑥ Dommel River Bridges
⑦ Memorial to the Fallen
⑧ Willem-Hikspoorsbrug

rebuilt and held the second gun to be eliminated where it was positioned to fire north or east. (51.457282, 5.468750) The first gun destroyed was 75 meters north on Tonnaerstraat and was sited to fire north. (51.457885, 5.469247).

The paratroopers encountered only random rifle and machine-gun fire from small infantry groups as they penetrated the city's northern outskirts until two 88-mm guns from KGr Köppel,[11] blocked Colonel Sink's progress. Not willing to delay the capture of the four Eindhoven bridges, Sink ordered Major Oliver Horton's 3rd Battalion to pin down the enemy while Major Robert Strayer's 2nd Battalion swung around the enemy's flank into the city.

11 KGr Köppel held the #3 Batterie, Flak Abt 654, Flak Regiment 87 in positions north at Woenselsestraat and south at the Tongelreep bridge at Aalst.

Company F left Pastoriestraat following a Dutchman north on Kloosterdreef toward the gun positions. Moving cautiously, two squads separated and deployed between the houses and rear yards. Working undercover to within 150 meters of the gun, Staff Sergeant John Taylor opened fire against the gun crew with his M1. Two enemy troops fell to the pavement wounded but the gun's first shell took off the corner the building shielding Sergeant Taylor. After the gun fired twice more, Privates Robert Sherwood and Homer Smith fired rifle grenades that chased the gun crew but failed to disable the gun. Finally, Sergeant Frank Griffin held his mortar tube between his knees and fired. The second shot landed directly on the gun finishing it. The second gun, up Woenselsestraat, now renamed Tonnaerstraat, came under rifle-grenade fire and the unnerved gunner blew the breach and attempted an escape. The Americans were too quick and trapped the gun crew in a nearby beet field. Forty-one enemy were taken prisoner and thirteen killed at the cost of one American wounded and one killed. By 13:00, Eindhoven had been liberated.

This area has seen redevelopment after the war, however the section of Tonnaerstraat, particularly the location of the second gun, presents visitors with the appearance of 1944 Eindhoven. The approach taken by the paratroopers from the magnificent Sint-Petruskerk on Kloosterdreef, along Runstraat, to Frankrijkstraat presents the small buildings, narrow passageways, and fenced gardens that required the utmost care by the 2nd Platoon of Company F.

Proceed east on Europalaan for 1.0 km, then turn right onto Baffinlaan and continue to the cemetery on the right. (51.455238, 5.482267)

Eindhoven (Woensel) General Cemetery
Baffinlaan, 5623 PK Eindhoven
Web: https://www.cwgc.org/find-a-cemetery/cemetery/2059000/eindhoven-(woensel)-general-cemetery/

The Woensel municipal cemetery contains a special section of 543 British, Polish, Canadian, Australian, New Zealand, and Czech airmen shot down over the mainland dating to as early as 1941. Because of the destructive force of an aircraft hitting the ground, many of the bodies were only partially identified resulting in some aircrew buried in common graves with gravestones bearing the RAF symbol with a simple 'An Airman of the 1939-1945 War' followed by rank if known, Commonwealth nation, and date of death. Finally, at the bottom, 'Known unto God.' A separate plot holds the Cross of Sacrifice with a mix of ground and air servicemen – the majority having died in 1945 in local hospitals. The entire cemetery holds a total of 686 burials.

Thirteen airmen from 207 Squadron are buried in the cemetery, but the most celebrated became that of the first, Flight Lieutenant John Siebert, RAAF. On 29 March 1941, the German *Ortskommandantur* (Town Commander) requested a burial in the military part of the municipal cemetery for a downed pilot. The rumor that an English airman was to be buried quickly spread through the city and thousands of people filled the cemetery and lined approach roads. A German chaplain, military band, and firing party commemorated the internment as Luftwaffe personnel carried in the flag-draped coffin. The band played *Ich hatte einen Kameraden* and a salute was fired. Not surprisingly, the German commander was not amused. Future burials of Allied military personnel took place in the early morning hours and all access to the cemetery was blocked.[12]

His grave can be found immediately ahead from the main entrance in Plot FF, slightly to the right and behind one of the two flagpoles. (51.455572, 5.481256) The place of honor in this cemetery also holds the graves of two polish airmen from 305 Squadron, RAF: Navigator Józef Malak Wacław, and Tail Gunner Mieczysław Ryszkiewicz whose Wellington bomber was shot down on 3 May 1941 by night fighters while on a mission to bomb Emden, Germany. An unidentified airman was also killed, and four other crew members were taken prisoner. To their left is Antoine den Hartog, a Dutch infantryman killed on 15 May 1940. Five additional RAF servicemen are buried to Siebert's right.

The four Eindhoven bridges crossed the Dommel River in the central district of the city. Only three remain since a small branch of the river has been covered over. The remaining three bridges are at Kanalstraat near the termination of the Eindhoven Canal (51.437506, 5.485476); at Vestdijk (51.436382, 5.484564); and at Wal (51.434329, 5.480723). Although the shrub-bordered river makes a beautiful contrast to the modern city buildings, these locations present little of interest.

Return north on John F Kennedylaan. Turn right on Sterrenlaan then bear left onto Soeterbeekseweg, which appears to be a bicycle path, but is indeed a narrow brick lane bordered on each side by mature trees. The lane goes directly to a bridge over the Soeterbeek. (51.468849, 5.509812)

On 19 September, Willem Hikspoors, a gardener on the Soeterbeek estate, encountered German reconnaissance units from Panzer Brigade 107 and he immediately realized that the Germans were planning an attack upon Eindhoven or the Son bridge. Hikspoors convinced them that the apparently fragile wooden bridge would not hold the weight of a tank. Hikspoors's advice distracted German attention away from the son of the estate owner, who was being held by the Germans as a spy for taking photographs of what the boy thought were approaching British tanks. The boy made a run for safety and escaped. The German force backtracked and passed through Nederwetten toward Son. A legend has arisen that the bridge's weakness was its strength in being able to repel the enemy. For his cool-headed act, Hikspoors received a medal and in 1984 the bridge was named after him.

Willem-Hikspoorsbrug passes over the Dommel River at the northeastern border of Eindhoven. A small sign signifies its capture in September 1944. **Liberation Route Marker #112** on the opposite side of the bridge retells Hikspoor's story in 'The Cold-blooded Gardener' audio.

---

12   Flight Lieutenant John Aloysius Siebert, aged 23 from Kingswood, South Australia, had received a Distinguished Flying Cross for his grim determination in carrying out attacks on enemy forces. He was killed during the night of 27/28 March 1941 during a mission against Dusseldorf when his twin-engine Avro Manchester medium bomber was shot down by a German night fighter Messerschmitt Bf 110 flown by Sergeant Gerhard Herzog. The rest of the crew parachuted to safety and were taken prisoner.

While the story is enchanting, it is just as likely that the German commander thought better of engaging in an urban battle in Eindhoven and retraced his route through Nederwetten because destruction of the Bailey bridge at Son offered a more vulnerable opportunity to severe XXX Corps' supply line.

> Return to Europalaan and continue east 2.7 km to a traffic circle. Take the third exit onto Parkstraat in western Nuenen and stop at the memorial wall. (51.470547, 5.545231)

On 20 September, a troop of Cromwell tanks from A Squadron, 15th/19th Hussars left Eindhoven to counterattack von Maltzahn's force as it withdrew from its second attack upon the Son bridge. Led by Captain Christopher Weatherby, the British force crossed the same rickety bridge and intercepted the German armor in Nederwetten. A seven-hour exchange destroyed two Panthers, a half-track and truck before Panzer Brigade 107 disengaged.

The Panzer Brigade reformed at Nuenen. Receiving reports of a strong German force in the town, Colonel Sink dispatched Company E (Captain Richard Winters), 506th with B Squadron, 44th Royal Tank Regiment (RTR)[13] to reconnoiter. The first two Shermans were knocked out, but the Panzer Brigade was discovered. Colonel Sink strengthened his attacking force, but congestion in Eindhoven delayed the added units. At 17:00 an attack along Europalaan started with Company E and A Squadron on the right and Company F with B Squadron on the left approaching from Boord. The Company E attack came from the southwest along Opwettenseweg and Geldropsedijk. The German main line of resistance ran along Europalaan anchored by an 88-mm cannon sited near the intersection of Parkstraat and Europalaan which marks the furthest advance of the Allied attack.

Two Panthers were destroyed, but failing light caused the attack to be called off. Von Maltzahn, feeling pressure from British VIII Corps closing in on his flank, withdrew farther to Helmond. In total at Son and Nuenen, the brigade lost eight of its thirty-six Panther tanks and numerous other vehicles.

A monument in the form of an open **sarcophagus** symbolizes the liberation of Nuenen. The now free citizens are shown on the lid celebrating with Dutch flags. A wall constructed with bricks from the destroyed Vink family farm which once stood 100 yards up the road backs the monument. A barely legible stone block imbedded in the wall once marked the graves of two tankers[14] from the 44th RTR killed in the assault and who were buried at the farm by Mr Vink. The stone was relocated after the postwar demolition of the original farm buildings. A plaque behind the benches

---

13   The 44th Royal Tank Regiment arrived in Normandy on 9 June 1944 as part of the 4th Armoured Brigade. The regiment was temporarily attached to the 101st Airborne Division on 17 September. The regiment comprised three squadrons and also held a squadron of the Royal Dragoons, and one artillery battery of the 86th Field Regiment.

14   Corporal Ralph Stothard, aged 28 from Creswell, Nottinghamshire, and Trooper Basil Nicholls, aged 21 from Huddersfield, were reburied in the Mierlo War Cemetery in Plot II, Row B, Graves 1 and 2.

commemorates the fallen from **Company E**, 506th PIR during MARKET-GARDEN.[15] A second bench commemorates the 44th RTR.

Continue through central Nuenen leaving on north Broedijk toward Spekt and Son en Bruegel. The route passes through the Panzer Brigade's accumulation area for its attacks upon the Son bridge. Cross over the Hooijdonk Ophallbrug in Breugel. (51.506696, 5.509833)

A single lane lift bridge in Breugel crosses the Wilhelmina Canal. The original was blown several days before the paratroop landings and the location played no part in the Son battles.

Continue into Son by following signs toward Sint-Oedenrode. Cross highway N265, then turn right onto Europalaan. Park near the large lake on the left. (51.513496, 5.489532)

The white marble **Airborne Memorial** presents a paratrooper carrying his machine gun under his arm and dramatically lunging forward in attack. The plaque on the plinth reads:

Liberated 17 September 1944 by the 506th PIR and elements of the 326th Airborne Engineers. This memorial plaque was placed in honor of the Screaming Eagles who gave their lives in this campaign as a token of esteem and friendship for the people of the Netherlands. Placed by comrades of the 101st Airborne Division Association 1969.

Battle for the Best Bridge
17 to 19 September

Battle

Uncertain of XXX Corps' arrival time, the status of the Son bridge, and believing the 30-meter-long concrete road bridge at Best to be lightly defended, Colonel Michaelis sent Company H led by Captain Robert Jones, a platoon from 326th Airborne Engineers, and a section of light machine-guns from battalion headquarters to move southwest along the edge of the Son Forest on Schietbaanlaan toward Best. The company met more resistance than expected and their first assault got no farther than a road junction of Schietbaanlaan and Hoeveweg east of Best, where they engaged in an unsuccessful firefight against 20-mm cannon fire from newly arrived but poorly trained I Bataillon, SS Police Regiment 3 (Oberst der Politzei Hans Otto Böhmer).[16]

---

15   Killed in the Nuenen attack were: Pfc William T Miller from St Louis; Pfc Vernon G Menze, aged 20, buried in Golden Gate National Cemetery, San Bruno, California; Pfc James W Miller, aged 20, from Wabash, Indiana buried in his home town; and Pfc Robert van Klinken, aged 24 from Washington buried in Netherlands American Cemetery, Margraten, Netherlands Plot C, Row 8, Grave 32.

16   SS Police Regimenter were formed as early as 1939 to provide security in rear areas. They were later used in a military capacity but their quality as frontline troops was questionable. By 1944, the various battalions had been grouped into regiments and strengthened with a tank scout and a tank destroyer company

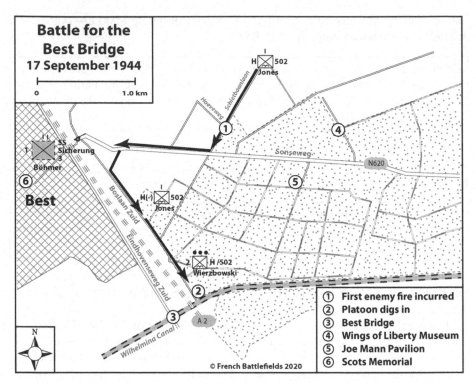

Battle for the Best Bridge
17 September 1944

0 ———————— 1.0 km

Hoeveweg
Schietboomlaan
H ⊠ 502
Jones

SS Sicherung
1 II 3
Böhmer

⑥
Best

Boslaan Zuid
Eindhovensweg Zuid

H(-) ⊠ 502
Jones

Sonseweg
N620

④

⑤

2 ⊠ H /502
Wierzbowski

②

③ A 2

Wilhelmina Canal

N

① First enemy fire incurred
② Platoon digs in
③ Best Bridge
④ Wings of Liberty Museum
⑤ Joe Mann Pavilion
⑥ Scots Memorial

© French Battlefields 2020

By 20:14 twelve truckloads carrying 300 infantry troops of KGr Rink,[17] 59th Infantry Division arrived and entered the vicious fighting and Jones pulled his company back towards the forest along what is now Boslaan Zuid.

Battalion commander Lieutenant Colonel Robert Cole ordered Jones to send his 2nd Platoon (2nd Lieutenant Edward Wierzbowski) with attached engineers and machine gunners toward the bridge. As darkness fell, Wierzbowski's unit became increasingly disoriented in the newly planted pine plantation while under attack from machine guns firing along the forest fire breaks. Rain began to fall effecting unit cohesion and men got separated from the main force. Eventually Wierzbowski's much-reduced force emerged onto the canal bank some 250 meters east of the bridge. Attempting to approach the bridge, the small group unknowingly passed through enemy lines and became surrounded. Wierzbowski carefully withdrew his group back along the canal and into the woods and dug in for the night. Night attacks were particularly terrifying and only the dawn brought realization of who had survived and

---

Oberst der Politzei Hans Otto Böhmer was arrested and tried in the Netherlands for ordering raids to round up Dutch Jews for deportation to death camps and slave labor camps. He was convicted and sentenced to two and one half years in prison. He was released to German authorities less than one year later.

17   KGr Rink held I Bataillon Grenadier Regiment 723 and Feld Ersatz Bataillon (Field Replacement Battalion) 347. Feld Ersatz Bataillone (FEB): temporarily held replacement troops while in training for combat operations. Oberstleutnant Berthold Rink was seriously wounded that day, captured, and brought to a Brussels hospital for treatment but died two months later.

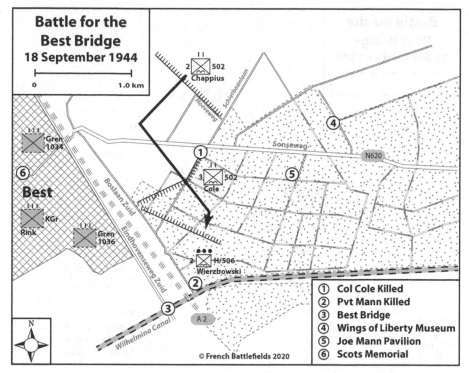

Battle for the Best Bridge
18 September 1944

0   1.0 km

2 ⊠ 502 Chappius

④

Horseweg   Schietbaanlaan

① Sonseweg   N620

Gren 1034

⑥

Best

3 ⊠ 502 Cole   ⑤

Boslaan Zuid

KGr Rink

Gren 1036

Eindhovenseweg Zuid

2 ⊡ H/506 Wierzbowski

②

③   A 2

Wilhelmina Canal

N

© French Battlefields 2020

① Col Cole Killed
② Pvt Mann Killed
③ Best Bridge
④ Wings of Liberty Museum
⑤ Joe Mann Pavilion
⑥ Scots Memorial

who had not. Captain Jones became concerned and sent out patrols to find the missing unit, but they only encountered enemy and returned. German infantry, lacking artillery and experiencing shortages of ammunition, could not evict even the lightly armed paratroopers.

Despite the darkness and rain, FEB 347 arrived along the road from Boxtel accompanied by 88-mm guns from Flak Abt[18] 428. At 05:20 on 18 September, the Germans unleashed their increased firepower upon the paratroopers' front and left flank. Artillery, mortar, and 20-mm antiaircraft fire increased through the morning inflicting serious casualties upon 3rd Battalion as the battle escalated. Now facing over 1,000 enemy troops. General Taylor threw Michaelis's 2nd Battalion (Lieutenant Colonel Steve Chappuis) into the battle with instructions to swing around the 3rd Battalion's right flank and make for the bridge. At about 10:00, the 2nd Battalion relieved the pressure with its arrival using infantry fire and maneuver to cross open fields dotted with haystacks but at a terrible cost of twenty percent casualties. Michaelis's regiment was now facing Poppe's Grenadier Regiment 1034 to the north and Grenadier Regiment 1036 to the south. Chappuis pulled his men back into the forest. P-47 Thunderbolts arrived after the mist cleared from their airfields to strafe and bomb inflicting heavy losses upon the enemy.

At precisely 11:00, the Germans blew the bridge showering Wierzbowski's men with concrete and steel debris. Later that afternoon the Second Lift brought sorely

---

18   Abteilung or Abt: a German military term that refers to a military unit ranging in size from a detachment to a division. Most frequently, the unit would be battalion in size.

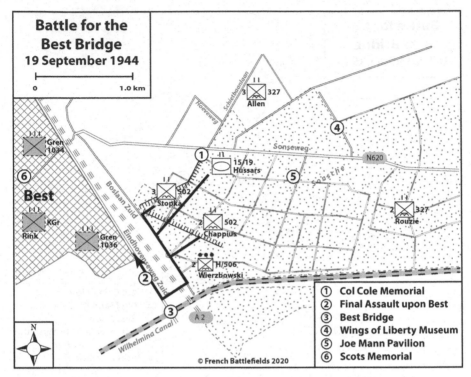

Battle for the Best Bridge
19 September 1944

0   1.0 km

① Col Cole Memorial
② Final Assault upon Best
③ Best Bridge
④ Wings of Liberty Museum
⑤ Joe Mann Pavilion
⑥ Scots Memorial

© French Battlefields 2020

needed reinforcements of the 327th GIR, but the hit and run attacks in the forests east of Best continued into the morning of 19 September. The Germans had established dug-in positions running north from the canal roughly along modern Boslaan Zuid supported by 88-mm guns on the south bank and troops in buildings to the west. Discovering that the bridge had been blown, Chappuis' battalion attempted to draw back, but fierce close-quarters fighting continued – killing three hundred 101st Division paratroopers.

General Taylor had had enough. That afternoon, he threw the entire 502nd PIR, the newly arrived 327th GIR, and some British Cromwell tanks from the 15th/19th Hussars into the forest fighting. When pushed relentlessly back to the Wilhelmina Canal, the Germans broke, and 1,056 German soldiers surrendered after leaving 600 dead in the fields and forests. General Taylor had the first major victory of MARKET-GARDEN. Wierzbowski, with his platoon down to three unwounded and out of ammunition, had earlier surrendered. During the German rout, he captured a German field hospital and returned to his company with his prisoners.

Battlefield Tour

The route leaves Son to follow the actions in the forested area east of Best where the paratroopers struggled to overcome the German defense of that canal bridge. Construction of the A2 Autoroute through this part of the battlefield has disrupted the terrain. The tour returns toward the drop zone to visit the excellent Wings of Liberation Museum.

Leave Son west on Boslaan which becomes Bestseweg (N620). Turn south after 3.0 km to pass through Nieuwe Heide and achieve the road along the north bank of the Wilhelmina Canal. Continue west for 1.7 km then right onto Boslaan Zuid, frontage road for the A2 Autoroute. Turn right at the first opportunity into the forest. (51.502770, 5.419226)

On 18 September 1944, Wierzbowski's platoon became surrounded and isolated by a superior enemy force. As leading scout, Pfc Joseph Mann crept to within bazooka range of an enemy artillery position and, in the face of heavy enemy fire, destroyed its ammunition dump. Despite the great danger involved, he remained in this exposed position and killed enemy troops one by one with his M-1 rifle until he was wounded in both shoulders. Mann successfully returned to the platoon position and was treated by a medic.

Later that same afternoon, the Germans again attacked the patrol's position in the woods. Mann was hit by two more bullets causing excessive bleeding. The medic bound Mann's arm tightly to his torso attempting to stem the flow. Two men volunteered to return to battalion with a request for help. Neither was successful as both men were wounded, and one was captured. The next morning the enemy launched a concerted attack and advanced undetected in the swirling river fog to within a few yards of Mann's position before throwing five hand grenades. One grenade landed behind Private Mann in a foxhole sheltering six wounded paratroopers. Unable to raise his bandaged arms, he yelled 'grenade' and lay back over the grenade and took the full force of the explosion. 'My back's gone,' he told Wierzbowski before dying a few moments later.[19] Out of ammunition and with most of his men dead or wounded, Wierzbowski surrendered his unit.

The granite **Joe Mann Cross,** chiseled in the shape of a parachute, roughly marks the location of Joe Mann's heroic sacrifice. The inscription states, 'On 19 September 1944 Joe E Mann, an American soldier sacrificed his young life at this spot to save the lives of his comrades.' Autoroute construction required relocating the memorial stone 200 meters to the east of its original location where it indicated that the engagement took place much closer to the Best bridge approximately 180 meters farther west along Ncb-Weg.

Visible remnants of foxholes 100 meters into the woods locate Wierzbowski's position where seventy-eight Americans and over three hundred Germans were killed. The final German positions were across the Autoroute to the west. A more modern bridge has replaced the 1944 **Best Bridge**.

Return to the canal frontage road (Ncb-Weg) and pass under the Autoroute bridge to the Best Bridge. From the Best Bridge, follow Eindhovenseweg Zuid to the north for 2.0 km. In the traffic circle exit toward Best and continue into the town. Parking can be a problem on the streets; try the Aldi parking lot adjacent to Koctshuistuin Park and proceed west on foot. (51.512939, 5.393910)

---

19   Pfc Joseph Mann, aged 22, the fifth of nine children from near Spokane, Washington, was posthumously awarded the Medal of Honor for giving his life for his comrades. He is buried in Greenwood Memorial Terrace, Spokane.

The 15th Scottish Division, as part of British XII Corps, was assigned to widen The Corridor in the Best sector. On 21 September, after the 101st Division had moved on to the north, the 7th Seaforth Highlanders (Lieutenant-Colonel PU Campbell) were able to establish a bridgehead across the canal using rafts to transport men and vehicles. The Germans had constructed strong defenses in Best and contested any effort by the British to dislodge them.

On 22 September, D Company led a movement into Best with reports that the town was not defended. The reports were wrong and when the troops entered the town square, a fierce firefight broke out. The two leading platoons were hit hard by German troops pouring out of the buildings. The 18th Platoon lost thirty-three men and the 17th Platoon completely disappeared.

The 2nd Glasgow Highlanders (Lieutenant-Colonel Hunt) followed with three of its companies against a German defensive line sited along the rail line that passes north-south through the center of the town. Fighting in the city center near the railway line and in De Vleut to the north continued until 26 September when a stalemate developed that lasted until 24 October. At that time a renewed British attack found that the enemy had withdrawn.

The **Scottish Memorial** in Best honors the 120 deaths from the battle to liberate the town. The metal memorial presents three figures of Scottish soldiers jumping through a tartan. The plaque below recognizes the unit's liberation of the town.

Proceed southwest on foot to Hoofdstraat 31. (51.511904, 5.391941)

Liberation Route Marker #130 presents the 'Fortress Best' audio which recalls the extended fighting to liberate Best and its impact upon the civilian population.

Reverse direction to Nieuwstraat and cross over the Autoroute onto highway N620. Follow for 1.5 km to the intersection with Schietbaanlaan; enter the forest to the south along this dirt road to the memorial immediately on the left. (51.515623, 5.421659)

Lieutenant Colonel Robert Cole had commanded the 3rd Battalion, 502nd PIR since its drop into Normandy on 6 June. During the attack upon Best and its bridge on the morning of 18 September, enemy troops infiltrated between Cole's thin positions and German artillery kept the paratroopers sheltering in their foxholes. Colonel Cole called for air support. The engaged troops were separated by only 100 meters when the P-47 'Thunderbolts' strafed 3rd Battalion's positions at the edge of the wood. The paratroopers broke out their orange panels and smoke grenades to identify friendly positions to the pilots and the planes shifted their attack accordingly. Cole walked out in front of his men and into the clear to review the situation with his hand shading his eyes from the sun. It was a fatal error. A shot rang out from a nearby building and Cole fell to the ground instantly dead with a bullet to the head. Moments later a German soldier was spotted leaving the house and the battalion's machine gun cut him down. Executive Officer Major John Stopka received an ambiguous message, 'You are in command of the battalion.' It was not until an hour later that he learned the reason.[20]

A flat slate slab with the outline of a parachute and bearing the 'Screaming Eagle' insignia of the 101st Airborne and a photograph of **Lieutenant Colonel Cole** marks the site at the edge of the forest where he was shot and killed. The Dutch at the bottom of the stone translates as, 'Killed for us.' The white farmhouse 325 meters down the road to the west probably sheltered the German sniper.[21]

Joseph Mann and his battalion commander Robert Cole were the only two men in the 101st Airborne Division to receive their country's highest award during the Second World War. Both received it posthumously, both killed the same day within only one kilometer from each other.

The **Liberation Route Marker #115** 'Robert Cole and Joe Mann' audio relates the sacrifices of Lieutenant Colonel Cole and Private Mann.

Continue east on highway N620 (Sonseweg) to the unattractive totems designed to look like cacti flanking a side road on the right. Enter Joe Mannweg and follow to a parking area. (51.515141, 5.436472)

The **Joe Mann Memorial** is on the small path on the right as you enter the parking area. The metal structure is topped with a large mother pelican spreading its wings to sacrifice its life to feed her babies with her own blood. Below, a group of stylized men portray Mann's heroic action. Behind the monument and hidden by shrubs is a sunken amphitheater with bench seating and a slightly raised earthen stage. Several popular walking paths crisscross the woods and the Joe Mann Pavilion holds a restaurant and café for hikers.

Return to highway N620 and continue east. After 400 m turn left on Sonseweg to the museum complex. (51.516216, 5.441656)

Museum Bevrijdende Veleugels (Wings of Liberation Museum)
Sonseweg 39, 5681 BH Best
Tel: +31 (0)49 932 9722
Email: info@bevrijdendevleugels.com
Web: https://www.bevrijdendevleugels.nl/
Open Tuesday through Sunday from 10:00 to 17:00. Entrance to the museum is through a brasserie; do not be put off by the signage or the restaurant which offers an

---

20   Major later Lieutenant Colonel John P Stopka, aged 29 from Sheridan, Wyoming, who received a Distinguished Service Cross for heroism displayed during the 11 June 1944 attack upon Carentan, was killed during the Battle of the Bulge on 14 January 1945 when American aircraft bombed 3rd Battalion positions. He is buried in Luxembourg American Cemetery, Luxembourg City, Luxembourg in Plot E, Row 9, Grave 38.

21   Lieutenant Colonel Robert Cole led his men in a bayonet charge against Oberstleutnant von der Heydte's FJR 6 in an attack near Carentan, Normandy on 11 June. The battle lasted almost all day until settled when American artillery fire forced von der Heydte to withdraw. Lieutenant Colonel Cole was later awarded the Medal of Honor for leading his men in that charge, but he died before he knew of the award. Cole, aged 29, is buried in Netherlands American Cemetery, Margraten, Netherlands, in Plot B, Row 15, Grave 27.

extremely large and attractive outdoor terrace. Museum information is presented in Dutch, English, German, and French. Handicap accessible. Admission fee.

The museum, founded by Fritz Driessen,[22] presents an enormous collection spread across five large buildings in a park-like setting of maple trees. The presentation begins with the inter-war years from 1918 to 1939 and continues through Dutch mobilization, German invasion, occupation, and liberation. An introductory movie and a large timeline are at the rear. Wall posters cover each of these time periods accompanied by full-size dioramas and large photos. An outdoor section presents military vehicles including a Sherman tank, an American 155-mm 'Long Tom' gun pulled by a half-track once held by the British 43rd Division, and a Bailey bridge. A separate building is dedicated to Operation MARKET-GARDEN displaying military equipment ranging from an American quad 50-mm AA gun to a C-53 Skytrooper, a variant of the C-47 transport aircraft and a Waco CG-4A Glider. German equipment includes a Kugelwagon, a half-tracked motorcycle known as a Kleines Kettenkraftrad HK101, and an 88-mm AA gun. A special display pays homage to members of the 101st Airborne who died in the liberation of the Netherlands. A book lists all their names alphabetically – page after page. A secondary building is dedicated to posters and maps showing the locations of operational air bases and more military hardware.

Capture of Sint-Oedenrode
17 September 1944

The 502nd PIR's 1st Battalion (Lieutenant Colonel Patrick Cassidy) left DZ 'C' on 17 September to secure Sint-Oedenrode's two road bridges over the Dommel River. The river in this area is a lazy stream that wanders through Sint-Oedenrode in a boggy valley with several branches and loops. Although not a deep or wide waterway, the terrain would be difficult for wheeled or tracked vehicles and the road bridges were prime objectives.

Battle

Upon approaching Sint-Oedenrode, the battalion's three companies diverged toward their individual objectives: Company C moved to secure the two undefended road bridges; one platoon of Company B detached east to Nijnsel to investigate reports of enemy activity; and Company A was held in reserve. The remaining two platoons of Company B advanced to secure a footbridge at the eastern edge of town now a bicycle bridge bordering highway N637 (51.565144, 5.473362) when it discovered a second highway bridge that was part of a bypass that was not marked on planning maps. The road bypassed the old center of town — usually difficult areas for tanks to traverse at speed. Company B engaged the enemy and quickly overcame German small-arms opposition from headquarters troops of Flieger-Regiment 93.[23]

---

22   Fritz Driessen was arrested by the German occupation authorities in 1941 then released on medical grounds. Driessen entered France and became a member the French Underground assisting the escapes of downed airmen. He joined the Americans in 1944 as a guide and interpreter. After the war, he became a successful industrialist and retired to collect military vehicles and weapons. This museum is the result of his efforts.

23   Flieger-Regementer were Luftwaffe basic training units for individuals already screened for

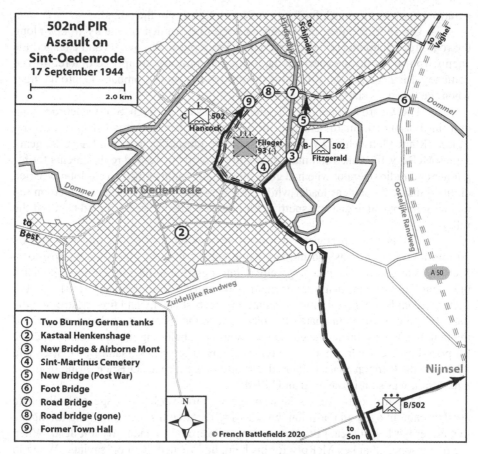

**502nd PIR
Assault on
Sint-Oedenrode**
17 September 1944

0   2.0 km

① Two Burning German tanks
② Kastaal Henkenshage
③ New Bridge & Airborne Mont
④ Sint-Martinus Cemetery
⑤ New Bridge (Post War)
⑥ Foot Bridge
⑦ Road Bridge
⑧ Road bridge (gone)
⑨ Former Town Hall

© French Battlefields 2020

Moving into Sint-Oedenrode, Company C encountered a German skirmish line. Third Platoon Commander Lieutenant Morton Smit sheltered from enemy fire when a hand grenade sailed over a hedge. Lieutenant Smit covered the grenade with his steel helmet and laid on top. The blast broke his hip and arm but prevented injury to his comrades.[24]

The fighting was over by 18:00 that evening and all the bridges were secured intact. In all, twenty enemy had been killed and fifty-eight captured.

On 18 September, approximately 700 troops of Bataillon 'Ewald'[25] (II Bataillon, FJR 2 commanded by Major Werner Ewald) launched ferocious counterattacks in their efforts to cut the Allied corridor. For days the bridge over the Dommel River was the focus of these counterattacks. However, the young German

potential pilot assignments. Flieger-Regiment 93 had a special assignment to defend the V-2 rocket launch sites.

24   Lieutenant Morton J Smit survived his injuries and received a Silver Star. Lieutenant Smit died in 2012, aged 92, and is buried in Arlington National Cemetery, Arlington, Virginia, Section 36A.

25   Bataillon 'Ewald': composed of fallschirmjäger trainees rapidly organized into what the German Army called 'March' units which were thrown into the battle.

paratroopers were no match for the experienced fighters of the 502nd.

On 19 September, the Dutch underground warned of enemy troops along the road from Schijndel (N637). A reconnaissance patrol discovered and engaged the enemy troops, but the unexpectedly large German unit was comprised of a reinforced company. Lieutenant Colonel Cassidy committed his entire Company C into the fight when the Germans started flanking the patrol.

The Guards Armoured Division had passed through Sint-Oedenrode that morning but an Irish Guards tank with mechanical problems had crawled into the central square (Markt) left behind by its unit. Cassidy requested its help and Lance Sergeant James McRory, the tank's commander, readily agreed but needed replacements for his gunner and radio operator who had gone on with the main body. Private John O'Brien climbed inside the tank as loader while Staff Sergeant Roy Nickrent remained on top manning the machine gun and spotting for targets while the still-crippled tank left the village.

The tank's appearance was opportune as Company C was under assault by 20-mm and 88-mm guns and mortars while enemy infantry closed on its positions. McRory maneuvered the creeping vehicle into position to take on the three vehicles mounting 20-mm guns that were engaging Company C from the flank. He slowly but accurately laid the tank's 75-mm gun onto the nearest enemy and fired destroying the gun. Two more shots eliminated the other two guns. Sergeant Nickrent ran behind the tank firing his submachine gun at enemy troops sheltering in the roadside ditches. Surprised by the American armor support and the aggressive assault by O'Brien and Nickrent, the German attack collapsed. Unfortunately, Private O'Brien, firing from the tank turret, was shot in the head and killed.[26]

McRory continued his slow progress northward to engage and eliminate another camouflaged gun position, but Cassidy recalled his men unwilling to engage in a larger battle just then. Fifty-three prisoners were taken and thirty left dead. When the paratroopers thanked McRory for his help, he brushed them off saying, 'When in doubt, lash out', which became the battalion's new, but unofficial, motto.[27]

With the battle for Best over, Colonel Michaelis had his three battalions together and support from a squadron of the 44th Royal Tank Regiment. Groups of Germans continued to cause problems in the area, so on 21 September Michaelis sent his three battalions each supported by troop of tanks in different directions to clean out stray enemy soldiers. The 1st Battalion headed north and northwest on roads toward Schijndel and Olland; the 2nd Battalion south toward the landing zone; and 3rd Battalion southwest toward Best. All three battalions engaged the enemy and stopped attempts to regain Sint-Oedenrode.

---

26   Sergeant Roy W Nickrent was awarded a Silver Star and Bronze Star during the war. Afterwards, he became town marshal and waterworks superintendent for the village of Saybrook, Illinois. He died in 2000, aged 80 and is buried in his hometown.
Private John J O'Brien, Jr, aged 25 who had been wounded in Normandy and returned to action, is buried in Allegheny County, Pennsylvania.

27   Lance-Sergeant James 'Paddy' McRory, aged 27 and recipient of the Military Medal for his support of the 502nd PIR, was killed in action on 25 April 1945 shortly before the war's end. He is buried in the Becklingen War Cemetery, Lüneburg Heath, Lower Saxony, Germany in Plot 4, Row B, Grave 11.

Battlefield Tour
      Sites of various engagements in and around Sint-Oedenrode are briefly visited.
VVV Sint-Oedenrode Sint-Paulusgasthuisjes
Kerkstraat 20, 5492 AH Sint-Oedenrode
Tel: + 31 (0)41 347 4100
Email: info@vvvsintoedenrode.nl
Web: http://www.vvvsintoedenrode.nl
Open daily from 10:00 to 17:00.

> From highway N620 or Son, take one of several roads north toward Sint-Oedenrode. The narrow, slow, and very rural Brouwarskampweg is an interesting choice because it passes directly across the drop zones.
> More conventionally, leave Son north on Nieuwstraat which changes name several times, turning toward Sint-Oedenrode on Nijnselseweg. The A50 Autoroute is not convenient.
> Pass through a traffic circle at (51.558172, 5.466438).

      Two more tanks from the Hermann Göring AuE Bataillon laid in wait in an orchard behind a line of trees at the southern end of the village. On 17 September, their tank fire upon the drop zone attracted the attention of P-51 fighters circling high overhead. Dropping in sweeping power dives, pilots fired rockets that eliminated the threat. When forward elements of Company C reached the crossroads that afternoon, they found one German tank with its engine still running blocking the intersection with a dead German soldier halfway out of the hatch. Private Wendell Stackhouse climbed aboard the tank intending to move it aside. Upon attempting to move the body, Stackhouse triggered a violent explosion which killed him instantly.[28]

> From the large traffic circle exit northwest onto Corridor. Pass over a bridge crossing a branch of the Dommel River and after 350 m find a parking space near the monument on the left along a walkway that fronts the long narrow park. (51.563078, 5.464746)

      Company B discovered a German squad attempting to blow a newly constructed bridge that did not appear on army maps. (51.562423, 5.464493) The squad was eliminated with a bazooka rocket, but the explosion attracted fire from a larger enemy group in the large cemetery of Sint-Martinuskerk west of the river. Pressured by Company C to its west and Company B to its east, the enemy force slowly withdrew to the northeast. The liberation of Sint-Oedenrode had been easy.
      The **Monument to the Dutch** is dedicated to the people of The Corridor from veterans of the 101st Division for their courage, compassion, and friendship. The dark metal casting around the central granite plinth depicts various actions of the airborne troops – studying maps, pulling jeeps out of gliders, parachuting, and helping small children.

---

28   Private Wendell Stackhouse, aged 22, is buried in Hartford, Connecticut.

The bridge north of the monument (51.564163, 5.465550) did not exist in 1944 because the Dommel branch extending east did not connect with the main river at that time. That bridge dates from 2008 when the connecting channel was opened. The section of roadway between the two large roundabouts is officially named 'Corridor' even though the original plan sent XXX Corps through the town center.

Continue north to the large traffic circle; take the third exit, cross over the Dommel River, and follow toward the town center. The targets of the battalion's efforts were two small road bridges approximately 190 meters apart over two arms of the Dommel River. They were taken by Company C, which passed through the town square and approached the key river crossings from the southeast. The first bridge, 350 meters north of the monument, at (51.565511, 5.464895), carried what was then the main highway northeast toward Veghel. The second bridge near (51.565504, 5.462417) no longer exists due to postwar redevelopment of the area.
Park near the old Town Hall (51.564937, 5.461435)

The wall of the former town hall bears several plaques. One demonstrates Sint-Oedenrode's long history by commemorating a visit by King Henry I in 1232. The largest plaque speaks to the community's losses during the First World War; another to losses in 1940. Place of prominence is given to a stone plaque headed by a 'Screaming Eagle' commemorating **Company B, 502nd PIR** which lost eleven men in Sint-Oedenrode, six in one blast of artillery fire. The men's names are listed.[29]

Exit Sint-Oedenrode north on Philippusstraat then west toward Olland / Boxtel on Ollandseweg for 1.6 km to the marker almost hidden in shrubbery on the right . (51.569460, 5.438335)

An easy-to-miss **single post** bears a metal plaque bearing the names John Thorogood and Stanley Matthews. Both men were troopers in a Sherman tank from C Squadron, 44th RTR accompanying Company B toward Olland on 21 September when it was struck by a shell from an antitank gun. The two men were killed, and three crew members were wounded.[30] The simple remembrance identifies the spot where the engagement was fought. The enemy force was too strong, and Company B withdrew back to Sint-Oedenrode.

---

29   The men were: Radio operator Technician Fifth Class Henry F Bilodeau, aged 23 from New Hampshire; Sergeant Cecil F Miller, aged 28 from Georgia; Pfc Ralph J Zerbe, aged 21 from Pennsylvania; Private Ivie A Ward, aged 27 of North Carolina; Pfc Orin F Keyes Jr, aged 26 from Massachusetts; and Private Redmond D Wells Jr, aged 29 of North Carolina are buried in Netherlands American Cemetery, Margraten, Netherlands. Sergeant John C Craine, aged 25 from Pennsylvania is buried in Long Island National Cemetery. Pfc Michael P Cherub, aged 27 from Connecticut is buried in Westport, Connecticut. Private Luther W Davis, aged 23 from Georgia is buried in Savanna. Pfc William J Heather from Ohio, who died of wounds in England, is buried in Cambridge American Cemetery. Sergeant Louis C See, aged 31 of Texas was wounded in Sint-Oedenrode but died of wounds during the Battle of the Bulge. He is buried in Fort Sam Houston National Cemetery;

30   Trooper Thorogood, aged 21, and Trooper Matthews, aged 22, are buried side-by-side in Uden Commonwealth War Graves Cemetery, Uden, Netherlands in Plot 1, Row D, Graves 4 and 5.

> Return to Sint-Oedenrode and turn right onto Lindendijk. Repass the bridges to the second traffic circle. Take the 1st exit on Hertog Hendrikstraat, left at Kofferen and continue to the Kasteel Henkenshage access road (51.559089, 5.456402)

After the repeated attacks upon Son by von Maltzahn's brigade, on 20 September the 101st Headquarters relocated to **Kasteel Henkenshage** in a large well-maintained park of enormous oak trees south of Sint-Oedenrode. While preparations for that move were being made, German self-propelled artillery brought the castle under direct fire. Lieutenant Colonel Cassidy drove off the intruders with a squad of paratroopers and two British tanks.

Henkenshage is a 14th century farmhouse which grew over the centuries into an attractive manor house. The towers and crenellations were not added until the 1850s by a local industrialist. The castle grounds are surrounded by a tall wall and moat with only the tops of the towers visible over the wall. The castle is owned by the municipality and only open to private functions, but several walking paths cross the attractive woods and are frequented by hikers and dog walkers.

Capture of Veghel
17 to 18 September 1944

Battle

The excellent drop pattern of 501st PIR's 2nd and 3rd Battalions (Lieutenant Colonel Robert Ballard and Lieutenant Colonel Julian Ewell respectively) permitted rapid assembly and movement toward their assigned objectives. Two sergeants and three pfcs from Company D took the main objective, the Zuid–Willemsvaart Canal bridge against minor opposition from rear echelon troops. Two platoons of engineers from the 326th Airborne Engineer Battalion, who dropped with the 501st specifically for the task, immediately began construction of a parallel truck bridge alongside what was in 1944 a single-track. The rail bridge 1.4 kilometers to the northwest was secured by Company E (Lieutenant Frank Gregg) slightly later. The regiment's 3rd Battalion moved on into Eerde and by 18:00 established contact with patrols from the 502nd PIR moving north from DZ 'C'.

Although misdropped to the northwest, the paratroopers of Lieutenant Colonel Harry Kinnard's 1st Battalion ran the distance to Veghel overcoming token resistance to join with 2nd Battalion before getting enmeshed with the local population's wild celebration. Nevertheless, by nightfall the battalion secured the rail and road bridges over the Aa River achieving all four regimental objectives.

Battlefield Tour

The Veghel tour reviews sites involved with the capture and defense of its canal bridges.

> Follow Autoroute A50 toward Veghel; take exit #10 toward Eerde-Veghel Centrum to regain the original Corridor.

The Corridor passes through a large industrial zone then over the **Zuid–**

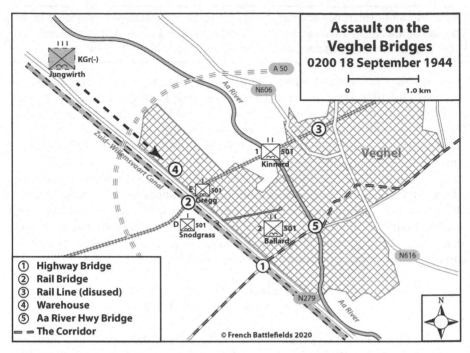

Assault on the Veghel Bridges
0200 18 September 1944

KGr(-)
Jungwirth
A 50
N606
Aa River
Zuid-Willemsvaart Canal
1 501 Kinnard
Veghel
E 501 Gregg
D 501 Snodgrass
2 501 Ballard
N616
N279
Aa River

① Highway Bridge
② Rail Bridge
③ Rail Line (disused)
④ Warehouse
⑤ Aa River Hwy Bridge
— = The Corridor

© French Battlefields 2020

Willemsvaart Canal on a new highway bridge. The 1944 draw bridge crossed over sluice gates but after the war a modern highway bridge was constructed directly east, and the drawbridge was removed leaving only the sluice gates.

Immediately after crossing the canal (51.608192, 5.532565) take the slip road on the right to Sluisstraat, pass under the bridge approach, turn south on Rembrandtlaan, and finally northwest on Rijksweg (N279). Unfortunately, no convenient stopping point is available near the bridge on this heavily traveled, high speed roadway. Continue northwest 1.5 km along the canal and briefly stop at the yard entrance. (51.617531, 5.515747)

In defense of Veghel, Kinnard sent Lieutenant Gregg's Company E to the northwest along the canal bank with Company D (Lieutenant Richard Snodgrass) extended to the west along the railroad track.

The Germans quickly responded to the threat. In a dense nighttime fog, three hundred fallschirmjägers of KGr Jungwirth (Major Hans Jungwirth)[31] first struck Company E at 02:00 driving along the canal to Gregg's outposts stationed at the large warehouse northwest of the rail bridge. The fallschirmjäger presented overwhelming firepower against the platoon of paratroopers blocking their progress. At 04:00, 2nd Platoon commander, Lieutenant Joseph McGregor, ordered a rapid withdrawal

---

31   Major Hans Jungwirth was a veteran commander having previously fought in Poland, France, Crete, Russia, and Tunisia. His kampfgruppe held various units during MARKET-GARDEN including a fallschirmjäger training battalion and attached grenadier and fusilier infantry battalions.

to the main line of resistance near the rail bridge while he remained fully exposed in the center of the road directing his men between delivering bursts of protective submachine-gun fire. Wounded, he was taken prisoner but rescued the following day during a counterattack.[32]

The German attack was beaten back, but the enemy maintained the pressure with additional attacks during the night. Gregg held the rail bridge line reinforced by a platoon from the 326th Airborne Engineer Battalion which was constructing a second bridge over the canal. The engineers ambushed an enemy contingent with a flurry of hand grenades. As daylight approached Gregg was able to commit his reserve platoon and Jungwirth withdrew. American casualties were seven killed and twenty-six wounded with Lieutenant Gregg among the wounded.[33]

After the American capture of the highway bridge, the **Veghel rail bridge** played no further part in the battle. After the war, the rail line fell into disuse and was removed. Only a few segments of rail remain imbedded in the pathway. The canal crossing 75 meters to the east is a modern pedestrian bridge. The large warehouse visible along the canal bank to the northwest marks where the company's outpost line fell to KGr Jungwirth's attack early on 18 September.

Defense of Hell's Highway
20 to 26 September 1944

By 19 September, all the waterway crossings in the 101st sector were in Allied hands. However, British VIII and XII Corps were making slow progress widening narrow salient against German units fighting to cut it. Constant flank attacks threatened to overrun American positions. General Taylor lacked the fire power to destroy the circling Germans or to even maintain a solid defensive line. In places the front line was literally the shoulders of the Eindhoven to Nijmegen highway.

Taylor's efforts to keep open the vital 22 kilometers of road that the paratroopers labeled 'Hell's Highway' were limited to offensive thrusts to keep Student's First Fallschirmjäger Army off balance. Receiving reports of German armor threatening The Corridor north of Veghel, Taylor ordered the 506th PIR from Best to Uden.

Meanwhile, Model ordered the lifeline to be cut by destroying the bridge over the Zuid–Willemsvaart Canal at Veghel. When the German attack began, Brigadier General Anthony McAuliffe, the division artillery commander, was in Veghel to establish a new division headquarters. He took command of available troops and led

---

32   First Lieutenant Joseph C McGregor, a Scottish citizen who lived in Bronx, New York before the war, had been a star soccer player and weight lifter winning the title 'Mr New York City.' He was awarded a Silver Star. McGregor was killed during the Battle of the Bulge near Recogne, Belgium and is buried in Henri-Chapelle American Cemetery, Plombières, Belgium in Plot G, Row 6, Grave 32.

33   First Lieutenant Frank 'Foxy' Gregg was the sixth of seven children to a farm family in Mars Bluff, South Carolina. Seriously wounded at Bastogne, Gregg spent the final months of the war in a British hospital. He fought in all three major 101st Division operations receiving a Silver Star, Bronze Star, and three Purple Hearts. He remained in the Army serving in Korea and Vietnam eventually retiring at the rank of colonel. Gregg was a technical advisor on the motion picture about MARKET-GARDEN – *A Bridge Too Far*. Colonel Frank Alexander Gregg died on 16 January 2019, aged 96, and is buried in Arlington National Cemetery, Arlington, Virginia.

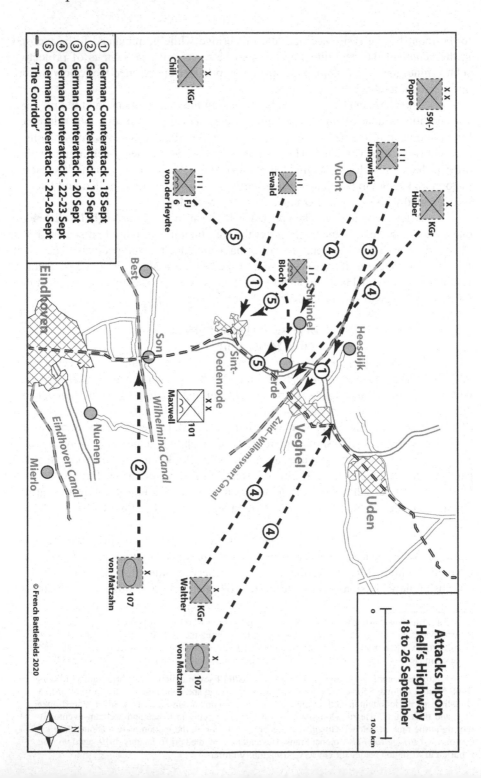

Attacks upon Hell's Highway 18 to 26 September

Legend:
- ① German Counterattack - 18 Sept
- ② German Counterattack - 19 Sept
- ③ German Counterattack - 20 Sept
- ④ German Counterattack - 22-23 Sept
- ⑤ German Counterattack - 24-26 Sept
- – – 'The Corridor'

© French Battlefields 2020

the defense of the bridges. McAuliffe used arriving units to beat off German attacks such that much of the 101st Division was defending the Veghel perimeter.[34]

Battle of Heeswijk-Dinther
20 September 1944

On Wednesday, 20 September, American patrols established that Fallschirmjäger AuE Bataillone 'Ewald' and 'Tuchstein' from KGr Jungwirth with approximately 700 men were in an isolated position along the canal south of Heeswijk-Dinther. Colonel Johnson dispatched Lieutenant Colonel Kinnard's battalion to eliminate the persistent threat to the Veghel bridges. Company C, which had previously established positions in Heeswijk and Dinther, was ordered to move down to the canal to cut off the kampfgruppe's retreat while Companies A and B moved to attack.

Both groups attacked at 09:30 with Company B along the canal and Company A several hundred meters to the right straddling the Aa River. Dutch locals assisted in their sweep up the Aa River valley pushing enemy troops from prepared positions and forcing numerous small group surrenders. During the initial skirmishing, 2nd Platoon's Lieutenant Billy Turner and his platoon sergeant crawled ahead of his main body and plopped into a drainage ditch. Upon command, the squad opened fire and moved forward from ditch to ditch. At one point, Turner jumped up, ran into an open field, and yelled for the enemy to surrender. Some did and came forward to American lines. Emboldened by his success Lieutenant Turner ran to the next field to repeat the effort again calling for a surrender. He was shot through the head and died.[35]

On the opposite side of the river, 3rd Platoon's Lieutenant Henry Puhalski eliminated a machine gun in a windmill and pressed on toward Dinther. Two Germans directly to his front waved white handkerchiefs. Lieutenant Puhalski walked forward only to fall in a hail of bullets. Thereafter, white flags were ignored.[36]

By 15:00 the Germans had been squeezed into a narrowing strip of land between the canal and river. They attempted to break out of the trap toward a wooded area along the canal only to be caught enfilade by a well-placed machine gun. By 17:30, Kinnard had destroyed the German battalion inflicting eighty casualties and capturing 418 prisoners at the cost of four dead and six wounded — a major victory.

Battle of Schijndel
21 to 22 September 1944

Dutch resistance indicated that a strong force under the command of Major Huber[37] was concentrating for an attack upon The Corridor through Schijndel. Colonel

---

34   General McAuliffe's action at Veghel using whatever units were available to withstand a strong armored force foreshadowed his defense of Bastogne, Belgium during the Battle of the Bulge later that year.

35   First Lieutenant Billy A Turner Jr, aged 23 of Garland, Texas, is buried in the Southland Memorial Park, Dallas.

36   First Lieutenant Henry J Puhalski, aged 29 from Oswego, New York, is buried in Netherlands American Cemetery in Plot M, Row 21, Grave 2. He is a recipient of the Silver Star.

37   KGr Huber: composed of three battalions of infantry totaling approximately 2,000 men from Panzergrenadier Regiment 1035, a battalion of 105-mm howitzers, a battery of 150-mm howitzers,

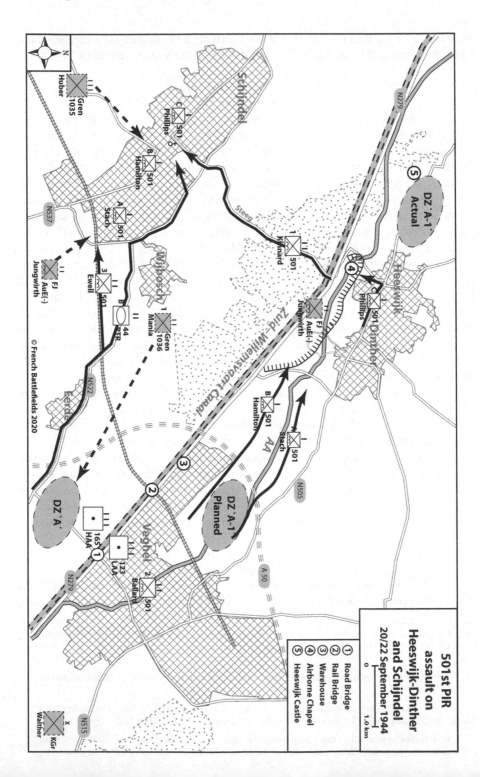

501st PIR
assault on
Heeswijk-Dinther
and Schijndel
20/22 September 1944

① Road Bridge
② Rail Bridge
③ Warehouse
④ Airborne Chapel
⑤ Heeswijk Castle

© French Battlefields 2020

Johnson decided to effect a double envelopment against the accumulation of German forces by sending the 501st PIR's 1st Battalion from its victory at Heeswijk and 3rd Battalion from positions in Eerde to become the hammer from the north while Colonel Michaelis's 502nd Regiment was the anvil coming from Sint Oedenrode in the south. Both American paratroop regiments were supported by squadrons from the British 44th Royal Tank Regiment.

Lieutenant Colonel Kinnard's 1st Battalion started out at 19:00 on 21 September from Heeswijk along Steeg roadway. His lead company brushed aside a vehicle mounting multiple 20-mm antiaircraft guns and found Schijndel weakly defended. By 01:50 1st Battalion controlled the town center. Lieutenant Colonel Ewell's 3rd Battalion approached Schijndel from Eerde following the railway line in the darkness. It encountered stiffer resistance from I Bataillon, Grenadier Regiment 1036 (Hauptmann Mania) delaying its arrival until after dawn the battalion fought small groups of enemy to their front and rear. Ewell's movement was fortuitous because it split KGr Huber to the west from Mania's battalion to the east weakening the attack upon Veghel.

The unexpected arrival of both groups surprised the enemy billeted in the town and units returning from night duties outside of it. Much of the morning was spent in small unit encounters against snipers or German vehicles attempting to enter the town through paratrooper roadblocks. The actions netted 250 prisoners, 170 wounded, and 40 killed.

At 07:15 and shrouded by ground fog, 200 infantry from Huber's Panzergrenadier Regiment 1035 supported by two Jagdpanthers approached Schijndel from the southwest along Schootsestraat and struck against the forward platoon of Company B (Lieutenant Ian Hamilton), 501st PIR. Hamilton gathered his 2nd Platoon and circled around the column's left flank by passing through the grounds of the convent of the Sisters of Charity. Emerging from sheltered positions, Hamilton's platoon burst upon the advancing enemy between the advance group and the main body. Rapid fire downed ten German troops and twenty more, stunned by the sudden assault, quickly surrendered. Huber's main body halted but held its ground. Hamilton dispersed the enemy later that morning with the assistance of two British tanks.

At 09:30, Company A (Captain Stanfield Stach) in the eastern part of town was hit by Jungwirth's training battalion approaching from the south along Koeveringseweg. Bazooka fire held off enemy armor although German infantry was able to divide into small groups and infiltrate into town. A final assault upon German troops south of Schijndel by Kinnard and Ewell from the north and Cassidy's 1st Battalion, 502nd PIR from the south started successfully but alarming news of a German penetration at Veghel forced a halt. Schijndel was abandoned to the Germans when Ewell returned to Eerde and Kinnard took up positions in Wijbosch.

On 22 September, the regiment launched an attack northeast against German forces when a tree burst exploded above an impromptu meeting of the regimental

---

a battery of 20-mm antiaircraft guns, and a squadron of four Jagdpanthers from #1 Kompanie, Panzerjäger Abt 559.
Jagdpanther or hunting panther: specially designed tank destroyer built upon the chassis of the Panther tank and mounting a 88-mm gun.

staff. Colonel Michaelis, three members of his staff, four visiting officers, and five enlisted men became casualties. Lieutenant Colonel Chappuis assumed command of the regiment.[38]

Battle of Veghel
22 to 23 September 1944

General Student's attack upon Schijndel from the west, with the final objective being Veghel, was complemented by an attack upon Veghel from the east by the reconstituted KGr Walther, the same formation that had opposed XXX Corps breakout, under command of newly formed LXXXVI Corps (General der Infanterie Hans von Obstfelder).[39]

Early on 22 September, under low gray clouds and amid swirling ground mist, units of KGr Walther dispersed to their assigned attack positions on either side of the Gemert–Erp road. An armored engineering company waited behind the attack force for the moment to race forward and blow up the Veghel bridge.

At 09:00, German troops rose from the water-logged meadows and started forward. Armor raced toward their initial objectives and artillery fired upon pre-identified targets. Erp was overrun against only weak resistance. II Bataillon (SS-Captain Friedrich Richter), SS Panzergrenadier Regiment 21 assaulted the Veghel canal bridge from positions east of Erp advancing along the canal line with two companies supported by three StuG IVs from Roestel's SS Panzerjäger Abt 10. However, the meadowland offered no cover and the water-soaked ground was slippery for even tracked vehicles. After an all-day struggle, Roestel's[40] StuGs brought the canal bridge under fire, but marshy terrain halted further progress. The attackers ran short of ammunition while under a heavy fire from the 123rd Light Antiaircraft Regiment.[41]

While Richter proceeded east, the bulk of KGr Walther continued northwest against The Corridor between Veghel and Uden by outflanking Veghel. By 11:00, Panzer Brigade 107 successfully severed Hell's Highway 400 meters north of Veghel. Panther tanks then turned left to charge into Veghel only to encounter a 57-mm antitank gun from the 81st Airborne Antiaircraft Battalion, which destroyed the leading Panther and caused its followers to pause.

---

38   John Hersey Michaelis recovered from his wounds and returned to duty in December. He commanded the 27th Infantry Regiment during the Korean War in defense of the Pusan perimeter earning a Distinguished Service Cross and the nickname 'Iron Mike.' Michaelis eventually retired at the rank of full general in 1972. He died in 1985, aged 73, and is buried in Arlington National Cemetery, Arlington, Virginia in Section 1-QQ.

39   Hans von Obstfelder was an infantryman who had received the Iron Cross First and Second Class during the First World War. He commanded army groups in Russia, Normandy, defended Caen in Operation GOODWOOD, and later the German Seventh Army. After the war, von Obstfelder spent two years in American captivity. He died in 1976, aged 90.

40   Captain later Lieutenant Colonel Franz Rudolf Roestel served in the Wehrmacht before transferring to the Waffen-SS in 1943. Roestel was awarded the Knight's Cross of the Iron Cross for defense of the Neerpelt bridgehead. He briefly commanded the 10th SS Panzer Division during the chaos of May 1945. Roestel died in 1974, aged 72.

41   123rd Light Antiaircraft Regiment of XXX Corps carried 40-mm Bofors guns. The unit held three antiaircraft batteries with 405 Battery and 408 Battery taking part in this action.

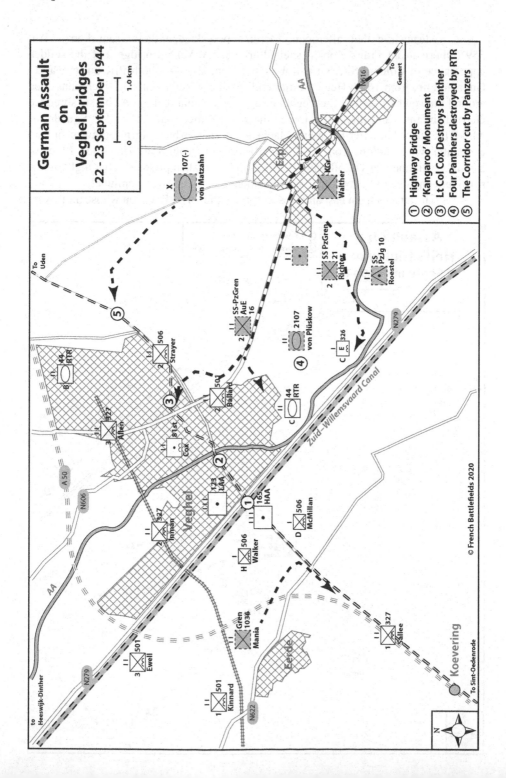

German Assault on Veghel Bridges 22 - 23 September 1944

0   1.0 km

① Highway Bridge
② 'Kangaroo' Monument
③ Lt Col Cox Destroys Panther
④ Four Panthers destroyed by RTR
⑤ The Corridor cut by Panzers

© French Battlefields 2020

Meanwhile that afternoon, Mania's two Jagdpanthers from Panzer Abt 559 (Oberleutnant Franz Kopka) shelled around the Veghel bridge, but the sudden appearance of Colonel Sink's truck-mounted Company D, 506th PIR on its way to Uden and fire from 165th Heavy Antiaircraft Artillery Regiment's 3.7-inch guns sited around the southern end of the Veghel bridge sent Mania reeling. Airbursts shredded German infantry and direct fire forced the Jagdpanthers back. B and C Squadrons, 44th RTR pushed into Eerde leaving Mania no alternative but to turn southwest only to encounter two battalions from the 327th GIR arriving from Sint-Oedenrode. Much of Mania's battalion was cut off with 75 killed and 170 taken prisoner. That night, a few survivors and one of the two Jagdpanthers managed to return to Schijndel.

The attacks from east and west surprised the 101st Division whose units were

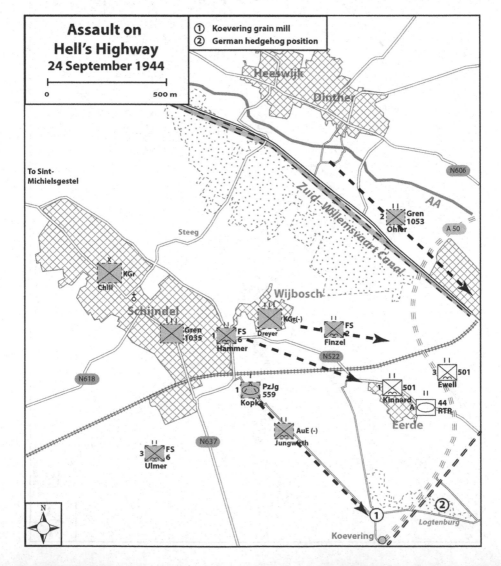

dispersed on missions outside Veghel leaving only 2nd Battalion, 501st PIR inside the city. General Taylor was swift in recalling available units to defend the city and its critical bridges. Specifically, 2nd Battalion, 506th PIR was recalled from the road to Uden, 3rd Battalion, 506th PIR was sent north from Sint-Oedenrode and 327th GIR northeast from Son. The 1st and 3rd Battalions, 501st PIR came from Schijndel. Firepower was provided by B and C Squadrons 44th RTR, two self-propelled howitzer batteries from the 86th Field Regiment, and the 123 LAA and 165 HAA Regiments which all converged upon Veghel.

Horrocks received the distressing news of these attacks during the afternoon of 22 September. He ordered the Grenadier Guards and Coldstream Guards Groups to turn back from Nijmegen and break the German hold from the north while the 506th PIR attacked from the south. Gathering darkness delayed further operations until the next day when the Grenadier Guards found that German defenders had dispersed during a night of punishing artillery fire. However, columns of vehicles were stalled on The Corridor for more than 25 hours and became easy targets for German guns. The delay of 22 September was fatal to the 43rd (Wessex) Division's attack in relief of the British paratroopers holding the perimeter around Oosterbeek.

Oberst Walther, recognizing the threat posed by British VIII Corps approaching his left flank from the south, began an orderly withdrawal by noon on 23 September but continued heavy shelling of the city for most of the day. When the two battalions of 506th PIR reached the blockage of Hell's Highway north of Veghel at 15:20 that afternoon, they found only minimal resistance and British armor driving southwest from Uden. Bulldozers were again clearing the roadway of wrecked vehicles.

Battle of the Sand Dunes
24 September 1944

After events at Schijndel, Lieutenant Colonel Kinnard's 1st Battalion took up positions along the now abandoned rail line north of Eerde. Sand dunes west of town were the prominent terrain feature.

On 23 September, FJR 6 arrived after a two-day, 70-kilometer-long forced march east from Boxtel. Von der Heydte was ordered to assault the Veghel bridge from the south while Walther resumed his assault from the east. However, the lack of radio communications prohibited coordination of the attacks. In morning fog on 24 September, 500 paratroopers from FJR 6 supported by the last remaining four assault guns of Panzerjäger Abt 559 struck Kinnard's outposts. Von der Heydte's fallschirmjägers were again facing the 101st Airborne Division in vicious close-quarters fighting that featured small-arms fire and snipers. An immediate call went out to Colonel Johnson for armored support and Johnson dispatched A Squadron, 44th RTR which arrived about 10:00. By 12:00, the German advance stalled amid the sand dunes west of Eerde while losses mounted. Two assaults by Kinnard's Company A (Captain Stach) pushed the Germans back inflicting serious casualties. The engagement ended around 16:00 when von der Heydte started a movement to the southwest.

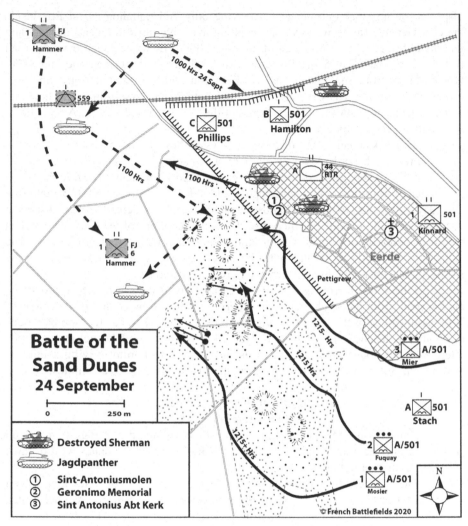

Battle of the Sand Dunes
24 September

0   250 m

- Destroyed Sherman
- Jagdpanther
- ① Sint-Antoniusmolen
- ② Geronimo Memorial
- ③ Sint Antonius Abt Kerk

© French Battlefields 2020

Battle of Koevering
24 to 26 September 1944

Also on 24 September, KGr Jungwirth left Schijndel with 952 men from 'March' battalions and four attached armored vehicles from Kopka's Panzerjäger Abt 559. The units swung around to Eerde's south to avoid the sand dunes and moved along secondary roads devoid of Allied troops to pass through gaps in the 501st Regiment's defenses. They destroyed three British Sherman tanks that were moving north on The Corridor to assist at Eerde. The flaming wrecks once again halted movement toward Arnhem. From a high point, Major Jungwirth saw The Corridor roadway lined with vehicles, nose-to-tail, all blocked by the burning Shermans. Rapidly issuing target objectives to his panzerjäger assault guns, the shooting gallery-like attack began at 19:00. Allied vehicles exploded one-by-one when struck by shells from Kopka's guns. Secondary explosions rocked the countryside as ammunition cooked off. Jungwirth later reported fifty vehicles destroyed.

No other example was needed to demonstrate the fragility of the British transport and supply line to Arnhem. The basically one-roadway-wide Corridor was cut for the final and most critical time. The advance of desperately needed boats to transport Polish and 43rd Division troops across the Rhine were trapped for forty hours.

Outposts near Sint-Oedenrode noticed the German troop movement and Companies C and H, 502nd PIR were immediately dispatched but were repulsed by 88-mm guns dug into concealed positions on either side of the road which presented commanding fields of fire up and down the highway. Shortly later, 88-mm fire knocked out three Sherman tanks from C Troop (Captain Bill Watkins), 44th RTR traveling south from Veghel. Finally, a 57-mm antitank gun managed to lay shells on the camouflaged position and one 88-mm gun was destroyed. In a firefight that lasted until 18:00, two other 88-mm guns continued to lay fire on approaching infantry until automatic weapons fire forced both to withdraw.

As the day progressed, the reinforced 1st Battalion, 502nd PIR and 52nd Recce Regiment (Lieutenant-Colonel JBA Hankey) attacked north while all three battalions of the 506th PIR moved south from Veghel. Both groups made slow progress pressuring the enemy. However, as it became dark, a friendly fire incident convinced General Taylor to halt operations for the night.

With darkness approaching, Jungwirth established a hedgehog defense flanking the highway in the Logtenburg Woods north of Koevering. Later that night he was strengthened by the arrival three more 88-mm guns, what remained of Major Huber's Grenadier Bataillon 1035, and #9 and #10 Kompanie from FJR 6, thereby becoming a sizeable force. The trapped enemy suffered Allied artillery fire from British 7th Armoured Division, 50th (Northumbrian) Division, and the 907th Glider Field Artillery Battalion (Lieutenant Colonel Clarence Nelson). The intermingling of Allied and German units along the highway precluded a massive artillery barrage. Thus, the enemy had to be removed by direct infantry assault.

At 07:30 on 25 September the attack resumed, but the early morning mist and rain slowed progress. The road congestion delayed arrival of the 1/7th Queens Royal Regiment until early morning. Using his 1st and 3rd Battalions to occupy the enemy's attention, Colonel Sink sent 2nd Battalion, supported by #5 Troop (Lieutenant Herbert Dutton), B Squadron, 44th RTR, on a flanking maneuver to the east. Again, tank progress was difficult over the rain-softened ground.[42] German armor seemed be behind every bush while paratroopers approached the enemy over open ground against ground-grazing machine-gun fire. Finally, at 19:40 2nd Battalion established contact east of the highway with Queens Regiment. That night the Germans withdrew to the northwest through a gap in the line leaving three hundred British bodies littering the shoulders of the highway.

Although the Corridor was free of German troops by the morning of 26

---

42   British Lieutenant Herbert K Dutton was awarded a Distinguished Service Cross by the American government for heroism for repeatedly pressing the attack, dismounting from his tank to perform personal reconnaissance while under heavy fire, and thereby playing a substantial role in destroying the enemy.

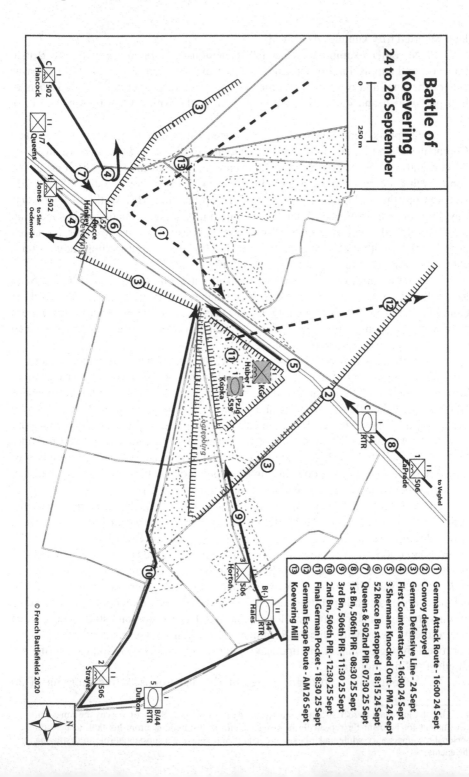

Battle of Koevering
24 to 26 September

0 — 250 m

① German Attack Route - 16:00 24 Sept
② Convoy destroyed
③ German Defensive Line - 24 Sept
④ First Counterattack - 16:00 24 Sept
⑤ 3 Shermans Knocked Out - PM 24 Sept
⑥ 52 Recce Bn stopped - 18:15 24 Sept
⑦ Queens & 502nd PIR - 07:30 25 Sept
⑧ 1st Bn, 506th PIR - 08:30 25 Sept
⑨ 3rd Bn, 506th PIR - 11:30 25 Sept
⑩ 2nd Bn, 506th PIR - 12:30 25 Sept
⑪ Final German Pocket - 18:30 25 Sept
⑫ German Escape Route - AM 26 Sept
⑬ Koevering Mill

© French Battlefields 2020

N

September, Jungwirth's assault guns were still within range and engaged anything moving along the highway. There was not much of that, because the roadway was strewn with wreckage and engineers were faced with the dangerous and time-consuming task of removing numerous antitank and antipersonnel mines.

Aftermath

Eerde remained in American hands despite recurring small assaults through 28 September when British infantry reached Eerde and relieved the paratroopers.

Veghel was not captured and the bridge remained intact. The roadway to the south was lined with parked vehicles and its ditches filled with waiting infantry. Vital supplies and reinforcements remained stuck in rear areas. As a result, the 43rd (Wessex) Infantry Division took 48 hours to cover the 64 kilometers to Arnhem. It was too late for the men at Oosterbeek. This delay turned out to be the death knell for Operation MARKET-GARDEN.

Battlefield Tour

The Veghel tour reviews areas of the extensive engagements to defend 'Hell's Highway.'

Continue northwest from the Veghel rail bridge for 8.4 km and follow signs through Heeswijk to Kasteel Heeswijk. (51.655549, 5.440802)

Immediately after landing on 17 September, Lieutenant Colonel Kinnard left Medical Officer Captain David Kingston to establish a first aid post for the eight jump casualties and a squad from HQ Company (Captain William Burd) as rear guard while the battalion advanced towards Veghel to capture the bridges.[43] Father Francis Sampson, regimental chaplain, also remained with the injured, but left to find transport to Veghel. Upon his return with two horse-drawn carts driven by Dutch civilians, he discovered that a large German force had recaptured the castle and most of the rear guard. A platoon sent from Veghel attempted to rescue the captives but were stopped by an enemy patrol as night fell. The next morning the American platoon disengaged and returned to Veghel.

Although latter retaken by Kinnard, the castle was again abandoned upon the unit's move against Schijndel. The area was only finally liberated in late October 1944.

Kasteel Heeswijk (Heeswijk Castle)

Kasteel 4, 5473 VA Heeswijk-Dinther
Tel: +31 (0)41 329 2024 or +31 (0)41 329 2352
Web: http://www.kasteelheeswijk.com/en/castle/
Open daily except Mondays from 11:00 to 17:00. The grounds are handicap acces-

---

43   Captain William Burd, aged 33 from Williamsport Pennsylvania, was wounded during the Normandy invasion. After recovering in England, he dropped in the Netherlands where he was killed at Heeswijk Castle. He is buried in Netherlands American Cemetery Margraten, Netherlands, in Plot G, Row 3, Grave 11. He never met his only son, William Jr, who became a Navy pilot and flew missions off an aircraft carrier during the Vietnam War.

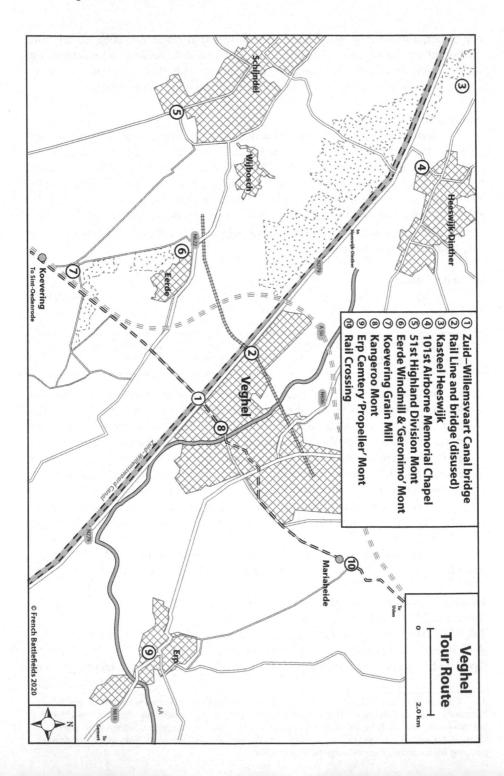

① Zuid–Willemsvaart Canal bridge
② Rail Line and bridge (disused)
③ Kasteel Heeswijk
④ 101st Airborne Memorial Chapel
⑤ 51st Highland Division Mont
⑥ Eerde Windmill & 'Geronimo' Mont
⑦ Koevering Grain Mill
⑧ Kangeroo Mont
⑨ Erp Cemtery 'Propeller' Mont
⑩ Rail Crossing

Veghel Tour Route

© French Battlefields 2020

sible. Parking and grounds are free; admission fee for the castle.

Heeswijk Castle has a turbulent history dating back to 1080. Over the centuries it was destroyed and rebuilt numerous times. The current building dates from 1835 and is the result of numerous renovations and extensions performed as recently as 2005. The building now accommodates cultural events and is owned by a foundation. The architectural details are fascinating and worth a brief visit just to view the exterior. Guided tours of the castle are available and view the castle's salon and Knight's Hall, the Chinese room and the Baron's Library. The tower rooms and the servant's room are also explored. The museum gives visitors a glimpse into life during the medieval era.

A memorial to the **101st Airborne Division** stands in woods southwest of the castle surrounded by its own small moat. A nondescript stone structure bears a dedication to Lieutenant Colonel Francis Sampson, chaplain of the 101st who parachuted with the troops on 17 September and, along with another paratrooper, unavoidably landed in the castle moat. Both men climbed out, but Father Sampson dove back into the water to recover his sacramental kit. (51.655131, 5.440273) [44]

Liberation Route Marker #121 stands at the edge of the southwest corner of the castle moat. The 'Father Sampson' audio retells the story of Father Sampson's perilous drop into the castle moat and his subsequent search for transport for the wounded only to find they had been captured. (51.6554398, 5.44022)

> Return to central Heeswijk; turn right onto Monseigneur van Oorschotstraat and follow to the chapel on the left. (51.648934, 5.466623)

US Airborne veterans funded the elaborate **Heeswijk Airborne Memorial and Liberation Chapel**. An inscribed stone embedded in the brick walkway remembers the heroes of the 101st Airborne Division who landed nearby to begin the liberation. Plaques on opposite sides of the chapel interior present thanks from the citizens Dinther and Heeswijk to those who gave their lives for the people of the Netherlands. A newer memorial wall built in the same style bears a polished, granite stone inscribed with twenty-nine names of civilians ranging in ages from eight months to seventy-nine years who died from 1940 to 1945. The memorial is shaded by four very large oak trees along the street that, based upon their size and age, may have been planted during the original dedication ceremonies. The street separates suburban housing from a vacant field and the wooded area of the final action in the Heeswijk battle.

---

44   Lieutenant Colonel Francis Sampson, a Catholic priest from Cherokee, Iowa, had jumped into Normandy where he received the Distinguished Service Cross for heroism when he remained behind with fourteen seriously wounded paratroopers and was captured by the enemy when their unit withdrew. Then-Captain Sampson spent the night under artillery bombardment while treating the wounded. Sampson was nearly executed by German paratroopers but was saved at the last minute by the intercession of a Catholic German NCO. In December 1944, Sampson was again captured near Bastogne and sent to Stalag II-A in northern Germany where he was held until the Soviet Army overran the area. Father Sampson continued his military service in Korea. Father Francis Sampson died in 1996, aged 83, and is buried in Luverne, Minnesota.

Leave Heeswijk on Baron van den Bogaerdelaan and follow across the Aa River and canal toward Schijndel. Take the first exit at the traffic circle before entering Schijndel, then the second exit at the next traffic circle onto Floralaan and follow west across the town. Turn right onto Boschweg and after 650 m turn left onto Gasthuisstraat. Turn right onto Lidwinastraat and finally turn left onto Lidwinahof. (51.627294, 5.414620)

Not all aircraft reached their destination or returned safely to England. Ground fire from rapid-fire 20-mm or more accurate radar controlled 88-mm antiaircraft guns, difficulties with tow cables, mechanical breakdowns, weather, poor navigation, and the occasional appearance of enemy fighter planes resulted in paratroopers and aircrew falling into enemy territory. In many instances they were rescued and hidden by local citizens and sometimes passed on to the Dutch underground. In the **Sint Lidwina Hospital** in Schijndel the Sisters of Love sheltered twenty-seven Americans in the large structure despite it also being occupied by German officers and hundreds of local refugees. The men were kept hidden until the town was liberated on 23 October 1944. A symbolic bronze memorial was erected to commemorate the risks to their own lives taken by the sisters. The work presents a large mother hen sheltering her baby chicks from attack from above by a hawk.

Reverse direction and return to Structuurweg and follow southeast to the Liberation Memorial along a broad curve near the intersection with Rooiseweg. (51.604321, 5.449519)

After the Americans left Schijndel, the town's liberation had to wait until the arrival of British infantry. On 23 October the 51st (Highland) Division launched an offensive from near this point. By 7 November, hundreds of square miles south of the Maas River had been cleared of the enemy. The division took 2,800 prisoners with minimal ninety-seven casualties.

The **51st Highland Division Monument** depicts a kilted Highlander greeting a welcoming Dutch child as the town is liberated. The statue rests upon a base of Scottish granite bearing a plaque listing liberated towns. Fronting shrubs are trimmed in the circular 'HD' symbol of the Highland Division.

Reverse direction on Structuurweg and at the second traffic circle (Nieuwe Eerdesebaan, N622) take the first exit and follow for 2.6 km to Zandvliet in Eerde. Turn right and continue to the windmill. (51.605768, 5.491989)

The fallschirmjäger attack started from a hillock 150 meters west of the windmill. A Jagdpanther's 88-mm zeroed in on the obvious observation post and its repeated fire slowly dismantled the brick structure. Colonel Johnson dispatched nine tanks from A Squadron, 44th RTR. One British tanker pulled up between the windmill and a house being used as Company C's command post. Lieutenant Wallace Hooper, the troop commander, refused Captain Robert Phillips's order to attack until so ordered by the tank battalion commander. While the discussion continued a Jagdpanther crept into a gap between two dunes and fired an armor piercing (AP) shell through the tank turret. Hooper flew through the air landing in a ditch fatally wounded. He yelled to the paratroopers 'Save my men. Get them out.'

The Jagdpanther's turret slowly rotated and another shell penetrated the second Sherman igniting ammunition that blew the hull apart. The turret then traversed to its far left and eliminated a third Sherman. At that, the squadron commander withdrew his remaining tanks leaving only the paratroopers to face the German attack. The Jagdpanther withdrew when paratroopers worked their way toward it carrying a bazooka.

At 12:15 Company C established a firebase upon one sand dune while three platoons from Company A moved from the south behind a rolling artillery barrage provided by the 907th GFAB directed by observers in the church steeple. First Platoon (Lieutenant Harry Mosier) charged around the south of the dunes across 100 meters of open fields through enemy machine-gun fire into enemy positions. In two and threes the infuriated paratroopers jumped on the fallschirmjägers in their foxholes, shooting, clubbing, and stabbing the enemy. The assault drove off forty or fifty while capturing seven and killing fifteen. Mosier established a fire base behind the dunes before being critically wounded. Platoon Sergeant George Adams was killed.[45]

The 2nd Platoon (Lieutenant Cecil Fuquay) continued moving north through the dunes from one scrub bush to the next until he reached the base of the highest dune. A German shell fell among the 2nd Platoon's command staff killing or wounding all except one squad leader. Nevertheless, the leaderless paratroopers held the sand dunes in a wild melee against a German counterattack.[46]

Third Platoon (Lieutenant Harry Mier Jr) led his men through a copse to the northern end of the strip of sand on the right flank and then drove into the dunes forcing Von der Heydte's attackers back into Mosier's repositioned machine guns. In the end the cost was high; Company A suffered eight dead and thirty-one wounded.[47]

Sint-Antoniusmolen
Mailing Address: Landvliet 11, Eerde
Web: https://www.eerdsemolen.nl/
Open Thursday evenings from 19:00 to 21:30 and Sundays from 10:00 to 16:00, Small admission fee.

The large windmill at the north end of the town became a beacon for the local

---

45   Lieutenant Harry L Mosier survived his wounds and remained in the US Army to also fight in Korea. Moiser died in 1997 aged 81 and was buried in Fort Bliss National Cemetery, El Paso, Texas. Staff Sergeant George Hubbard Adams, Jr, aged 23, is buried in Frankston, Texas.

46   Killed in the assault were Second Platoon commander Lieutenant Cecil O Fuquay and Corporal Bronislaw Kraska. Fuquay, aged 25, from Palm Beach, Florida, enlisted in the Florida National Guard before receiving officer training. Fuquay came from a pioneering Florida family; his great grandfather fought against the Seminole Indians and was a veteran of the Confederate Army in the Civil War. He is buried in West Palm Beach, Florida.
Corporal Bronislaw Kraka, aged 21, is buried in Clifton, New Jersey.

47   Lieutenant Harry J Mier Jr, from Uniontown, Pennsylvania, continued his military career rising to the rank of major general in the Pennsylvania National Guard. Mier died in 2011, aged 91, and is buried in Arlington National Cemetery, Arlington, Virginia in Section 54, Grave 1803.

fighting for its obvious observation capability. Similarly, the tall church tower in the center of town also attracted enemy attention. Both were heavily shelled and almost destroyed. Much of the Eerde sand dunes disappeared when Canadian engineers bulldozed the dunes to convert the open area into a temporary airstrip. Today, the ground is an electrical power relay station or enveloped within a campground and wooded area.

Plaques on the **Sint-Antoniusmolen** list the 71 casualties from the 501st PIR with special mention of Sergeant Jacob Wingard killed by a sniper at 11:00 on 18 September while acting as observer from an upper window. Plaques also commemorate five men of the British 44th RTR and nine civilians killed in the brutal engagements in this sector. Another plaque references the British Sherman tank that hid between the windmill and the house before being knocked out on 24 September.[48]

The rebuilt windmill is open for tours. Beautifully executed paintings displayed on the interior walls of the ground floor depict the local battle and show damage to the church and to the windmill. A steep staircase goes up to a second story, which opens onto an exterior platform offering views of the countryside to the west and south. The church is visible along Kapelstraat.

Walk 20 m to the south. (51.605565, 5.492144)

The **Geronimo Memorial**, so called because the name of the famous Apache Indian chief had become the 501st Regiment's battle cry, is adjacent to the reconstructed windmill. The colorful mosaic emblem of the unit tops a brick wall beneath shade trees. A basic concrete stele bears a plaque listing the names of the unit's eleven fatalities.

Between the memorial and the windmill, **Liberation Route Marker #128** commemorates the destruction of observation posts in the windmill and church steeple. 'The Observation Posts over the Battlefield at Eerde' discusses the tactical importance of the windmill and church tower in providing observation of enemy movements on the battlefield. Corporal Richard Klein, radioman, Sergeant Jacob Wingard, observer, and Lieutenant Nigel Hilton relayed target co-ordinates to mortars near the church until Wingard was killed and the other two are driven out of the windmill.

Continue east along Kapelstraat to the town church. (51.604979, 5.497216)

At the beginning of the German attack, the forward observer from the 907th GFAB refused to mount the exposed steeple of **Sint-Antonius Abt Kerk**. Lieutenant Harry Howard from the 1st Battalion ascended the steeple to observe for the artillery. Someone in Lieutenant Howard's group flew a large American flag from the structure

---

48   Sergeant Jacob H Wingard, aged 22 from Philipsburg, Pennsylvania, is buried in Netherlands American Cemetery, Margraten, Netherlands in Plot A, Row 4, Grave 29. The five British tankers, Trooper Gilbert L Astin, aged 21, Trooper James E Hardy, aged 30, Lieutenant Wallace R Hooper, aged 28, Trooper Jasper Jones, aged 27, and Trooper Frank W Stacey, aged 36, are all buried in the northeast section of Eerde churchyard. Trooper John Anderson, whose body was never found, is commemorated on the Groesbeek War Cemetery Memorial.

which German tankers took as a target and blew away the top of the steeple. Shortly later, the flag reappeared on the top of the now shorter steeple. The Germans blew it off again. This process was repeated several more times during the day. Eventually the dunes were recaptured, and the flag remained flying from a considerably shorted steeple.

Leave Schijndel south on highway N637. After 1.6 km turn left on Damianenweg and after 1.7 km turn right onto Koeveringsedijk. Continue 1.6 km to the small wooded triangle on the left formed by Koeveringsedijk and DeCoevering. (51.58687, 5.49246)

Liberation Route Marker #116 commemorates the fighting around Koevering where, from 24 to 26 September 1944, KGr Jungwirth succeeded in halting the Allied advance for almost 40 hours. The 'Hell's Highway' audio relates the experiences of a German soldier and the brutal fighting in German attempts to cut the British supply line. In the story, he eventually surrenders to a lone American paratrooper.

The **Koevering grain mill**, built in 1299, was a suspected German observation post and was destroyed on 25 September. The monument consists of a wooden frame suspending a milling stone above a second milling stone representing the grain processing capability of the mill.

Turn sharp left then right to access Molenweg leading to the frontage road for the A50 Autoroute which cuts straight through the battlefield.

The 1st Battalion, 506th PIR began 24 September with a march northward from Veghel to join the regiment's 2nd and 3rd Battalions in Uden. Around 03:30 the next day, the battalion received orders to return to Veghel the clear the road to Sint-Oedenrode. After a full day's march, Major LaPrade's battalion spread across both sides of the highway and cautiously approached the burned-out British convoy hit by Kopka's Jagdpanthers the day before. Flames still flared amid the vehicle wreckage and scattered cargo.

The flat terrain made the nighttime advance difficult. Any sound was greeted by German machine-gun fire grazing just inches above ground level. Visibility was practically zero on a night so dark that at one point a platoon fell in behind an advancing Sherman tank - unaware that it had been captured by the enemy. A trooper spotted a German cross that had been hastily applied. When the recognition was made, the German crewman threw a hand grenade that killed Lieutenant Warren Frye.[49]

Suddenly LaPrade faced Jungwirth's machine guns and 40-mm shell fire.

---

49   First Lieutenant Warren Hill Frye from Husted, Colorado left High School after one year to help support his mother and three siblings by joining the Civilian Conservation Corps where he learned carpentry. Frye enlisted twelve days after his eighteenth birthday and his leadership skills were soon recognized. He landed in Normandy on 6 June and was almost immediately wounded, but returned to his unit after convalescence. Lieutenant Frye, aged 21, is buried in Netherlands American Cemetery, Margraten, Netherlands in Plot A, Row 4, Grave 30.

In the darkness muzzle flashes and tracers seemed to come from everywhere in a sudden firefight that just as suddenly died out. Major Horton's 3rd Battalion had paralleled LaPrade's unit before swinging wide to the east. Horton's men stubbornly pushed along the rural track into Logtenburg to join LaPrade's men on Hell's Highway shortly before nightfall. The next morning a few rear guard troops put up only a brief resistance.

Although the Liberation Route marker is near the old mill, the German ambush occurred where Molenweg becomes Abenhoefweg and parallels the postwar Autoroute. The final German hedgehog position was in the forest on the opposite side of the Autoroute but it is difficult to access. They made their escape from the forest on the night of 25/26 September.

Continue north on the frontage road. Turn right onto MacArthurweg to cross under the A50 Autoroute, then a wide curve to the left rejoins The Corridor. Continue into Veghel. Turn left on Sluisstraat then right on Hoogstraat to the large memorial stone on Kolonel Johnsonstraat. (51.615402, 5.540088)

A huge stone memorial in the center of town commemorates the heroes of the **101st Airborne Division** and its leader, **General Maxwell Taylor**. A metal kangaroo tops the stone reflecting the 'Kangaroo' radio call sign used by the division. A plaque placed by the comrades of the 101st Division Association notes the town's liberation on 17 September by the 501st PIR and the intense combat of 22-26 September. The plaque continues to list each of the division's units that participated in the Netherlands campaign. A stone covers a buried urn symbolically holding soil from each American state.

The adjacent **Liberation Route Marker #129** 'A German Loose Cannon' audio recalls an odd episode during the first day of the town's liberation. A bizarre situation occurred when an American lieutenant, driving a captured German vehicle encountered a German tank south of Veghel. Facing bazooka fire from the Americans the tank commander realized too late that Veghel had fallen into the hands of the Americans. The tank fired at Colonel Johnson standing on the Veghel bridge and then roared through the town to re-join his own troops. Speculation holds that the tank may have been the one that escaped destruction at Wolfswinkel.

The former house of Doctor Kersemakers, which stands behind the memorial park but is more visible from around the corner on Hoogstraat, was used as Johnson's Regimental Headquarters during Operation Market Garden in September 1944. The inscription on the gate reads: **'KLONDIKE 1944'**, the call sign for the 501st PIR. A 'Screaming Eagle' adorns the frieze. (51.615369, 5.540556)

Follow Hoogstraat through central Veghel (changes name several times) to Hezelaarstraat, the main Veghel to Uden road until the postwar construction of the by-pass to the east. The tree-lined street has seen its rural fields developed into an upscale residential community. (51.618004, 5.554769)

On 22 September, alerted to the approach of German armor by General McAuliffe, Lieutenant Colonel XB Cox Jr,[50] commander of the 81st Airborne Antiaircraft Battalion, personally jumped into the nearest gun-towing jeep and tore north to intercept the panzers. Stopping in this intersection, Cox's ad hoc gun team swung the gun around to the west only 100 meters from the nearest Panther while the tank's turret began a slow turn to aim at them. The tank fired first, but the shot was high hitting a house behind Cox and showering the team with shattered masonry. Colonel Cox aimed the gun and its first shot disabled the tank and with the second shot the tank burst into flames discouraging the advance of the other Panthers approaching through the corn fields to the east. In their rush to engage the tank, the gun team had not set the spades that prevent recoil upon firing. The gun lurched back upon the first shot breaking gunner Pfc Roberts' kneecap[51]

The attack against Veghel resumed on 23 September with attacks from the north and east. Company F, 506th PIR was to lead the efforts to reopen The Corridor northward to Uden. Before daylight, just as the leading platoon was passing the still smoldering British convoy destroyed the previous day, one of the ammunition trucks exploded in a huge fireball. The concussion killed the platoon commander and his radioman. [52]

Von Maltzahn's commanders used the confusion to strike. Antitank guns of Captain Gueymard's Battery B were still in position from the previous day's heroics and disabled a Panther and two half-tracks, but the panzer attack continued. Three half-tracks and a PzKpfw IV with infantry hit and forced back the left flank of 2nd Platoon. Pfc Orel Lev entered a house and went to the upper floor to cover the withdrawal with his bazooka. Despite heavy enemy fire, Lev destroyed a half-track. Noticing the German tank commander directing its attack from his open turret hatch, Lev killed him. Artillery fire and the arrival of British tanks blunted the German attack. Despite Lev's actions the platoon suffered sixteen casualties that morning including Pfc Lev.[53]

Reverse direction to highway N616 and proceed east toward Erp.

50　Lieutenant Colonel XB Cox from San Angelo, Texas was a graduate of Texas A&M University. His unit was instrumental in defeating the German attacks upon Bastogne, Belgium during the Battle of the Bulge. After the war he married, became a rancher, and led numerous civic organizations. Cox died in 2014 at age 99 leaving a wife, two children, three grandchildren and three great-grandchildren. He is buried in his hometown.

51　Famed war correspondent Walter Cronkite reported the actions of the gun crew on 26 September 1944. Some postwar accounts credit the 327th GIR with this tank kill. Our version is from *Rendezvous with Destiny* by Rapport and Norwood, page 354 and it agrees with Cronkite's. Lieutenant Colonel Cox's ad hoc gun team included Captain Adolph Gueymard, Battery B commander from Baton Rouge, Louisiana, Corporal William Bowyer, Pfc Rogie Roberts from Port Arthur, Texas and a lone glider pilot. Flight Officer Thomas Berry, who was on his way back from Nijmegen and volunteered to help, was not identified as the glider pilot until years later.

52　First Lieutenant Raymond G Schmitz, aged 24 from Illinois, is buried in Netherlands American Cemetery, Margraten, Netherlands in Plot K, Row 18, Grave 7.
Radioman Carl E Pein Jr, aged 21, is buried in the family plot in Colonia, New Jersey.

53　Pfc Orel Henry Lev, aged 22, was awarded a Distinguished Service Cross for courageously remaining to cover his platoon's withdrawal. He is buried in Los Angeles, California.

KGr Walther's major effort was along Erpseweg (N616) toward eastern Veghel. During the morning, German Panthers moved against the flank of Company D when Tech/5 Jack Rider,[54] a company cook, and Private Benjamin Stoner picked up a bazooka, ran the entire length of the company line fully exposed to enemy fire and knocked out a Panther.

Around noon in fields south of the Veghel–Erp road (highway N616) along Kruigenstraat (in the vicinity of 51.603434, 5.556407), two Sherman Fireflies from C Squadron, 44th RTR crossed an open field in a misty rain while awaiting the arrival of supporting infantry. The leading Sherman fired at a Panther 500 meters away but missed. Before it could re-engage, its frontal armor was hit twice setting it burning. Meanwhile, a Panther targeted the second Sherman, commanded by Lieutenant Wally Arsenault by firing through a house. Lieutenant Arsenault spotted a third Panther exposing its rear while changing position. Arsenault got off four quick shots, three of which hit, setting the target on fire. At that moment, a fourth Panther appeared and its first shot penetrated Arsenault's turret forcing the crew to bail out and make their escape. Continued armored fighting eventually took out all four Panthers.[55]

The open terrain east of Veghel created excellent tank killing opportunities for both sides. The engagement described occurred only 1.75 kilometers due east of the Veghel canal bridges and provides an impression of the close approach of German armor to the vital canal crossings.

Continue to follow highway N616 into Erp to convenient parking available along the south side of the cemetery on Steengraaf. The cemetery entrance is on De Steen which is not a through street. The military graves are near the southeast corner of the cemetery. (51.598308, 5.606312)

On 17 September, forty-five C-47 'Dakota' aircraft from 304th and 305th Squadrons of the 442nd TCG took off from Chilbolton Airfield in England. The planes carried the 3rd Battalion, 501st PIR and 3rd Platoon, Company B, 326th Airborne Engineers. The planes were targeted to DZ 'A' near Veghel.

Pilot 2nd Lieutenant Herbert Shulman was flying #43-15111, nicknamed 'Sonya'. When the formation was hit by heavy antiaircraft fire as it crossed the Belgian front line. 'Sonya' was hit in the port engine and began to burn, but Shulman kept his plane on course determined to drop his human cargo and parapacks on target. After the last paratrooper left the plane, Shulman executed a broad left turn slowly losing altitude. Three crewmen parachuted from the aircraft, but the chute of his co-pilot 2nd Lieutenant Omar Kampschmidt did not open. Shulman struggled with the burning craft until it crashed into the Aa River near Erp. Mechanic Technical Sergeant Ralph Zipf and radio operator Staff Sergeant Roger Gullixon floated to the ground. Local resistance member Gerardus Otten ran to the crash site and discovered Shulman's

---

54   Jack B Rider, Sr served in the Second World War, Korea and Vietnam. He died in 1989, aged 69, and is buried in Clarksville, Tennessee.

55   Lieutenant Arsenault's third shot killed Major Hans-Albrecht von Plüskow, aged 34 and commander of Panzer Bataillon 2107. He is buried in Ysselsteyn German War Cemetery, Ysselsteyn, Netherlands, in Plot CC, Row 13, Grave 130.

body in a nearby field.[56]

A memorial in the **Sint-Servatius Roman Catholic Cemetery** consisting of a propeller from a C-47 embedded upright in the ground, recalls the action that was so typical of the courage and determination of the troop carrier pilots during MARKET-GARDEN to bring their planes through the flak and accurately drop their troopers. In all, thirty-five C-47s were shot down that day.

The memorial stands amid eight graves holding the British aircrew from 15 Squadron who died on 2 November 1944 when their Lancaster I aircraft collided at 20,000 feet with another Lancaster from the same squadron on a daylight bombing raid on an oil plant in Homberg. The second Lancaster also crashed killing five of its seven-man crew.[57]

Return to highway N616 in Erp then turn north on Voorbolst and follow 3.5 km into Mariaheide. Turn left onto Ericastraat, then right onto Pastoor van Haarenstraat, which becomes The Corridor, and continue 1.1 km to the cluster of trees that mark a now disused rail line. (51.642803, 5.588677)

Von Maltzahn's Panther tanks, moving northwest from Erp, cut The Corridor and isolated the 506th paratroopers that had just arrived in Uden. Although the city could easy have been taken, the German objective was not the city but cutting off the head of the British supply line to Nijmegen and thus consequently to Arnhem. At the rail crossing, the Panthers encountered four British trucks from E Troop, 123rd Light Antiaircraft Battalion (LAA) towing 40-mm Bofors guns. The German armor easily destroyed three of the guns before continuing south toward Veghel.[58]

Liberation Route Marker #120 identifies the former rail crossing. In the 'Surrounded in Uden' audio American paratroopers Bill and Babe discuss being surrounded on the road to Uden and the horrors of the battle.

Continue north on The Corridor into Uden. Uden is a big city and following The Corridor through the city streets can be difficult.

From Uden Centrum follow 'CWGC' signs onto Kerkstraat. Turn right onto

---

56   Both Shulman and Kampschmidt were buried in the Roman Catholic Cemetery in Erp. They were later reburied in the temporary cemetery in Wolfswinkel, then again in Netherlands American Cemetery, and finally brought home to the United States at the wishes of their next of kin. Lieutenant Herbert Shulman, aged 25 from Chicago, Illinois, is buried in Westlawn Cemetery, Norridge, Illinois. Lieutenant Omar Jean Kampschmidt, aged 19, is buried in Mountain View Mausoleum in Oakland, California.

57   The crew members were pilot Flight Lieutenant Bernard Earley, aged 24 and recipient of the Distinguished Flying Medal; flight engineer Pilot Officer Alfred Abraham Markovitch, aged 21; navigator Flying Officer James Easdale Campbell, aged 23, awarded the Distinguished Flying Cross; air bomber Pilot Officer Geoffrey William Lilley, aged 23; wireless operator Flying Officer Frederick John Frearson, aged 22; gunner Warrant Officer George William Morris, aged 23; flight engineer Sergeant William Hunter, aged 21; and gunner Flight Sergeant Peter Woollard, aged 20. A separate lone grave holds Private Frank Edward George Lentern, aged 22 of the Royal Army Ordinance Corps, who died on 11 October 1944.

58   Major Berndt-Joachim Freiherr von Maltzahn died in 1964 at age 61.

Piusplein, then another right turn to the cemetery surrounded by red brick wall on Burgemeester Buskensstraat. (51.663828, 5.612440)

Uden War Cemetery was originally a Roman Catholic cemetery that had been unused since 1918; the civilian graves having been removed. During the early years of the war Allied servicemen, mostly downed air crews, were buried in the garden of the parish priest. As the number of graves grew the municipality purchased the unused cemetery grounds. The grounds now hold 701 Commonwealth burials and 2 Polish graves all relocated from the priest's garden or from isolated graves around the community. The Cross of Sacrifice is street side in front of the cemetery, which occupies a plot in a residential neighborhood. The graves frequently bear fresh red roses, poppy wreaths, or floral displays.

The cemetery holds the graves of nineteen members of the Royal Australian Air Force (RAAF), eight of whom were from 460 Squadron, which boasts of the highest tonnage, heaviest casualties with 978 dead, and most decorations in Bomber Command flying Lancaster and Wellington bombers over northern Europe.

Side Trip: Sint-Michielsgestel

Several memorials in Sint-Michielsgestel recall events in the town. From Veghel follow highway N279 to Heeswijk, Steeg to Schijndel, and N617 to Sint-Michielsgestel.
Total round trip distance: 34 km from the Veghel bridge.

A seminary in Sint-Michielsgestel became a prison camp in May 1942 where the Germans held 460 prominent Dutch politicians, writers, religious leaders, lawyers, and educators. Their captivity was an 'insurance' against unrest in the country, but they were lightly treated and even allowed to receive visitors. The intellectuals formed study groups, debating societies, and established relationships which greatly influenced postwar Dutch political movements. Other captives, especially those involved in espionage were treated more severely. On 15 August five inmates were executed in retaliation for an attempted resistance bombing of a train carrying German personnel on leave. On 16 October 1942, a second execution took place for local resistance activity. Survivors were liberated on 17 September 1944. The building currently houses the **Gymnasium Beekvliet**, a Catholic secondary education school. (51.641619, 5.364026)

A **monument to citizens of Sint-Michielsgestel** shot by the Germans stands in front of the village church. The impressionistic memorial stands over a bronze book bearing the names of those who died fighting the Germans in the Netherlands and combating the postwar independence movement in the Dutch East Indies. (51.640891, 5.352789)

The graves of the pilot and co-pilot of a British Horsa glider are immediately to the right of the entrance to the **religious cemetery** in Sint-Michielsgestel. The glider carried a Polish antitank crew and was shot down by German antiaircraft fire west of the village on 19 September.[59] (51.642697, 5.352703)

    The **51st (Highland) Division Monument** in Sint-Michielsgestel consists of a light-colored brick wall bearing three plaques. Two plaques commemorate C Squadron, 1st Northamptonshire Yeomanry and the 7th Black Watch which liberated the village on 22/23 October 1944 during its drive upon Vught. The central plaque remembers those units' casualties in the village. (51.637916, 5.355958)

Side Trip: Vught Concentration Camp

General Student's command post on 17 September was Huize or Villa Bergen in Vught. (51.650273, 5.301318) The approach to Camp Vught passes the Dutch Engineers (Genie) Museum on the left while the road terminates at the camp entrance. (51.665311, 5.258973)

Total Distance: 12 km northwest of Sint-Michielsgestel; 25.2 km northwest of the Veghel Bridge

National Monument Kamp Vught
Lunettenlaan 600, 5263 NT Vught
Email: info@nmkampvught.nl
Web: http://www.nmkampvught.nl
Open Mondays from April through September and Tuesday through Friday the remainder of the year from 10:00 to 17:00; Saturday, Sunday, and public holidays from 12:00 to 17:00. Closed certain dates throughout the year; see website for information. Admission fee; recommended only for those over 10 years of age. The camp's Visitor Center provides an English language guide sheet to translate the camp's Dutch signs.

    Known as 'The Gateway to Hell,' the vast site housed victims before the German officials transported them to extermination camps in Poland. Construction started in 1942 on what the Germans designated as *Konzentrationslager Herzogenbusch*. The work was performed by slave labor prisoners from other camps, many of whom died as a consequence of the grueling work schedule. Twenty-three watch towers, each equipped with machine guns and searchlights guarded the barracks.

    In February 1943, the first prisoners, many of them Jews, arrived and workshops for Philips Electronics were established. Employment in the German war effort rescued Jewish employees of the company from extermination camps — at least temporarily. Unfortunately, their protection ended in June 1944 when they were sent to Auschwitz. When the Allied armies approached in early September the camp was emptied with 2,800 men sent to Sachsenhausen and 650 women to Ravensbruck. Accurate information is impossible to obtain because the retreating guards burned the camp records, but an estimated 31,000 prisoners including 1,800 children passed through the camp. Approximately one half of which were Jewish. After liberation, the camp became a German PoW camp and also held Dutch collaborators.

---

59   Those killed were Staff Sergeant Ronald Ernest Osborn, aged 26 from Brighton, Sussex, and Sergeant Norman Whitehouse, aged 36 from Edmonton, Middlesex, both of The Glider Pilot Regiment; Polish troopers Ogniomistrz (Sergeant Major of Artillery) Piotr Maslorz, aged 37, and Kanonier (Gunner) Kazimierz Nowak, aged 21, are buried in Arnhem Oosterbeek War Cemetery Plot XXXIII, Row A, Graves 8 and 9.

The camp's grounds are enclosed in wartime barbed wire mounted upon concrete posts with watchtowers outside the captive areas. An outdoor scale model presents the camp's 1943 appearance. A recreated sleeping area, toilet, and the original crematorium demonstrate camp life. The ovens were not for mass killings but to dispose of bodies of those who died of other causes. A replica cell presents the story of seventy-four women crammed into the nine square meter (eighty-one square feet) cell on the night of 15/16 January 1944 for protesting the imprisonment of their barracks leader. Fourteen hours later, ten women had died, others were unconscious or insane. The camp commandant, SS-Major Adam Grünewald, was tried by a SS Court in Velp and found guilty of causing the women's deaths. Although sentenced to three and one half years in prison, he was pardoned one month later, joined an SS division, and died in January 1945 during the Russian siege of Budapest.

Most disturbing is the Children's Memorial where bronze tablets bear the names and ages of 1,269 child victims and lists their shockingly young ages. The base of the tablet holds bronze replicas of children's toys.

Although a signpost near the entrance to Camp Vught indicates a path through the Vughtse Heide to the *Fusilladeplaats* (execution grounds), the long walk can be significantly shortened by driving to the access road on Loonsebaan opposite Heiweg at (51.654251, 5.269399). Proceed north 800 m along the partially paved roadway to the parking area and walk the remaining 240 m to the memorial wall at (51.661711, 5.263451)

The road and path pass into one of the three lunettes that are survivors of a line of nine such fortifications that swept along the west and south sides of the town.[60] The fortifications were dug during the Belgian Revolution of 1830-1 when the southern provinces seceded from the Kingdom of the Netherlands. Dutch King William II ordered the construction of a ring of defenses to protect 's-Hertogenbosch from Belgian or French attacks from the south. The three remaining lunettes mark Fort Isabella army camp. The *Fusilladeplaats* is located on Lunet 2.

The sand hill to the rear of the wall was back drop for a German execution site where approximately 450 Dutch resistance fighters were shot during July, August and September 1944. A memorial wall has been constructed to record the names of the 329 known victims. In 1995 panels were defaced by vandals. They have been replaced, but the original, damaged panels remain encased near the camp gates as a symbol of mindless vandalism.

Side Trip: Peel–Raamstelling Bunker Line
The Peel–Raamstelling was a 1940 defensive sector of personnel bunkers that ran from Grave to the Belgian border. Bunkers were built on the west bank of the Peel Canal every 200 to 400 meters. Each bunker sheltered three to four people. S-type bunkers had three loopholes, one for a machine gun and the other two for riflemen. Surrounding terrain usually held foxholes for additional troops.

---

60   Lunette: a crescent shaped fortification surrounded by a moat.

Leave Uden to Hoogstraat on the western edge of Mill (N264). (51.686800,
5.776495)
Total distance: 15 km east of Uden

The casemate at the edge of Mill on Langenboomseweg is a prime example
of the pre-war Peel Bunker Line. This casemate belongs to the so-called 'porcupine'
type with three loopholes having 190 degrees fields of view and equipped with one
light machine gun. Casemate #538 received hits from German artillery, antitank guns,
and Stuka bombers as the pot-marked surface demonstrates. The casemate commander
Sergeant N Blokland staunchly stood here on 10 May until he died about 15:00.

The armor and hardware are intact, and a wooden platform allows close-up
viewing from the canal side. Views through the glassed embrasure display typical
bunker interior including a manikin holding a machine gun. The footpath follows the
canal defense for 4.25 kilometers to the west and 4.75 kilometers to the east.

Other bunkers can be viewed by following the Peelkaanal walk path south for 1.1
km or driving the narrow Nieuwenhofweg to where it crosses the canal and walking
west along the canal for 80 meters. (51.679736, 5.766717)

Around 04:30 on 10 May 1940 a German armored train with 500 infantrymen
was able to pass behind the Peel–Raamstelling. Three quarters of an hour later the
armored train returned, probably to pick up reinforcements. In the meantime, Dutch
soldiers had placed asparagus roadblocks and land mines which caused the train to
derail. The German soldiers jumped out and attacked the Dutch soldiers who had
hidden themselves in nearby casemates. After a day of fierce battle, the Germans
succeeded in breaking the opposition and advancing farther towards the German
parachutists at the Moerdijk bridges.

This relatively difficult to reach location passes Casemate #534 whose
southeast side was severely damaged by artillery fire and two of its three embrasures
penetrated by armor piercing shells. Continue to two S-type casements, #532 and
#533, which are connected by a reconstructed trench line. Nearby sections of railroad
track have been inserted into the ground resembling the asparagus design used in 1944
to block the now-disused rail line.

About 180 m west of casemate #538 a park holds a tracked vehicle as a memorial.
(51.686653, 5.774037)

The 1st Canadian Armoured Carrier Regiment was formed in August 1944.
The units utilized M7 'Priest' self-propelled guns as armored personnel carriers which
they nicknamed 'Kangaroos' — a first for any army — as devised by Lieutenant-
General Guy Simonds, II Canadian Corps. The M7 saw its 105-mm gun and
ammunition storage compartments removed, but a machine gun added. Later other
obsolete tank models were similarly converted. The vehicles were used in a variety of
missions from attack to rescuing wounded. The concept proved so successful, that it
was adopted after the war by most armies.

An armored troop carrier from the **Canadian 1st Armoured Carrier Regiment** stands on display. A bronze plaque on a nearby stone lists the seventeen members of the unit who were killed during the war, mostly during the early 1945 Rhineland battles.

1. The reconstructed 1955 version of Joe's Bridge shows no similarity to the trestle bridge captured during the battle, below.

The relocated Irish Guards Monument stands beside Liberation Route Marker #100 on the banks of the Bocholt-Herentals Canal, inset.

The sun brightly illuminates crosses in the nearby Lommel Polish War Cemetery.

2. Sherman tanks of the Irish Guards Group advance past others which were knocked out earlier during the initial Irish Guards advance on 17 September. (IWM – BU925)

Memorial Gate of Liberation Bergeijk commemorates the passage of the first Allied units into the Netherlands.

3. Parachutes open overhead as waves of paratroops land in the Netherlands. (NARA – 111-SC-354702)

This Waco glider, carrying three men and a jeep from the 501st PIR, crashed on LZ 'W' after being hit by a second glider whose pilot had been blinded by enemy fire. Men of the 506th PIR rescued all three victims. (NARA – 194180-SA)

4. A Grenadier Guards Group tank crosses the Bailey bridge in Son on the morning of 19 September to resume the assault toward Nijmegen and Arnhem. (NARA)

The 101st Memorial behind the Zonhove Sanatorium where shrapnel from German 88-mm guns hit Major LaPrade's Company A, killing five and wounding eight, below left.
A 'Screaming Eagle' parachutist statue, commemorating those who died in the campaign in the Netherlands, stands near the lake in Son en Bruegel, below right.

5. The War and Liberation Memorial in central Eindhoven commemorates the inhabitants of the city who were killed during the Second World War, below left.
Located on the former premises of the Philip factories in Eindhoven, the Monument to the Fallen commemorates company employees killed or missing during the Second World War, below right.

The Airborne Memorial celebrates the liberation of Eindhoven by the 101st Airborne Division and the British Second Army on 18 September.

6. The Netherlands American Cemetery in Margraten, Netherlands holds the remains of 8,291 American dead. The grave of Lieutenant Colonel Robert Cole is shown, inset.

German Second World War dead are buried under 31,598 gray concrete crosses which extend into the distance in the Ysselsteyn German War Cemetery. The mausoleum is centered amid the First World War German burials of German soldiers killed elsewhere but whose bodies washed ashore in the Netherlands. Liberation Route Marker #203 is in the foreground.

7. This stone memorial to Lieutenant Colonel Robert Cole marks the location of his death from a sniper's bullet on 18 September at the edge of woods near Best.
Lieutenant Colonel Cole, recipient of the Medal of Honor for his actions in Normandy, is shown in the inset.

The Pfc Joseph Mann Battlefield Memorial, which has been relocated from near the Best bridge, commemorates his sacrifice of his life by falling upon a German handgrenade.
Pfc Joe Mann, posthumous recipient of the Medal of Honor, is shown in the inset.

8. Monument to the Dutch in Sint-Oedenrode was donated by 101st Airborne veterans to the citizens of the Netherlands in appreciation of their friendship and courage. Detail of the left side, inset.

The open sarcophagus in Nuenen represents the liberation of the town and identifies the site of the battle of 20 September 1944. The difficult to read stone inset in the wall behind states (in Dutch) 'In honor of them and our fatherland died here - killed in action Cpl R Stothard Tpr B.Nicholis' with the image of a tank and the date, inset.

9. Kastel Heeswijk, the congregation point and first aid post of the misdropped 1st Battalion, 501st PIR on 17 September.

Eerde Windmill and observation post that was central to the 24 September battle between Company A, 501st PIR and German paratroopers, below right.

'Geronimo' Memorial to the 501st PIR in Eerde, below left.

10. Wings of Liberation Museum period photo of Sherman tank crossing the Veghel Bridge on 19 September.

Major Hans-Albrecht von Plüskow's command Panther tank is examined by an American soldier after the battle for Veghel, right. (NARA)

The Propeller of a C-47A 'Dakota' in the Sint Servatius Roman Catholic Cemetery in Erp commemorates the crew of 'Sonya' which crashed on 17 September killing two crewmembers. The four graves in a row are a section of eight holding crew members of a British Lancaster bomber which crashed in November 1944.

11. American medics shelter in a ditch along an exposed stretch of 'Hell's Highway' between Eindhoven and Son while their column is under artillery and mortar fire on 20 September from von Maltzahn's Panzer Brigade 107. (IWM – BU1059)

A convoy of Bofors guns from a light antiaircraft regiment passes destroyed vehicles along 'Hell's Highway' on 20 September. (Stichting Liberation Route Europe)

12. Members of the 82nd Airborne Division have their gear checked by the jumpmaster for the last time before entering their C-47 'Dakota' on 17 September. (NARA)

The John S Thompsonbrug over the Maas River near Grave, below.
Casemate Zuid on the southern end of the Grave bridge displays real and artificial gun embrasures, inset.

13. Aerial view of the Heumen Lock and Bridge in 1944 showing the island between the canal and spillway which was well, but only briefly, defended. (NARA)

Mook War Cemetery displays the attention paid to Commonwealth War Grave Cemeteries with their precise alignment of grave plots and generous use of trees and shrubs. Liberation Route Marker #4 is on the right of the entrance gate.

14. The footbridge crosses over Voerweg in Valkhofpark, Nijmegen. During medieval times Voerweg was a defensive ditch surrounding the Valkhof fortifications. SS-Captain Karl-Heinz Euling used the roadway as his escape route when his positions were overcome on 20 September, above.

Sint-Nicolaaskapel in Valkhofpark, Nijmegen still projects its medieval appearance, left.

Ruins of the ancient Valkhof ramparts remain despite centuries of local conflict.
Hunnerpark is to the right and Belvedere is visible in the distance, below.

15. A British convoy passes wreckage on the bridge at Nijmegen on 21 September. (IWM – B10173)

Aerial view taken after the battle of the bombed city of Nijmegen with its now famous bridge in the distance. (NARA – 208AA-274W-1)

16. The area of the 504th PIR's dramatic crossing of the Waal River with the new De Oversteek Bridge as viewed from the south bank.

The original, taller Waal Crossing Memorial was erected in 1984. After relocation, a replacement stone listing the 49 names of the paratroopers who died in the assault was added. The De Oversteek Bridge is viewed from the north bank. The electricity pilons roughly mark the downstream border of the crossing area but did not exist in 1944.

Chapter Four
American 82nd Airborne Division 'All-American'

The 82nd Airborne Division was originally organized in 1917 during the First World War as an infantry unit. Since its initial members came from all forty-eight states, its nickname became 'All-American.' The division participated in the St-Mihiel and Meuse–Argonne Offensives in 1918.

The division was redesignated shortly after the Japanese attack on Pearl Harbor and in August 1942 became the US Army's first airborne division under the command of Lieutenant General Matthew Ridgway. It first combat mission was a parachute assault into Sicily in July 1943 followed shortly later into Salerno, Italy in September 1943. The third parachute jump was into Normandy in June 1944 again quickly followed by the Netherlands in September. The division is the only combat group to have performed four parachute attacks. The unit entered the Battle of the Bulge in December 1944 by truck. During the Second World War, the 82nd Airborne Division suffered 9,073 casualties with over 1,600 killed in action.

The division's objectives were the intact capture of bridges over the Maas River at Grave, the Waal River at Nijmegen, and at least one of four bridges over the Maas–Waal Canal. As important as the bridges were to MARKET-GARDEN, even greater emphasis was placed on protecting the Corridor from counterattack from the German Reichswald Forest only 12 kilometers from the Nijmegen bridge. The forest was known to shelter German units, but their size and composition were unknown. The Groesbeek Heights, an escarpment southeast of Nijmegen, held the key high ground and the ridgeline faced the Reichswald and dominated the canal crossings. Physical possession of the bridges would be worthless, argued General Gavin, if the heights remained in German hands.

Specifically, 504th PIR (Colonel Reuben Tucker) dropped on DZ 'E' and 'O' to seize the Grave bridge over the Maas River and a bridge over the Maas–Waal Canal. The 1st Battalion, 505th PIR (Colonel William Ekman) targeted DZ 'N' immediately south of Groesbeek to seize the rail bridge over the Maas River at Molenhoek and to gain control of the Groesbeek escarpment near Riethorst. The regiment's 2nd Battalion was to attack the Maas–Waal Canal bridge from the east to facilitate the 504th in its attack on that same objective from the west. The 3rd Battalion was to move east to establish a defensive line facing the Reichswald. The 508th PIR (Colonel Roy Lindquist) dropped on DZ 'T' northeast of Groesbeek to establish a defensive perimeter facing Germany. Colonel Lindquist established his regiment's principle defense on high ground overlooking Beek, which was closer to Germany than to Nijmegen. Once the landing zone for Monday's glider landings was secure and if he felt appropriate, one battalion would be sent into Nijmegen for an attempt to quickly capture the Waal bridge against expected low-quality occupation and training units.

The troopers well knew the mission objectives having studied aerial photographs and sand tables of the terrain that morning. On 17 September, 480 planes left England at 11:09 and in less than ninety minutes the leading pathfinders marked Drop Zone 'O'. Thirty minutes later the main body started delivering 7,277 paratroopers to the four landing zones east and south of Nijmegen. Forty-eight Waco gliders carried Brigadier General Gavin's divisional headquarters, antitank platoon,

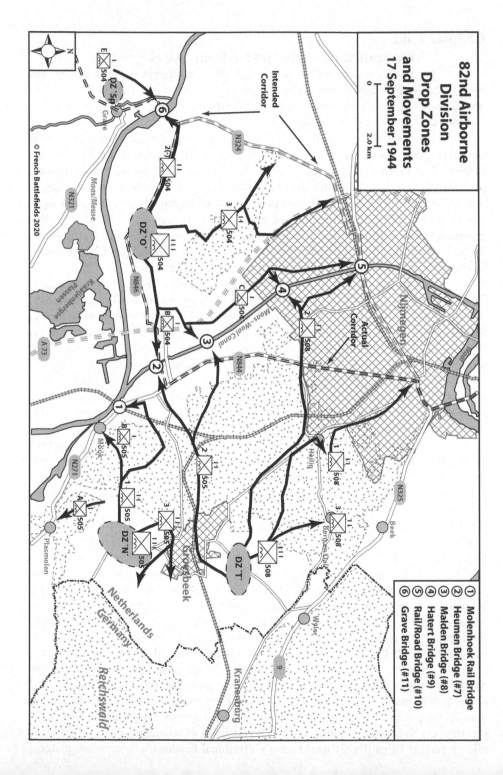

engineers, and support troops, and thirty-eight Horsa gliders held Lieutenant-General Frederick Browning's I Airborne Corps headquarters.

The flight was relatively uneventful until the planes neared their objectives, where flak and small-arms fire came from the bridges and wooded areas including the Reichswald. The planes were especially vulnerable upon the final approach when they dropped to an altitude of 500 feet and slowed to 100 miles per hour. Nevertheless, only one plane and two gliders failed to reach the target area. Eight planes did not return because of ground fire; two suffered a mid-air collision. Twenty-five flight crew members were killed but only six wounded; two paratroopers were killed, 122 wounded or injured, and 26 missing — a spectacular success by any measurement for a paratroop assault.

As the day progressed, the German defensive strategy became clear. Model felt that the major threat was not the British paratroopers surrounded in unconnected positions in Arnhem and Oosterbeek, but the advancing British armored column joining the airborne troops at Nijmegen. To hold the British armored column at Nijmegen, Model needed time for the arrival of the entire 10th SS Panzer Division; time to be gained by attacks from the east and from the Reichswald against the Groesbeek Heights. The assignment was given to SS-Colonel Heinz Harmel.

Harmel's division was dispatched toward the Nijmegen bridge to establish a bridgehead south of the river for a possible counterattack. But Harmel's forces were north of Arnhem and by the time they collected, British forces held the northern end of the Arnhem bridge. Harmel had only one alternative to get across the Rhine to Nijmegen — the river ferry at Pannerden which was 13 kilometers southeast of Arnhem. Such a crossing was a slow, tedious effort and required construction of stronger raft ferries that could bear the full weight of his tanks thus delaying their appearance on the Nijmegen battlefield.

Capture of the Grave and Heumen Bridges

At 06:45 on 10 May 1940 two bridge sections of the Maas bridge near Grave, one of the longest bridges in Europe at 520 meters, were destroyed by the Dutch Army rendering the bridge and canal locks below unusable. Temporary replacement sections were later constructed which remained in use until after the war. The nine-span bridge over the Maas was an important strategic point on the route of Operation MARKET-GARDEN. The span was not only essential for XXX Corps' movement to Arnhem, but also for the 82nd Airborne Division's survival as well. Without the Grave crossing, the airborne troops north of the Waal River would be cut-off from ground resupply and reinforcement.

The Maas River known as the Meuse River in France runs predominantly north to Mook where it turns west for 7 kilometers to Grave. After Grave, the river continues generally northwest before joining the Waal River and flowing into the North Sea. The Maas–Waal canal, which brought Maas River traffic directly to the Waal River at Nijmegen, was opened in 1927. Numerous bridges allowed train and road traffic to cross the canal.

Four crossings became the targets of 1st Battalion (Lieutenant Colonel Willard Harrison), 504th PIR who identified the bridges by number starting with the vertical-lift bridge across canal locks in Heumen as bridge #7. Major Harrison identified bridges farther north at Malden as bridge #8 and at Hatert as bridge #9. Bridge #10 in De Kamp, the last of the four canal bridges, carried a rail line and thus assuredly could support the weight of the 35-ton Sherman Mk V tanks. The Germans knew its importance as well and heavily defended it with pillboxes, barbed wire, and mine fields.

Battle

At 13:15, 2,016 men of Colonel Tucker's 504th PIR jumped onto DZ 'O' north of Overasselt assigned to capture the Maas bridge at Grave and the four bridges over the Maas–Waal Canal. Tucker decided to attack both ends of the Grave bridge to improve chances of capturing it intact. A small section of eleven C-47s left the main body to carry Company E (Captain Walter van Poyck), to small special drop zone west of Grave. Platoon leader Lieutenant John Thompson watched from the open door of his C-47 as the men from the other planes jumped. When the jump light came on in his plane, Thompson hesitated for a few seconds to more closely approach the target bridge. It was a fortuitous delay. Jumping over open fields, his 3rd Platoon landed only 700 meters from the southwestern edge of the target bridge.

Despite leading only sixteen men, Lieutenant Thompson decided to attack before the enemy became fully alerted to his threat to the bridge. Two squads waded through drainage canals toward the river at times in neck deep water holding their weapons above their heads. The third squad swung around to the west to approach along the river and come up under the road span.

They could see German soldiers scurrying in and out of a building 250 meters west of the bridge on the opposite side of a narrow creek known as Graafsche Raam. Thompson's men raked the small pumping station with machine-gun fire fearful that it stored bridge demolition equipment. A 20-mm antiaircraft gun on a wooden flak tower build upon the roof of Casemate Zuid near the southern approach road fired but because of shoulder-high, sandbagged walls, the gun could not depress sufficiently to hit Thompson's position. While two squads maintained fire on the gun emplacements and foxholes, platoon bazookaman Private Robert McGraw fired three rockets; two hit the roof and the antiaircraft-gun fire ceased. Thompson's men rushed the casemate and captured the lone survivor. They then turned the gun upon the German flak tower at the opposite end of the bridge, cut all visible wires to the bridge, mined the roadway, and awaited the arrival of reinforcements. Sergeant Roy Tidd led seven men against the second flak tower of Casemate Nord protecting the bridge, which mounted twin 20-mm antiaircraft guns. Tidd rushed the tower and single-handedly captured it killing one and wounding three enemy.[1]

While the attack upon the casemate continued, two German trucks led by a command car appeared racing along the highway from Grave. A bazooka team fired and the doors of the command car flew open and two men fell out. A second bazooka team fired at the leading truck, blowing off the left front wheel causing the truck to

---

1   Sergeant Roy E Tidd received a Silver Star for actions on 27 September near Nijmegen where he directed fire from a British tank against an attacking force of 100 infantry and four tanks supported by artillery and mortars while exposing himself to enemy fire.

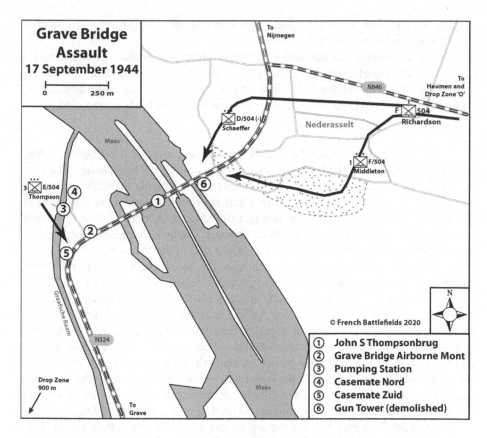

Grave Bridge
Assault
17 September 1944

0   250 m

To
Nijmegen

To
Heumen and
Drop Zone 'O'

N846

D/504 (-)
Schaeffer

Nederasselt

F   504
Richardson

Maas

1   F/504
Middleton

3   E/504
Thompson

4
3
1
6
2
5

Graafsche Raam

N324

Drop Zone
900 m

Maas

To
Grave

© French Battlefields 2020

N

① John S Thompsonbrug
② Grave Bridge Airborne Mont
③ Pumping Station
④ Casemate Nord
⑤ Casemate Zuid
⑥ Gun Tower (demolished)

crash over the high road bank. The second truck halted and struggled to reverse back down the road. German soldiers poured from both vehicles but immediately withdrew when faced with heavy fire from the American platoon. Thompson formed a roadblock to the south joined by men from Company F arriving over the bridge.

The bulk of Company E fell on the drop zone west of the city of Grave; however, small-arms fire from the town prevented them from reaching the bridge that afternoon. Sensitive to the 19-kilometer gap between his southern-most 82nd Airborne unit and the closest 101st Airborne unit at Veghel, van Poyck installed a roadblock facing south. A night patrol into Grave found that enemy troops had abandoned the town, much to the joy of local inhabitants.

Thirty-five men of 1st Platoon (Lieutenant Martin Middleton) followed closely by the remainder of Company F (Captain Beverly Richardson) moved from DZ 'O' at Overasselt against the northern end of the Maas bridge and used a .30-caliber machine gun to engage German troops manning 20-mm guns on a flak tower and on troops on the flat land between the dike road and the river. A flanking action led by Lieutenant John Schaeffer brought ten men from Company D (Captain Victor Campana) west of the northern bridge approach. Lieutenant Schaeffer charged across open ground into the fire of a machine-gun nest and captured the four-man crew. Schaeffer then assaulted the northern flak tower capturing two more German soldiers. He turned the captured 20-mm gun upon a German mortar team setting up in the flat lands and eliminated it.[2]

After clearing the flak tower and although under fire from German snipers who had tied themselves to the upper girders, two troopers used their entrenching tools to hack the demolition wires from the superstructure. The first major objective of MARKET-GARDEN had been taken at the cost of one killed and fifteen wounded.

Company B (Captain Thomas Helgeson)[3] approached the Heumen bridge in column along the roadside ditches that passed through apple orchards. The road sloped up near the canal crossing which was seven meters higher than the surrounding countryside. A fifty-man German guard detail opened fire with rifles and machine pistols on the leading platoon. Machine-gun fire also came from a house on a small island formed by the lock and the sluice channel. Captain Helgeson's paratroopers sought shelter in the roadside ditches on the right side of the roadway.

The bazooka team fired four rockets at the house, but all failed to detonate. Finally, two high explosive (HE) rifle-grenades temporarily silenced the enemy position. Two paratroop machine-gun teams attached from HQ Company established strong defensive fire on the dike road while Lieutenant Maurice Marcus with eight men infiltrated to near the bridge and sprayed the island with machine-gun fire keeping enemy troops from moving toward possible bridge detonators. First Platoon established a base of fire on the top of the dike by occupying foxholes previous dug by the German defenders. Its three BARs fired at the crossroads on the opposite side of the canal and along the road. Company Executive Officer Lieutenant Henry Dunavant established his mortar teams behind the powerhouse and fired upon the island building.

Corporal Charles Nau led three paratroopers up the stairs from the roadside ditch and into enemy automatic weapons fire from bridge defenders. Nau quickly killed or wounded six guards forcing the remaining Germans on the bridge to take shelter in the control house.[4]

The regimental demolition platoon used a half-sunken rowboat to cross the canal. Two of its members climbed the girders cutting all the wires that they could find. An additional seven men crossed the canal but were pinned down at the crossroads on the opposite side. At 17:00 an attempt to assault the enemy strongpoint from the powerhouse was beaten back by heavy fire. One hour later, a patrol established a fire

---

2   Lieutenants John S Thompson and John E Schaeffer were awarded Silver Stars for their initiative in capturing the bridge. Thompson from Beverly, Massachusetts became a major league baseball pitcher playing four years with the Philadelphia Phillies. He died in 1988, aged 71.

3   Thomas Helgeson, from Ripon, Wisconsin, survived the war despite fighting in North Africa, Sicily, France, the Netherlands, and Belgium. He received the Silver Star for his leadership during an engagement against a German Panzer Division during the Battle of the Bulge. Other awards included two Bronze Stars and three Purple Hearts. He remained in the Army until the 1960s, then became a corporate executive and raised three children. Helgeson died in 2004 at age 85.

4   Corporal Charles Elmer Nau from Osceola, Pennsylvania was awarded a Distinguished Service Cross for disregarding his own safety by exposing himself to withering small arms fire and for his leadership in assuming command of the assault force. Corporal Nau died in 2003, aged 79, and is buried in Tyrone, Pennsylvania.

base in farm buildings opposite the north side of the island. At dusk around 19:30, 3rd Platoon Leader Sergeant Shelton Dustin with nine men moved around the right side of the powerhouse to form a skirmish line unnoticed by the island defenders in the approaching darkness. Sergeant Dustin threw Gammon grenades[5] into the house and an air raid dugout capturing an officer who then ordered his thirty-nine troops to surrender.[6] Company B had six killed and one wounded.

Aftermath

      Within three hours the bridge over the Maas River was captured and after six hours the Heumen bridge over the Maas–Waal Canal was taken in some of the most successful episodes of MARKET-GARDEN. The importance of the Heumen bridge was magnified when the Malden (#8) and the Hatert (#9) canal bridges were both blown almost in the faces of approaching paratroopers. The next day, while engaged in a fire fight with two platoons from 508th PIR, the Germans blew the De Kamp rail bridge (#10). The explosion weakened the nearby road bridge rendering it unusable and forcing a rerouting of all Corridor traffic over the Heumen bridge.

      At 08:20 on 19 September, the armored cars of B Squadron, 2nd Household Cavalry Regiment crossed the Maas–Waal Canal at Heumen followed two hours later by tanks of the 2nd (Armoured) Battalion, Grenadier Guards which had replaced the Irish Guards as XXX Corps' leading armored unit.

Battlefield Tour

      The tour route starts at the southern end of the Maas bridge and continues along DZ 'O' on the north bank of the Maas River to the Heumen lock bridge.

> Follow highway N324 through Grave crossing the Graafsche Raam, which once formed a medieval defensive moat around the town. On the approach to the Maas Bridge, enter the side road to the left stopping at the Airborne Monument. Technically the bridge traverses the river in a southwest to northeast direction, but most accounts identify it as going south to north in keeping with the predominant direction of the main highway. (51.767964, 5.731774)

      Three flagpoles stand around a polished stainless-steel parachute that forms the **Grave Bridge Airborne Monument** commemorating the capture of the bridge and all troops who fought for liberation. A plaque states in part:

This liberation sign has been placed in honor of those who fought for our freedom and gave their lives for our sake and will live in our memories forever.

      The second plaque on the memorial recalls the events of the bridge's capture.

---

5   Gammon grenade: a hand-thrown bomb used particularly by the Special Air Service, parachutists, and the Resistance composed of plastic explosives of variable size wrapped in fabric and sewn to a fuse that detonated upon impact.

6   Sergeant Shelton Dustin from Farmington, Maine, who led his eight-man squad in the attack upon the strongly fortified island, was awarded a Distinguished Service Cross for leadership in attacking the German defenses at the canal bridge. Sergeant Dustin died in 1982, aged 64, and is buried in Fort Rosecrans National Cemetery, San Diego, California.

Unfortunately, some minor details do not mesh with other histories of the events. The bridge is now known as the **John S Thompsonbrug** after its capturer.

Liberation Route Marker #123 stands in the copse across from the Airborne Monument and commemorates the capture of the Grave bridge. 'The John S Thompson Bridge' audio recording retells Thompson's actions at the bridge that was to be named after him and a Dutch farmer who had been conscripted into the German Army.

A bicycle path from the airborne monument south along highway N324 leads to stairs that go down to **Casemate Zuid**. The two gun embrasures point in the direction of the bridge and held either a 50-mm antitank gun or a water-cooled Dutch-made 7.9 mm machine gun in addition to the rooftop antiaircraft gun. This two-story casemate is designed to shoot over the embankment with the gun ports level with the bridge's roadway. The bottom floor served as a warehouse for ammunition and explosives. A few shell-scars mar its sides, undoubtably from attacking Germans in 1940 or Americans in 1944. Four phony embrasures are painted on its front. There are two doors at the rear that may have been an escape hatch from the upper level. (51.767350, 5.730920)

Continue west toward the building beside the creek but turn into the gravel parking area before crossing the creek. (51.769280, 5.731007)

The powerhouse described by Thompson's men is actually the Gemaal van Sasse pumping station which was used as headquarters for the flak batteries defending the bridge.

Graafs Kazematten Museum
Mars en Wythdijk, Grave
Tel: +31 (0)48 647 6351
Web: http://www.graafskazemattenmuseum.nl/
Open April to October on Saturday and Sunday from 13:00 to 17:00. Small admission fee; unaccompanied children under 12 years not permitted. The museum incorporates the two bunkers that guarded the southern approach to the Maas Bridge.

The reinforced concrete bunkers, constructed in 1936, formed part of the Dutch bridge defensive system and were permanently manned by approximately seventy men of the Dutch Korps Politietroepen.[7] **Casemate Nord**, the museum office near the parking area, holds displays of photos, uniforms, weapons, and other artifacts describing local events of May 1940.

Casemate Zuid focuses upon 17 September 1944 and the capture of the Maas bridge.

Cross the Maas bridge on highway N324. The white brick building on the north-eastern approach marks the site of the long-gone flak tower captured by Lieutenant Schaeffer. The planned Corridor route was to continue straight on highway N324

---

7   The Dutch Korps Politietroepen (Police Troops) was created in 1919 within the Dutch armed forces. The new corps was tasked with policing the Dutch Army and Navy and to assist the regular police when necessary. The Politietroepen were absorbed into the *Koninklijke Marechaussee* (National Police or Gendarmerie) in 1940 when the German occupation authority disbanded the Dutch Army.

into Nijmegen, but reconnaissance indicated that bridge #10 ahead had been blown, thus making the Heumen bridge the critical passage into Nijmegen.
Turn right towards Overasselt (N846) at the next traffic light and proceed 2.0 km to the memorial on the left. (51.768526, 5.770227)

Colonel Tucker's 2nd and 3rd Battalions dropped on the flat ground of DZ 'O' at 12:47 delivered by 135 C-47s of the 315th and 316th Troop Carrier Groups. On 23 September, after days of delays caused by poor flying conditions, 3,500 men of the 325th GIR, artillery, and antitank guns arrived on the same drop zone by glider. Because the Arnhem area landing zones near Wolfheze were no longer under British Airborne control and the drop zone near Driel was threatened by German troops, elements of the 1st Polish Independent Airborne Brigade dropped at Overasselt that same day.

The **82nd Airborne Division Memorial** in Overasselt or the **Parachutists Monument** identifies drop and landing zones 'O'. Three symbolic metal parachutes in the field among the peacefully grazing cows bear witness to the drop zone. A brick entrance frames a concrete plinth in front of shrubs with flagpoles to the rear. A bronze model of parachute and glider craft are sealed under glass. The regiment established its aid post in a farmhouse 290 meters to the east and its regimental headquarters in the town hall of the Schoonenburg district of Overasselt, which is no longer standing. Gaasseltsedam, the nearest rural road to the west, led to the farm of the same name which stands on the center of DZ 'O'.

Liberation Route Marker #2 audio describes the landings and objectives of the 82nd Airborne Division and relates the excitement of a local family witnessing 'Freedom Fall from the Skies.'

Continue east toward Heumen but, where highway N846 turns to the left, continue straight on Dorpstraat, under the Autoroute, and into the village. The road becomes De Boomgaard, then Kapitein Postmalaan before ending at the canal. Stop at the statue on the left. (51.76775, 5.8504722)

A statue in the traditional *Pieta* form, a mourning mother holding her dead son in her arms, forms the backdrop for a memorial to twenty-four Dutch soldiers of the 26th Regiment of Infantry killed at this site on 10 May 1940 while defending the canal crossing from the invading German Army.

Liberation Route Marker #35 bears testimony to the bridge's capture four years later. The 'Bridge Number 7' audio describes the American paratroopers' assault upon German defenders at the Heumen lock bridge.

Continue on the roadway to view the lock and the island where the Germans attempted to resist the paratroopers. (51.768146, 5.851894)

The paratrooper assault ran from the intersection bordered by the 1940 memorial, past the red brick powerhouse to the now absent bridge. The tree-shaded artificial island created by the sluice by-pass still holds the two-story stone house used as quarters by the German defense detail. The **Heumen bridge** that once went over the canal lock was removed in 1992 and replaced by a modern highway bridge 300 meters to the north carrying highway N271. The locks remain in operation to accommodate barge traffic on the canal. The tall white structures hold the counterweights that open and close the lift span. The opposite side of the canal locks holds an information panel that describes the history of the locks — in Dutch only. (51.768627, 5.853519)

Return through Heumen to highway N846 and proceed north. Turn right onto highway N271 and cross the Maas–Waal Canal. From highway N271 (Rijksweg) turn right onto Molenstraat and follow to the monument on the right. (51.764548, 5.864021)

Starting on 20 September American and British soldiers were buried at this site behind what was the Van den Broek brewery. By the end of the fighting, the ground held 836 American soldiers killed around Groesbeek and Nijmegen, as well as 38 British and three Canadians. Four years later all the graves were removed with Americans reburied at Netherlands American Cemetery in Margraten and the British and Canadians at Mook War Cemetery.

Tall columnar yews and large boulders almost hide a plaque identifying the location of the **temporary American Cemetery.** The memorial states the number of burials incorrectly:

Here rested the remains of 637 gallant soldiers and airmen of the United States and British armed forces in the Fall and Winter of 1944. They gave their lives to free the Netherlands from Nazi tyranny.

Battle for the Nijmegen Bridges

Recognition of the importance of a city on the south bank of the Waal River extends back to Roman times when a fortification was constructed upon a hill overlooking river crossings. The Valkhof, as it became known, later held chapels and forts dating to Holy Roman Emperor and King of Germany Frederick I 'Barbarossa' (1122–1190). The great Waalbrug across the river was not built until 1937 and, at almost 600-meters-long, it was longer than the bridge at Grave. A single-track Spoorbrug or rail bridge also crossed the river one kilometer downstream. In 1944 Nijmegen was a city of slightly less than 100,000 people

Nijmegen was known as the 'City of the Towers' until 22 February 1944 when American bomber aircraft mistakenly dropped their loads upon Nijmegen thinking that they were over Germany and destroyed the city center. Almost 800 people died; their bodies were laid to rest in mass graves in the *Begraafplaats Graafseweg* (General Cemetery). (51.831491, 5.831920)

A short distance inside the cemetery an open field on the left holds a stunning memorial to those who died as a result of the bombing. A polished granite stone erected in 2005 bears an inscription by HH Ter Balkt, a Dutch poet. The stone is dramatically torn in two representing the families torn apart by the bombing and the physical damage to the city.

On the morning of the MARKET-GARDEN assault, only a few German soldiers guarded the Nijmegen bridges. By the afternoon of 17 September, local garrison troops had been augmented by II Bataillon, FJ-Panzer AuE 'Hermann Göring' Regiment, and companies of newly conscripted trainees.[8] The 1,000-troop force was under command of FJ Reserve Training Bataillon 'Henke' (Oberst Fritz Henke) which also held one company from the schwere Flak Bataillon 572 with four 88-mm flak guns and eight 20-mm antiaircraft guns. Oberst Henke's diverse forces established positions around the south ends of both bridges connected by strongpoints through Keizer Karelplein and Keizer Lodewijkplein later renamed Keizer Traianusplein. An additional strongpoint across the river at Lent guarded the northern approach to the highway bridge.

About 200 men from #1 Kompanie, SS Panzer Pionier Abteilung 10 under the command of SS-Lieutenant Werner Baumgärtel were the first reinforcements to reach Nijmegen on the morning of 18 September and they took up positions between the two bridges. In addition, II Bataillon SS Panzergrenadier Regiment 22,[9] led by 25-year-old SS-Captain Karl-Heinz Euling, arrived from Arnhem after crossing the Waal at Pannerden. Baumgärtel joined with Euling that afternoon forming KGr Euling and established positions in Hunnerpark. Later that day, Nijmegen defenses were reorganized with SS-Major Leo Reinhold in overall command of Henke around the rail bridge and Euling around the highway bridge. Reinhold, commander of II Bataillon, SS Panzer Regiment 10, established positions around the north end of the bridge. His unit was without its tanks but incorporated strong artillery support from Batterien 19 and 21, SS Artillerie Ausbildungs Regiment 5 (SS-Captain Oskar Schwappacher). In all, the mix of troops totaled almost 3,000 men. The rapid changes in the command structure may seem confusing but they typify the flexibility of the German Army command system.

Battle
17 September
At 18:30, Colonel Roy Lindquist of the 508th PIR sent his Company A (Captain Jonathan Adams) into Nijmegen in a *coup de main* attempt at the bridges after receiving reports that they were lightly defended. The planned approach avoided the city center by attacking the bridge from the southeast. However, Geert van Hees, a local Dutch underground member, suggested an alternative route along broad Groesbeekseweg (S106) that passed the resistance headquarters where valuable information could be obtained. The leading platoon encountered German machine-gun fire as it approached Keizer Karelplein, the main traffic circle surrounded by large apartment blocks and office buildings. Entrenched enemy troops denied the paratroopers' advance in a gun battle that continued well into the night.

---

8   The companies were from an NCO Training School, three companies of a replacement battalion from the 406th Infantry Division, and railway guards.

9   Some confusion remains over the name of Euling's unit. In months prior to the battle, he had commanded I Bataillon, SS Panzergrenadier Regiment 21 and II Bataillon SS Panzergrenadier Regiment 19. At the outbreak of Operation Market-Garden, he commanded the 9th SS Division's replacement battalion known simply as Bataillon 'Euling.' Shortly later the unit was referred to as II Bataillon, SS Panzergrenadier Regiment 22. All of these designations appear in various historical works and reflect the efforts of the German Army to rapidly rebuild divisions that had been shattered in France.

At 10:00 the next morning, Lieutenant Colonel Shields Warren received instructions to withdraw his battalion to clear LZ 'T' of enemy troops in preparation for the afternoon glider landings.

18 September

At dawn, Lieutenant Howard Greenwalt led a platoon of Company G (Captain Russel Wilde), 508th PIR from Berg en Dal to seize the highway bridge from the south along Berg en Dalseweg. Company G was two blocks from Mariaplein when hit by 20-mm and 88-mm antiaircraft guns situated in dug-in positions along the southern end of Hunnerpark. The Germans had converted the level, tree-shaded grounds into a major strongpoint with deep trenches, well-positioned guns, four Jagdpanzer IVs, and forward positions in the houses surrounding the traffic circle to control all the surrounding roadways approaching Keizer Lodewijkplein.

Captain Wilde deployed his men and by that morning held some buildings around the south side of the traffic circle. At 15:30, after the remainder of the company arrived, it attempted an advance toward the bridge, but well-placed salvos from SS-Captain Schwappacher's 88-mm battery on the north riverbank directed by observers in the city's historic Belvedere observation tower stopped the assault. Just as battalion commander, Lieutenant Colonel Warren prepared to renew the assault, he received instructions to return to the Groesbeek area to defend LZ 'T'. At 15:30, Wilde received orders to withdraw to Berg en Dal. The second attempt to capture the Waal Bridge had failed.

Although General Gavin outlined a plan to send two battalions against the Nijmegen bridge on 18 September, the assault was cancelled by General Browning who ordered the battalions to the high ground south of Groesbeek and the flatland east of the Maas–Waal Canal. Browning felt no urgency since XXX Corps was far from Nijmegen, but the delay allowed further strengthening of the German bridge defenses.

19 September

The renewed effort on 19 September was spearheaded by the 505th PIR's 2nd Battalion, (Lieutenant Colonel Benjamin Vandervoort)[10] under overall command of Lieutenant-Colonel Edward Goulburn of the Grenadier Guards Group. The combined American paratrooper and British armor attack against the highway bridge left Sionshof Hotel headquarters at 15:45 and quickly achieved the city's southern districts where Goulburn's forty tanks split into three columns.

In western Nijmegen, Grenadier Guards Captain John Neville led an assault upon the rail bridge with a troop (Lieutenant GR Merton) of five Sherman tanks, a platoon of infantry (Lieutenant John C Moller) from the No 2 Company, 1st Grenadier Guards mounted in Bren carriers, and Company D (Captain Taylor Smith), 505th PIR. Guided by Dutchman Herman van der Poll, Captain Neville's combined force

---

10   Lieutenant Colonel Benjamin Vandervoort received his second Distinguished Service Cross for his leadership during the Nijmegen fighting. He later suffered mortar fire injuries that resulted in the loss of his left eye and ended his combat career. After the war, Vandervoort joined the Foreign Service and held numerous military advisory positions. Colonel Vandervoort, from Gasport, New York, died in 1990, aged 73 and is buried in Beaufort National Cemetery, Beaufort, South Carolina.

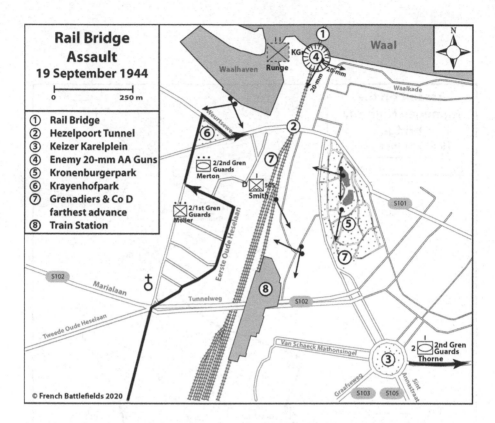

Rail Bridge Assault
19 September 1944
0   250 m

① Rail Bridge
② Hezelpoort Tunnel
③ Keizer Karelplein
④ Enemy 20-mm AA Guns
⑤ Kronenburgerpark
⑥ Krayenhofpark
⑦ Grenadiers & Co D
   farthest advance
⑧ Train Station

© French Battlefields 2020

swung far to the west to approach the rail bridge from the west side of the rail yards. Neville's force was only 200 meters from the rail bridge when it first encountered an impenetrable defensive screen of machine guns, panzerfausts, two 20-mm flak guns, and a 45-mm antitank gun all manned by 750-man kampfgruppe commanded by Hauptmann Runge.

The steep embankment limited the Shermans' movement toward the bridge, so the tanks drove toward the Hezelpoort tunnel under the bridge approach. The first two tanks nearing the tunnel were disabled by German artillery firing across the river. Infantry attempts to cross the rail yards were met with intense machine-gun fire from German troops dug in on the embankment and in nearby houses. With the light fading, Neville withdrew his troops to a church on Krayenhofflaan.

A second column of Grenadier Guards commanded by Major George Thorne separated from the highway bridge attack force and proceeded north to check the situation at the post office. His tanks blasted any suspicious building along the way before crossing Oranjesingel. They seized the undefended post office building and an inspection found no demolition equipment. Later that evening Major Thorne led a strong patrol along Oranjesingel attempting to gain Keizer Lodewijkplein, but

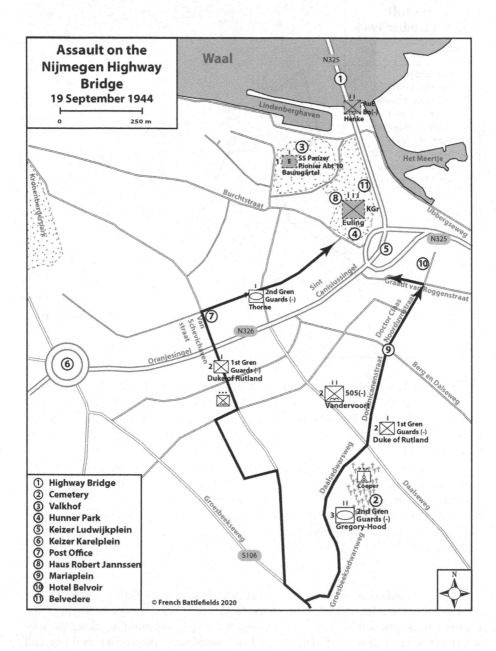

Assault on the Nijmegen Highway Bridge
19 September 1944

0   250 m

① Highway Bridge
② Cemetery
③ Valkhof
④ Hunner Park
⑤ Keizer Ludwijkplein
⑥ Keizer Karelplein
⑦ Post Office
⑧ Haus Robert Jannssen
⑨ Mariaplein
⑩ Hotel Belvoir
⑪ Belvedere

© French Battlefields 2020

concealed SP guns in Hunnerpark fired and Thorne withdrew back to the post office.[11]

The main effort third column, guided by Dutch volunteer Geert van Hees, moved toward Hunnerpark from the southwest. Six hundred men from 2nd Battalion, 505th PIR stalked the sides of the streets or rode upon the tanks from No 3 Squadron (Major Alec Gregory-Hood), 2nd Battalion, Grenadier Guards. Three platoons of motorized infantry from No 2 Company (Captain the Duke of Rutland),[12] of the Guards' 1st Battalion rode in Bren carriers. While the tanks provided suppressive fire with shell and machine gun, the paratroopers of Companies E and F cleared a two-block-wide corridor fighting through the gardens and alleyways and over the roof tops of the two-story brick and stone houses lining the tree shrouded streets. In labyrinthine Nijmegen, the fighting frequently reduced to close-quarters showdowns between small, momentarily isolated groups. Cooperation between the seasoned veterans assured relentless pursuit, block after block, against a resourceful and courageous enemy who scrambled to alternative positions frequently forced to abandon heavy weapons and ammunition.

First Platoon (1st Lieutenant James E Smith), Company E worked through heavy fire to reach Keizer Lodewijkplein. The well-placed enemy immediately hit Lieutenant Smith's platoon with small-arms and mortar fire while artillery shells came from across the river directed by radio-equipped observers. Camouflaged antitank guns covered the intersections protected by interlocking fire from MG-42s.

To his left, Company F (Captain Robert Rosen) slowly approached the park until stopped by a log barricade that barred the British tanks. The Germans had placed an 88-mm gun on the western edge of the roundabout protected by SP guns concealed in Hunnerpark. At Graadt van Roggenstraat, an 88-mm shell hit the first Sherman to move into the intersection engulfing it in flames and exploding ammunition while killing the troop leader, Lieutenant John A Moller.[13] Seconds later, a second tank, attempting to locate the hidden gun, was disabled, but the crew managed to escape. The third tank was damaged, leaving the troop with only one operational Sherman. The paratroopers quickly dispersed into the surrounding buildings – the open streets had become killing fields.

Despite the intense fighting, paratrooper casualties had been minimal. A dozen Shermans and troopers manned a Line of Departure in houses along the southern edge of Hunnerpark for the final assault. Colonel Vandervoort reported his men ready

---

11   Major Thorne's mixed unit held a troop of tanks from No 1 Squadron, 2nd Battalion, Grenadier Guards, two infantry platoons of No 3 Company, 1st Battalion, Grenadier Guards, and a platoon of 505th paratroopers.
Major George Thorne came from a sterling military family. His father General Sir Andrew Thorne was awarded two Distinguished Service Orders during the First World War. His brother Peter and brother-in-law Lord Wigram were also Grenadiers. Major Throne was wounded at Nijmegen and received the Military Medal for actions in Lower Saxony, Germany just before the end of the war. Major George Thorne died in 2008, aged 95.

12   Charles John Robert Manners, 10th Duke of Rutland, inherited the title in 1940. The Rutland title originated in 1373 awarded to the grandson of King Edward III. Charles Manners remained in the position until his death in 1999, aged 79.

13   Lieutenant John Alan Moller, aged 21 from Knightsbridge, London, is buried in Jonkerbos War Cemetery, Plot XXII, Row F, Grave 1.

to go for the park and highway bridge. They had momentum, the enemy on the run, and they wanted to finish the job while still retaining the upper hand. To Vandervoort's disappointment, instructions came back to consolidate for the night. The Grenadier Guards infantry would mop up in the morning. Another opportunity lost.

SS Panzergrenadiers set fire to houses around their perimeter to illuminate possible avenues of Allied advance. They also sent out night patrols to infiltrate the American positions. For their part, the paratroopers carefully improved their positions to assault German strongpoints the next day. Despite the arrival of tanks onto the battlefield, the third effort to seize a bridge across the Waal had failed.

20 September

After the failed attempts at capturing the two bridges on 19 September, General Gavin argued that the only way to capture any bridge intact was to take both approaches simultaneously. That night Gavin proposed a daytime river assault to take the north bridge approaches. Stiff with their walking sticks and old school scarves, British officers incredulously gaped at Gavin and Colonel Tucker, the cigar-chomping commander of the 504th PIR, whose unit was selected for the attack. Gavin would have preferred to wait until darkness on that Wednesday, but thoughts that the British 1st Airborne Division at Arnhem might not survive an additional day's delay convinced him that action must be taken as soon as possible. During the night, British engineers rushed to bring forward twenty-eight small, canvas and plywood boats to be used in the river crossing attempt.

The German defenses were formidable. Defending the north bank of the river was Henke's fallschirmjäger headquarters staff, Reich laborers, and a flak battery. Captain Schwappacher held his training regiment behind the dike road south of Oosterhout. The German side of the 310-meter-wide river offered no protection. Flat ground ran inland from the river's edge for 200 to 800 meters, the sloping embankment was 5 to 7 meters high, and the dike road was 7 meters wide. Enemy machine-gun positions lined the dike and covered the flat ground. Mortars and artillery were positioned behind the dike and 20-mm guns were stationed on the rail bridge and in Fort Hof van Holland. Twenty-seven-year-old Major Julian Cook, 3rd Battalion commander, viewed the enemy positions from the ninth floor of the PGEM regional electrical power plant, which had been liberated by a Dutch Resistance group two days earlier. He determined that the river assault was a true suicide mission.

Colonel Tucker, also observing the crossing area from the power station, turned to General Horrocks and asked, 'If we take the bridge, what assurance do we have that your troops will get to Arnhem immediately?' Horrocks indicated that the tanks of the 2nd Grenadier Guards were posed to cross the bridge. 'Nothing will stop them', he added. It was, as we shall see, a lie.[14]

All morning on 20 September, British and American forces prepared for the dangerous crossing attempt. Tucker's Company D took up positions in German trenches along the riverbank to provide suppressive fire. Approaches to the riverbank

---

14   In fact, after the war General Horrocks claimed in his memoirs that the idea of a river assault was first suggested by himself and General Browning. Records clearly indicate that Gavin initiated preparations for the crossing before Horrocks even arrived at Nijmegen.

were strengthened to allow British tanks to line the waterfront and supply suppressive cannon fire. Typhoons were alerted to strafe and rocket the north bank thirty minutes before launch. At H-hour the tanks would switch to smoke shells to hide the crossing boats.

Companies I (Captain T Moffatt Burriss) and H (Captain Carl Kappel) were to lead the river assault. Captain Burriss was to clear out the dike and area immediately west of the landing zone establishing a basic defensive perimeter against a flank attack from the west. Captain Kappel's Company H was assigned to clear the trenches from the river to the dike road, reorganize, then attack northeast to the Arnhem highway.

However, the boats did not arrive. The river assault experienced delays while trucks carrying the boats inched their way through the snarl of Corridor traffic. Originally scheduled for 08:00 the assault was repeatedly postponed eventually to 15:00. Major Cook nervously paced the riverbank. Thirty Shermans of Lieutenant-Colonel Giles Vandeleur's Irish Guards mounted the river embankment at H-30 minutes and lined up track to track. Twenty-four 25-pounder guns of the 153rd Field Regiment added their firepower from positions in De Goffert Park, 4 kilometers to the southwest, and eleven pack howitzers of the 376th Parachute Field Artillery Battalion were sited closer to the river because of their shorter range.

British Typhoons strafed the entire north bank with rockets and machine-gun fire as planned. The Germans answered with a barrage of antiaircraft fire. Paratroopers witnessing the density of German flak knew what they could expect during the river crossing. On the ninth floor of the power plant General Horrocks, General Browning, Colonel Tucker, and Lieutenant-Colonel Giles Vandeleur gathered to witness the attempted crossing. General Gavin had left to tend to another hot spot near Groesbeek.

Only twenty minutes before launch, with the Typhoons already overhead and the tanks on the embankment, twenty-six boats arrived. The paratroopers were shocked when they first viewed the flimsy, canvas-sided craft. The 19-foot-long boats had a flat reinforced plywood bottom and canvas sides supported by 30-inch, folding, wooden slats.

At 14:57, 260 men including Cook's two companies, engineers, and members of the battalion staff began to cross the river fanatically paddling the twenty-six assault boats with Company I on the left and Company H on the right. Each boat carried thirteen paratroopers and two engineers to man the boats and return them to the south bank for the second wave. Everything went wrong for the men, most of whom had never before rowed a boat. Some boats bogged in the mud when loaded in water that was too shallow, others overturned when men climbed aboard, and some, overloaded, just sank.

The river water ran at 12-to-16 kilometers per hour swiftly pushing the boats downstream and forcing wide changes in their direction. A few got caught in the eddy near they shore and spun crazily as they drifted downstream. Rifle butts replaced lost paddles. Cook, a Catholic, kept time rowing by praying 'Hail Mary' on one stroke, 'full of grace' on the second stroke repeatedly interspersed with 'Keep going! Keep going!' Someone made a crack about being in the airborne navy.

When a stiff wind dissipated the smoke screen to reveal the boats on the river, enemy light machine guns, mortars, artillery, rifles, and 20-mm antiaircraft guns

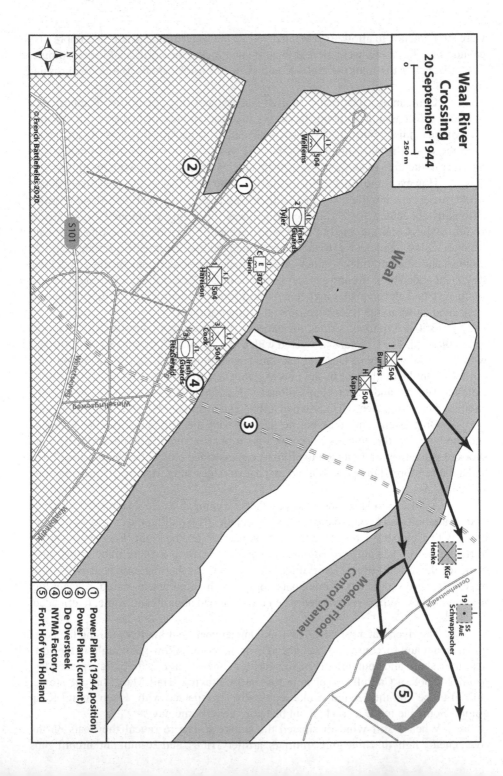

Waal River
Crossing
20 September 1944

0 ___ 250 m

© French Battlefields 2020

① Power Plant (1944 position)
② Power Plant (current)
③ De Oversteek
④ NYMA Factory
⑤ Fort Hof van Holland

opened fire from across the river, from Fort Hof van Holland, from the right on the south side of the river, and from guns along the rail bridge. Mortar and heavy machine-gun fire potted the water's surface like a summer hailstorm while multiple shell explosions churned the water. The volume of enemy fire made a successful crossing seem impossible. Complete boats disappeared in a shower of water with direct hits. Heavy equipment dragged men to the bottom. Dead paratroopers were simply heaved overboard.

The engineer steering Captain Burriss's boat said, 'Take the rudder. I'm hit!' Burriss leaned backward to take the rudder and the engineer was hit again in the head; Burriss caught shell fragments in his side. The engineer's body fell overboard but his foot caught the gunwale causing his body to act as a rudder and sending the boat into a spin. Burriss heaved the dead man overboard.

Schwappacher's Batterie 19 put direct fire on the crossing boats – shells ripping through the canvas-sided craft and their occupants. The only answer was to paddle — and keep paddling.

At 15:20 when the boats approached the enemy-held shore, the men were gasping for breath with the exertion of pushing the unseaworthy craft with rifle butts and a few paddles. Captain Kappel dropped off the back of his boat and gave it a final shove towards the shoreline. Of the thirteen men in the boat, only three were unwounded, six were dead. He noted that the bottom of the boat sloshed with bloody water. Burriss was so happy to have survived the crossing that he vomited.

Dazed paratroopers slumped on the beach to regain their breath then struggled for a moment before engaging the enemy. They moved up the riverbank bayoneting the few enemy troops in their foxholes or eliminating machine gunners with hand grenades.

Individual determination, bravery, and tragedy ran in bewildering sequence while the paratroopers fought across the exposed flood plain. Only a line of outposts held the Oosterhoutsedijk or dike road, but five trench lines along the dike embankment dominated the 600 meters between the water's edge and the roadway. Germans on the railway bridge raked the paratroopers with enfilade fire from the right flank and rear. Irish Guards tanks concentrated their fire upon the opposite shore's dike where enemy guns dominated the flat flood plain.

The one hundred or so survivors of the first wave scrambled for the Oosterhoutsedijk shooting and throwing grenades into German foxholes as they advanced. There was no unit cohesion, no squads or platoons – only a line of skirmishers firing their weapons from the hip. At the dike, they briefly sheltered from German fire behind the slight elevation. From there, they exchanged hand grenades with German troops on the opposite side. A few troopers had prepared Gammon grenades, which effectively cleared stretches of dike road with their powerful explosions, after which came a moment of silence before the moaning sounds of wounded German soldiers. The survivors started to stand arms raised in surrender, but the frenzied paratroopers with a lust for blood borne by the savage deaths of their comrades were not accepting their surrender and continued firing until all were dead.

In less than 30 minutes the paratroopers overcame resistance along the dike. They then divided to assault their next objectives. Some continued inland, pursuing withdrawing enemy troops; others headed for Fort Hof van Holland or the rail and highway bridges. There was no unit cohesion, just individuals from different squads, platoons, even different companies. Confused and chaotic pursuit of the enemy denied them an opportunity to regroup. The several hundred-meters-wide bridgehead was littered with 168 German bodies.

Only eleven boats returned for a second wave. An additional five waves ferried across Companies G, C, A, 1st Battalion HQ, and B in that order. The antitank guns of the 80th AA/AT Battalion were ferried across on two rafts built by Royal Engineers.

The American force divided to charge continued against support positions. Captain Burriss led a group to expand the perimeter to the northwest using rifle grenades to eliminate a 20-mm flak tower northeast of a holding pond. Burriss left twelve men to hold the position and led the remaining ten men along the dike road.

Captain Kappel moved with two partial platoons against the railroad embankment where he encountered heavy enemy fire. Machine guns applied grazing fire along the embankment while heavy fire from one 88-mm and two 20-mm guns repulsed all efforts to cross the embankment. Kappel directed the attack south along the embankment toward the northern end of the rail bridge searching for a passage. As they passed a concrete shelter dug into the side of the embankment, they heard voices inside. Not waiting to find out who, they threw in Gammon grenades killing an unknown number of Dutch civilians who were sheltering from the gun fire.

Lieutenant Edward Sims, Company H Executive Officer, with eighteen men overcame a small group at the northern end of the rail bridge. Sims ordered his men to sever any wires leading to the bridge that might control explosives and established a defense around that end of the bridge.

Lieutenant Richard LaRiviere, 2nd Platoon Leader who was known to his men as 'Lieutenant Rivers' led fifteen to twenty men south eliminating groups of enemies as large as thirty men along the way. Grenades were exchanged over the embankment; then Lieutenant LaRiviere threw over a Gammon grenade. A German reached out to grab it and throw it back. The detonation killed all the enemy in the vicinity. LaRiviere left five men to guard the west side of the culvert while he continued with the others toward the north end of the rail bridge to join Sims.

Three to five hundred German troops under pressure from Neville's assault on the southern end of the rail bridge approached the northern end. Fearful that all thoughts of surrender would disappear if the Germans determined how few Americans held the bridge, Sims' and LaRiviere's detachments opened up with their BAR and several machine guns. Some enemy climbed the bridge girders to escape the fusillade; others jumped into the swift waters of the Waal to escape; some wounded fell between the ties into the swirling waters. Some Germans reversed and tried to go back south where the now trapped men met the same fate. Those sheltering among the bridge girders were slowly eliminated. Afterwards, 267 bodies were found on the bridge.[15]

---

15   Lieutenant Edward J Sims was awarded a Silver Star for his leadership and aggressiveness in the fight for the rail bridge. He fought in the Battle of the Bulge and received a second Silver Star in Korea. Lieutenant Sims also received two Bronze Stars, two Purple Hearts, and six Commendation Medals. After the war Sims wrote that he regretted the slaughter at the Nijmegen rail bridge as a terrible waste

At 16:00 Kappel radioed Colonel Tucker that the rail bridge was secure. Moments later Tucker ordered a halt to the Allied artillery fire. Kappel hoped that British tanks would join him by crossing the bridge, but attention had shifted to the more desirable highway bridge. Sims remained at the rail bridge while the remainder of Company H moved to assist Company I seize the highway bridge.

Captain Burriss continued with a group of four to five men along the hedgerow north of the dike eliminating small pockets of resistance while Pfc Leo Muri followed the dike road. They joined again at the rail embankment 450 meters north of the rail bridge, before edging south along the embankment. LaRiviere joined Burriss and continued east toward the highway bridge along Oosterhoutsedijk into Veur-Lent. At the first building, Oosterhoutsedijk 51, Burriss kicked open the door to find a dozen German soldiers resting inside. He threw in a Gammon grenade and dove away from the door. The force of the explosion blew out all the windows and the door and killed everyone inside.

At 19:38, the small force reached the tunnel that passed underneath the Waalbrug. An eerie silence was broken only by the gunfire in Hunnerpark across the river. Burriss, LaRiviere, and Private John Hall Jr ran up the stairs that led to the bridge ramp. On the bridge above, a lone German soldier dropped his rifle and immediately surrendered. The three Americans stood for a moment before a shot from the direction of the bridge girders killed Private Hall as he stood between the two officers.[16] LaRiviere quickly whirled, fired, and killed the sniper. Burriss sent Pfc Muri and a second man south to cut demolition wires.

Burriss saw tanks charging toward him in the dimming light. Unsure as to whose tanks, he ordered his small group onto the embankment and to prepare Gammon grenades. When the tanks got closer, he could tell that they were Grenadier Guards' Shermans.

General Browning, watching the effort from the roof of the power station along with the other senior British officers, exclaimed, 'I have never seen a more gallant action.' General Dempsey, commander of British Second Army, met with General Gavin days later, shook his hand, and said 'I am proud to meet the commander of the greatest division in the world today.'

The German response was equally incredulous. SS-Colonel Harmel later remarked, 'Crossing one of Europe's widest and fast flowing rivers in daylight was inconceivable and dismissed as suicidal.'

The crossing of the Waal River was a feat unequaled by any force in the entire European Theater of Operations. American casualties amounted to 48 dead and 140 wounded — a seventy-two percent casualty rate.

KGr Runge guarded the southern approaches to the rail bridge, the rail

---

of young men. He attributed the hasty decision to the emotions raised by the loss of comrades during the Waal River crossing. Sims died in Tinton Falls, New Jersey in 2013, aged 93, and is buried in Arlington National Cemetery, Arlington, Virginia.

16   Private John W Hall Jr, aged 20 from Arizona, died of his wounds. Hall is buried in Liberty Veterans Cemetery, Fresno, California.

yards, and Kronenburgerpark against Company D and Neville's Grenadiers. Runge's troops were an odd mix of SS and young soldiers who fought savagely and old men, mainly Polish and Russian foreign conscripts, who surrendered at the first opportunity. Company D Platoon Leader Lieutenant James Meyers renewed the attack on the southern end of the rail bridge from the rail yard that had been such a problem the previous day. A paratrooper charge silenced the heavy automatic weapons fire and the two 20-mm guns. To the east on the opposite side of the rail yard along the edges of Kronenburgerpark progress was rapid until the paratroopers came under fire in the open areas of the park. Buildings around the park had to be cleared room by room. Paratroopers and guardsmen tossed in grenades followed by a burst of automatic weapons fire. The combat was savage against the stubborn SS troops. The paratroopers took to the rooftops of the multistory buildings to fire down upon enemy foxholes and gun positions.

The pressure increased on the Germans as the Americans and British steadily gained ground. By mid-afternoon, the southern end of the rail bridge had been captured, but SS troops held sectors of Kronenburgerpark trapped between Allied troops holding both ends of the bridge. At dusk, two to three hundred German soldiers walked south from the middle of the bridge to surrender.

Meanwhile in Nijmegen, after four unsuccessful attempts to reach the highway bridge through Keizer Lodewijkplein, a new plan was formulated. Calculating that the German defenders in the Valkhof would not anticipate an attack from the city center, Grenadier Guards led the final coordinated assault upon the Valkhof and Hunnerpark from the west while 2nd Battalion, 505th PIR attacked positions across Keizer Lodewijkplein.

Starting at 08:30, No 2 Company, No 4 Company, and King's Company, of the 1st Grenadier Guards Battalion each supported by a troop of tanks advanced along parallel streets through central Nijmegen carefully jumping from one intersection to the next.

A troop of Sherman tanks under command of Lieutenant Peter Prescott from No 2 Squadron, 2nd Grenadier Guards, and No 2 Company, 1st Grenadier Guards, received orders to clear Oranjesingel from Keizer Karelplein to the bridge. The advance made good progress while the infantry methodically cleared the houses lining the broad boulevard. Nevertheless, it took five hours to reach Kelfkensbos where the Grenadiers forced Euling's SS troops to fall back into Hunnerpark.

King's Company similarly cleared areas southwest of Valkhof. From morning to early afternoon, 2nd Battalion, 505th PIR cleared buildings south and southwest of Keizer Lodewijkplein. The attacking units were poised for the final assault against the German stronghold.

By 13:30 while No 2 Company acted as reserve in central Nijmegen, No 4 Company (Major HF Stanley) Grenadier Guards assaulted Hunnerpark across Kelfkensbos on a two platoon front, but the attack did not start well despite each platoon being supported by a Sherman tank from Lieutenant Peter Prescott's troop. Upon entering the open area, the leading tank was hit by a panzerfaust and exploded.

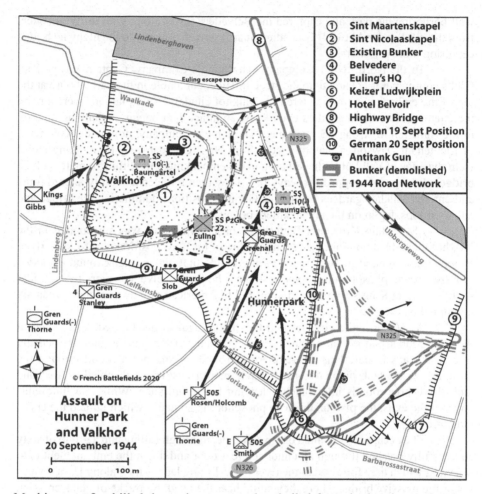

Assault on Hunner Park and Valkhof
20 September 1944

© French Battlefields 2020

Machine-gun fire killed the entire crew as they bailed from the burning tank. Then Lieutenant Prescott's tank was also hit on his rear deck by a panzerfaust fired from an upper story window. Prescott tried to maneuver away but was discovered by an AT gun hidden among shrubbery. Both fired. Prescott's shot missed, but the German armor piercing shell did not and Prescott and his crew bailed out. Infantry suffered withering small-arms fire making crossing the street impossible.

Major Stanley shifted his assault to the right tying in with the paratroopers on Sint Jorisstraat, now under fire from the Belvedere to the front and buildings around Keizer Lodewijkplein to the rear. Under the cover of smoke grenades, the company dashed across Sint Jorisstraat and into Hunnerpark.

Two weak companies of SS Pioniere held strongpoints in the Valkhof and Belvedere connected by shallow trenches behind barbed wire entanglements. The site resembled the worst of a First World War battlefield. The Belvedere was the key position. From the heights of its tower, an observation post dominated the bridge's southern approaches. Lieutenant Peter Greenall led a 10-man platoon along the high wall bordering the park and captured the Belvedere tower along with thirty prisoners from the SS Pionier Abt 10.[17] Grenadier Guards moved down onto the highway bridge capturing more prisoners.

To the North, No 1 Company (The King's Company, Captain Vicary Paul Gibbs commanding) charged up the steep hillside, cut a hole in the barbed wire at the top of the embankment, and entered the Valkhof citadel.[18] Two platoons were among the enemy before the defenders even knew an attack had begun. A flanking attempt to the right fell to strong SS resistance. The King's Company, now under command of Lieutenant Dawson, a platoon leader from No 2 Company, sent a flanking patrol from the edge of Valkhof to the left around the embankment to within 50 meters of the bridge where it was stopped by heavy fire. They then retraced a slightly altered route and entered Valkhof gardens behind the German positions dominating the bridge and enemy troops dug in on the embankment below.

SS-Captain Krueger's Batterie 21 observation post was surrounded in the Valkhof citadel but continued directing the fire of his guns positioned across the river. Bloody hand-to-hand fighting raged until around 20:30 when a tank round exploded in a trench and phosphorous grenades forced the final twelve survivors to surrender to the charging King's Company, but all fell to American bullets that night when six attempted an escape.[19]

At 16:00, while Greenall led the charge against the Belvedere, Lieutenant Adriaan Slob's platoon surrounded Euling's headquarters and around 150 enemy troops in Haus Robert Janssen. A Sherman rolled up and put a round through the building. As the tank pivoted to fire again, a panzerfaust round disabled it. A second tank fired three rounds into trenches leading to the entrance. While machine guns covered the exits, the platoon threw in phosphorous grenades which ignited the entire structure.[20]

The occupants streamed out to surrender although Euling and a group of sixty successfully escaped through an unnoticed rear door and down the embankment onto Voerweg which they followed to the river bank. Euling led his men along Ubbergsweg under the massive bridge where they could hear the clanking tracks of tanks crossing the river into Lent. Suddenly Euling encountered thirty to forty British soldiers taking a rest break. Euling brazenly used American hand gestures and voice commands to

---

17   Lieutenant Peter Michael Benson Greenall was killed moments later by a German escaping across the bridge in a motorcycle sidecar. He is buried in Jonkerbos War Cemetery, Plot XXII, Row G, Grave 3.

18   The 23-year-old Captain The Honorable Vicary Paul Gibbs from Ware, Hertfordshire was killed during the assault. He is buried in Jonkerbos War Cemetery in Plot 22, Row G, Grave 4.

19   After the war, Schwappacher reported that six or seven severely wounded German soldiers were executed by their American captors.

20   Lieutenant Adriaan Slob, aged 27, was born in the Netherlands but fled Nazi occupation to England in a boat with Jewish boys. Some confusion exists whether he joined the Grenadier Guards as a grenadier or as a Dutch Liaison Officer. In either case, he was killed in a road accident in Nijmegen in February 1945 and was buried in Jonkerbos War Cemetery originally under a Grenadier headstone. The headstone has since been replaced with that of Royal Netherlands.

wave his men safely passed.[21]

Vandervoort's paratroopers concentrated upon clearing enemy positions along Sint Canisiussingel, the deadly Keizer Lodewijkplein traffic circle, and Hunnerpark by moving forward through the houses, advancing along the rooftops of the buildings, or using bazookas to blow passages between the buildings. Company E attacked out of Graat van Roggenstraat against Keizer Lodewijkplein and the southern side of Hunnerpark while Company F attacked Hunnerpark from the west.

At 14:30, under covering fire from the second story windows of houses fronting the park and traffic circle, Company F, now commanded by the company XO, Lieutenant Joseph Holcomb and Lieutenant Smith's Company E formed a skirmish line and charged into the traffic circle four platoons abreast. Six hundred SS troops held their fire until the Americans were fully exposed in the open before filling the circle with tracer fire. Machine guns in the upper floors of the Villa Belvoir and SS gunners in Valkhof added to the carnage. Men fell wounded or dead as survivors sprayed enemy positions with their Thompson submachine guns. Snipers targeted anyone appearing to give instructions. Lieutenant Holcomb was shot in the head,[22] Platoon Leader Lieutenant William Savell was shot in both arms, platoon leader 1st Lieutenant John Dodd was hit by an exploding 20-mm cannon shell and slowly died.[23] His incensed platoon furiously attacked the enemy gun crew without quarter. Medics were not exempt from the carnage, Pfc Vernon Carnes was killed.[24]

Sergeant Spencer Wurst led his men through the barbed wire entanglements taking on one German foxhole after another using rifle fire, grenade or bayonet.[25] Sergeant Wurst's group was the first to achieve the east side of the park quickly followed by British infantry.

After many of the company officers had become casualties,[26] Vandervoort strode onto the battlefield to direct his sergeants and corporals to get the men moving

---

21   Karl-Heinz Euling received the Knight's Cross for leading his daring escape. Euling died in 2014, aged 95.

22   Lieutenant Joseph Holcomb survived his near fatal wounds, remained in the army, and retired at the rank of lieutenant colonel.

23   First Lieutenant John Dodd, aged 28, is buried in Richmond, Virginia.

24   Medic Pfc Vernon D Carnes, aged 22, is buried in Sunrise, Minnesota.

25   Squad Leader Sergeant Spencer F Wurst, who lied about his age to join the Pennsylvania National Guard in 1940 at age 15, was awarded a Silver Star for his personal courage and leadership during the assault upon Hunnerpark. After four of his officers had already been killed or wounded, 19-year-old Sergeant Wurst stood exposed, directed his men, and provided targeting directions to a British tank. Spencer Wurst had fought with the 82nd Airborne Division since North Africa and was additionally awarded a Bronze Star, a Purple Heart with Oak Leaf Cluster, six Campaign awards, and six awards from the French, Belgian, and Dutch governments. His story is told in *Descending from the Clouds* by Spencer F Wurst and Gayle Wurst.
He remained in the US Army for 35 years to eventually command the 112th Infantry Regiment, the unit he joined as a youngster. Spencer Wurst died on 16 March 2015, aged 90, and is survived by three children, seven grandchildren, and ten great-grandchildren. He is buried in Arlington National Cemetery, Arlington, Virginia, Section 55, Grave 5589.

26   Lieutenant Jack Carroll, 3rd Platoon Leader, had been wound by artillery fire earlier that morning.

under the machine gun fire of the British tanks. The combat was without mercy and without quarter and men of neither side considered surrendering. By late afternoon on 20 September, assault guns south of Hunnerpark had been overrun and the buildings near the traffic circle were reduced to flaming ruins.

Grenadier Guards tanks on both flanks converged upon the park attracting much of the German automatic weapons fire. The tanks fired at point blank range into air-raid shelters and drove over trenches. Company E's 2nd Platoon left the buildings and moved toward the highway bridge approach road engaging the enemy in a hand-to-hand battle with fixed bayonets despite being exposed to fire from German antiaircraft and antitank guns. The tanks provided the advantage, rolling over trenches despite the threat of antitank panzerfausts or 88-mm shellfire. Of the five hundred men of KGr Euling over three hundred-fifty died and approximately sixty others were captured.

The American assault was also costly. Company F suffered nineteen dead and fifty wounded including almost all its officers and Company E suffered eleven dead. Dutch civilians emerged from their hiding places shortly after the gunfire ceased. They covered the American wounded with blankets and the dead with flowers.

British tanks had difficulty navigating the rubble-choked roadways around the southern bridge approach. Some number of Shermans stood abandoned where panzerfausts had shot off their tracks. Smoke from the burning houses surrounding Keizer Lodewijkplein obscured visibility and made breathing difficult for the troops.

At 17:40 Major Cook sent a radio message for tank support from the rail bridge. The message and the appearance of an American flag on that bridge was misinterpreted to mean that the highway bridge had been captured.

Lieutenant-Colonel Goulburn, ignoring the risks, sent a troop of four tanks from No 1 Troop under Sergeant Peter Robinson, a 29-year-old veteran of Dunkerque, accompanied by Lieutenant AGC Jones and a troop of 14th Field Squadron, Royal Engineers to defuse demolitions. Squadron leader Major John Trotter dispatched the troops telling them not to stop for anything.

At 18:13 Robinson led his four-tank troop onto the bridge. Almost immediately, a shell from an antitank gun positioned at the far end of the bridge hit the roadway in front of Robinson's Sherman Mk V[27] 'Firefly' tank #26 damaging a bogey wheel and knocking out the radio. Robinson threw smoke and rapidly reversed while Lance-Sergeant Jack Billingham and Lance-Sergeant Cyril Pacey fired against an enemy obscured by smoke from burning houses in Lent. All four tanks reversed off the bridge into the traffic circle. Robinson jumped out, commandeered the next Sherman Mk IV tank #27 of Billingham and continued forward. Billingham took Robinson's quickly repaired tank.

At 18:20 Robinson's troop again charged onto the bridge with their machine guns blazing against snipers and German pioneers attempting to repair broken demolition circuits. Dead and wounded fell from the girders onto the roadway. Grenades dropped from above set Billingham's #26 tank on fire.

---

27   British Sherman Mk V: American-built Sherman M4A4. Similarly, the British Mk IV was the American built M4A3.

When the leading Sherman approached the center of the bridge 88-mm shells screamed past the tank's turret each a near miss. Robinson's gunner fired its cannon as fast as he could load it while his .30-caliber machine gun sprayed the roadway. Suddenly the 88-mm went silent its recoil mechanism hit by the machine gun's armor piercing rounds.

The northern end of the bridge held four large concrete blocks, surmounted by wooden flak towers, that forced any vehicle to turn sideways to maneuver through the staggered opening. The effort exposed the tank's broadside to an 88-mm antitank gun farther down the road. The original third tank, Mk IV #25 commanded by Pacey, now in the lead because of the exchange between Robinson and Billingham, slewed sideways through the gap in the barrier and fired at potential targets followed by Robinson's tank. Robinson's gunner, Guardsman Leslie Johnson, spotted the antitank gun sandbagged into the side of the roadway approximately one hundred meters from the north end of the bridge. They each threw four shells at each other. Johnson struck a hit and the 88-mm was silenced. Although Sergeant Pacey's tank had been hit, Robinson continued forward driving over the damaged gun and its wounded or dead crew. Once through the gap, Robinson spotted another 88-mm gun 300 meters ahead on the left. Johnson fired again, one shot, and hit the gun. At the loss of the weapon, German infantry attempted to scatter, but Johnson mowed them down with the tank's machine gun.

The fourth tank Sherman Mk IV #28 of Lance-Sergeant Knight had driven 500 meters into Lent before it was hit by a panzerfaust shell and set on fire. The entire crew bailed and all, except for Sergeant Knight, were captured. Knight hid in a ditch until the enemy patrol passed, put out the fire, and drove the tank by himself. During the confused fighting in Lent, of the nineteen tankmen involved, eight became PoWs including Billingham.

By 19:15 the highway bridge was in Allied hands, although the threat of demolition remained. Lieutenant Jones and his engineers found and cut six wires on the side of the bridge. Jones next discovered ten Teller mines in a slit trench near the roadblock. He removed their detonators and threw them into the river. While inspecting the bridge more thoroughly, Jones captured seven German soldiers hiding among the bridge's structure. Now guided by one of the captives, Jones discovered 200-pound explosive charges shaped to fit within the bridge girders hidden below the road deck. A methodical search of all the pier compartments revealed no more explosives, but his men took eighty-one prisoners who were sheltering in the rooms within the bridge's piers.[28] Afterward 180 German bodies were removed from the bridge and its northern approach road.

Meanwhile, Robinson charged ahead into Lent to encounter a swarm of German troops seeking shelter in the church. A tank armor piercing shell followed by several high explosive shells set the structure aflame. The tank's coaxial machine gun

---

28   Lieutenant Anthony George Clifford Jones, son of an British Army colonel, received the Military Cross for bravely defusing the bridge demolitions unknowing if or when they might be detonated. After the war he attended Cambridge University, Sandhurst, and Staff College between duty stations in India, Malaysia, Germany, and England. He retired in 1978 at the rank of major-general. Jones died in 1999, aged 76.

sprayed the escaping survivors.

Robinson and Pacey continued along the Nijmegen to Arnhem highway until reaching the viaduct where the rail line crosses over the highway. Spotting shapes in the ditches, barely discernible in the growing gloom, Robinson's machine-gunner swung his gun to engage. Two hastily thrown Gammon grenades exploded immediately in front of the tank without damage. Before more serious exchange took place, the two groups recognized each other. The thirty men in the ditches were American paratroopers.

Immediately after passing through the rail tunnel in Lent, the two tanks were surprised by fire from two German 88-mm guns. Unable to locate the guns' positions in the total darkness, the tanks drew back behind the tunnel. Later the British tanks returned to the bridge. Robinson's orders had been to hold the northern end of the bridge and that was what he would do.[29]

However, the author having visited the site before recent reconstruction, he noted that the roadway entered a sweeping turn immediately after passing under the rail line. An approaching tank would have no possibility of engaging a properly positioned German antitank gun much less two guns. Road construction has completely altered the intersection.

After Robinson's tanks had continued into Lent the squadron second-in-command, Captain Lord Peter Carrington, greeted Captain Burriss on the northern approach ramp. The tanks laagered for the night and their crews started to brew tea. This incident became the center of great controversy between British and American commanders. American paratroopers expected an immediate rush of British armor across the bridge toward Arnhem, but nothing happened. Burriss was furious and demanded an explanation from Carrington, volunteering his men to eliminate the 88s ahead that had stopped Robinson. Burriss reported the conversation as, 'You mean to tell me you're going to sit here on your ass while your own British paratroopers are being cut to shreds – and all because of one gun?' He [Carrington] shook his head. 'I can't go without orders.' ... Burriss continued, 'You yellow son of a bitch. I've just sacrificed half of my company in the face of a dozen guns and you won't move because of one gun.' Carrington refused stating again that he had to wait for orders. Burriss threatened to shoot Carrington with his submachine gun if he did not proceed, but the British officer ducked into his tank and slammed the hatch shut.[30]

---

29   Sergeant Peter Robinson received the Distinguished Conduct Medal and was much honored by local residents during return visits to Nijmegen. He died in 1999 at age 84. The DCM, now replaced by the Conspicuous Gallantry Cross, was a second level award to enlisted ranks and falls only below the Victoria Cross in importance.
Lance-Sergeant Knight and Sergeant Pacey each were awarded the Military Medal.

30   Captain Thomas Moffatt Burriss, the youngest of three children from Anderson, South Carolina had been left fatherless at age twelve. Nevertheless, he graduated from Clemson University in 1940 and was activated into the Army Reserves shortly after Pearl Harbor. Burriss was awarded a Silver Star, three Bronze Stars, a Purple Heart, and three Presidential Unit Citations. After the war, he was a member of the South Carolina House of Representatives for 15 years. T Moffatt Burriss died on 4 January 2019, aged 99, and is buried in Columbus, South Carolina.
Captain Lord Peter Carrington was awarded a Military Cross, then a third level award reserved for officers of the rank of captain or below. The citation gave Carrington credit for pushing Robinson's troop of tanks across and capturing the bridge. Peter Carrington, 6th Baron Carrington, served as

Major Cook could not understand the delay. Colonel Tucker fumed finding that British strictures meant armor waited for the infantry to catch up. Gavin was downright irate and argued with Horrocks to no avail with Horrocks replying, 'We don't move our tanks at night.' Horrocks believed that the straight elevated road to Arnhem was a job for infantry. Tanks would have to wait until infantry could move up and pass through the Guards Armoured. Despite the bridge being firmly in American hands by 19:15, indirect fire from a SS Artillerie Abt 10 sited near Pannerden continued to pummel the southern approaches effectively preventing infantry from crossing the river. Later that night, No 2 and No 4 Companies, Irish Guards did cross the bridge to strengthen the perimeter.

Aftermath

Whatever the rationale, the opportunity to save what remained of British 1st Airborne Division was thrown away. Three hours later the Arnhem bridge was in German hands. The Germans spent the night ferrying more troops and vehicles across the canal at Pannerden — they were not reluctant to move at night.

At 10:40 on 21 September, the Irish Guards' No 1 Squadron (Captain Roland Langton) was ordered to make a 17-kilometer dash for Arnhem with twenty minutes advance notice, without formulated plans, and without maps. The unit crossed the Nijmegen bridge at 13:30, almost eighteen hours after its capture.

The Germans launched repeated counterattacks against the bridgehead north of the Waal over the next several days. The British 231st Infantry Brigade relieved the 504th PIR. British tanks attempting to move north to Arnhem on the elevated dike roads were subject to antitank fire and the effort was essentially abandoned.

Despite the end of the fighting in Arnhem, German Luftwaffe continued its efforts to destroy the bridge at Nijmegen with daily attacks from 25 to 29 September. Most of the attacks took place at dusk or night to avoid Allied antiaircraft fire, resulting in many of the bombs falling upon the city. On 25 September, a Focke-Wulf 190 scored a hit on the bridge roadway blowing a hole in the surface that was quickly repaired.

Although ground combat within Nijmegen ended on 20 September, the terror for its civilian population was far from over. German artillery north of the river and in the Reichswald continued to fire on the city until February 1945. Civilians were repeatedly driven to seek shelter in cellars or the stoutly built religious schools and monasteries. Casualty estimates from sporadic bombardments range as high as 800. In all, 2,200 Nijmegen civilians were killed and 10,000 injured. Approximately twenty-five percent of their homes were destroyed and another fifty percent severely damaged.

Battlefield Tour

Nijmegen

The battles for the Nijmegen bridges are reviewed in detail as it constitutes one of the major and most difficult actions during MARKET-GARDEN. The tour route begins on the southeast section of Nijmegen where the first American troops entered the city to launch their initial assault, then continues to the sites of attacks upon the rail

Defense Secretary, Foreign Secretary, chairman of British General Electric, and Secretary General of NATO. He died on 9 July 2018 at age 99.

bridge, the launch of the Waal River crossing including the new 'De Oversteek' bridge, battles against the stiff German defenses in Hunnerpark and the Valkhof, historical sites in central Nijmegen, the bridge crossed by British tanks, and, finally, battles on the north bank of the Waal River.

VVV Nijmegen
2 Keizer Karelplein 32H, 6511 NH Nijmegen
Tel: +31 (0)900 1122344
Web: https://en.visitnijmegen.com/
Open daily from 10:00 to 17:00.

The Information Center WW2 Nijmegen
Ridderstraat 27, 6511 TM Nijmegen
Tel: +31 (0)24 2200102
Email: welcome@infocentercentrumWO2.nl
Web: https://europeremembers.com/destination/infocentre-ww2-nijmegen/
Open Monday through Saturday from 10:00 to 17:00, Sundays and public holidays from 12:00 to 17:00. Closed on Christmas Day and New Year's Day. Free.

The Information Center assists visitors in touring the historical and cultural sites in and around Nijmegen with emphasis upon events of the Second World War. The center offers suggestions for walking tours and for educational programs.

> The tour begins in Heilig Landstichting at the traffic circle intersection of Nijme-gensebaan and Sionsweg (S100). (51.812276, 5.886663)

The **Hotel Sionshof** had been a German headquarters for four years. It became shelter for the officers of the Guards Armoured Division and accredited journalists, and the 508th PIR regimental command post. Lieutenant Colonel Warren's Companies A and B left their positions near the Sionshof Hotel at 20:00 on 17 September in the first attempt to capture the Nijmegen bridges.

The Sionshof, now the Hotel Courage Sionshof, is a sprawling white brick complex of hotel, restaurant, bar, and outdoor terrace on the southwest corner of the main road. The hotel celebrates its role in the battle with an **Airborne Plaque** on the hotel wall depicting a landing American paratrooper and the Nijmegen bridge. A standing tree trunk carved into a landing paratrooper is on the north side of the hotel.

Liberation Route Marker #48, 'Hotel Sionshof,' describes the transit of paratroops across the English Channel and the Dutch countryside and General Gavin's Dutch Liaison officer Captain Arie Bestebreurtje's efforts to contact members of the local Dutch underground

> Proceed northwest along Groesbeekseweg (S106); after 3.4 km pass Fransestraat on the left. (51.838831, 5.864859)

On 17 September, machine-gun fire struck Company A's leading platoon as it approached the intersection wounding the platoon leader, Lieutenant Fred Layman,[31] and killing his assistant, Lieutenant Boyd Alexander.[32] The 2nd Platoon (Lieutenant George Lamm)[33] took the lead and cautiously advanced with the scouting assistance of local underground leader Geert van Hees.

As the column approached Keizer Karelplein an MG-42 sat 350 meters ahead at the intersection of Groesbeekseweg and Sint Annastraat, the main road to Mook. (51.840882, 5.860491) The point squad moved along opposite sides of the tree-lined street keeping close to houses and the low iron fences that bordered the small front gardens. The machine gun fired again sending tracer bullets careening wildly off the cobblestone pavements and brick houses. The squad's BAR responded silencing the menace. Squad scout Private Walter Dikoon moved up to the intersection and turned right to enter Keizer Karelplein. A second machine gun, sited in the large central circle, fired and killed Dikoon.[34]

A German half-track drew parallel to the troops but was disabled by two bazooka rockets forcing the troops aboard to disperse in all directions. Under orders to engage the enemy with bayonets, Company A took on the scrambling SS troops in hand-to-hand combat among the gardens and between the houses.

The red brick and white stone apartments lining the wide avenue of Groesbeekseweg are, for the most part, postwar reconstructions after the destructive bombings that occurred during the war. Most buildings retain the small front gardens of shrubs and trees.

Continue to follow Groesbeekseweg northwest to Sint Annastraat and into Keizer Karelplein. Parking may be a problem. (51.842193, 5.859365)

Lieutenant Colonel Warren gave the order for Company A to attack the traffic circle. The paratroopers dispersed and a confused firefight erupted among the buildings illuminated only by flashes of exploding grenades. While Company A fanned out to capture Keizer Karelplein, trucks carrying SS troops could be heard screeching to a halt on the opposite side of the broad traffic circle. Tailgates crashed down and the enemy soldiers urgently dismounted hurried by their NCOs. Tracer rounds flashed across the circle amid loud detonations of grenades.

After taking several casualties, Company A regrouped among the buildings

---

31 Lieutenant Fred Layman recovered from his wounds and returned to his unit in November. He received more serious facial wounds during the Battle of the Bulge. He remained in the Army serving in Korea and numerous supervisory positions before retiring with the rank of major in 1959. Layman died in 1994. aged 78, and is buried in Willamette National Cemetery, Happy Valley, Oregon.

32 Second Lieutenant Boyd A Alexander, aged 21 from Webb City, Oklahoma, is buried in Netherlands American Cemetery, Margraten, Netherlands Plot M, Row 14, Grave 7.

33 Lieutenant George D Lamm received the Silver Star for his leadership against the enemy on the night of 17/18 September. He later received the Distinguished Service Cross for his disregard of his personal safety against heavy enemy fire when blowing bridges over the Salm River in St-Vith on 22 December 1944 during the Battle of the Bulge. Lamm died in 1992, aged 73, and is buried in Massachusetts National Cemetery, Bourne, Massachusetts.

34 Private Walter Dikoon, aged 20 from Providence, Rhode Island, is buried in Netherlands American Cemetery, Margraten, Netherlands in Plot F, Row 4, Grave 10.

lining the southern half of the circle. The Germans held the northern half and dug-in positions along the intersecting boulevards. German trenches and a 20-mm gun occupied the traffic island in its center near the statue of Charlemagne.

Warren then added Company B (Captain Woodrow Millsaps) to the struggle for the intersection with orders to sweep the right flank. A German counterattack overran Company A on the left which pulled back to reorganize. The plan changed with Company B keeping the Germans occupied while Company A moved to the right and headed for the highway bridge.

The **Keizer Karelplein** and the six roads that radiate from it constitute one of the busiest intersections in Nijmegen. The statue of Charlemagne remains, but structures circling the park have been extensively modernized. The intersection became the key position during later battles for the bridge. To the east, Oranjesingel led to Hunnerpark; Kronenburgerpark and the rail bridge are to the north; the train station and the heavily defended rail yards are to the west.

Exit Keizer Karelplein to the north moving along the west side (S101) of Kronen-burgerpark to the northern end of the park and locate a plaque mounted in the side-walk. (51.8483611, 5.85663611)

On 19 September, Dutchman Herman van der Poll led Captain Neville's tanks and supporting infantry for the rail bridge following a circuitous route west to approach the rail bridge from the southwest eventually paralleling the rail yards along Eerstre Oude Heselaan as far as Oude Weurtseweg. Although the tanks moved swiftly through German outposts utilizing their 75-mm guns, a warning was relayed to KGr Runge. The bridge's rail marshaling yards were strongly defended with interlocking machine-gun fire and antitank guns. A direct assault failed when Neville sent his infantry up and over the embankment surrounding the marshaling yard and his tanks toward nearby Hezelpoort tunnel. German artillery north of the river fired upon the Shermans when they entered open ground sending two British tanks up in flames. The appearance of two SP guns from the tunnel convinced Neville to retire for the night to a church. The force was low on ammunition and lacked communications with the other forces.

After the failure to pass through the Hezelpoort tunnel, Company D Executive Officer Lieutenant Waverly Wray ordered Lieutenant Isaac Michelman with his rifle squad and Platoon Leader Lieutenant James Meyers to join him in moving around the rail station to take on the German armor near the railway switching yards.

Lieutenants Meyers and Michelman guarded Wray's flank and rear as Wray accompanied by a bazooka team and Private Frank Aguerrebere carrying a rifle grenade launcher moved to the west side of the rail yard. The small group started taking casualties from the intense enemy fire which wounded both bazookamen. Wray, leading his men, brought Private Aguerrebere forward to eliminate a tank, but the target was too distant and the grenade fell short. Wray took the unmanned bazooka, loaded it, and moved forward to attempt to hit the tank. Suddenly, enemy fire resumed, and Wray crumpled to the ground. He was dead. [35]

The two lieutenants became pinned under a box car by automatic weapons fire coming down the rail tracks from the direction of the bridge. Michelman was seriously wounded. Meyers, deciding the positions to be too exposed, ordered a withdrawal leaving Michelman to be recovered later. Later that afternoon the company pulled back to the street running along the west side of Kronenburgerpark.[36]

Controversy continues over who cut the fuses to the highway bridge demolitions. Some fuses had already been cut on 18 September by 22-year-old Dutch student, scout, and resistance member Jan van Hoof. Perhaps these were repaired to be later cut by British engineers who stormed the bridge. In any case, on 19 September van Hoof rode on the fender of a British Humber scout car guiding it through the darkened streets from the post office toward the rail bridge. While approaching the bridge on Lange Hezelstraat a German 20-mm gun sited in the front garden of the red brick house across Kronenburgerstraat fired and set the car on fire. An American and two British soldiers inside the thinly armored car fell onto the pavement in flames. They died on the spot. Van Hoof jumped clear and when called to by the Germans he defiantly yelled 'Dutchman, free Netherlands' as the Germans approached. Taken prisoner, van Hoof was beaten and executed.[37]

The next day, while the 504th paratroopers were crossing the Waal River, Neville charged at the rail yards against KGr Runge which had so stubbornly defended the southern end of the rail bridge. Despite intense fire from machine guns and 20-mm flak guns, Neville's force drove back Runge's men securing the southern end of the rail bridge.

The **plaque** in the pavement identifies the spot with the words, 'Here fell Jan van Hoof, savior of the Waal bridge.' The plaque also marked the spot where Pfc Corney Ward, Lance Sergeant William Berry and his driver, Guardsman Albert Shaw, died in the flames of their burning vehicle. All four were hastily buried in Kronenburgerpark.[38]

Liberation Route Marker #14 lies at the north end of Kronenburgerpark just east of the railroad bridge. The 'Once in your life do something good' audio describes van Hoof's espionage efforts and his final moments.

---

35   Lieutenant Waverly Wray, from Batesville Mississippi, had been nominated for a Medal of Honor but awarded the Distinguished Service Cross for his actions on 7 June near Ste Mère-Église when he single-handedly eliminated the commanding officer and entire staff of a Panzergrenadier battalion, turning the tide of the German attack upon the critical Norman town. His death on 19 September was 8 days before his 25th birthday. Wray is buried in Panola County, Mississippi.

36   That night, Lieutenant Meyers returned to rescue Lieutenant Michelman, but Michelman was gone. It seems that he crawled out and made his way to the aid station.

37   Jan van Hoof was reburied in an official war grave and now lies in the General Cemetery Vredehof in Nijmegen. After the war, van Hoof was posthumously decorated by both the Netherlands and the United States. Since the Second World War, many scouting groups have been named in his honor.

38   Lance Sergeant William Thomas Berry, aged 30, is buried in Jonkerbos War Cemetery, Plot 1, Row D, Grave 2. Guardsman Albert Shaw, aged 23 from Worksop, Nottinghamshire, is also buried in Jonkerbos War Cemetery, Plot XXII, Row A, Grave 2. Pfc Corney M Ward, of Dexter, Missouri died on his 23rd birthday and is buried in Netherlands American Cemetery, Margraten, Netherlands in Plot D, Row 19, Grave 28.

> Proceed west on Lange Hezelstraat (S101), through the Hezelpoort tunnel (becomes Weurtseweg). Turn right onto Winselingsweg and follow to the De Oversteek under-pass; parking is currently possible despite the entire area undergoing extensive rede-velopment. Enter the elevator column that borders the bridge. (51.856118, 5.840129)

The river assault force assembled near the power station and now forlorn factory areas along Winselingsweg to the west. The PGEM power plant has been torn down and a coal storage yard removed from north of the canal port. A new power plant with a single chimney now stands south of the canal port.

The growth of industry and commerce in Nijmegen required an additional crossing of the river and the most logical place to construct a new bridge was 20 to 30 meters east of the historic airborne crossing site. The planners took great pains to include the historical events in the design of the bridge. In 2013 the city of Nijmegen finished the construction of a new single arch bridge named **'De Oversteek' (The Crossing)** which crosses the river at an angle rather than the more usual perpendicular orientation. The bridge is a structurally gorgeous work of art and functionality with twenty sweeping brick arches, in keeping with Nijmegen tradition of brick construction supporting the approach road (Generaal James Gavinsingel) and supporting metal hangers along the length of the roadway. The entire construction presents an image of grace and beauty.

De Oversteek passes immediately east of the NYMA building, a prewar textile factory that marks the eastern edge of Major Cook's launch site.

> As of this writing, the riverbank can be reached by walking 70 meters across a weedy field from the stairway/elevator tower toward the river. The steep five-to-seven-meter drop from the bank level to the water's edge remains apparent. The opposite bank can be seen, but extensive efforts to improve flood protection for the ancient city has resulted in reshaping and rerouting the river.

Captain Burriss thought the river crossing plan was suicide. Loaded with equipment but with a shortage of paddles, a whistle blew, someone yelled 'Go' and the most daring river crossing in history began when his company hoisted their boats and staggered over the dike and through gaps in a barb wire fence. Major Cook held the wire down with his foot and, as each man passed through the opening, gave them personal encouragement. Paratroopers carried the boats down to the escarpment where they passed the craft down onto the shoulders of men near the river. The weight of the equipment-loaded boats drove the troopers' legs into the soft riverbank mud. The launch surprised the enemy troops manning the opposite shore, for the first few moments their guns were ominously silent.

German fire from across the river had prohibited studying the routes over the dike. When the order was given to launch the boats, Captain Kappel led Company H's charge over the flat-topped dike to discover a chain-link fence topped with barb wire barring his unit's access to the river. Two Gammon grenades solved that problem, but instead of entering the water in a lateral line, the men and boats were funneled through the narrow gap. When Kappel finally got to the riverbank he found Private

James Legacie drowning a short distance offshore. Kappel threw his equipment into his boat and strode into the water to rescue the private.[39] Occupants of Kappel's boat stretched out and pulled both men into the boat before they began paddling for the opposite shore.

Company C (Captain Wesley Harris), 307th Engineers provided the boatmen to transport the paratroopers across the river. A forward artillery observer team from the 376th PFAB (1st Lieutenant Whitney Russel)[40] and a section of the Regimental Demolition Platoon (1st Lieutenant William Mandle) accompanied the first wave. Cook crossed in the first wave like, as he described it, 'Washington crossing the Delaware.' Colonel Tucker crossed in the third wave; both men were field grade officers who were willing to expose themselves to the same dangers as the men they commanded.

A stairway and elevator provide access to **De Oversteek** bicycle lanes from which one is presented with a spectacular view of the crossing area, the rail bridge to the east, and the highway bridge in the farther distance. The NYMA factory building is immediately west of the bridge and the power lines that locate the crossing area are slightly farther west.

Since 19 October 2014, the **'Sunsetmarch'** has been a daily tribute to the forty-eight American soldiers who died during the crossing fighting for the liberation of the Netherlands. Forty-eight pairs of lighting columns line the bridge. At sunset the streetlights illuminate, pair by pair, at a slow marching pace. Each night a veteran walks the Sunsetmarch across the bridge paced by the lights. The total duration of igniting all the streetlights is almost twelve minutes.

Liberation Route Marker #17, which commemorates the Waal River crossing, stands at the base of the bridge in 20 Septemberplein near the elevator. (51.855940, 5.839960)

Return to Keizer Karelplein. Continue northeast on Oranjesingel and turn onto Van Schevichavenstraat. The large red brick building is the post office. (51.843406, 5.865894)

On 17 September while the battle raged at Keizer Karelplein, Captain Adams and Lieutenant Lamm moved east from Keizer Karelplein with 2nd Platoon to check out the building on Van Schevichavenstraat. According to the Dutch Resistance, the Nijmegen Post Office held the demolition controls for explosives attached to the highway bridge 800 meters to the northeast. Paratroopers stormed the building, quickly overwhelmed the guards, and destroyed whatever appeared to them to be a firing mechanism.

They set the building on fire and resumed movement toward the bridge against sporadic fire from buildings along the broad boulevard. Along the route, Platoon Staff

---

39   After the war, James Legacie learned to operate heavy equipment during construction of an Alaskan military base and continued in road construction after his return to his North Dakota hometown. Legacie died in 2012, aged 91, and is buried in Lawton, North Dakota. He is survived by five daughters, twelve grandchildren, and eighteen great-grandchildren.

40   First Lieutenant Whitney Swithin Russell Jr aged 23 from Maryland, was killed in action on 28 January 1945 during combat in Germany. Russell is buried in Baltimore, Maryland.

Sergeant Alvin Henderson killed two Germans in hand-to-hand fighting, bayoneted four others, and assisted in the capture of six prisoners.

Company A continued toward Keizer Lodewijkplein to find it occupied by SS Aufklärungs Bataillon 9 (SS-Captain Victor Gräbner), recently arrived from Arnhem. During the assault upon the broad open square, the point became pinned down by enemy machine-gun fire. S/Sergeant Henderson led a squad and pushed forward destroying the enemy position. He attacked Keizer Lodewijkplein personally destroying two machine gun positions and causing the crew of the third to withdraw. Continuing his personal assault upon enemy positions, Henderson was killed by a burst of machine-gun fire while attempting to throw a phosphorus grenade into one of the buildings surrounding the traffic circle.[41]

Despite Henderson's heroics, Company A suffered another counterattack by fresh German troops, which set fire to nearby buildings to illuminate the square and silhouette anyone attempting to advance. Unable to bypass the German strongpoints, Captain Adams and his men sheltered for the night in an abandoned warehouse.

> Return to Oranjesingel and continue east as it becomes Sint Canisiussingel. Turn right onto Berg en Dalseweg and continue 300 m into Mariaplein (51.842751, 5.873968)

The third column of Grenadier Guards and Vandervoort's paratroopers pushed from the southwest along Dominicanenstraat towards the Waalbrug. Only the leading tank troop and a few vehicles carrying a platoon of infantry made it across heavily defended Mariaplein before further movement across the open square was cut off by heavy German fire from surrounding buildings. Fifty men of 1st Platoon (Lieutenant James Coyle), Company E sprinted across the square under the cover of smoke grenades to enter Doctor Claas Noorduynstraat. Heavy fire from MG-42s and 20-mm antiaircraft guns isolated Lieutenant Coyle's platoon from the following column, but the platoon continued forward to approach the last houses before Keizer Lodewijkplein. Again using smoke grenades, Lieutenant William Meddaugh succeeded in bringing the remaining two platoons of Company E across the deadly square.

The **route along Oranjesingel, Berg en Dalseweg,** and into **Mariaplein** is lined with a mix of old and modern buildings, because the firebombing of the city reduced much of its center to rubble. Nevertheless, the two-story brick and stone structures are representative of wartime apartment style. Mariaplein is an attractive circle but lacks any reference to its September 1944 importance.

> Leave Mariaplein northeast on Doctor Claas Noorduynstraat to the intersection with Graadt van Roggenstraat. (51.844393, 5.875688) The rebuilt Hotel Belvoir is on the corner.

A large house, then named Villa Belvoir and since replaced by the Amrath Hotel Belvoir, stood east of Keizer Lodewijkplein. A company of fallschirmjäger from

---

41 Staff Sergeant Alvin H Henderson, aged 22, was posthumously awarded the Distinguished Service Cross for leading his squad in destroying enemy positions. He is buried in Oklahoma City..

the Hermann Göring AuE Regiment occupied the large structure on 17 September and encircled the position with slit trenches and barbed wire entanglements. Its windows bristled with machine guns.

On 19 September, British tanks moved forward, but an undisclosed 75-mm antitank gun took out two Shermans in quick succession and the rest backed into safer positions. Company E's Lieutenant Coyle led his platoon through the backyards of buildings along Graadt van Roggenstraat sheltered from enemy view by the four-foot-high brick walls that separated the gardens to spot the antitank guns in Hunnerpark that had knocked out the tanks. The platoon entered the houses at the west end of the street and automatic weapons teams placed a .30-calibre machine gun and BAR on tables near second story windows. They observed German troops active in the park bringing up more ammunition. Troops entered other houses across from the Villa Belvoir. Coyle had his men hold their fire despite the tempting targets allowing as many men as possible to be in position before disclosing their presence.

A British forward artillery observer, not hearing the young lieutenant's orders to not fire, walked into a room facing the park and fired. Immediately, thinking it was the awaited signal, all the paratroopers' barrels open up. A German 50-mm antitank gun, which had taken up position in the street directly below the paratroopers, was hit with a rifle grenade. A German gun turned its attention toward the men in the buildings and fired a shell that ripped through the walls of three buildings in succession, staggering the men and seriously wounding one. The concussion of a second shell killed the British artillery observer.

Finally, at 19:00 with daylight failing, and despite Vandervoort's signaling that the paratroopers were ready to take Hunnerpark, the attack was called off when British commanders decided to consolidate for the night and send in the Grenadier Guards infantry the next morning. The third attack upon the bridge had failed.

The structures around this intersection were severely damaged by shells or resulting fires during the battle requiring their removal after the war. The original Villa Belvoir sat upon an entire city block surrounded by gardens, but the current hotel stands upon more modest grounds.

Proceed northwest on Graad van Roggenstraat into Lodewijkplein. Circle around counterclockwise and exit onto Sint Jorisstraat going northwest. Parking in this crowded area can be a problem, but the Kelfkensbos underground garage in front of Museum Het Valkhof offers an ideal solution. (51.846655, 5.869195)

The area is best viewed on a 1.6 km walking tour. The garage's pedestrian exit accesses **Voerweg** where an elevator raises to the plaza facing the museum. Cross the plaza to the south side and walk east along Kelfkensbos.

Immediately after passing the corner of the museum, turn left to proceed on an uphill path formed by remains of the Valkhof's ramparts. (51.845943, 5.871683)

The stone wall forms the limit of Hunnerpark and provides broad views over the park, Keizer Lodewijkplein, and the buildings across the square which were the limit of the paratroopers advance on 19 September.

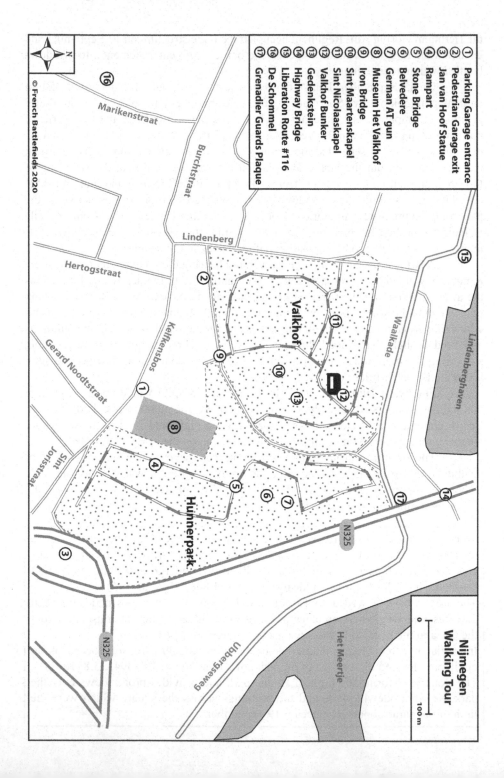

① Parking Garage entrance
② Pedestrian Garage exit
③ Jan van Hoof Statue
④ Rampart
⑤ Stone Bridge
⑥ Belvedere
⑦ German AT gun
⑧ Museum Het Valkhof
⑨ Iron Bridge
⑩ Sint Maartenskapel
⑪ Sint Nicolaaskapel
⑫ Valkhof Bunker
⑬ Gedenkstein
⑭ Highway Bridge
⑮ Liberation Route #116
⑯ De Schommel
⑰ Grenadier Guards Plaque

Nijmegen
Walking Tour

0   100 m

© French Battlefields 2020

Although the final assault was planned for one hour later, at 14:30, Captain Robert Rosen, commanding Company F, decided on his own authority to assault Hunnerpark from Derde Walstraat. Lacking help from Company E or British tanks, his company advanced through the streets south of the park attracting 20-mm fire from enemy positions. His men reached the yards across the street from the park. Rosen led a charge of approximately 20 troops across the open ground.

Rosen's assault was met by machine-gun, small-arms fire, and grenades from Euling's SS troops in foxholes and trenches sited from the traffic circle back 100 meters into the park. Captain Rosen was seen running back across the street with a fatal facial wound and the assault collapsed.[42]

An American medic rushed forward to tend a wounded paratrooper in the park before returning for assistance to recover the man before he bled to death. Assistant platoon leader Lieutenant William Hays and another officer left their weapons and advanced to recover the wounded man. In a remarkable incident, German soldiers witnessed the rescue but held their fire.

The nearly flat **Hunnerpark** terrain was heavily fortified with trenches and air-raid shelters used as dugouts. Three bunkers guarded approaches to the highway bridge.

A bronze statue of a male figure symbolizing **Jan van Hoof** with a Dutch tricolor flag was erected in Keizer Traianusplein to honor resistance members who died and in particular van Hoof. The statue is difficult to access, but views of it from Hunnerpark are especially good and it marks the location of one of the German 88-mm guns. (51.845537, 5.873258)

> Continue up the rampart and cross a stone bridge to the viewing platform in front of the Belvedere. (51.847517, 5.872533)

The **Restaurant Belvedere** offers great views of the bridge. The Belvedere tower was built in 1511 as an observation point over the river. The cellars underneath held a powder magazine until 1818. The building now houses a private party facility. The Belvedere high point overlooks all access to the south end of the bridge and indicates the problems in overcoming the fierce resistance. (51.847497, 5.872530)

A **German 50-mm PaK 38 antitank gun** that was used against attacking British tanks stands upon a concrete platform on the downward slope of the hillside below the Belvedere. The position is accessed from the stairway that descends from the Belvedere, even though it cannot be seen from the terrace. (51.847640, 5.872557)

> Leave the Belvedere by the alternate path that gently slopes down toward the Museum Het Valkhof. The path reenters the plaza passing the northern corner of the museum, which approximates the location of Haus Robert Janssen. (51.847035, 5.871366)
>
> Proceed across the plaza to the ironwork gateway on the right. Cross the bridge into

---

42   Captain Robert Rosen, from Brooklyn, New York and a graduate of the United States Military Academy, died. Rosen, aged 28, is buried in the United States Military Academy Post Cemetery in West Point, New York.

Valkhofpark. (51.846925, 5.870419)

The iron bridge presents views down onto Voerweg, which follows the defensive ditch dug in 1250 surrounding the ancient fortifications and now separates Valkhof from Hunnerpark. The brick wall and bases of medieval towers can be seen.

The first recorded structure in the **Valkhof** was a Roman fortress (*Oppidum Batavorum*) large enough to accommodate the entire Tenth Legion known to have been stationed at Nijmegen from 71 to 103 AD. The castle complex was expanded during later centuries with various additional buildings, towers, and a ring wall. The centerpiece was the massive donjon or Great Tower which had no windows on the lower floors instead holding supplies and water to survive sieges. In 1796 the Valkhof was sold by the province to be used as building material. The two chapels are all that has survived from the castle.

Sint Maartenskapel, built in 1155 by order of German Emperor Frederick I 'Barbarossa', stands on the right upon entering the park. The chapel was part of the Reich Hall which held the emperor's crown, scepter, and throne. The construction material used was from the 8th century castle of Charlemagne which had previously stood on this same spot. Numerous modifications resulted in the structure becoming unstable and demolition of the castle caused the collapse of all but the remaining semi-circular choir niche. Two surviving Roman pillars with Carolingian capitals supported a second story separated by arches in the wall. The doorway on the left accessed the crypt or lower level. Later centuries saw the chapel used as a kitchen. (51.847568, 5.870555)

Ahead on the left is **Sint Nicolaaskapel**, built around 1030 on the sixteen-sided pattern of the palace chapel at Aix-le-Chapelle or Aachen in German. The present form of the chapel resulted from rebuilding around 1400 when the eight-sided core was raised to form a defensive tower. The citadel held the SS Pioneer Abt 10 – mostly experienced combat troops who had fought in Russia. The chapel's thick walls provided a useful defensive position and although shelled during the battle, it was repaired after the war.

The chapel remains in use as a Greek-Orthodox church and for exhibitions and performances. Volunteers provide guided tours every day except Monday April to October from 11:00 to 16:45. (51.848111, 5.869623)

The Valkhof was the highest point for kilometers around and dominated approaches to both bridges. The overlook 50 meters east of the medieval chapel provides dramatic views over the river, the old harbor, all three bridges and the opposite shore. The old concrete on the left side of the promontory is the roof of the German bunker. (51.848128, 5.870481)

Valkhof Bunker
Mailing Address: Van der Duyn van Maasdamstraat 19, 6535 VS Nijmegen
Email: info@valkhofbunker.nl
Web: https://www.valkhofbunker.nl
Open hours are erratic but can be found on its website. (51.848141, 5.870626)
The Valkhof Bunker was part of a series of three bunkers constructed in

the Valkhof during 1943 with the goal of covering all approaches to the bridge. The bunkers were connected by a system of trenches and manned by SS Pionier Bataillon 10.

This bunker is the only survivor of the three as the other two were heavily damaged and were removed in 1947 and 1984. In September 2016, the remaining bunker was opened to the public by the volunteer Valkhof Bunker Foundation and now houses an exhibition that tells the story of the liberation of Nijmegen and the battles for the Waal Bridges.

A white marble **memorial stone** 30 meters south of the promontory records the medieval rulers of the Valkhof starting in 777 with Charles the Great (Charlemagne) through Otto II in 1247. (51.847917, 5.870619)

Steps immediately west of the bunker lead down to a pathway that circles around to the front of the bunker presenting its two machine-gun embrasures targeting the bridge. The path accesses Ubbergseweg and a tunnel under the bridge approach. SS-Captain Euling made his escape along this roadway. The left side of the bridge support at the bottom of the hillside on Ubbergseweg bears a dull gray metal plaque commemorating the 50th Anniversary of the Grenadier Guards' capture of the bridge. (51.848704, 5.872482)

From the Sint Nicolaaskapel, follow a path west that descends the slope and accesses Lindenberg. (51.848147, 5.868868)

The King's Company assaulted up the slope from the old police station that now is the Lindenberg cultural center.

Driving north of Valkhofpark is tortuous, therefore we suggest to continue on foot north on Lindenberg for 290 m to the riverfront district. (51.849309, 5.868773)

On the night of 28/29 September 1944, divers from the German Marine Einsatzkommando (MEK) 60 (Oberleutnant Hans-Friedrich Prinzhorn)[43] and MEK 65 were given the dangerous task of blowing up the river bridges in Nijmegen using 4-meter-long torpedoes buoyed by compressed air tanks. In the fast-flowing waters of the Waal, the men lost contact with each other. Frogmen assigned to blow up the highway bridge were seen and while under heavy fire, they desperately tried to sink their bombs to the correct depth and activate the detonators. One bomb eventually exploded too far out of position to inflict structural damage, but it did blow a 13-meter gap in the roadway. The second torpedo was disarmed and removed by Royal Engineers. Around 06:00, a huge explosion dropped the center span of the railway bridge. The frogmen, by then totally exhausted, floated to the banks of the river, where the Allies captured them. Of the twelve frogmen involved in the operation, ten were captured three of whom later died of wounds sustained during their attack. Two frogmen managed to escape capture and were later awarded high military honors for their action.

Liberation Route Marker #16 is found along the Waalkade that fronts the

---

43   Oberleutnant Prinzhorn successfully led Operation Bruno on the night of 16/17 September 1944 when German frogmen destroyed harbor buoys in Antwerp.

small inner harbor. On the 'German Frogmen Beleaguer the Bridges' audio German frogmen dramatically describe the difficulties of the operation. The city's three bridges can be viewed from this riverfront location.

Waalkade can provide a pleasant riverside walk 800 meters west to the **Belgian Prisoners of War Plaque** which is mounted upon the river barrier wall. The May 1940 destruction of the rail bridge trapped ten of thousands of Belgian prisoners of war. The famished and sick prisoners were transported to Nazi camps in open coal barges. The people of Nijmegen spontaneously responded with a relief campaign that saved many lives. The plaque was erected by the National Federation of Belgian Prisoner of War Survivors. (51.850392, 5.858064)

The Raadhuishof is a short distance west of the Kelfkensbos parking garage. The one way and pedestrian streets and a lack of parking in the old district of Nijmegen suggests walking from the Kelfkensbos garage.

Leave the plaza heading east along Burchtstraat. After 130 m turn left onto Marikenstraat and continue on the right hand upper level 100 m to the front of the Raadhuishof. (51.846056, 5.866164)

On 22 February 1944, the US Army Air Corps launched Operation ARGUMENT, commonly referred to as 'Big Week,' a series of aerial bombardments on German aircraft factories to weaken the Luftwaffe before the Normandy Invasion. The Messerschmitt factory at Gotha, Germany was shrouded in clouds and the bombers looked for alternative targets of opportunity. Upon the return toward England, twelve Liberators from 446th Bombardment Group selected the rail complex in Nijmegen as their secondary target. At 13:28 they dropped their bombs and much of the historic city center was destroyed.[44] Civilian casualties are officially stated at 763, but because refugees were sheltering in the cellars of burned-out buildings, it could certainly have been much higher. The Dutch government in exile in London, reliant upon American forces to reestablish control of the country after liberation, largely remained silent on the true scale of the tragedy for decades after the war.

In the Raadhuishof or town hall court in Nijmegen, **'De Schommel'** or The Swing monument was erected in memory of the twenty-four children and eight religious sisters who died in the bombing while tending an infant school which formerly stood on the site of the monument. The swing symbolizes movement between the past and the present.

Two courtyards contain several other memorials: **Liberation Route Marker #15** highlights 'The mistaken American bombardment' when anti-personnel and fragmentation bombs were dropped. The audio relates the reactions of the children and sisters during the tragic mistake. A plaque shows photographs of the twenty-four children who were killed. In addition, a **remembrance wall** contains the names of the residents of Nijmegen who died that day.

Return to your vehicle and exit the parking garage onto Kelfkensbos. Pass into

---

44　Daylight bombing accuracy defined the target to be a 300-meter circle around a central point. After action photo reconnaissance indicated that only 20 percent of the bombs hit the target.

Keizer Traianusplein and turn left to follow highway N325 onto the Nijmegen bridge. (51.849811, 5.872168)

Continue across the Nijmegen Bridge. Do not stop but note in passing an engraved stone mounted on an extension on the side of the Waal Bridge near the north end that commemorates **Jan van Hoof** with an image of him cutting the demolition cables. The memorial stands directly above the northern pier that held the main demolition charges. Van Hoof received the Netherlands highest award, the Militarie Willemsorde for his actions in saving the bridge. A postwar commission decided that the truth regarding the controversy over who cut the demolition line may never be known, but it was possible that van Hoof did cut the cables only for the damage to be discovered and repaired by German engineers. In either case, the explosives did not detonate and the single-span bridge stands today as it did in 1944. (51.852493, 5.870881)

At the northern end of the highway bridge, turn right at the first intersection (Turen-nesingel). As of this writing the four-lane bridge passes west of the Dutch casemate near the corner. Construction of four more lanes for the bridge is well underway and upon completion will reroute the northbound lanes to the east of this position.
From Turennesingel, after 160 m turn left onto Parmasingel and follow 700 m to the T junction at the rail line.

A pill box on the rail embankment, barely visible from the road below even at close range, had fields of fire toward the rail underpass and the full length of the embankment to the river. (51.858109, 5.859675)

Turn left onto Parallelweg, then right onto Oosterhoutsedijk. Immediately pass under the rail line and continue along this excitingly narrow dike road for 1.2 km to the memorial on the left. A small parking area is outlined on the side of the road. (51.863705, 5.847257)

The **Waal Crossing Memorial** consists of two upright stones placed upon a circular cobblestone platform. The left, topped with the 'AA' division insignia, records the units which crossed the river on 20 September. The right stone bears an inscription, in Dutch, that records, 'At this place on 20 September 1944 was the heroic crossing of the Waal.' A polished granite marker in front of the older stones lists the names of the men who died in the crossing. During the Waal crossing forty-eight American soldiers were killed. Remarkably, forty-nine names are on the monument. The name of radioman Norris Case, who was killed at the crossing, was not until recently listed on the Roll of Honor. Gerald Page Hereford who died later is wrongly on that list, but his name remains on the new memorial out of respect for his sacrifice.[45]

The historic battlefield on the north bank of the Waal River has been redeveloped as dictated by the need for flood control works along this entire stretch

---

45   The 3rd Battalion, 504th PIR received a Presidential Unit Citation for the capture of the Nijmegen bridges.

of the river. Although this section of Oosterhoutsedijk has been left unchanged, the section accessing Veur-Lent has been rerouted to accommodate the Spiegelwaal basin between the dike road and the original riverbank. Thus, the river crossing troops landed much farther from the memorial.

Standing amid the peaceful surroundings before the Waal Crossing Memorial, one cannot but reflect how different its was on that 20 September day. The individual soldiers' recollections describe events that occurred in dizzying succession.

In Company H's landings along the waterfront below this memorial, Sergeant John Toman survived the water crossing before being shot in the head by an enemy bullet.[46] Private Joseph Jedlicka burdened with a BAR, bandoliers of .30-caliber ammunition, and two ammunition containers, sank in 8 feet of water. He could not swim so he waded ashore holding his breath.

Captain Burriss recalled:

We were soaked, gasping for breath, dead tired, and constantly expecting to feel that searing sensation as a bullet tore through you. I wanted to vomit. Many did. Somehow or other we were three-fourths of the way across. Everyone was yelling to keep it up but there was little strength left in anyone. …But at last we reached the other side. We climbed over the wounded and the dead in the bottom of the boat and — up to our knees in water — waded to shore.[47]

Pfc Walter Muszynski had been in one of the first boats across the river manning his .30 caliber machine gun from the bow of the small boat. Upon reaching the shore he continued to provide protective cover as his squad moved toward the rail embankment. Fire from a German flak gun knocked the machine gun from his arms destroying it. Pfc Muszynski crept forward to within ten meters of the gun position and threw a hand grenade destroying the gun that was putting flanking fire into his platoon. During that act, he was mortally wounded.[48]

Company I's 1st Platoon Leader, Lieutenant Robert Blankenship, was one of the first men to cross. He saw the men from later boats pinned down by a machine gun on the left flank of the landing area. Lieutenant Blankenship crawled, ran, and leapt across 90 meters of open terrain to kill the four-man crew with rifle fire. Nearby a sniper fired upon Blankenship's scout. With his rifle empty, he battered the enemy with his fists. Blankenship then led two of his men to close on a German flak wagon, which they neutralized with hand grenades.[49]

---

46   Sergeant John J Toman had the bullet hit just above his ear. He was evacuated eventually to the United States. He lost his hearing, use of facial muscles and was confined to a wheelchair. After six years in a nursing home, he was transferred to a VA hospital where he remained until dying in 1999 — 55 years after the events that crippled him. Toman's name is not on the Waal Memorial, but he just as surely died of his wounds inflicted on 20 September 1944.

47   Burriss, T Moffat, *Strike and Hold: A Memoir of the 82nd Airborne in World War II*; Potomac Books, Inc; Washington, DC 2000

48   Pfc Walter J Muszynski, aged 23 from a large family of nine children from Cudahy, Wisconsin was awarded the Distinguished Service Cross. A product of the Depression era Civilian Conservation Corps, Muszynski had fought in North Africa, Sicily, Italy, and Netherlands during the war. He is buried in Netherlands American Cemetery, Margraten, Netherlands in Plot F, Row 19, Grave 26.

49   Lieutenant Robert C Blankenship, from DeRidder, Louisiana was awarded a Silver Star. During

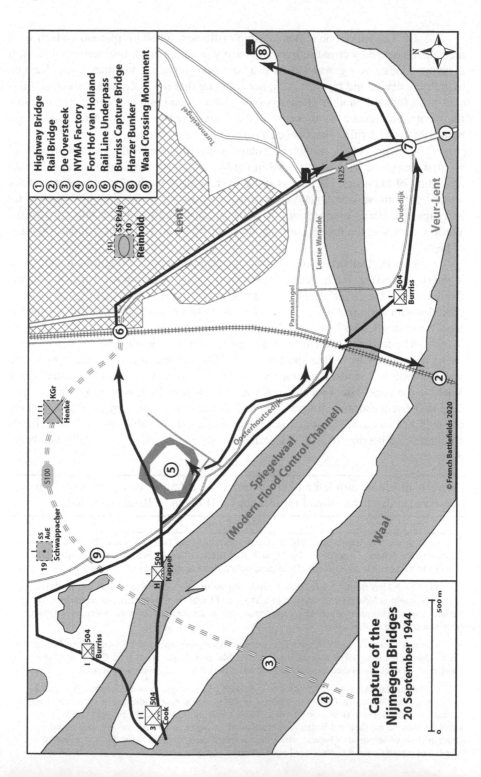

Capture of the
Nijmegen Bridges
20 September 1944

1. Highway Bridge
2. Rail Bridge
3. De Oversteek
4. NYMA Factory
5. Fort Hof van Holland
6. Rail Line Underpass
7. Burriss Capture Bridge
8. Harzer Bunker
9. Waal Crossing Monument

© French Battlefields 2020

Pfc Leo Muri, one of Blankenship's riflemen, found his platoon's advance off the beach blocked by crossfire from two enemy machine guns. Instinctively, Pfc Muri crept up to the nearest gun and threw in a Gammon grenade. A German soldier leapt up to grab the device and throw it back, not realizing that it was contact detonated. Muri continued forward another 18 meters to near the second gun and eliminated it with a fragmentation grenade. Two enemy soldiers attempted to flee, but Muri killed them both with his M-1 rifle. That opened a path up the steep bank.[50]

Captain Harris, Engineer Company Commander who crossed in one of the first assault boats, was wounded in the back and arm but continued to supervise unloading of the boats. He recrossed the river, refused medical treatment once back on the southern bank and again crossed the river during which time his boat was hit and capsized. Harris plunged into the water and assisted three men into other boats. While supervising the loading of boats for the third wave, Harris passed out from loss of blood.[51]

Captain Delbert Kuehl, Regimental Chaplain, was not required to participate in the river crossing, but he recognized the danger to the men of the 3rd Battalion and thought that if they ever needed him, it was now. On the river, Kuehl sat shoulder to shoulder with a trooper who was struck by a 20-mm exploding shell. The detonation blew the man's head off.

The fearless chaplain carried an aid kit and upon landing he began tending to the men's physical as well as spiritual needs. While attempting to bandage a man with severe stomach wounds, a mortar shell struck nearby and a piece of shrapnel struck Kuehl in the back. The force drove Kuehl onto the man he was treating. The trooper, despite the seriousness of his own wounds, showed his concern by asking, 'Chaplain, did they get you too?' Despite his wounds and a considerable loss of blood, Kuehl continued ministering to and evacuating the wounded which eventually numbered thirty-five.[52]

Reverse direction, turn left on Zaligestraat to the entrance road on the left. Stop and observe the derelict nature of fortifications at Hof van Holland on the left.

---

the course of the war, Blankenship also received a second Silver Star, a Bronze Star, five Purple Hearts, and the Military Order of the Knights of Willem from the Dutch government. After the war, he returned to his hometown and eventually became mayor. Blankenship died in 1970, aged 48.

50   Pfc Leo P Muri from Altoona, Pennsylvania was awarded a Silver Star for his heroic actions. Leo Muri fought in North Africa, jumped into Sicily, and landed in the Netherlands on his birthday. He later fought in Germany where he received promotion to sergeant. His brother, Albert, was a chief petty officer in the south Pacific.

51   Captain Wesley D 'Spike' Harris from Bronco, Texas, was awarded a Distinguished Service Cross. During the war, Harris also received a Silver Star and Purple Heart with Oak Leaf Cluster. Lieutenant Colonel Harris died, aged 45 in 1962 and is buried in Lovington, New Mexico.

52   Captain Delbert August Kuehl, born to a desperately poorly Depression-era family in Alexandria, Minnesota, was ordained a Protestant minister in 1942, and almost immediately volunteered for military service. Kuehl was awarded a Silver Star for bravery under fire during the Waal crossing. After the war, he married and began missionary work in Japan, where he and his wife raised five children, four of whom also became missionaries. Kuehl died in 2010, aged 93, and is buried in Abraham Lincoln National Cemetery, Elwood, Illinois.

Fort Beneden Lent also known as Fort Hof van Holland, a 17th century fortification surrounded by a water-filled moat, stood 600 meters from the water's edge. The small complement of one 20-mm gun and an 81-mm mortar section in the fort was reinforced by SS infantry. The fort was a particular target of the Irish Guards tanks using armor piercing shells.

Lieutenant James Megellas of 1st Platoon, Company H, who had lost half his platoon during the crossing when one boat was hit by mortar fire and sank without a trace, led three men around to the north side of the fort where they charged ahead throwing grenades that suppressed fire from the 20-mm antiaircraft gun and drove the gunners to seek protection inside the fort's galleries. The moat held only a few feet of dirty, black water covered with a green slime of algae. Sergeant Leroy Richmond shed his equipment, swam underwater to cross the moat, and climbed the sloped wall. Richmond signaled his men to indicate a narrow causeway on the south side of the fort. Aware that the fort needed to be silenced, but that it was not a major objective, Megellas set up his light machine gun to fire bursts directly along the causeway into the courtyard while his men threw hand grenades over the parapet. Megellas then moved on leaving the fort to the following 1st Battalion.[53]

The Lieutenant Colonel Harrison's 1st Battalion arrived on the northern bank and proceeded to protect the left flank while also resuming the attack on Fort Hof Van Holland which forced a German surrender after a brief engagement taking thirty prisoners. By 18:00 an American flag flew from the northern end of the rail bridge. The battalion relieved Company H at the railroad bridge, allowing them to follow Company I toward the highway bridge.

After the war **Fort Hof van Holland** briefly became a storage area, then was abandoned. Current plans to renovate the grounds and buildings as a historical and ecological site are planned to be completed in 2028. It is possible, however, to walk along the entrance road and view the weed-filled moat and the entrance bridge that was captured by the paratroopers.

> Continue east on Oosterhoutsedijk to the small siding at the north end of rail bridge. (51.856849, 5.859030)

The west side of the rail bridge embankment now bears plaques detailing the wartime history of the bridge. The upper plaque displays an image of the destroyed bridge resting in the river with text describing how the bridge was blown up by

---

53   Lieutenant James Megellas, from Fond du Lac, Wisconsin and a graduate of Ripon College, first saw combat in the mountains near Naples, Italy. Ten days after the Waal River crossing, Megellas single-handedly stormed an enemy machine-gun nest. For that action, he received the Distinguished Service Cross. In January 1945 during the waning days of the Battle of the Bulge, Megellas took on a German PzKpfw V 'Panther' tank disabling it with a well-placed grenade before finishing the job with a second grenade into the turret. For that action he was nominated for the Medal of Honor but received the Silver Star instead. Megellas was one of the most honored officers in the 82nd Airborne Division having received the Distinguished Service Cross, two Silver Stars, two Bronze Stars, and two Purple Hearts. At age 80 Megellas wrote his well-regarded recollections in *All the Way to Berlin: A Paratrooper at War in Europe*. Megellas died on 2 April 2020, aged 103, and is buried in Arlington National Cemetery, Arlington, Virginia.

retreating Dutch troops on 10 May 1940. During the late summer, the destroyed bridge was replaced by a single-track emergency bridge and the rail line was once again operational by November 1940.

The second plaque displays an image of the rail bridge and describes the 1944 capture of the bridge. It notes that an unknown number of Allied and German troops were killed and were buried in the dike wall east of the abutment. On 29 September 1944, the central span was again blown up by German frogmen. A single-track span was again repaired by August 1945.

The rail bridge embankment that Lieutenants Sims and LaRiviere overcame has been considerably altered by the flood control construction. The original embankment continued to the river's edge; the three white support piers have since been added.

The view to the west provides a perfect visual image of the Waal Crossing area with the new power plant, power lines, the slope up to the dike road, and, of course, the graceful lines and arches of the new De Oversteek bridge.

Continue through the rail abutment and turn right to cross the new De Lentloper bridge. Follow the roadway to the easternmost house, park at a convenient spot, and walk along Oudedijk to the bridge underpass. (51.854068, 5.869577)

The **stairway** that ascended from the riverbank level up to the bridge roadway has been completely modernized into a wide stairway with a ramp for bicycles. The shelter under the bridge remains and the sealed doorway is evident.

The Oudedijk cannot be driven because there is no parking east of the bridge. Continue on foot from the underpass 400 meters to the bunker. (51.856618, 5.873377)

Shortly after 16:00, SS-Colonel Harmel received a disturbing message at his headquarters in Doornenburg 10 kilometers to the northeast: 'a white smoke screen has been thrown across the river opposite Fort Hof van Holland.' While Harmel rushed to Lent, he could not believe his own conclusion. It meant only one thing: they were attempting to cross the Waal by boat.

Harmel wanted the highway bridge to be blown, despite specific instructions from Generalfeldmarschall Model, who wanted it preserved for a potential German counterattack. Harmel observed the four British tanks and Lieutenant Jones' scout car nearing the center of the bridge while waiting to give the order. A guard stood by the plunger hidden in a farm garden near the Lent bunker. Harmel waited, he had to be sure the bridge was lost before detonating it. Better yet if it was loaded with enemy tanks when detonated.

Harmel scanned the bridge with his binoculars. He saw Robinson's tank reach the half-way point and anxiously waited for more tanks to fill the bridge's roadway. Finally satisfied, he gave the order, 'Let it blow!' The engineer pushed the plunger – and nothing happened. A repeat, the plunger went down again. Again nothing. Harmel radioed the disappointing results to Bittrich and left to establish defenses at Elst.

The pre-war **Dutch Bunker**, officially Lent B676, in which Harmel sheltered while he made the difficult decision to blow the bridge, is similar in construction to the Grave Bridge Casemate Zuid with two embrasures above dike level aimed directly at the bridge and a doorway entrance to the lower level. The bunker also was the location for two 20-mm antiaircraft guns.

The surrounding terrain has been extensively modified including removal of the farm and garden where Harmel's engineer waited to detonate the explosive charges. Plans exist to relandscape the area and retain the bunker because of its historical significance.

Return to Lentse Warande, turn right and follow to its eastern end. (51.857246, 5.867324)

For those curious, the eastern end holds remnants of the **chicane** used by the Germans to slow vehicles crossing the bridge by having them navigate between the large concrete blocks. Their future is uncertain pending completion of the construction project.

Another pre-war **Dutch casemate** is visible across the highway. The bunker is not accessible, but its position is noted as one of historical significance.[54] (51.857440, 5.868129)

Battle of Groesbeek Heights
17 to 28 September 1944

The 300-meter-high glacial moraine of the Groesbeek Heights dominates the southern approaches to Nijmegen from the east putting the Corridor under the guns of enemy artillery hidden among the tree-shrouded slopes. General Gavin shifted his forces between those attacking the Nijmegen bridges and those defending the Corridor from flank attack as required.

On 17 September the Allied air armada started taking flak as its planes approached the Maas–Waal Canal. In 18 minutes, 4,511 men of the 505th and 508th PIRs landed on the opposite sides of Groesbeek in a nearly perfect operation. A co-ordination problem resulted in 2nd and 3rd Battalions, 505th PIR approaching DZ 'N' at the same time. A quick decision by Lieutenant Colonel Vandervoort brought the 2nd Battalion to DZ 'T' where the 508th PIR would not arrive until later. That afternoon, British and American gliders delivered vehicles, equipment, and 2,956 more men.[55]

Colonel Ekman's 2nd Battalion, 505th PIR came down near Kamp north of Groesbeek a district distinct from De Kamp to the southwest of Nijmegen and set off toward their objectives at 14:15. The battalion cleared Groesbeek of enemy and occupied Hill 81.8 (Hoge Hoenderberg at 51.780458, 5.902048) on the ridge line west

---

54 Conflicting accounts record which of these two bunkers sheltered Harmel and the bridge detonator. It is clear that both were constructed to defend against enemies crossing the bridge, but in a postwar newspaper account, Harmel clearly states that, 'I watched from the bunker on the riverbank.'

55 Famed CBS radio news commentator Edward R Morrow recorded his on-the-spot impressions while flying with 1st Battalion, 505th PIR. Morrow returned to London in the C-47 to deliver a vivid description of the airborne assault.

of the village without contest.

The 1st Battalion was to hold the southern perimeter from the Mook railway bridge to the Reichswald by occupying a ridge which overlooked the Nijmegen-Gennap highway which was the main road from Germany. A reconnaissance patrol entered the Reichswald and dispelled rumors of a massive German armored presence in the forest.

Colonel Lindquist's 508th PIR established a defensive perimeter anchored upon the Maas–Waal Canal at Hatert and swinging around the forest boundary south of Nijmegen to high ground at Berg en Dal overlooking Beek. An ambiguity in orders or a misunderstanding resulted in Lieutenant Colonel Warren's 1st Battalion's late start toward the Nijmegen bridges. Lindquist's 2nd Battalion moved westward to Hatert and De Kamp to secure bridges #9 and #10. Its attacks on the canal crossings were met with German demolition of both bridges. The regiment's 3rd Battalion secured the wooded hills around Berg en Dal by 16:30.

Two aircraft in the leading serial made a navigation error and dropped twenty-five men of Company A into Germany near Wyler two kilometers east of the drop zone. Platoon Leader Lieutenant Rex Combs, who was wounded during the approach, led the paratroopers back to their battalion killing twenty-one enemy troops, taking fifty-nine prisoners and destroying four antiaircraft guns without losing a man.[56]

General Kurt Feldt tasked the 406th Infantry Division to hold the line from east of Nijmegen to Wyler east of Groesbeek. Under command of Generalleutnant Gerd Scherbening, the 406th zbV Division had been a static, purely administrative organization without troops. The unit had six hours to collect its assigned units, establish attack routes and objectives, and transport men to their start positions.[57] The division eventually grew to 3,500 men equipped with 130 assorted machine guns, an unknown number of Russian-made 143-mm guns, and 24 mortars. Its perimeter stretched along a 16-kilometer front from Beek, through Wyler, then west to pass south of Groesbeek, to the Maas River south of Mook.

Battle

The flat riverside terrain between the wooded Groesbeek escarpment and the Maas River provided Model with his best opportunity to destroy the sole remaining bridge at Heumen. Its destruction would isolate the 82nd Airborne at Groesbeek and the British 1st Airborne at Arnhem from resupply and reinforcements. The wooded hills that looked down upon the roadway (now highway N271) and the Maas River were the scene of considerable combat for the next ten days.

---

56   Lieutenant Rex Garland Combs was awarded his second Silver Star for his courageous leadership. He had received a similar award for rushing an enemy force of sixty, killing fifteen and capturing forty-five near Chef-du-Pont, Normandy, a Purple Heart with three Oak Leaf Clusters, and was knighted by Queen Wilhelmina of The Netherlands. Lieutenant Combs, from Los Angeles, California, died in 1976, aged 64. He is buried in Allendale, Missouri.

57   Units of the 406th zbV Infantry Division were composed of NCO Train School students, Landesschützen or older conscripts used for a variety of domestic guard duties, men with ear or stomach problems in special companies, and inexperienced Luftwaffe troops from recently closed NCO training schools. These units were spread among kampfgruppen named after their commanders – Göbel, Greschick, and Stargaard.

Battle for Mook

On 17 September, Lieutenant Harold Miller's 1st Platoon, Company B approached within 400 meters of the rail bridge before encountering heavy small arms fire. At 19:00, while the firefight continued, German troops occupying the bridge detonated their explosives and destroyed the bridge. Miller took seventeen of the defenders prisoner and established BAR positions 200 meters on either side of the bridge ruins.

Meanwhile, 2nd Platoon (Lieutenant Stanley Weinberg), Company B cleared Plasmolen of enemy then moved northwest along highway N271. At the entrance to Riethorst, Weinberg and his troops ambushed an Opel staff car killing Oberstleutnant Siegfried Harmisch, commander of Wehrkreis IV's engineers.[58] A German detachment put accurate mortar and machine-gun fire onto Weinberg's leading troops bringing their advance to a halt.

By 20:00, 1st Platoon (Lieutenant Harold Gensemer) arrived as reinforcements and the platoon leaders decided to occupy Hill 77.2 (Sint Jansberg at 51.739166, 5.928611), a wooded ridgeline approximate 100 meters long and half that in width north of the highway, and establish roadblocks to the north and south. Weinberg and Gensemer's platoons dominated the road to Heumen until late the next day when a German Ostwind[59] stripped the hillside of vegetation forcing the paratroopers to withdraw.

The German attack against Mook began at 07:30 on 18 September. Around noon, German tanks and 300 infantry from the ad hoc KGr Göbel (Oberleutnant Günther Göbel)[60] hit at Riethorst four kilometers south of the Mook bridge. The initial assault made little headway against a determined defense. Unable to maneuver off the roadway, armored vehicles fell prey to rocket-firing American bazooka men. Stronger, more cohesive units would be needed in a coordinated attack.

Tuesday 19 September was generally quiet with only small unit incursions of the 505th PIR's sector.

At 11:00 on 20 September, KGr Hermann[61] (Oberstleutnant Harry Hermann) renewed the assault through Mook intending to achieve the canal at Hatert. A barrage of 88s, Nebelwerfers, and mortars rolled over the Company B roadblock in Plasmolen killing all but one man. The German assault cleared Riethorst, forcing the surviving paratroopers to withdraw to Kiekberg Hill.

KGr Hermann entered Mook by 14:10 where hand-to-hand fighting raged

---

58   Wehrkreis: German military district designed to provide a regular flow of trained recruits and supplies to the Field Army

59   Ostwind: a tracked vehicle built upon a Panzer Mark IV chassis mounting a 37-mm gun in a rotating open-roof turret.

60   KGr Göbel: three infantry companies and a reconnaissance company heavy in machine guns. Günther Göbel was a veteran of Stalingrad and a holder of the Knight's Cross of the Iron Cross with Oak Leaves. In May 1945 he was captured by the Soviet Army and interned in various labor camps until his release in 1955. He died in 1993, aged 75.

61   KGr Hermann composed of remnants of the FJ Training Regiment 21, eleven light and heavy artillery guns from FJ Artillerie Regimenter 5 and 6, KGr Göbel which had failed in its attack upon Mook two days earlier, and a weak flak troop.

through narrow side streets and houses against the remaining two platoons of Company B. One platoon was driven from the town while the other platoon sheltered in cellars and maintained harassing fire. Colonel Ekman rushed to Mook to organize a counterattack using the displaced Company B platoon and two platoons from Captain John Dolan's Company A. Ekman also requested Coldstream Guards tanks from the division reserve. Captain Dolan's two platoons supported by a troop of Shermans from No 3 Squadron launched an assault upon Mook from a wooden area across the road from the town cemetery.

The tide turned, and the combined Allied force drove KGr Hermann back to Riethorst. That night KGr Hermann withdrew toward the Reichswald. At Mook, the 1st Battalion suffered twenty killed and fifty-four wounded.

The Battle of Groesbeek Heights
The proximity of Allied troops to Germany could not go unchallenged. Model's plan was to hold on the line of the Waal River until eventual reinforcement by the 10th SS Panzer Division's arrival from the Arnhem area. A coordinated assault by Korps Feldt was to impose the vital delay. At 06:30 on 18 September, four battalions of rear echelon, security, and training units from Wehrkreis VI, the military district closest to the Dutch border, supported by half-tracks mounting 20-mm flak guns and five armored cars launched attacks against the most thinly held sector of the Groesbeek Heights perimeter towards Beek, Wyler, and Groesbeek.

German troops surged down the road from Wyler, threatening an ammunition dump and infiltrating Landing Zone 'T' where much of the sorely needed airborne divisional artillery was to arrive later that day. Pressured from three directions, Gavin recalled Company G, 508th PIR back eight kilometers from its efforts to capture the Nijmegen bridges. Colonel Lindquist recalled his 1st Battalion from the battle around Keizer Karelplein in Nijmegen to clear the landing zone.

German troops from an NCO training school and an engineer battalion formed an ad hoc kampfgruppe and attacked out of the Reichswald onto DZ 'N'. Gavin dispatched his only reserve, two companies of 307th Airborne Engineer Battalion into the gap between the 505th and 508th Regiments.

The battle over the landing zones was still raging when Monday's Second Lift arrived. Artillery from the 4th Flak Division sited in the Reichswald fired at the slow moving tugs and gliders with eight 88-mm flak guns and several batteries of 37-mm and 20-mm flak guns scattering the planes across the countryside – some even ending up in Germany east of Wyler. Despite the German welcome, the Second Lift delivered 454 Waco gliders with 1,899 troops which comprised one parachute battalion, two glider battalions, and three battalions of glider artillery. Altogether, a substantial strengthening of the division. [62]

Model insisted upon renewing the attack the next day. However, after a fierce argument with his commanders, Model conceded; his men were just not ready. The

---

62   Arriving were the 319th and 320th Glider Field Artillery Battalions and the 456th Parachute Field Artillery Battalion, delivered instead by glider. Also, the Second Lift delivered the 307th Airborne Engineer Battalion, medical battalion, signal company, and eight 57-mm antitank guns of Battery D, 80th Airborne Antiaircraft Battalion.

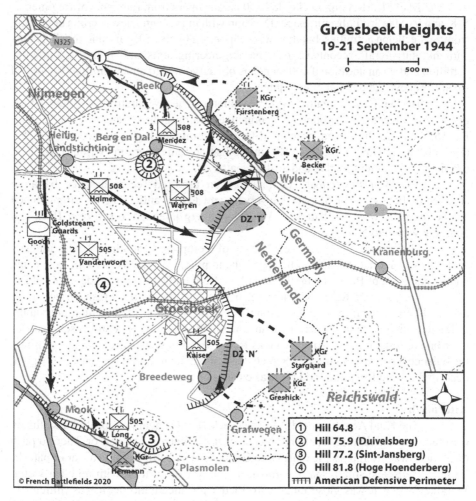

Groesbeek Heights
19-21 September 1944

① Hill 64.8
② Hill 75.9 (Duivelsberg)
③ Hill 77.2 (Sint-Jansberg)
④ Hill 81.8 (Hoge Hoenderberg)
ⅢⅢ American Defensive Perimeter

© French Battlefields 2020

German combat groups were strengthened by the arrival of 3,000 paratroopers from the 3rd and 5th Fallschirmjäger Divisions from Cologne.

At 06:30 on 20 September three battalion-size kampfgruppen named Becker, von Fürstenberg, and Greschick developed concentric attacks against the eastern and southern sectors of the 82nd's perimeter toward Beek, Wyler, and Groesbeek.

Major Greschick's kampfgruppe held 870 men composed of recently conscripted infantrymen from a Luftwaffe fortress battalion and an 'ear' battalion of old men with hearing problems supported by fourteen 20-mm cannon and batteries of 88-mm and 37-mm guns from the 4th Flak Division. His mission was to attack out of the Reichswald to envelop and by-pass Groesbeek before proceeding to the Maas–Waal Canal. A massive barrage opened against the outposted 505th PIR east of Groesbeek before an assault that pushed back the defenders to the outskirts of the town. KGr Greschick penetrated the fringe of Groesbeek but there it was held amid the snap of small-arms fire and the thump of exploding grenades.

Major Karl-Heinz Becker led 700 paratroopers from remnants of Regimenter 5, 8, and 9 of the 3rd Fallschirmjäger Division with many being new recruits or coming from rear echelon activities, but they were supported by five SP guns and the division's antitank, antiaircraft, reconnaissance, and engineering units and an attached infantry battalion adding an additional 300 men. His objective was to attack through Wyler and Beek to relieve the defenders in Nijmegen.

Becker's effort against Wyler encountered heavy paratroop artillery which drove the attackers to ground. A reorganized kampfgruppe renewed the assault. By 16:00, Wyler had been penetrated but the dominant high ground on Hill 75.9 (Duivelsberg in Dutch or Devil's Hill in English or Teufelsberg in German) was held despite bombardment by flak and artillery batteries.

KGr von Fürstenberg commanded an armored reconnaissance battalion (Panzer Aufklarüng Abt 6) with half-tracks and towed antitank guns strengthened by the remnants of a flak battalion. Von Fürstenberg intended to roll over Beek and continue west into Nijmegen.

His kampfgruppe hit two platoons of Company I, 508th PIR with a heavy artillery and mortar barrage. The subsequent massive infantry assault drove the paratroopers out of Beek and up the hillside to Berg en Dal where the defense held.

Korps Feldt fed newly arriving troops into the battle. Fresh battalions of about 300 men each from engineer, gunless fallschirmjäger artillery, and infantry units failed to reinvigorate the German advance while the Americans denuded segments of their line to respond. The arrival of tanks from the Nottinghamshire Yeomanry shifted the balance but it was not until 22 September that the flat terrain from Beek to the great bend in the Waal River around Ooij was cleared of the enemy.

Aftermath

The 82nd Airborne held the Groesbeek Heights against repeated assaults by German units attempting to, at first, recapture the Nijmegen bridges, or, later, to push the Allies away from possible routes into Germany. The battle became a war of patrols, artillery duels, and small, sharp skirmishes — a war of attrition with no clear victor. Woodland combat was close range and filled with uncertainty as it was difficult to identify friendly or enemy positions in the dense forest. The 325th GIR relieved the 1st Battalion after its arrival on 23 September, but the grim combat continued. The 325th GIR suffered repeated attacks against Kiekberg Hill near Mook on 27 – 30 September. The 508th PIR defeated the last German assault out of the Reichswald on the night of 30 September/1 October.

Canadian forces finally relieved the 82nd Airborne Division on 13 November after fifty-seven days in almost continuous combat. During the total period, the division suffered 535 killed, 622 missing, 2,617 wounded, and 523 injured.

Battlefield Tour

The tour reviews sites in and around Groesbeek including the landing sites of the 505th and 508th PIRs and a stop at the revamped Freedom Museum before moving towards the German border engagements at Wyler, Beek, and Berg en Dal.

VVV Berg en Dal (includes Groesbeek)
Dorpsplein 1a, 6562 AH Groesbeek
Tel: +31 (0)24 397 7118
E-mail: info@vvvbergendal.nl
Web: https://www.visitnijmegen.com/berg-en-dal
Open daily from 10:00 to 17:00.

> The Groesbeek Heights tour begins at the rail bridge in Mook. (51.757154, 5.872915)

On 20 September, KGr Hermann fallschirmjägers progressed to within two kilometers of the Heumen bridge and the British armored column crossing toward Nijmegen threatening the vital supply lifeline. General Gavin left his observation post in the PGEM plant overlooking the Waal River crossing and arrived in time to witness a lone bazooka man in a foxhole beside the road that passed under the rail line and into Molenhoek. His only protection was a string of mines laid across the road directly under the bridge. Behind him stood a single British Coldstream Guards tank. The tank attempted to withdraw under German infantry attack, but drove over an American mine blowing off a track. The crew escaped and ran for the rear. The general and two staff members climbed the railroad embankment to fire upon the advancing enemy while his jeep driver reversed to rely the order for the Coldstream Guards to double time to the location. Company A's assault into Mook from the northeast relieved pressure and the subsequent arrival of Coldstream Guards sealed the breech.

The now-repaired **rail bridge in Mook** marks the furthest German advance

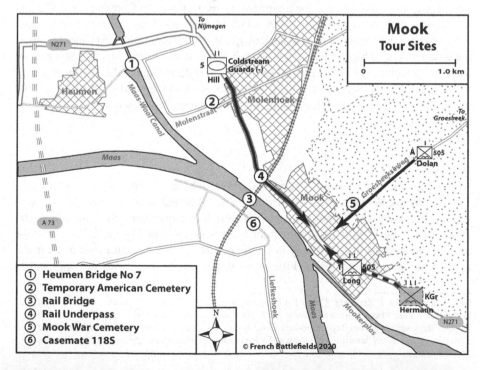

① **Heumen Bridge No 7**
② **Temporary American Cemetery**
③ **Rail Bridge**
④ **Rail Underpass**
⑤ **Mook War Cemetery**
⑥ **Casemate 118S**

© French Battlefields 2020

against American paratroopers towards Nijmegen from the southeast. A walking path (Halderweg) on the east side of the viaduct leads up to the five- to seven-meter-high dike which was constructed to hold back the flood waters of the Maas River. The site provides good observation across the river and of the rail bridge.

Maas Line Casemate 118S, vividly painted in a checkerboard pattern and with its two embrasures aimed at the rail bridge, stands 340 meters west of the rail bridge almost directly across the river. The bunker façade shows the damage of grenade impacts. The river is lined with thirteen such casemates spaced roughly every 250 meters constructed in 1939 by the Dutch Army to defend crossings of the Maas River. (51.753173, 5.870817)

Proceed southeast on highway N271 into Mook. Turn left toward Groesbeek on Groesbeekseweg and continue 450 m to the cemetery on the left. In 1944, the Mook-Groesbeek road was known as Adolf Hitler Allee. The Mook Communal Cemetery is opposite the military cemetery at the edge of town. (51.753731, 5.886060)

On 20 September, Company A officers, Captain Dolan, Lieutenant George Presnell, and Lieutenant Michael Chester, and two platoons from Company A approached Mook from the northeast through the wooded area to oppose the attack of KGr Hermann.

Near the entrance to the cemetery, Dolan's jeep ran over a land mine and all three were blown from the vehicle suffering injuries. Presnell and Chester eventually returned to the unit after Market Garden, but Dolan's injuries were more severe and he was sent to the United States for treatment, never to return to Company A.[63] Despite the loss of their officers, Company A attacked from the forest across a wide-open field astride Groesbeekseweg. In particular, the 2nd Platoon had just emerged from the wooded area to begin their attack when it received fire from rifles and Schmeisser MP40 submachine guns. The teams broke left and right to engage the enemy in a fight that was conducted with small arms. Combat was man-to-man and hand-to-hand. That night, fires started by an artillery bombardment consumed the town forcing the enemy to pull back.

Mook War Cemetery
Groesbeekseweg 6585 Mook
Web: https://
www.cwgc.org/find-a-cemetery/cemetery/2059101/Mook%20War%20Cemetery

Mook War Cemetery is within a small forested area set upon the side of a small hill. It holds 311 Commonwealth war casualties and eleven Polish nationals who died either in the vicinity during the fighting of September and October 1944 or at the time of the advance into Germany in February 1945. A few casualties occurred in the interim during patrol activities. Fifteen are unidentified. The graves are approached

---

63   Captain John J 'Red Dog' Dolan led his Company A's defense at the dramatic battle for the bridge at La Fère Manor from 6 to 9 June 1944. They held against enemy assault and artillery fire for four days suffering an eighty-six percent casualty rate. He was awarded a Distinguished Service Cross for extraordinary heroism. After the war, Dolan became an attorney and practiced law in Boston, Massachusetts.

through a metal gate and along a grass path to the Cross of Sacrifice with plots on each side. A pavilion in the rear houses the register. There is no War Stone as this is a relatively small cemetery.

In the right rear of the cemetery, war presents one of its peculiarities. An air crew died on 28 August 1942 when their Lancaster bomber from 49 Squadron was shot down by a night fighter while returning from a mission to bomb Nürnberg. Five men of four different Commonwealth nationalities are buried side-by-side just as they had died.[64]

Buried in the adjacent grave is Polish Paratrooper Mieczysław Krzeczkowski, who died 24 September in Oosterbeek, aged 19. Krzeczkowski's body was originally misidentified as being that of 'T. Cjczyzno'. No such person was carried in Polish records. In 1988, a Polish officer recognized that the 'name' was Polish for 'For You My Country.' Krzeczkowski was eventually properly identified by his registration number and the marker changed.

Nine Polish soldiers killed near Alphen, Netherlands were originally buried in field graves. The bodies were exhumed and reburied at Mook. Upon our last visit, the grave of Dragoon Robert Szramowski, 10th Polish Dragoons aged 23 who was killed on 12 October 1944, was adorned with a single yellow rose.

Liberation Route Marker #4 stands outside the cemetery gate asking the question about the vanished grave, that is, the only soldier buried in Mook who is not in the Mook War Cemetery. Private Eric Holmes was first buried and forgotten in the Roman Catholic churchyard. Forty years later, his grave was located but his family decided to let him lie. (51.75381, 5.885912)

Continue 3.7 km toward Groesbeek where Groesbeekseweg becomes Mooksebaan; turn sharply left on Rijlaan and stop after 1.2 km near the Heumensebaan footpath. (51.774319, 5.911004)

The drive thru the forest along the Mooksebaan towards Groesbeek is truly lovely; large pine and hardwood trees line the road, bike paths on both sides, and walking paths going into the Groesbeekse Bos. The 82nd Airborne Division established its divisional command post within these woods on 17 September. The location is easily achieved along Rijklaan although nothing identifies the command post, or the location of the incident described below.

General Gavin and the men from his plane, mostly engineers, dropped onto DZ 'N' roughly 1.6 kilometers to the southeast. Almost immediately upon entering the forest, they heard rifle shots that warned of enemy troops nearby. Initially an engineer officer led the small party toward the preselected divisional command post at the intersection of a forest road and the highway near the now abandoned Groesbeek-Nijmegen rail line. Judging the officer's pace to be overcautious, Gavin and Captain Bestebreurtje, assumed the point positions, one on each side of the sunken road

---

64   Buried in a collective grave at Plot IV. Row C. Grave 10 are Sergeant Eric Albert Berrett, RAF aged 22; Sergeant Reginald Patrick Dobson, RAAF, aged 26; Flying Officer John Lowrie, NZAF, aged 21; Flight Sergeant Norman Rae Mitchell, RCAF aged 20; and Sergeant William Dudley Peirce, RAAF aged 20.

through the thick pine forest.

The group advanced at a fast pace for five or ten minutes until a machine gun fired over the seven- or eight-foot embankment directly over Gavin's head apparently aiming for Captain Bestebreurtje on the opposite side of the road. Gavin charged up the embankment to see an enemy soldier scrambling through the forest. Thinking better of shooting in the dense forest, the general slid back down to the roadway to see a single German soldier sprawled over his machine gun a mere 10 meters ahead—with a bullet hole in his forehead. Bestebreurtje, with his weapon at his hip, had fired one deadly shot at the white forehead visible between the soldier's helmet and machine gun. The two officers resumed their fast pace toward the CP.

The fact that the division commanding general, so driven to complete the very first element of his mission, would take the point position in a column of troops is truly remarkable. The event demonstrates General Gavin's aggressive attitude to getting the job done. During the next four days he would be seen at the hot spots across the wide defensive area assigned to his division as he personally assessed situations, reassigned unit objectives, and encouraged his men by example.

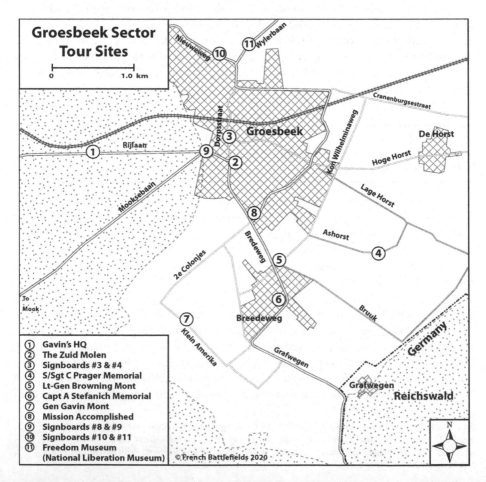

Born in Rotterdam, Captain Arie Bestebreurtje was well acquainted with the Nijmegen area. He was also well-known to the local Dutch underground having made a previous reconnaissance mission into the Netherlands. In fact, upon reaching the first house after the drop, he used the local telephone system to call underground representatives near Arnhem and received word that the British landings there had indeed taken place. Captain Bestebreurtje provided valuable assistance throughout Operation MARKET-GARDEN.[65]

> Reverse direction and return to Mooksebaan; turn left immediately upon exiting the forest into Groesbeek and park after 100 m opposite the small memorial on the right. (51.774225, 5.929516)

A metal sculpture presents **evacuating civilians** forced to leave their homes when Groesbeek became a battlefield. Standing figures show a father leading a child to supposed safety by her hand, a mother pushing a baby carriage which presumably contains their worldly possessions, and a grandfather faithfully pulling a laden hand cart. The inscription describes the suffering of civilians upon their return in the Spring of 1945 to find their property destroyed and the fields strewn with abandoned weapons of war that continued to kill and injure. The reconstruction took many years amid continued suffering and privations.

For the 70th anniversary of MARKET-GARDEN Groesbeek commemorated its central position in the battle for Nijmegen with a series of large outdoor historical photographs depicting places and events of 1944 at the actual site of their occurrence. The photographs are presented in pairs at various locations around the town. Two such signboards are on the opposite side of Mooksebaan short distances to the west.

At the intersection of Mooksebaan and Houtlaan an **unnumbered signboard** presents three photographs from 17 September 1944 showing Chaplain E van den Heuvel transporting wounded Lieutenant Colonel Wilbur Griffith commander of the 376th Parachute Artillery Battalion on his bicycle. The colonel had broken his foot during the landing. The other two photographs present a Mrs Kraft speaking with a German-American paratrooper while other residents of Mooksebaan watch; and an unidentified first sergeant speaking with a local teacher near the hamlet of Herwendaal. (51.774478, 5.929213)

Slightly farther west, **signboard #9** features two photographs of school headmaster Johan Tervoort. In the smaller photo, Tervoort is shown speaking to Captain Bestebreurtje. It was assumed that Bestebreurtje received information on the German garrison in Groesbeek. Teacher Cees van Beugen is shown pointing to the location of the local resistance leader Anton Melchers. Melchers informed Bestebreurtje that the telephone network remained functional. The second photograph shows a British tank

---

65   Tall and muscular, Captain Arie Bestebreurtje qualified for the 1936 Olympics in speed skating. Educated in law in Zurich, he escaped the Netherlands when the war broke out to eventually join the British Special Operations Executive (SOE) as an American officer. During the war, he was wounded twice, captured twice, and escaped twice. After the war, Bestebreurtje emigrated to the United States, became a Presbyterian minister and settled in Charlottesville, Virginia where he raised three children. Bestebreurtje died in 1983 at age 67 when he fell through ice while skating and drowned.

taking a short break in front of Tervoort's house on 19 September with local children on top. (51.774562, 5.928693)

Continue east on Mooksebaan to the traffic circle. Take the first exit and find parking around the large windmill. (51.773241, 5.933626)

Groesbeek was entered on 17 September by a detachment of the intelligence section of 3rd Battalion (Major James Kaiser), 505th PIR. Speaking German to the twenty-six second-rate garrison troops, Kaiser accepted their immediate surrender.

The Zuid Molen
Herwendaalseweg 1, 6562 AG Groesbeek
Tel: +31 (0)24 397 1283
Email: info@de-zuidmolen.nl
Web: https://www.de-zuidmolen.nl/
Open from 8:00 to 12:00 and 13:00 to 17:00, Monday thru Friday and Saturday 8:00 to 16:00. Free.

The windmill was built in 1857 and this high point for the surrounding area was a Dutch Underground locating beacon for escaping airmen and became the 505th PIR's observation post during MARKET-GARDEN. Later it served as the critical artillery observation post for the spring offensive of 1945 when the officers of General Henry Crerar's Canadian Army units climbed to the cupola to view the battlefield terrain.

The mill is now owned by the fourth generation of the original builder and features baked goods, a variety of flours, nuts, seeds, and seasonal food items.

Drop and Landing Zone 'N' is surrounded with monuments and memorials to commanders who landed here and those who defended the landing zone from attack. The area is difficult for tourists to approach from the west because of the narrow, frequently gravel roadways. A longer route to view the drop zone and memorials is more practical after leaving the Zuid Molen.
Leave Groesbeek east on Gooiseweg which passes in front of the windmill. After 600 m turn right onto Kloosterstraat and follow for 800 m. After passing directly through a traffic circle, turn right onto Kon Wilhelminaweg and after 850 m left onto Ashorst. Follow for 800 m to a short private drive. (51.763626, 5.958084)

A brass plaque affixed to private home reads, 'In memory of **Staff Sergeant Clarence Prager** Company I, 505th PIR.' At dusk on 17 September, Prager was leading the unit's 3rd Platoon with orders to establish a perimeter of four outposts near the edge of the Reichswald to protect LZ 'N'. As Prager and his men approached the forest, they encountered established German machine gun positions. Prager single-handedly attacked and destroyed two German positions then led his men to attack the third forcing the enemy to withdraw after a fierce firefight. When the platoon moved to establish its fourth and final outpost, they encountered a numerically superior German force that waved for them to surrender. Prager's unit was soon surrounded, and he ordered the small detachment to withdraw to the remainder of the platoon while he held off the enemy with his Thompson submachine gun. No sooner had the men started to move back when Prager was struck and killed.[66]

This memorial is on private property and cannot be visited at all times.

Return to Kon Wilhelminaweg and turn left. Stop after 400 m at the memorial on the right in the outskirts of Breedeweg (51.763247, 5.942528)

A segment of brick wall bears a **polished granite plaque** headed by the British Airborne Pegasus emblem identifying the landing of Horsa gliders in these fields on 17 September which carried Lieutenant-General Frederick Browning and his I Airborne Corps field headquarters. The plaque refers to the Horsa gliders used to transport the headquarters as 'their winged horses.'

Continue into Breedeweg and turn left at the next intersection. After 350 m enter Kerkplein on the right and follow to Sint Antonius Church. (51.758573, 5.942312)

On 18 September, the Division's Second Lift arrived while segments of LZ 'N' were still occupied by German troops. One flak-riddled glider overshot the landing zone and landed in Grafwegen particularly close to German lines almost on the fringe of the Reichswald. Captain Anthony Stefanich, commander of Company C, 505th PIR, courageously led a flanking attack to retrieve the occupants of the glider. The enemy scattered with one group hiding in a building 200 meters away. After personally running across 50 meters of open terrain to rescue the glider pilot, Stefanich again exposed himself to small-arms fire from the building to save other men in the glider. During the effort he was mortally wounded. As he lay dying, he told his lieutenant, 'We've come a long way. Tell the boys to do a good job.'[67]

Three stones imbedded into the side wall of Sint Antonius church commemorate the actions of **Captain Stefanich** noting his name, his death, and the battlefields of Europe on which his division fought—Sicily, Italy, Normandy, Netherlands, Belgium, and Germany. The brick fence posts also bear stone plaques listing the names of eleven MIA-KIA from the September to October battles around Plasmolen.[68]

66　Sergeant Clarence Prager, aged 31, was awarded Distinguished Service Cross and is buried in Morgantown, West Virginia.

67　Captain Anthony Stefanich, aged 27, was born in Bradley, Illinois. He enlisted as a private in the Illinois National Guard, rose to officer rank, and volunteered for parachute training. Captain Stefanich served in Africa, Sicily, Italy, France and Netherlands and became the 82nd's Divisional boxing champion. He had received a Bronze Star and two Purple Hearts for directing effective counterfire while twice wounded on 6 June 1944. His actions on LZ 'N' earned him a posthumous Silver Star. Captain Stefanich is buried in Bourbonnais, Illinois.

68　The listed names are: Pfc Guy E Belcher from Alabama died of his wounds on 6 October 1944; medic Private Alpheus E Fowlkes Jr, aged 24 and recipient of a Silver Star also from Alabama, died 2 October 1944; Pfc Kenneth H Lau, aged 23 from Minnesota, died of wounds on 6 October 1944; Private Sonnie J Rockford, aged 21 from Missouri; Captain Anthony M Stefanich; Corporal Roger F Coffin, aged 21 from Herreid, South Dakota; Pfc Stanley Creswick, aged 21 from New Jersey. Corporal Russel O Meade, aged 26 from Anne Arundel County, Maryland, and Private Raymond J Dionne, aged 21 from Strafford County, New Hampshire are Bronze Star recipients; Private Walter Faranfontoff, aged 20, is buried in Los Angeles; and Private JD Shelton, aged 20 from Cocke County, Tennessee, is buried in Baltimore, Tennessee. All of the men except Stefanich, Faranfontoff, and

> Leave the church by continuing south on Breedeweg, which curves to the southwest and becomes Sint Antoniusweg. After 650 m enter a double intersection and exit southwest on Klein Amerika. Follow Klein Amerika for 1.2 km to the memorial sited among roadside trees on the right. (51.756611, 5.924510)

Klein Amerika draws its name from efforts in the 1930s to duplicate the large scale farming methods then prevalent in America's Midwest in the Netherlands.

A brick memorial stands upon the highest point of DZ 'N' across the road from a farm. The brick wall carries two granite plaques; one dedicated to **Brigadier General James Gavin** and the **All-American Division** who landed in these fields and the second to the **First Canadian Army** which guarded the area during the brutal winter of 1944-1945. Both plaques are inscribed with weapons of war: the airborne plaque with a C-47 transport aircraft and the Canadian with jeep, half-track, and Ford truck

> Continue 300 m on Klein Amerika to the curve in the road. (51.758398, 5.920911)

Liberation Route Marker #9 identifies the landing zone where American paratroopers appeared as 'Liberators like Stars from the Sky'. The audio presents a Dutch minister praying for landing paratroopers, giving comfort to dying German soldiers, and the German soldiers reactions to the Groesbeek landings.

> Follow Klein Amerika for another 300 m to the main farm complex and park in the parking area on the left. The final 170 meters to the Waco model are over a rutted dirt road and it can be approached if desired, but views across the field are possible. (51.761758, 5.921645)

On 17 September 2014 a full-size rebuilt **Waco CG4** glider without its outer fabric covering was unveiled to commemorate the 70th Anniversary of the Airborne landings. Visible from the parking area for Klein Amerika, the tubular construction displays the small size of the Waco design.

> Continue on Klein Amerika which becomes 2e Colonjes for 1.3 km straight through the traffic circle to the monument on the right. (51.767555, 5.937922)

A natural stone in the shape of a star forms the platform upon which a two-section brick wall rests. The wall bears two granite plaques in English and Dutch bearing the insignia of the airborne forces and the words: '**Mission Accomplished**.' An additional table monument expresses the 'feelings of gratitude and respect of the people of Groesbeek towards the 82nd Airborne Division under command of General James Gavin who liberated Groesbeek on the 17th of September from terror and oppression.'

Shelton are buried or commemorated in Netherlands American Cemetery, Margraten, Netherlands.

Reverse direction and return to the traffic circle. Take the 1st exit (Bredeweg) and follow for 1.2 km into central Groesbeek observing that the road changes name several times. Park on Kloosterstraat near Dorpsstraat.

Two more 1944 images are on opposing sides of the old rectory at the corner of Dorpsstraat and Kloosterstraat in central Groesbeek. **Signboard #4** pictures a British Sherman tank as it drives past the rectory of HH Cosmas and Damian Church on its way to support American efforts at Wyler on 20 September 1944. While holding a roadblock west of Wyler, the paratroopers of 1st Battalion, 508th PIR requested fire support. The tank took a position behind the roadblock and fired upon German attackers in Wyler bringing their advance to a halt. (51.776313, 5.932707)

Around the corner **signboard #3** presents civilians observing the first American Paratroopers entering the center of Groesbeek on 17 September 1944. A member of 3rd Battalion, 505th PIR crosses Dorpsstraat heading toward positions to the east. (51.776293, 5.932669)

Continue north on Dorpsstraat which becomes Molenweg and follow for 1.1 km. Enter the traffic circle and park near the Total gas station on Nieuweweg.

Directly east of the gas station **signboard #11** shows Colonel William Ekman, commander of 505th PIR, conferring with Executive Officer Lieutenant Colonel Edward Krause along Nieuweweg. A second view from down the roadway observes the same scene. (51.784634, 5.931829)

West of the gas station **signboard #10** presents three photographs depicting the 508th PIR moving via Nieuweweg which becomes Njimeegsebaan toward Heilig Landstichting while being watched by curious civilians. The images include a 1944 aerial photograph of the location. (51.784811, 5.930968)

Reverse direction and turn left on Wylerbaan and continue 240 m to the museum on the right. (51.785674, 5.936452)

Freedom Museum (formerly known as National Liberation Museum 1944-1945)
Wylerbaan 4, 6561 KR Groesbeek
Tel: +31 (0)24 397 4404
Web: https://www.bevrijdingsmuseum.nl/
Open daily Monday to Saturday from 10:00 to 17:00; Sundays and public holidays 12:00 to 17:00. Handicap accessible, admission fee.

The museum recently completed a substantial expansion. The new building has the form of a 'shaded dome' which evokes association with the parachutes of the airborne liberators. The museum's name changed as did its focus to 'The Story of War and Freedom without Borders.'

New displays relate the Second World War history of this border region to postwar developments and current European Union events considering issues of freedom, international cooperation, and human rights from a European perspective.

The museum grounds display Sherman tank 'Robin Hood' donated appropriately by the Nottinghamshire Sherwood Rangers Yeomanry which suffered 268 fatalities in local fighting. The unit supported 508th PIR until the end of September. It also participated in Operation VERITABLE in the Reichswald. Nearby stands a German 75-mm PaK 40 antitank gun that was captured by the 53rd (Welsh) Division in February 1945. Text painted upon the latter's shield states, 'This piece caused death and destruction in Nijmegen from September 1944 to February 1945' when the gun frequently shelled Groesbeek. Text on the other side of the gun, 'Silenced on 8 February 1945 by Sergeant Mick Savage, Corporal LS Maso, and Corporal A Britton RCA.' (Royal Canadian Artillery)

Continue northeast on Wylerbaan for 1.4 km to the memorial on the left near the intersection with Derdebaan. (51.795181, 5.950050)

On 18 September, 1st Battalion, 508th PIR was called upon to respond to the attack upon the Groesbeek perimeter by Korps Feldt. After an eight-kilometer march back from Nijmegen, Lieutenant Colonel Warren's three companies attacked from the wood line west of Wylerbaan overlooking LZ 'T'. Despite 20-mm shells fired into the woods, the paratroopers charged downhill almost at a run. As they approached a farm complex, the enemy added machine-gun and small-arms fire to the antiaircraft guns. Companies B and C took shelter in a slightly sunken farm track looking for any protection from the massive volume of fire directed at them. Small groups of men from both companies jumped up and rapidly moved forward, firing as they advanced. Company C First Sergeant Leonard Funk led a three-man patrol that took on three 20-mm guns firing at the gliders that were now beginning to land. They eliminated the infantry protecting the gunners, then, well ahead of the group, Funk singled-handedly killed or wounded approximately twenty crew members.[69]

It soon became apparent that these diverse troops in uncoordinated units were no match for the battle-hardened American paratroopers. Machine guns and bombs from the protective air umbrella cleared the fields and broke the back of the German attack. The landing zone was cleared minutes before the 454 gliders of the division's Second Lift approached at 14:00. Sixteen 20-mm antiaircraft guns were destroyed. German casualties amounted to 50 killed and 149 taken prisoner. The paratroopers sustained fifteen casualties.

Tuesday, 19 September was relatively quiet along the Groesbeek Heights as German commanders gathered their forces. On the morning of 20 September, the batteries of KGr Greschick zeroed in on a platoon of Company D, 508th PIR sited among the farms to the west. The following assault drove the paratroopers back, almost to the edges of Groesbeek where it was halted by small-arms fire.

On 24 September, the 3rd Battalion, 504th PIR relieved 2nd Battalion, 508th PIR in the sector with Company H near Groesbeek and Companies G and I in the Den

---

69   First Sergeant Leonard Funk was awarded the Distinguished Service Cross for his actions that day. Funk, from Wilkinsburg, Pennsylvania later received the Medal of Honor in January 1945 for recapturing a force of eighty German soldiers who had escaped their guards near Holzheim, Belgium. He died in 1992, aged 76, and is buried in Arlington National Cemetery, Arlington, Virginia, Section 35, Grave 2373-4.

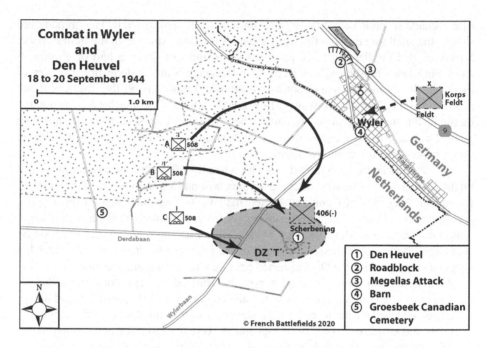

Combat in Wyler
and
Den Heuvel
18 to 20 September 1944

0   1.0 km

① Den Heuvel
② Roadblock
③ Megellas Attack
④ Barn
⑤ Groesbeek Canadian Cemetery

© French Battlefields 2020

Heuvel Woods. Ownership of the woods around the farm changed hands with each attack and counterattack. At 11:45 on 26 September, Company G, 504th PIR with a platoon from Company I and four British tanks assaulted the woods eliminating approximately one hundred enemy troops. The expected German counterattack occurred at 14:00 by a battalion of infantry. The fighting resumed, but with the assistance of the 376th PFAB, Company G prevailed and held the sector.

A parachute supply cannister forms the **508th PIR Monument** and identifies **DZ 'T'**. This double monument also commemorates the starting point of Operation VERITABLE, in which over 300,000 British and Canadians soldiers moved toward Wesel, Germany and the Rhine River in February 1945.

The tree-lined side road on the right north of the 508th monument goes to the **Den Heuvel** apple orchard and campground which was the central focus of the area combat.

Continue into Wyler crossing the German border in the process and turn right after 1.7 km then almost immediately left on Hauptstrasse. After 350 m turn right on Krummestrasse and stop at the John the Baptist Church on the left. Park across the street from the church. (51.808148, 5.966657)

On 19 September, a patrol into Wyler led by Lieutenant Edward Gleim from Company B, 508th PIR found the German village abandoned. Corporal Edward Boccafogli established a roadblock backed by a 57-mm antitank gun on the eastern edge of Wyler along Hauptstrasse. After a quiet night, a truck carrying German soldiers approached the roadblock around dawn on 20 September. Boccafogli fired a rifle grenade seconds before the 57-mm antitank gun fired its shell. The grenade fell short—the shell tore through the truck's canvas top and exploded in the field beyond. Survivors fled the flaming truck and escaped to the east under a hail of gunfire. A short time later, fallschirmjäger from KGr Becker advanced along the shoulder of the road; then a machine-gun company established positions on the southern flank. A short artillery barrage from the 319th GFAB silenced the machine guns for the moment, but the engagement escalated when SP guns arrived to back the machine guns. Company B, now outnumbered and outgunned, fell back through the village under severe pressure from the German assault.

American troops returned to Wyler when the 504th PIR established positions on the high ground to the west after the fighting around Den Heuvel. On 30 September, Lieutenant Megellas of Company H, led his twenty-four-man platoon on a patrol across the Wylermeer to capture prisoners for interrogation about a suspected large-scale German attack. Megellas went ahead of the platoon to survey the situation by crossing a footbridge at the southern end of the lake. For his heroism and leadership Megellas was awarded the Distinguished Service Cross. To quote the award:

> Arriving at the enemy observation post, he crawled forward alone and killed two outpost guards and the crew of a machine gun nest. He brought forward his patrol, attacked the main enemy defenses and single-handed secured three prisoners and killed two more. Two blockhouses were then attacked and destroyed. The aggressiveness of this patrol action thoroughly demoralized the enemy in the sector. His mission completed, First Lieutenant Megellas withdrew his platoon through the enemy's lines and under mortar fire. He personally carried a wounded man while firing his Thompson submachine gun with one hand.[70]

Proceed on foot to the cemetery area behind the church. (51.808530, 5.967258)

Although no memorial exists to commemorate the Wyler battles, the importance of the Wyler position is obvious from the **church cemetery's vantage point**. The terrain flattens to the east and views miles into Germany are possible from the higher elevations in the village. The differing bricks in the church bell tower show the postwar reconstruction to repair the obviously damaged high observation post.

The Wylermeer is east on the opposite side of Highway 9 and runs along the highway for miles to the northeast forming much of the Dutch – German border in this area. The footbridge crossing used by Megellas has been replaced with a road bridge which is visible from the church grounds. The German observation post attacked by Megellas was farther east along Häfnerdeich, making the engagement one of the first in this sector to have been fought inside Germany.

Reverse course and return to Wylerbaan and at the edge of Wyler stop after the sweeping curve at the side road on the left (Lagewald). (51.803890, 5.965970)

---

70   The wounded man was Sergeant John M Fowler III, who had been shot in the stomach with the bullet lodging near his spine. Fowler spent three months in English hospitals before being reassigned to another unit just before the Battle of the Bulge. Sergeant Fowler was awarded the Silver Star for his efforts during the Waal River crossing. He died in 1975.

After a morning of house-to-house fighting, Company B, including Corporal Boccafogli and his squad, were pushed back near a barn on the Dutch side of the village. Private Hebert Ellerbusch crawled up to a stone wall and subtly opened a gate with his bazooka. Ellerbusch fired setting the barn aflame but was mortally wounded in the effort. Seven German soldiers surrendered; others escaped back to Wyler deflating the attack.[71]

Company B suffered increasing casualties because its proximity to attacking enemy troops brought friendly fire upon the unit from British tanks up the hill to their rear in addition to harassing fire from the enemy. Captain Millsaps directed Company B back up the hill that evening with German PoWs carrying the wounded on doors, ladders, or anything that they could find. A haystack set afire by tracer rounds illuminated the withdrawal and German troops inflicted further casualties.

Liberation Route Marker #36 stands at the intersection and describes the beginning of 'Operation VERITABLE' in February 1945. Without possession of bridges over the Rhine River, the only access to Germany was through the countryside between the Maas and Rhine. Operation VERITABLE was the largest British / Canadian operation since Normandy and entailed half a million soldiers and 34,000 vehicles along a 10-kilometer front. An untimely warm spell softened the ground and days of rain turned soil into soupy mush. The audio presents British conversations with General Horrocks describing the difficult terrain and weather.

The barn at the sharp turn in Wylerbaan 100 meters to the east, where Boccafogli's men made their stand, remains identified by the solar cells which cover its roof. (51.804720, 5.966525)

Continue southwest on Wylerbaan for 1.5 km, then west on Derdebaan for 1.4 km. Turn north on Zevenheuvelenweg to the cemetery entrance. (51.797735, 5.930755)

Groesbeek Canadian War Cemetery and Memorial
Zevenheuvelenweg 38, 6561 Groesbeek
Web: https://www.cwgc.org/find-a-cemetery/cemetery/2063900/groesbeek%20canadian%20war%20cemetery

Construction began in August 1945 and by the next spring the first burials occurred. All but eleven of the 2,610 burials in the cemetery are Commonwealth troops of whom 2,331 are Canadian. Most died in the Battle of the Rhineland when the 2nd and 3rd Canadian Infantry Divisions and the 4th Canadian Armored Division took part in the drive to clear the territory between Nijmegen and the Rhine in March 1945. General HDG Crerar, who commanded Canadian land forces in Europe, ordered that Canadian dead were not to be permanently buried in German soil. They were instead reburied in Groesbeek.

Each of the Canadian tombstones is inscribed with the Maple Leaf above the name and many bear touching epitaphs such as: 'Private, aged 22, Some day we will understand.' The trees within the cemetery are all Canadian maples in keeping with

---

71   Private Herbert W Ellenbusch, aged 21 from Minnesota, is one of five soldiers who went missing that day and whose remains have never been recovered. He is commemorated on the Wall of the Missing in Netherlands American Cemetery, Margraten, Netherlands.

their tradition.

Within the cemetery stands the **Groesbeek Memorial** formed by two L-shaped porticos which record the names of more than 1,600 men who died during the campaign from 30 August 1944 to 5 May 1945 and whose graves are not known. The frieze bears the carved Latin inscription 'We live in the hearts of friends for whom we died.' Galleries record the names of the major rivers that the Canadians crossed during their advance toward Berlin — the Seine, Schelde, Maas, Rhine, and Elbe.

The cemetery is sited on high ground and presents views over the 82nd Airborne drop and landing zones. The Reichswald Forest can be seen five kilometers distant to the southeast.

Continue north on Zevenheuvelenweg for 2.5 km. Upon entering Berg en Dal, stop at the park on the left. (51.817960, 5.922460)

Berg en Dal was peacefully liberated on 17 September by a platoon from Company H. The next day the quiet was broken by sporadic artillery fire when the town was counterattacked by remnants of FJ Artillery Regimenter 2 and 4 fielding only seven howitzers and a naval cadet company. The German force was easily defeated by the paratroopers.

Events heated up on 19 September when paratroopers of 3rd Battalion 508th swept into the outskirts of Beek, 1.5 kilometers downhill from Berg en Dal to forestall a potential German attack against Nijmegen along the highway from Kleve, Germany. Despite a battalion of German infantry supported by dug-in tanks and 88-mm guns, the town was cleared by noon with the help of the 82nd's divisional artillery.

The **stone obelisk** in the small park represents the town's liberation memorial and commemorates twenty-eight civilian deaths of those killed during the war.

Continue to the next intersection and turn right, take the second exit from the traffic circle and proceed 1.1 km. Turn left onto an unnamed access road. The access road becomes a one-way, dirt track loop for the last 900 m. Park across from the De Duivelsberg - Pannenkoeken Restaurant. (51.819388, 5.943475)
From the east end of the parking area, take the path northwest through a short section of forest to the knoll. (51.820602, 5.943606)

On 19 September, to cut the approach toward Beek from Wyler, Lieutenant William Call led a patrol from 508th PIR's Company G to secure the wooded height of Hill 75.9 (Duivelsberg[72]) which dominated highway N325 between Wyler and Beek. The long, narrow ridgeline offered excellent observation and artillery positions overlooking the surrounding countryside.

Devil's Hill was defended by a detachment of German fallschirmjäger. A local teenager led Lieutenant Call to a knoll that overlooked the enemy on lower ground to the east. Deciding that the German force was too large to overcome, Call ordered one

---

72   In 1944 Duivelsberg was in Germany. A postwar border alteration put it 300 meters inside Netherlands.

quick volley into the relaxing fallschirmjäger before executing a rapid withdrawal. The task of taking the position was reassigned to the two remaining platoons of Company A led by Lieutenant John Foley in the absence of Captain Adams who was still trapped in central Nijmegen. Company G attached a platoon led by Lieutenant Kenneth Covey. The combined force totaled seventy-six men.

Foley established a skirmish line north of the summit. A screaming, 200-meter charge closed upon the rear of the main enemy body sited upon a small knoll at the edge of the forest and facing the opposite direction. The Germans turned their eight light machine guns on the paratroopers. Foley's men overcame each foxhole on succession until the diminished fallschirmjäger force broke and ran down the hillside to the east. The two lieutenants moved downhill to check German foxholes on the downward slope when a sniper in a farmhouse at the base of the hill fired killing Lieutenant Covey.[73]

Attempts at infiltrating the American line continued through the night, frequently defeated by the warnings given by the rustling of dry leaves. Fighting in heavily wooded terrain is always dangerous. Sight lines are hampered by the trees, enemy and friendly positions are difficult to identify, disorientation among the undergrowth is common. The confused fighting saw small groups advancing only to be surrounded. Brief firefights eliminated enemy positions or patrols only for the enemy to do the same. These were trained fallschirmjägers after all, not rear echelon troops or hospital cases thrown into battle.

The next day, that is 20 September, fallschirmjägers from KGr Becker supported by five SP guns fell upon the three platoons. German artillery and mortar fire subsided just before dawn, when the fallschirmjäger began a frantic assault up the hillside. The charge reached within three meters of the paratroopers' line of five light machine guns sited on the crest of the hill before being thrown back. German troops ceased fire while an officer slowly approached the paratroopers' strongpoint. He explained to Lieutenant Foley that his men were surrounded and continued resistance would be hopeless. He suggested that Foley surrender his men and enter German captivity. Foley replied, 'If you want me, come and get me!' The fighting continued for an hour before the Germans were thrown back. Relief in the form of the 325th GIR arrived before sunrise on 24 September. Foley and his men had repulsed four company-sized attacks.

An appreciation of the difficult combat conditions around **Duivelsberg** can be had by hiking the 280 meters to the observation area upon the hill summit. Deep cut ravines wind through the forested hillsides. The rounded hilltop, first fortified in 1012, is reached by a steep, wooden staircase. The more important German observation post was ahead to the east and slightly lower in elevation at the edge of the forest. The commanding view over the Wylermeer and onto the flatland to the east — all the way into Germany — attests to the tactical importance of the high ground.

Reverse course to Oude Kleefsebaan. Follow for 1.3 km through Berg en Dal to a

---

73   Lieutenant Kenneth A Covey, aged 24 from Cook County, Illinois, is buried in a Lincoln, Nebraska cemetery. The gravestone incorrectly lists the date of death as 26 September 1944.

right turn onto Nieuwe Holleweg. After 300 m, turn right on Van Randwijckweg and follow for 900 m into Beek. Turn left onto Rijksstraatweg and after 400 m turn north on Verbindingsweg. Stop at the park immediately on the right. (51.829997, 5.922246)

Korps Feldt's attack of 20 September also hit the paratroopers in front of Beek where a 500-man battalion of reserve reconnaissance troops of KGr von Fürstenberg fell upon two platoons of Company I, 508th PIR. Half-tracks mounting 20-mm antiaircraft guns poured fire into buildings while infantry threw stick grenades through the windows. Buildings were cleared room by room and strongpoints were assaulted and overrun in deadly combat. Grossly outnumbered, the paratroopers resisted as their officers fell to enemy fire. Eventually command of the two platoons devolved to Corporal Robert Chisholm. When the Germans brought a fifteen-minute saturation artillery bombardment followed by a massive attack, Corporal Chisholm realized his position was about to be overrun and organized an orderly withdrawal up the wooded hill to the Hotel Erica in Berg en Dal. A destroyed half-track on a sharp S-bend blocked the uphill road into Berg en Dal impeding the enemy's armored advance. Von Fürstenberg ended the attack at nightfall.[74]

Later, around 19:00, Company H (Lieutenant Louis Toth) executed a spoiling attack from the south. Savage street fighting continued well into the night. Each attack generated a counterattack in attrition warfare as both sides committed more units while the paratroopers forced the enemy back down the hill. Entering the town at dawn on 21 September, Toth's troops supported by Companies F and G secured Beek by 18:00 after an all-day battle.

The park is dedicated to **Lieutenant John Foley**, Company A, 508th PIR, 82nd Airborne Division, the company commander who took Duivelsberg and held it against repeated enemy assaults. A combination of a brick platform inscribed with an American star supporting several brick columns linked with stone plaques celebrates the liberation of the town from occupation on 17 September 1944. A particularly daring element depicts a 508th PIR parachute-borne 'devil in baggy pants,' as the Germans referred to the paratroopers, parachuting into battle with rifle in one hand and a hand grenade in the other. To the right a brick-framed polished granite stone lists the forty-three members of the communities of Beek and Ubbergen who perished during the war.

Liberation Route Marker #12 at the east end of the small roadside park tells of 'The Diary of Rose Jakobs', a young Jewish twin who fled Germany with her family of six. Rose hid with an aunt and uncle, first in a cramped attic in Nijmegen then in Beek where she reunited with her parents. Her short life ended on 2 October 1944 when a German fragmentation bomb dropped upon a group of American soldiers also killed Rose. Three school notebooks recorded her thoughts and experiences from August 1942 to September 1944 and were published as '*The Rose that Never Bloomed.*'

---

74   Robert Chisholm parachuted into Normandy on D-Day, led his company in Beek, and was wounded from a tree burst during the Battle of the Bulge. His extensive wounds brought him back to the United States for treatment. Chisholm re-enlisted after the war and remained in the Army for thirty years rising to the rank of lieutenant colonel. He now lives in Anthony, New Mexico at the age of 94.

Reverse direction and proceed southeast on Rijksstraatweg. After 350 m turn right onto Nieuwe Holleweg and carefully follow it around the church where it curves left to become Oude Holleweg and follow up the hill 1.0 km. Turn right onto Oude Kleefsebaan and immediately left onto Molenbosweg and follow for 450 m to the Fletcher Hotel-Restaurant Erica entrance on the left. (51.821925, 5.908570)

The airborne platoons led by Corporal Chisholm exited Beek through the forest and approached the **Hotel Erica** along the route just driven to take shelter in the surrounding woods.

Liberation Route Marker #45 stands beside the entrance driveway. The 'Hotel Erica' audio relates the wartime memories of Ms Julia van Vliet, who, at age seven, hid with other civilians in the hotel cellar while the battle raged outside.

Side Trip: Jonkerbos War Cemetery

The cemetery is located in southwestern Nijmegen. (51.822461, 5.830707)

Jonkerbos War Cemetery
Burgemeester Daleslaan 35, 6532 Nijmegen
Web: https://www.cwgc.org/find-a-cemetery/cemetery/2062100/jonkerbos-war-cemetery/

The American 504th PIR assembled in preparation for the crossing of the Waal River in a small wood in the southwestern district of Nijmegen known as Jonkers Bosch. The grounds now hold the Jonkerbos War Cemetery, containing 1,629 Commonwealth burials from the Second World War, of which 99 remain unidentified. Also included within its walls are fourteen war graves of other nationalities, including five Belgian, one Dutch, seven Polish, and one Russian. The graves are oriented in a sweeping arc centered not upon the Cross of Sacrifice, which is at the far end of a central avenue, but upon the Stone of Remembrance.

Jonkerbos was created in 1946/7 when the initial 400 burials came from temporary cemeteries near hospitals in Nijmegen. Later, airmen downed in the air war over Germany were transferred from Venlo and Oosterhout. Finally, Jonkerbos received transfers from cemeteries on the Frisian Islands. These included Royal Navy sailors, Polish airmen, and victims from the Dunkerque evacuation who washed ashore. Isolated burials continued as battlefield graves were discovered during reconstruction activities.

Five of seven men who died in the crash of an Avro Lancaster on 17 December 1942 are buried in the right rear of the cemetery. The brand-new plane was lost during a bombing of oil refineries in Nienburg, Germany. The bodies were discovered in 1951 during road construction. The aircraft was part of 44 (Rhodesia) Squadron, which suffered the third highest casualties in RAF Bomber Command with 214 planes lost. The Rhodesia name celebrates the 25% of field and air crew who were from Southern Rhodesia. The unit's First World War commander was later Air Chief Marshal Arthur 'Bomber' Harris.

In a special ceremony held on Christmas Eve, each grave is illuminated by a votive candle.

Chapter Five
British 43rd (Wessex) Infantry Division 'Yellow Devils'

The 43rd (Wessex) Infantry Division was first formed in 1908 as the Wessex Division in the voluntary Territorial Force. The division never fought as a unified command during the First World War. Instead battalions were dispatched first to India then later to the Middle East. As part of the Territorial Army, the division was mobilized in 1939 and remained on defensive status in England for the next four years. The division landed in Normandy as a follow-up formation on 24 June 1944 as part of XII Corps and engaged in heavy fighting in the Odon River area. As part of XXX Corps, the division made slow progress following the Guards Armoured Division up the Corridor arriving in Nijmegen on 21 September.

The Betuwe, or 'The Island' as the floodplain between the Waal and Rhine rivers was known, consists of reclaimed, marshy polder crisscrossed with drainage ditches and water routes. The nearly straight, elevated dike road across the Betuwe from Nijmegen to Arnhem could not have been more unsuitable for tanks. The roadway had steep banks with ditches on both sides. The terrain negated the potential for British armor to maneuver, constricting it to the raised dike roads that were fully exposed to enemy artillery and antitank guns. In this exposed and difficult to traverse terrain, elevated, solid ground of any sort became routes of advance or retreat or areas of defense.

After the Allies had captured the bridges over the Waal River, they sought to continue their advance towards Arnhem. However, unknown to British tankers that had crossed the Nijmegen bridge, the path to Arnhem on the night of 20/21 September held only a few enemy outposts. For whatever the explanation, they stopped and spent the night in Lent. Afterward any forward movement was bitterly contested by German forces and it soon became clear that the goals of MARKET-GARDEN would not be achieved.

The ever more energetic Germans, with the Arnhem bridge now open to traffic after 21 September, sent KGr Knaust reinforced with ten Tiger I tanks from schwere (Heavy) Panzer Kompanie 'Hummel' and assault guns to Elst. Lieutenant Colonel Harzer swiftly moved to establish a new *Sperrverband* or blocking line along the Nijmegen-Arnhem railway embankment less than 3 kilometers east of Driel. By the next morning KGr Reinhold established positions one kilometer north of Lent and one kilometer southwest of Ressen. That afternoon, KGr Knaust arrived at Elst from Arnhem. Although composed of miscellaneous battalions – 'Schörken' (Wehrmacht), Machine Gun Battalion 47, 'Kauer' (Luftwaffe), 'Köhnen' (Marine), and 'Stocker' (Dutch SS) – the 2,400-man line was strengthened by detachments of artillery and flak regiments which provided 105-mm howitzers and 88-mm and 20-mm antiaircraft guns. The opportunity for an easy armor passage to Arnhem was lost. The Betuwe, became the new front line. Fighting continued with heavy shelling from both sides. The civilian population was caught in the middle and soon the decision was made to evacuate the area.

Battle
21 September

　　Irish Guards, led by Captain Roland Langton's No 1 Squadron, left the Nijmegen bridgehead at 11:00 for Arnhem. The movement was almost spontaneous. Colonel Joe Vandeleur possessed only a captured road map and one reconnaissance photo of enemy antiaircraft gun positions south of Elst with which to brief Captain Langton who was given only 20 minutes to plan the advance and brief his troop

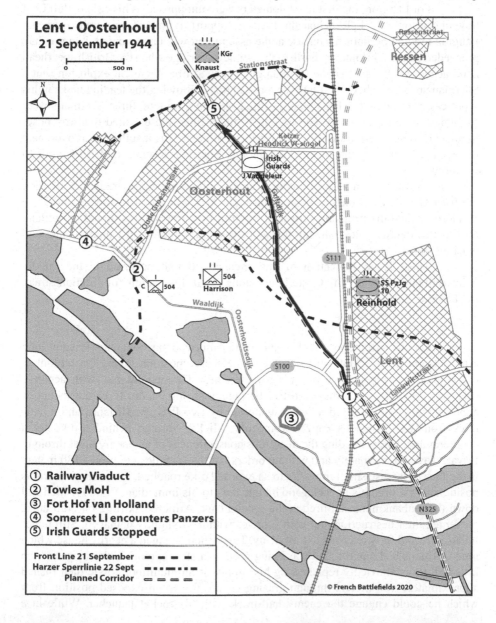

Lent - Oosterhout
21 September 1944

0   500 m

N

KGr Knaust

Stationsstraat

Ressen

Ressenstraat

Keizer Hendrick VI-singel

Irish Guards
J Vandeleur

Oosterhout

Oude Groenestraat

Griftdijk

S111

SS PzJg 10
Reinhold

4

2

1 504 Harrison

C 504

Waaldijk

Oosterhoutsedijk

S100

Lent

Laauwikstraat

3

Railway Viaduct

N325

① **Railway Viaduct**
② **Towles MoH**
③ **Fort Hof van Holland**
④ **Somerset LI encounters Panzers**
⑤ **Irish Guards Stopped**

Front Line 21 September
Harzer Sperrlinie 22 Sept
Planned Corridor

© French Battlefields 2020

commanders. Langton was to be followed by a second squadron. A reconnaissance of the German position led Lieutenant-Colonel Giles Vandeleur to conclude that '...it's a ridiculous place to try to operate tanks.' Brigadier Gwatkin told them, 'Simply get through.'

KGr Knaust had arrived in Elst during the afternoon of 21 September and a force of two 88-mm guns, seven French-made 75-mm flak guns, one Tiger I tank, and 300 infantrymen held an intersection on Griftdijk north of Oosterhout.

For Langton, the first few kilometers were unopposed as his column left Lent traveling at only 12 kph. When the first air support Typhoons appeared overhead, Langton thought perhaps his unease at the assignment was unwarranted. Langton had proceeded only 4.3 kilometers north of the Nijmegen bridge when the British spearhead approached the crossroads and German guns opened fire. A violent explosion sent a Sherman sprocket wheel high into the air. Langton, following the leading tanks in his scout car, then knew his fears were justified. Within a minute, three Shermans were in flames blocking the road. The trailing vehicles lined the elevated roadway nose-to-tail. The tanks were trapped on the road; the infantry was insufficient to overcome the enemy. Knaust's guns knocked out another Sherman forcing the Irish Guards to withdraw.

Unable to maneuver off highway and with their air support radio out of order, the Irish Guards were unable to break through. At 15:30, No 4 Company and No 3 Squadron exited the protective cover of the fruit orchards and attempted to outflank the blocked roadway along the rail line to the east, but fell afoul of Knaust's tanks and machine guns.

There is no indication of this engagement that occurred in the rapidly industrializing district of Oosterhout along Griftdijk south of Stationsstraat. (51.884856, 5.843118)

On the afternoon of 21 September, American bazookaman Private John Towle, Company C, 504th PIR occupied a defensive position facing Oosterhout in the Nijmegen bridgehead where his battalion kept Germans at bay with accurate rifle fire. Following a German artillery barrage, a strong enemy force consisting of approximately one hundred infantry supported by two PzKpfw III tanks and a half-track from KGr Knaust's Panzer Kompanie 'Mielke' formed behind a dike for a counterattack. Understanding the disastrous consequences of an enemy breakthrough, Private Towle immediately and without orders left his foxhole and moved 180 meters in the face of intense small-arms fire to an exposed dike roadbed. From this precarious position Towle fired his bazooka and hit one tank to his immediate front. He then slid down the embankment and fired at the second tank. Armored skirting on both tanks prevented their destruction, but both vehicles withdrew slightly damaged. Still under intense fire and fully exposed to the enemy, Towle then engaged a nearby house which nine Germans had entered and was being used as a strongpoint. With one round, he killed all nine. Hurriedly replenishing his supply of ammunition, Towle then rushed approximately 100 meters through grazing enemy fire to an exposed position from which he could engage the enemy half-track with his rocket launcher. While in a kneeling position preparatory to firing on the enemy vehicle, Towle was mortally wounded by mortar fragments.[1]

The German forces regrouped to resume the assault while Company C's commander requested help from British tanks. At around 17:00, after sitting trapped on the Nijmegen bridge for the past four hours by the column of stationary Irish Guards vehicles, Cromwell tanks of the 2nd Welsh Guards with infantry from 1st Welsh Guards passed around Oosterhout and took on the Germans with their 17-pounder guns. They knocked out three PzKpfw III and machine gunned the infantry.

Unfortunately, no remembrance identifies the location of Towle's heroism west of the Waal Crossing on Waaldijk road. (51.873655, 5.832486)

22 September

In the early morning fog two reconnaissance troops of C Squadron, 2nd Household Cavalry left the Nijmegen area in Daimler Dingo scout cars moving west for approximately 10 kilometers then north directly toward Driel using secondary roads. Two and a half hours later, the fast-moving, twenty men of No 5 Troop (Captain Lord Richard Wrottesley) and No 2 Troop (Lieutenant Arthur Young) established the first contact between the airborne forces near Arnhem and the armored forces moving up the Corridor. They had not fired a shot. The third troop (Lieutenant Harry Hopkins) encountered the enemy when the fog suddenly lifted near Oosterhout where its leading scout car was knocked out on the dike road. German tanks forced a retreat and the road to Driel was once again closed.

Major-General Ivor Thomas was determined to relieve the trapped force at Oosterbeek. His 43rd Division engaged in a two-pronged operation: an attack east to seize Elst and a drive north to Driel. However, the Dutch road network had its way of hampering large-scale troops movements. Both brigades, 3,000 men each, attempted to move through the same crossroads while being shelled by German artillery positioned in Elst. The 129th Infantry Brigade (Brigadier GHL Luce) was to advance directly toward Arnhem along both sides of the elevated highway led by the 4th Wiltshire Battalion, but encountered Major Knaust's twenty tanks along the elevated highway near Elst and could go no further.

The 214th Infantry Brigade (Brigadier Hubert Essame) aimed to move farther west, through Oosterhout before turning north toward Driel. The brigade's departure was delayed when a leading battalion, the 7th Somerset Light Infantry, became lost passing through Nijmegen the previous night. Its late arrival cost Essame the advantage of launching his movement hidden by the early morning mist.

D Company (Major Sidney Young) led the first attack. While on an early reconnaissance Major Young was killed and the resulting attack failed.[2] The second

---

1   Private John Roderick Towle from Cleveland, Ohio was awarded the Medal of Honor posthumously for his sacrifice in breaking the enemy attack. Towle, aged 19, is buried in Calvary Cemetery in his hometown.

2   Major Sydney Charles Young, aged 30 from Yeovil, Somerset and considered to be one of the division's most esteemed officers, had been awarded the Military Cross for his attack upon enemy antitank guns during fighting near the Odon River the prior July. He is buried in Jonkerbos War Cemetery Plot 1, Row F, Grave 2.

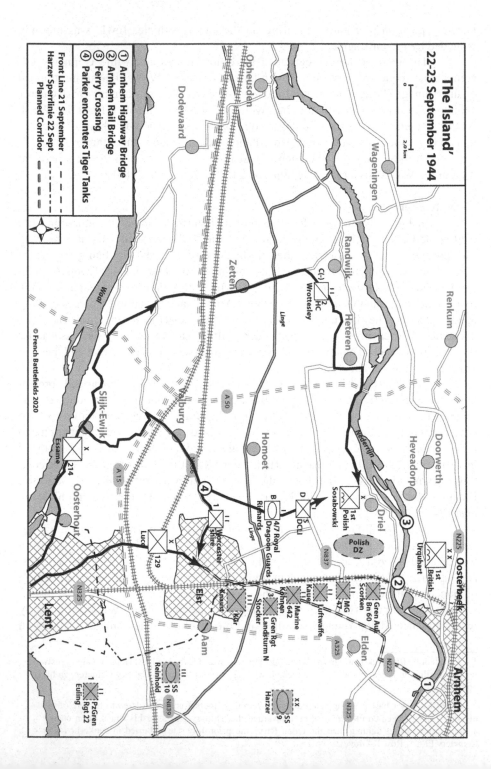

The 'Island'
22-23 September 1944

① Arnhem Highway Bridge
② Arnhem Rail Bridge
③ Ferry Crossing
④ Parker encounters Tiger Tanks

Front Line 21 September
Harzer Sperrlinie 22 Sept
Planned Corridor

© French Battlefields 2020

attack around the right flank also failed when German tanks and artillery pinned the Somersets to a forested area surrounding Huis Oosterhout. Brigadier Essame gathered the entire division artillery to support a third attempt starting at 15:20. Within two hours a gap had been blasted in the German defenses and at 18:50, B Squadron (Captain David Richards), 4th/7th Royal Dragoon Guards carrying D Company of the 5th Duke of Cornwall's Light Infantry (DCLI, Lieutenant-Colonel George Taylor) on its decks turned north toward Driel. The main body reached the Polish positions forty-five minutes later to contact the 750 Polish parachutists who had landed the previous day. Sosabowski asked, 'How am supposed to cross the river?' The answer he received was 'Be clever; make rafts.'

       While the 5th DCLI sped toward Driel, Bren carriers from DCLI's A Company (Major Harry Parker) were trailing the main body because they had stopped to pick up marching personnel. Near the de Hucht crossroads north of Elst the column encountered two Tiger tanks from schwere Panzer Kompanie 'Hummel' coming from Elst. Company Sergeant Major Reg Philp opened fire with a Bren gun at the commander of the leading tank in the column. The tank then sprayed his carrier with its machine gun forcing the men to dive into a ditch while the tanks continued south.

       Alerted by Philp, Parker returned from Driel, stationed six PIAT teams along the German armor's withdrawal route, and strung mines across the road. The leading motorcycle hit a mine and disintegrated in the explosion. Next came five tanks – three Tigers and two Panthers – led by another motorcyclist. The first tank to approach the crossroads was hit by six PIATs and exploded. The PIAT men similarly attacked the next tank. When the third, a Panther, tried to reverse out of the trap, Parker's men pulled mines behind and finished it with a PIAT. The remaining two tanks also attempted to reverse but crashed into the ditch. CSM Reg Philp[3] climbed aboard each in succession and dropped grenades into the turrets, the lightly armed infantry accounting for all five enemy tanks.

       The terrain of this engagement has been somewhat altered over the years. Widening of the roadway and creation of the bicycle path has filled the ditch. The DCLI relief force approached this intersection (51.915276, 5.807062) from the west and turned north toward Driel 1.8 kilometers farther east. Modern housing subdivisions do not permit following the route.

       General Horrocks called 22 September 'Black Friday' when weather in the Netherlands and England grounded all aircraft depriving Horrocks of fighter coverage and Urquhart of resupply attempts, but the ground fighting persisted. Although desperate to get to Oosterbeek, Horrocks now had to send his 32nd Guards Brigade south to help the 101st Airborne reopen the 'Hell's Highway'.

23 September

       The 1st Battalion Worcestershire Regiment, 214th Brigade attacked the German stronghold at Elst astride the road from Valburg (N836). Knaust's Panther

---

3   CSM Reg Philp was awarded the Distinguished Conduct Medal for his exploits. Philp died in 2012, aged 92, and is buried in Hartland, Devon.

tanks barred the way. Bittrich put the pressure on Knaust to hold for another 24 hours, enough time he figured to eliminate the British airborne pocket at Oosterbeek. Six Panther tanks of Knaust's dwindling armored forces were knocked out. Three days of constant fighting left the smouldering ruins of Elst in British hands.

Aftermath
        After MARKET-GARDEN the front line stalled along the Linge River. Autumn rains caused serious flooding made worse by the German explosion of the Rhine River dike at Elden flooding of much of the Betuwe.
        By December 1944 only 4,000 male civilians remained on 'The 'Island', refusing to leave their cattle and other possessions. The area between the Waal and Rhine river came to be known as 'Men's Island' since almost all the women and children had been evacuated. The Betuwe was liberated in April 1945, just weeks before the German surrender. The citizens returned to find their homes looted and destroyed. Abandoned explosives made some areas unsafe. The reconstruction efforts took years

Battlefield Tour
        No convenient route provides access to the 'The Island' sites. Visitors can select topics of interest from the various sites described or proceed directly to the Arnhem battlefield by passing through Ressen and past Elst via Autoroute A325.

In Gendt 8 km northeast of Lent (51.874221, 5.966482)

War Museum 'No Man's Land'
Nijmeegsestraat 19, 6691 CK Gendt
Tel: +31 (0)63 493 0790
Email: info@museumniemandsland.nl
Web: http://www.museumniemandsland.nl
Open Mondays from 20:00 to 22:00 and Fridays from 10:00 to 17:00. Reservations recommended.
        A small private museum of collected battlefield relics dedicated to events in the Betuwe between 1939 and 1945.

On Dorpstraat in Slijk-Ewijk. (51.886370, 5.789595)

        Combat along the dike north of the Waal River is remembered in Slijk-Ewijk where the 101st Airborne Division established its divisional command post on 4 October. The small village hall bears a plaque featuring the '**Screaming Eagle**' insignia above the inscription:
        In October- November 1944 the US 101st Airborne Division fought
    on the 'Island' for our liberty.

On Bonegraafseweg between Dodewaard and Ochten (51.913335, 5.615178)

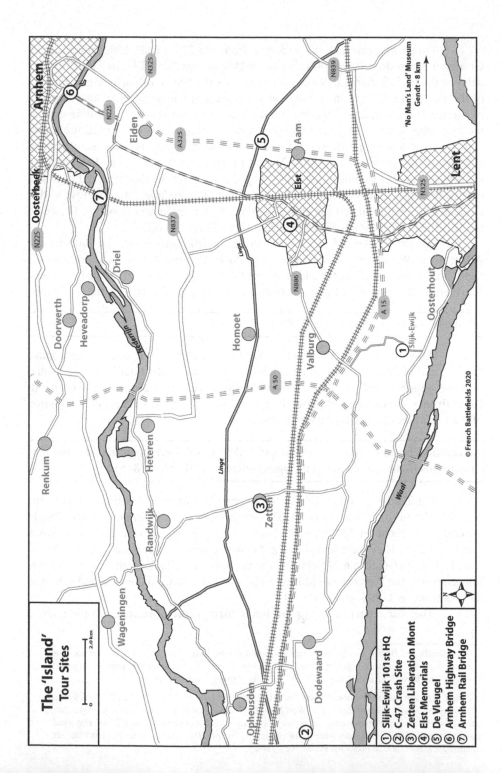

The 'Island'
Tour Sites

'No Man's Land' Museum
Gendt - 8 km

© French Battlefields 2020

① Slijk-Ewijk 101st HQ
② C-47 Crash Site
③ Zetten Liberation Mont
④ Elst Memorials
⑤ De Vleugel
⑥ Arnhem Highway Bridge
⑦ Arnhem Rail Bridge

On 18 September, C-47 'Dakotas' from the 314th and 315th Troop Carrier Groups were to drop British 4th Parachute Brigade on Ginkel Heath. Bad weather delayed the takeoff. Serial 619 carried one half of the Medium Machine-gun Platoon of the British 156th Parachute Battalion when the left engine and fuel tank were hit by German antiaircraft fire. The plane left the formation and lowered landing gear as the pilot attempted to land the crippled aircraft. Upon impact one of the fuel tanks exploded, the plane flipped over and caught fire trapping the six crew members and eighteen paratroopers. One of the eighteen British troopers survived by being thrown from the plane, but despite care provided by the villagers, he died the next day. The twenty-four dead were buried at the crash site and villagers marked each grave with a wooden cross, unfortunately the graves were washed away in later flooding. The death toll was the highest for any aircraft crash during MARKET-GARDEN. [4]

An impressive red and black marble obelisk was erected in 2000 by the Adriaan van Westreeman Foundation. The attached plaque features the outline of a C-47 aircraft, record of events, and names of the American crew[5] and British troopers. The memorial is one of the most beautiful and expressive of its type on the battlefield.

Wilhelminaplein in Zetten (51.927854, 5.714669)

Another impressive **Liberation Monument** worthy of a visit commemorates the loss and violence of war with a symbolic dug-out and the final liberation with a massive stainless steel 'V' rising from its depths. Five tiles bear the coats of arms of Great Britain, the United States, Belgium, Canada, and the Netherlands in recognition of their sacrifices for the country's liberation.

In central Elst, turn onto Dorpsstraat and follow to the large open square. Find the memorials in the rear corner of the open square. (51.918945, 5.845502)

On 22nd September, British troops marched along the narrow roads to the west of Elst on their way to Driel. The 7th Somerset Light Infantry (SLI) fought through Oosterhout on 22 September but could not overcome resistance of German tanks near Elst. They were joined by the 1st Worcestershire Regiment and the 4th/7th Royal Dragoon Guards on 24 September to engage enemy tanks in the center of town. Subsequently, the Worcesters and Dragoons attacked Elst from the west and achieved its liberation on 25th September 1944.

The rear corner of the square holds **three remembrances**. On the right, a

---

4   Tragically the British paratroopers' remains could not be individually identified after the war. They are buried in eighteen adjacent graves in Jonkerbos War Cemetery in Plot 8, Row A, Graves 1 through 9 and Row B, Graves 1 through 9 under the inscription, 'Buried near this spot.'

5   Staff Sergeant Joseph W Bobo of Ohio, Technical Sergeant George A Collier, aged 27 of Alabama, Staff Sergeant Xon C Connett, aged 20 of West Frankfort, Illinois, 2nd Lieutenant Henry G Honeysett, aged 22 of Glenside, Pennsylvania, and pilot Captain Leonard A Ottaway, aged 27 of Haviland, Kansas are buried in the Ardennes American Cemetery in Neupré, Belgium. Captain Herbert Pluemer, Jr, aged 29 was reinterred in Scotch Plains, New Jersey.

symbolic metal disc suspended above a stone plinth bears inscription dedicated to the three British units involved in the local fighting. A brick framed stone plaque stands in the center. Its inscription names three hostages executed by the Gestapo in this square during the night of 13/14 September 1944. The executions were in reprisal for destruction of a segment of the Arnhem-Nijmegen railway line. Four other hostages were held to encourage 500 workers to dig antitank ditches before being released. [6]

The **Liberation Route Marker #31** on the left identifies Elst as 'The Key to Success' by the British and German forces in their battles for the Nijmegen and Arnhem bridges. British troops describe facing their armored enemy and the trap that they set for German tanks.

Proceed toward the Elst train station via Dorpstraat and Van Oldenbarneveltstraat. Continue east on Nieuwe Aamsestraat before turning north on the frontage road (Lingestraat) for Autoroute A325 and follow for 1.4 km to Kampsestraat which crosses over the autoroute. Follow Kampsestraat an additional 300 m to the memorial on the right. (51.928047, 5.877509)

The bicycle path now fronting the northern bank of the Linge has been labeled *Patrouillepad* or **Frontline Path**. Ten information signs along the path highlight post-MARKET-GARDEN exploits of an American reconnaissance patrol, the crash of a Messerschmitt, existing foxholes, and German activities in the area. Metal mesh coverings along the Linge preserve foxholes used during the battle.

Monument the Wing (De Vleugel) presents a 7-meter-tall steel wing sticking out of the ploughed earth at an angle. It serves as a metaphor for the people that still have not detached themselves from the pain and suffering caused by the war. One of the Frontline Path panels stands near the Wing and describes the suffering of the local population and the symbolism of The Wing in three languages.

---

6   The victims were: WL van Dijk, G de Koning, and AMM Puthaar, two local teachers, and a councilman.

Chapter Six
British 1st Airborne Division 'Red Devils': The Landings
17 to 19 September

Elements of the British 1st Airborne Division had seen prior action in Tunisia, Sicily, and Italy. The division did not participate in Normandy being held instead in reserve. During the autumn of 1944, the unit, now under command of Major-General Robert 'Roy' Urquhart, was frequently poised for action only to have the proposed mission cancelled – usually by the capture of the drop zone by rapidly advancing Allied ground forces.

In September 1944, the 1st Airborne Division, composed of 1st and 4th Parachute Brigades, the glider-borne infantry of the 1st Airlanding Brigade, and the attached 1st Polish Independent Parachute Brigade, planned for Operation COMET, an effort considered similar to MARKET-GARDEN but one cancelled on 10 September for being too ambitious for a single airborne division.

The division's objectives in MARKET-GARDEN were the capture of a highway bridge across the Nederrijn that led into central Arnhem and the railway and pontoon bridges farther west. The city of Arnhem was a risky drop zone for parachutists and was to be avoided. British planners assessed the southern bridge approach as soft, mucky polder completely unfit for the accompanying glider landings. They also felt that heavy antiaircraft defenses around Deelen airfield north of the city were to be avoided. Thus, Urquhart selected the elevated, dry and firm pastures and heath between Wolfheze and Renkum 10 to 13 kilometers to the west. The distance between landings and objectives were to become a major issue in the Arnhem assault.

Three battalions of the British 1st Airlanding Brigade (Brigadier Philip Hicks) were to secure the drop zones for the paratroopers.[1] This seemingly reversed order was selected because glider borne troops arrive in complete platoons and are therefore able to concentrate more rapidly that dispersed paratroopers. Hicks' brigade did not participate in the initial assaults upon the Arnhem bridges, instead being required to hold the drop zones for the D+1 and D+2 lifts.

The 1st Parachute Brigade (Brigadier Gerald Lathbury) intended to capture the three Nederrijn bridges in Arnhem. Three routes were selected for the brigade's movement into the city to achieve maximum speed such that at least one group could quickly capture a bridge before it could be detonated. Specifically, the 275-man 1st Airborne Reconnaissance Squadron (Major CFH Gough) on jeeps and motorcycles and 1st Battalion (Lieutenant-Colonel David Dobie) were to follow the rail line for some distance before passing through the forest to the Ede-Arnhem road (Amsterdamseweg, N224) on a route code-named 'Leopard.' Once in Arnhem the 1st Battalion would peel off to occupy high ground in the northern districts of the city. The Reconnaissance Battalion would continue to the highway bridge executing a *coup de main*.

The 3rd Battalion (Lieutenant-Colonel JAC Fitch) would leave the drop zone to the south into Heelsum to reach the Utrecht–Arnhem road (Utrechtseweg,

---

1   The 1st Airlanding Brigade was composed of 1st Battalion, Border Regiment; 2nd Battalion, South Staffordshire Regiment; and 7th Battalion, King's Own Scottish Borderers. Landing at the same time were the 1st Airborne Reconnaissance Squadron, the artillery of the 1st Airlanding Light Regiment, and their associated antitank, engineers, and other support personnel.

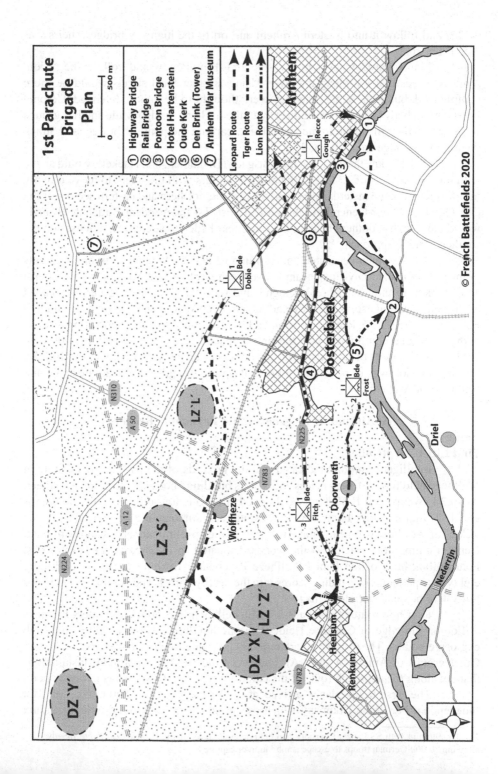

1st Parachute Brigade Plan

500 m

① Highway Bridge
② Rail Bridge
③ Pontoon Bridge
④ Hotel Hartenstein
⑤ Oude Kerk
⑥ Den Brink (Tower)
⑦ Arnhem War Museum

Leopard Route
Tiger Route
Lion Route

© French Battlefields 2020

N225) and follow it into western Arnhem and on to the highway bridge. Theirs was the 'Tiger' route.

Lieutenant-Colonel John Frost's 2nd Battalion would follow the 'Lion' route on roads that ran along the river. Using smaller local streets would be more complicated, but at the same time they were thought to be lightly defended. Colonel Frost's main body would proceed directly to the highway bridge while smaller groups would cross the rail bridge to the south bank, capture the pontoon bridge, and attack the highway bridge from the south.

On Monday, the 4th Parachute Brigade (Brigadier John Hackett) would arrive with the Second Lift of 2,119 additional paratroopers with the intent to move directly into Arnhem along Amsterdamseweg to occupy the northern and eastern sectors of the city. On D+2, Major-General Sosabowski's Polish 1st Independent Parachute Brigade would land on the southern bank of the river near Elden to strengthen defenses on the southern bridge approach.

On 14 September Dutch underground leaders in Arnhem identified elements of the 9th SS Panzer Division encamped between Arnhem and Apeldoorn to the north and Zutphen to the east for replacements and refitting. After having barely escaped encirclement at Falaise, Normandy and having been driven across France by the US First Army, the 9th SS Panzer Division had been reduced to barely operational status with its original compliment of 9,000 men reduced to a still formidable 6,000 men but having lost most of its equipment, vehicles, and artillery. In addition, the 10th SS Panzer Division was to be similarly brought up to strength while stationed east and southeast of Arnhem.[2]

1st Airlanding Brigade and 1st Parachute Brigade

Battle

First Lift 17 September

Intelligence reports indicated that the grounds of the psychiatric institute in Wolfheze held forty artillery pieces and that its buildings housed 750 German soldiers. At 10:38, twenty-four B-17 bombers dropped thirty-one tons of high explosive bombs and 150 fragmentation bombs on the hospital and surrounding private houses. The village of Wolfheze was nearly flattened by the Allied preliminary aerial bombardment. German ammunition caches in the woods detonated in ever expanding explosions. Four outbuildings of the famed Wolfheze Psychiatric Institute were leveled killing eighty-five patients and sending scores into the nearby forest. The bombardment killed thirty-five hospital staff and villagers.

Four hours later eighteen B-25 'Mitchell' bombers attacked artillery barracks at Ede on the edge of Ginkelse Heide with one hundred forty-four 500-pound high explosive bombs. The results were reported as poor due to cloud cover over the target. Other groups of American and RAF bombers struck at 117 antiaircraft installations that lay along the approach route of the paratroopers. Results were again mostly poor.

The first troop planes arrived at 12:40 carrying the Pathfinders of 21st Independent Parachute Company which was assigned to mark the drop and landing

---

2   The 9th and 10th SS Panzer Divisions had held open the jaws of the Falaise Gap in Normandy allowing 50,000 German troops to escape annihilation or capture.

zones for following aircraft. The first to touch down was 3rd Platoon and HQ Company on LZ 'S' quickly followed by 1st Platoon on DZ 'X' and 2nd Platoon on LZ 'Z'. German patrols offered some opposition but were quickly eliminated. 'Eureka' transponder beacons, used for short-range radio navigation, were activated and soon responded to the 'Rebecca' airborne transceiver through the planes' highly directional antennas.

1st Airlanding Brigade

The first of 284 Horsa and Hamilcar gliders started arriving on LZ 'S' at 13:00 and nineteen minutes later at LZ 'Z' carrying Brigadier Hicks' 1st Airlanding Brigade. The four companies of the 1st Borderers went south with the intent of protecting DZ 'X' and LZ 'Z' south of the railroad. The 7th King's Own Scottish Borderers (KOSB) went northwest to DZ 'Y' near Ede which was to be utilized the following day. Two companies of the South Staffords gathered around a farm that once housed the Dutch Cavalry to guard LZ 'S'. Each British glider had two pilots who were also trained as infantry fighters; as a result, there were approximately 1,100 additional infantry soldiers – bigger than a battalion of extra men – formed into the Glider Pilots Regiment. The pilots rendezvoused west of Wolfheze to form a central reserve under divisional command.

Despite the hazardous nature of unpowered glider landings, remarkably few deaths occurred. Of the 320 gliders, all but 36 reached their destination. The main cause of those that failed was breakage of the tow rope over England — generally the result of low cloud cover requiring sudden course corrections which stressed the tow ropes. One glider fell apart while in the air, the resultant crash killed all twenty-three men aboard. Seven gliders came down in enemy territory. In all, only eleven pilots died in glider crashes.

1st Parachute Brigade

At 13:53 and for the next fifteen minutes the sky above DZ 'X' was filled with 2,283 parachutes as three battalions of the 1st Parachute Brigade[3] jumped from 145 Dakotas flown by the US Air Force accompanied by 650 parapacks color-coded to indicate their contents – guns, ammunition, or equipment in an operation as smooth as any practice jump. Paratroopers scurried to collect their equipment, locate themselves on the drop zone, and reach their unit's rendezvous (RV) as identified by colored smoke. The RVs were on or near the Arnhem side of DZ 'X'. Casualties were light; four refused to jump, one died, and few were injured. The formations left for their objectives around 15:00 hours.

But there were difficulties. Major Freddie Gough's Reconnaissance Squadron had three troops, each with eight jeeps mounting a single .303-inch Vickers machine gun, chartered to race for the highway bridge. A Troop arrived without its vehicles after its gliders were among those downed by German antiaircraft fire in transit. In addition, British communications radios, designed for a 5- to 8-kilometer range, saw their faint signals disappear at a fraction of that distance. Similarly, two hastily

---

3   The 1st Parachute Brigade held the 1st, 2nd, and 3rd Parachute Battalions, 1st Airlanding Antitank Battery, 1st Parachute Field Squadron of Royal Engineers, and 16th (Parachute) Field Ambulance.

assembled American forward observer teams found themselves unable to locate the ground-to-air VHF radio sets needed to direct fighter close support. The lack of firm communications complicated division actions for most of the battle.

German Response

The swiftness of the German response had much to do with the eventual British defeat. Generalfeldmarschall Model, a witness of the airborne landings, commanded Army Group B and, as such, personally authorized the redistribution of German troops. SS-General Bittrich's headquarters were in Doetinchem, only 35 kilometers to the east. The two experienced and high-ranking commanders immediately took matters in hand avoiding the usual period of confusion that follows an airborne assault. They immediately understood the target to be the Arnhem bridge. The 9th SS Panzer Division was detailed to concentrate upon the British landings, while the 10th SS Panzer Division headed to defend the Waal River crossing at Nijmegen.

The defense of Arnhem was initially entrusted to KGr Spindler (SS-Lieutenant Colonel Ludwig Spindler), an ad hoc unit formed around 120 Normandy survivors of the 9th SS Division's Panzer Artillerie Regiment who now fought as infantry. Spindler quickly gathered his artillerymen from around Deelen Airfield and immediately started to form a blocking line five kilometers west of the bridge along Dreijenseweg.

The line expanded to the north and south as units arrived on the scene and were added to KGr Spindler. SS-Captain Hans Möller's[4] kampfgruppe of engineers from SS Panzer Pionier Bataillon 9 fighting as infantry worked its way along Utrechtseweg toward Oosterbeek and the Renkum Heath landing zone but was stopped in Den Brink park a few hundred meters west of Sint Elisabethshof when it encountered tracer bullets whizzing across the road. SS-Lieutenant Heinz Gropp's 87-man force from the SS Flak Bataillon 9 left a loading exercise with one 88-mm flak gun and a 20-mm cannon to join Möller in positions in the railway marshalling yards in central Arnhem. Late that night various 'alarm' or quick response units added another 100 men to his total.

The German commanders redirected other units toward Arnhem. KGr von Allwörden (SS-Captain Klaus von Allwörden), comprised of the remnants of SS Panzerjäger Bataillon 9 left Siegen, Germany between 14:30 and 15:00 for Arnhem with two Jagdpanzer IVs and some number of towed 75-mm PaK guns. It arrived the next morning and extended Spindler's *Sperrlinie* or blocking line north of Amsterdamseweg. Other units continued to join Spindler as the battle progressed: SS Panzergrenadier Regimenter 19 and 20 arrived early morning of 18 September; the next day, Sturmgeschützbrigade (Assault Gun Brigade) 280 arrived with ten StuG IIIs; survivors of KGr Gräbner on 21 September; Pionier Lehr Bataillon 'Glogau' on 22 September; and, finally, fifteen powerful PzKpfw VI 'King Tiger' tanks of schwere Panzer Bataillon 506 on 24 September.

SS-Major Josef Krafft's 435-man SS Panzergrenadier AuE Bataillon 16 (Bataillon 'Krafft') was on exercises two-to-three kilometers east of LZ 'S'. Krafft, in

---

4   Hans Möller was a sergeant in 1940 in the SS 'Der Führer' Regiment when he led an engineering platoon across the Ijssel River and cleared snipers along the Nederrijn to Renkum. Four years later he was back on he same battlefield.

the deep forest, could not see the actual landings so he sent #2 Kompanie from Hotel Wolfheze toward the landing zone as a reconnaissance in force while #4 Kompanie established defense line near Hotel Wolfheze. Krafft summoned #9 Kompanie from Arnhem as a battalion reserve. Krafft recalled the German defensive response:[5]

> From previous experience we knew that a small force of superior troopers was only effective if it could attack immediately. It was therefore imperative that we intercept their attack as quickly as possible.

No 2 Kompanie became disoriented in the forest before emerging directly facing the center of LZ 'S'. Their heavy machine guns shot up four gliders before the company withdrew back to the line established by #4 Kompanie along the

---

5   Krafft's unit originally trained replacement soldiers for the 12th SS Panzer Division *'Hitlerjugend.'* With the need to establish a defensive line in the Netherlands, the unit was transferred to Division von Tettau. It was composed of two infantry companies and a heavy weapons company containing mortar, antitank, flak, flamethrower, and heavy mortar sections.
Krafft was an ex-police officer, who joined the SS Panzer Division *'Das Reich'* in 1941. An experienced combat soldier having fought in Russia, he came to the personal attention of Reichsführer Heinrich Himmler who advanced his career within the Waffen-SS. Krafft survived the war and died in 1986 at age 79.

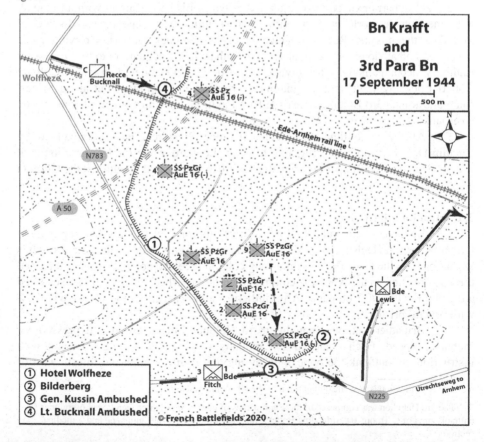

Wolfheze Road. Krafft correctly assumed the British objective and formed hedgehog positions astride the two main routes into Arnhem – the Ede–Arnhem railroad cut and the Wageningen–Arnhem road (Utrechtseweg, N225). By 15:30, Krafft's had #9 Kompanie as a mobile reserve, with mortars in the center and antitank guns along the main approaches.

Reconnaissance Squadron

Major Gough's Reconnaissance Squadron left LZ 'Z' and moved along Amsterdamseweg the 'Leopard' route at 15:00 despite his A Troop's vehicles not having arrived. Led by two jeeps under the command of Lieutenant Peter Bucknall of C Troop, he expected the *coup de main* action against the highway bridge to be a pushover against the assumed few old men in Arnhem. Krafft's #4 Kompanie ambushed the section and the occupants of the first two jeeps were killed or captured. The surprise assault ended only two kilometers from the landing zone.

Despite his unit now being pinned down, Gough responded to a message from Urquhart to report to headquarters. He turned his jeep around and headed back to the landing zone. Gough's efforts to locate Urquhart were fruitless and resulted in separating him from his unit for the remainder of the battle.

Urquhart anxiously paced up and down in his headquarters without contact with the outside world or even with his own units. Messengers were dispatched to locate the missing Reconnaissance Squadron without success. Growing more frustrated and anxious for speed, at 16:30 Urquhart left headquarters to find Brigadier Lathbury accompanied by his divisional artillery commander, Lieutenant-Colonel Robert Loder-Symonds and a signalman. Urquhart and Lathbury met along 'Tiger' route and joined 3rd Battalion near the Rijn Pavilion, a restaurant complex along the riverbank.[6]

At the same time, the Reconnaissance Squadron, now commanded by Captain David Allsop, was struggling to open 'Leopard' route for 1st Battalion as it was subjected to Krafft's hit-and-run attacks. Allsop attempted to outflank the German *Sperrlinie* to no avail.

3rd Parachute Battalion

Lieutenant-Colonel John Fitch's 3rd Battalion[7] quickly left the drop zone to Utrechtseweg in Heelsum and followed 'Tiger' route east with Major Peter Waddy's B Company in the lead. The one-mile-long column received no opposition as it passed through forested areas. When the column entered Oosterbeek, it came under scattered attack by Krafft's #9 Kompanie. After inflicting some casualties, the enemy withdrew with several prisoners.

Brigadier Lathbury caught up to Colonel Fitch's group and pressed for increased speed. Fitch detached C Company (Major RPC 'Pongo' Lewis) with instructions to outflank the opposition by moving north through the forests west of

---

6   The Rijn Pavilion is now the dining room of the NH Arnhem Rijnhotel.

7   The 3rd Battalion was composed of three companies of paratroopers, three jeep towed 6-pounder antitank guns of C Troop, 1st Airlanding Battery, one half troop of Royal Engineers, and a medical section.

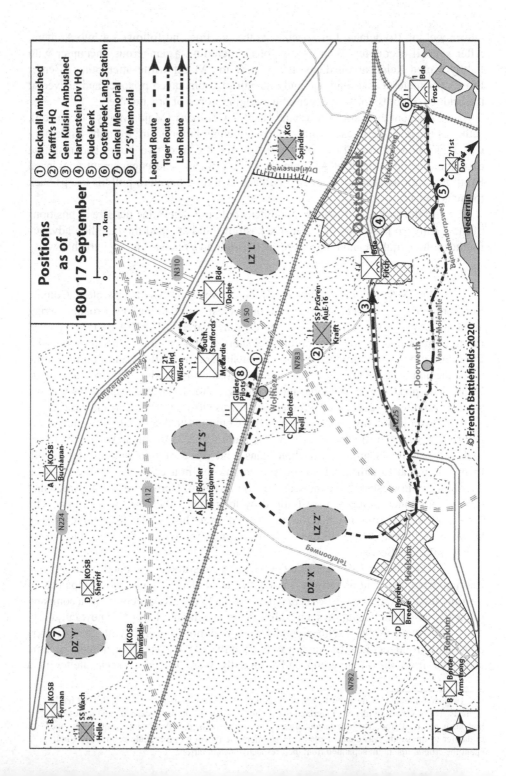

Positions as of 1800 17 September

① Bucknall Ambushed
② Krafft's HQ
③ Gen Kuisin Ambushed
④ Hartenstein Div HQ
⑤ Oude Kerk
⑥ Oosterbeek Lang Station
⑦ Ginkel Memorial
⑧ LZ 'S' Memorial

Leopard Route
Tiger Route
Lion Route

© French Battlefields 2020

Oosterbeek on Bredelaan. Lewis achieved the rail line and followed it into Arnhem. After several encounters with enemy forces including a dangerous encounter with lightly armed Reichsarbeitsdienst troops near the Markt while attempting to enter Frost's perimeter, Lewis had one-and-one-half platoons taken prisoner and arrived at the bridge with only forty-five men of his original force of one hundred.

At about the same time around 18:30, A Company (Major Mervyn Dennison), acting as the rear guard, came under machine-gun and mortar fire from the Bilderberg woods. Fighting amongst the trees went on for the next two hours and resulting casualties included three of A Company's five officers. The engagement convinced Krafft that he was in danger of being outflanked and he began to pull his troops back to the northeast.

In the darkness, Lathbury and Fitch could not determine the size or positions of the enemy, so they took up defensive positions and stopped the battalion advance for the night. Urquhart and Lathbury spent the night in a mansion along Utrechtseweg.[8]

On 18 September, aware that 'Lion' route to the south was clear, Colonel Fitch ordered his 3rd Battalion to pass through Oosterbeek to the lower road. Leaving at 04:30, progress was rapid through the darkened streets. The 3rd Battalion passed through the Benedendorpsweg train tunnel shortly after dawn on 18 September with little difficulty. As it continued east, German snipers on rooftops and in attics broke unit cohesion by applying murderous fire on British units passing in the narrow streets below. The paratroopers scattered into buildings, shops, gardens, and sheds seeking shelter until the snipers could be rooted out. It was slow, laborious, deadly work.

Split by enemy small arms fire, HQ Company lost sight of the leading units and took a wrong turn separating from the main force. Unfortunately for Fitch they took the battalion's mortars, machine guns, and three of four antitank guns with them. Fitch had to call a halt to regroup among the houses between Utrechtseweg and the river in western Arnhem near the Rijn Pavilion. German armor appeared and kept Fitch's much-reduced force trapped by long range shellfire for six hours. The 1st Parachute Battalion reached the train tunnel a few hours later then Utrechtseweg between 16:00 and 17:00, all the while losing men to German fire from the houses lining Hulkesteinseweg.

KGr Harder (SS-Lieutenant A Harder) constituted a second blocking line running from the central railway station to the Nederrijn with two companies of dismounted tank crews, logistics personnel from SS Panzer Regiment 9, and a company of hastily assembled naval personnel all fighting as infantry. Frost was now cut off.

Around 16:00, Lathbury and Urquhart, who were still with the battalion command group, decided to find a way back to their HQ. The senior officers became separated from the main group and eventually were forced to seek shelter in a

---

8   Brigadier Lathbury's decision to halt for the night has been roundly criticized in post battle analysis. There was no evidence of German troops along 'Tiger' route in Oosterbeek and a message had been received from Brigade headquarters at the Arnhem bridge that 'Lion' route, only one kilometer to the south, was clear of enemy. In addition, the division and brigade commanders both spent the crucial first night separated from their respective headquarters.

Dutchman's attic to avoid capture.

Fitch decided to attempt moving to a more northerly route but made little headway against German gunners which appeared to be covering every intersection. The men sheltered in houses west of Sint Elisabethshof Hospital. They had suffered sixty-five casualties, with A, B, and HQ Companies involved elsewhere, the battalion was down to 140 men.

1st Parachute Battalion

Colonel Dobie's 1st Parachute Battalion's mission was to occupy high ground along the main road north toward Apeldoorn. Receiving word of the enemy in front of the Reconnaissance Squadron, Dobie altered his route by leaving Wolfheze to the north toward Amsterdamseweg. Leading R Company (Major 'Tim' Timothy)[9] entered a wooded area along Wolfhezerweg. The company encountered a hastily gathered Luftwaffe signals unit from Deelen airfield and fought until darkness with little progress while suffering fifty percent casualties.

With R Company engaged along the road, Dobie swung the remainder of the column east into the woods and moved parallel to Amsterdamseweg until faced with the five tanks and fifteen half-tracks of KGr von Allwörden.

Dobie turned south and when informed of Frosts' being at the bridge decided to move to re-enforce 2nd Battalion. Dobie spent the night forcing his vehicles through the dense forest aiming for the most direct route to the bridge, the route already abandoned by 3rd Battalion. They entered Oosterbeek along Stationsweg before dawn on 18 September. Upon approaching the rail overpass on Utrechtseweg, the leading platoon came under fire from German infantry on the embankment. Dobie's mission was to reach the bridge not to engage enemy troops that he encountered along the way. So, 1st Battalion withdrew, moved south, and passed through the rail underpass along Benedendorpsweg.

The leading unit came under fire soon after passing through the underpass and entering the built-up district. Taking casualties but continuing to press forward, it was nearly 16:00 before attacking platoons reached the intersection of Klingelbeekseweg and Utrechtseweg just 200 meters short of the Rijn Pavilion where 3rd Battalion had been stopped earlier that day. And like 3rd Battalion, the 1st Battalion sought shelter in the neighborhood west of Sint Elisabethshof.

Krafft gathered his units along Amsterdamseweg (N224) and followed it east into Arnhem. Augmented by additional Naval and Police detachments, KGr Krafft established positions near the Arnhem rail yards. KGr Spindler formed beside Krafft to establish an irregular line of strongpoints from Krafft's new positions to the river. British attempts to penetrate Spindler's line continued through the night, frequently in

---

9   Major John 'Tim' Timothy participated in the famous Bruneval Raid to capture German radar technology in February 1942. He received a Military Cross for leadership and initiative while leading raids into enemy territory in Tunisia during February and March 1943 and a second MC or bar for rescuing five hundred PoWs from behind enemy lines in Italy in October 1943. Major Timothy would receive his second bar for actions along Amsterdamseweg and for leading attacks upon German armor along Onderlangs on 19 September. He was captured and spent most of the remainder of the war in Oflag VIIB. After the war, he returned to Marks and Spencer as a store manager. John Timothy died in 2011 aged 97, and is buried in Timberscombe, Somerset.

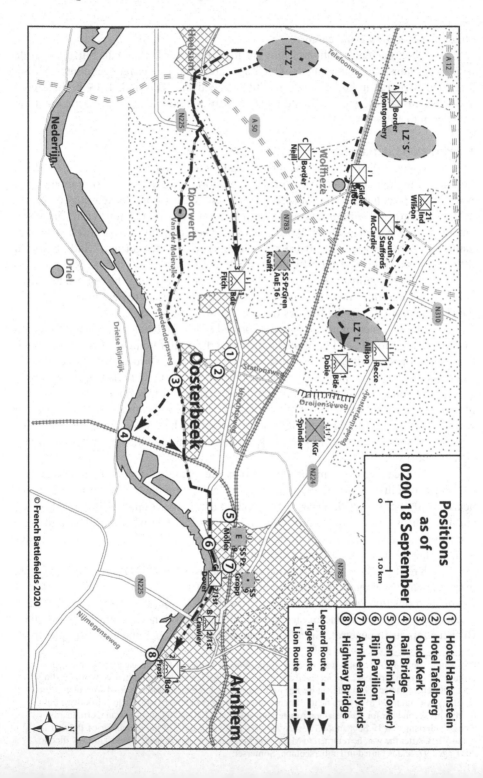

Positions
as of
0200 18 September

0 — 1.0 km

① Hotel Hartenstein
② Hotel Tafelberg
③ Oude Kerk
④ Rail Bridge
⑤ Den Brink (Tower)
⑥ Rijn Pavilion
⑦ Arnhem Railyards
⑧ Highway Bridge

Leopard Route
Tiger Route
Lion Route

© French Battlefields 2020

house-to-house fighting as they probed for a weakness, but each attempt was repulsed. It was not obvious at the time of course, but Spindler's line was to become decisive in the battle for Arnhem.

2nd Parachute Battalion

The smaller, 481-man 2nd Battalion[10] of Lieutenant-Colonel Frost left the drop zone at 15:00 making for its southern or 'Lion' route led by the rifle platoons of A Company (Major Digby Tatham-Warter). After two miles, Lieutenant Andrew McDermont's No 3 Platoon ambushed a German column from Krafft's #2 Kompanie and took thirty or so prisoners, destroying all the vehicles.

With No 2 Platoon (Lieutenant John Grayburn) now leading, progress through the wooded area along Oude Oosterbeekseweg / Benedendorpsweg was rapid. By 18:00, the battalion entered built-up areas of Oosterbeek to wild acclaim of the Dutch people.

An attempt to capture the rail bridge over the Nederrijn failed when German guards on the opposite bank blew the central span. After a brief delay to clear snipers at Oosterbeek Laag Station, the 2nd Battalion column crossed the boundary between Oosterbeek and Arnhem on Klingelbeekseweg. A Company passed through the western outskirts of Arnhem encountering light resistance at times which forced the paratroopers to leave the road for the back gardens of nearby houses. B Company reached the pontoon bridge to find its central span removed rendering the crossing useless. Thus, both crossings to the south bank of the Nederrijn prohibited Frost from attack against the Arnhem highway bridge from the south.

The column, with Grayburn still in the lead, moved along Onderlangs before dropping down to the towpath (Rijnkade). Along the route, paratroopers quickly overcame small groups of German soldiers, killing and wounding some and taking about forty prisoners. At 19:30 Grayburn's platoon reached the Arnhem bridge, having covered the 13 kilometers in six hours. The 2nd Parachute Battalion story will be continued later.

4th Parachute Brigade

Second Lift 18 September

By Monday morning, the KOSB had moved 6 kilometers farther away from the Arnhem bridge to secure DZ 'Y' at Ginkelse Heide siting its B, C, and D Companies in the farthest corners of the drop zone. Similarly, A and D Companies of the 1st Borderers took up positions in the north and south edge of LZ 'Z' and C and D Companies on the eastern and western edges.

Second Lift take-offs on 18 September were delayed four hours until a night mist cleared from English airfields. Accidents and mishaps during take-off claimed a small number of aircraft, but weather improved over the English Channel. The streams of aircraft met heavy flak upon crossing the Dutch coastline, because the Germans were now fully alerted.

Unlike the British First Lift, American C-47 and a few C-53 aircraft brought

---

10   Attached to the battalion was one half of B Troop, a partial platoon of Royal Engineers from the 1st Parachute Squadron, and four jeep-towed 6-pounder antitank guns.

the parachutists in first followed by RAF tugs towing 296 Horsa and Hamilcar gliders. The gliders carried vehicles, guns, and the remaining infantry; ten Horsas delivered the first of the Polish Brigade's antitank troops.

The operational plans that had been captured and delivered to General Student alerted the Germans and they were ready. SS and antiaircraft units disengaged from Arnhem and hurried to Ginkelse Heide's DZ 'Y' and Wolfheze. When the first transports carrying paratroopers approached Arnhem, the flak once again intensified. Six planes were hit and crashed killing thirty-one soldiers and seventeen aircrew. Courageous pilots in other planes maintained their low, slow approach until all the parachutists had jumped.

The Second Lift's transports and gliders were greeted by German mortar and machine-gun fire. Smoke obscured the drop zone. The courage and tenacity of the plane and glider pilots braved an inferno of enemy fire and, frequently in flames, delivered 2,119 men of Brigadier Hackett's 4th Parachute Brigade. [11]

Despite the German antiaircraft defenses and problems with the jump, 90% of the paratroopers managed to land in the designated zone. They started their advance towards Arnhem at around 17:00 straight into the teeth of the German *Sperrlinie*.

By the afternoon, Division von Tettau's mixed training units were steadily clearing the landing zones of British troops. SS NCO School 'Arnhem' (SS-Colonel Hans Lippert) captured Renkum and entered Heelsum moving swiftly until encountering the 1st Border Regiment at the outskirts of Oosterbeek. The Renkum brickworks were taken by a naval battalion later in the day. At least three gliders were hit by German fire from the southern end of LZ 'X' where the enemy had infiltrated between the 1st Border Regiment's companies. Six obsolete Renault tanks drove north from Renkum only to fall victim to British antitank teams. The heath, however, eventually proved to be too big to defend and part of the drop zone was lost.

With the delivery of the Second Lift troops, Ginkelse Heide was abandoned. The 1st Battalion, Border Regiment moved toward Oosterbeek to become part of the airborne perimeter around Arnhem as originally planned. The KOSB, under temporary command of 4th Parachute Brigade, was released to perform the same function securing LZ 'L' around the Johannahoeve Farm[12] for the Polish Brigade's transport and artillery delivery during the Third Lift scheduled for the next day.

10th Parachute Battalion
The 10th Battalion (Lieutenant-Colonel Kenneth Smyth), Parachute Regiment dropped into the enemy's rear area and stormed into enemy fire to clear the northeast corner of Ginkelse Heide of the Dutch SS battalion which had forced the

---

11   The 4th Parachute Brigade was composed of 10th, 11th, and 156th Parachute Battalions, 4th Parachute Royal Engineers, the remaining two companies of the 2nd South Staffordshire Battalion, 2nd Airlanding Antitank Battery, and numerous rear echelon and administrative troops.

12   Johannahoeve Farm was 320 acres of mixed farm and woodland that no longer exists. The property was bounded by Amsterdamseweg, Dreijenseweg, the rail line, and Wolfhezerweg. The main buildings were roughly near the current Abbey Koningsoord, a Cistercian convent.

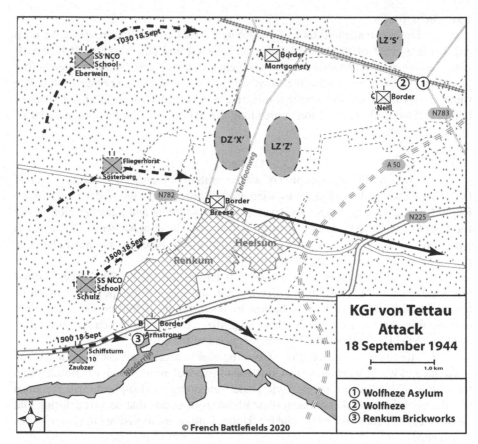

KOSB headquarters and support staff from the edge of the drop zone. After a small action against the Zuid Ginkel Café, the 10th Battalion advanced to the west edge of LZ 'S' before stopping for the night.

11th Parachute Battalion

Lieutenant-Colonel George Lea's 11th Battalion rendezvoused quickly and left the drop area to enjoy a quiet afternoon's walk into Oosterbeek. Command confusion at divisional headquarters left the battalion waiting for five hours before receiving instructions to proceed toward the bridge. After the unnecessary delay, a Dutch guide led the unit into Arnhem ending the day near the Sint Elisabethshof Hospital.

156th Parachute Battalion

Lieutenant-Colonel Sir Richard des Voeux's 156th Battalion left the drop zone to the south, then followed the rail line through Wolfheze, past the Reconnaissance Squadron's ambushed jeeps finally halting for the night just west of Dreijenseweg after encountering *Sperrlinie* Spindler.

Battlefield Tour
The first battlefield tour of the Arnhem / Oosterbeek area reviews the drop and landing zones of the 1st Airlanding and the 1st and 4th Parachute Brigades. It passes along the 1st Brigade's early engagements on 17 and 18 September before traversing Oosterbeek leaving the town's important sites to be reviewed later. The route passes under the rail line that effectively separates Oosterbeek from Arnhem before following along the 'Lion' route along the river to the Rijn Pavilion bivouac of 1st and 3rd Battalion.

Arnhem
Arnhem's history as capital of what eventually became the Dutch province of Gelderland goes back to 1233. Its location on the north bank of the Nederrijn or Lower Rhine River greatly influenced its development as a trading and transportation center for areas of the Netherlands and Germany to the north and east. Movement to the south was more restricted. The new highway bridge across the Nederrijn that was to become the focus of MARKET-GARDEN opened in 1935.

The prosperous pre-war city held a population of 96,000. Large forested tracts surrounded Arnhem, quite different from the flat, treeless polder of much of the Netherlands. The forests were broken by open, flat heath that provided excellent opportunities for landings by parachute or glider. The pre-war Dutch Air Force had built an airfield at Deelen only 9 kilometers north of the city.

The citizens of the Arnhem–Oosterbeek area regard their participation in the great Second World War battle as an important historical event and they commemorate the events of 1944 with respect. Civic leaders encourage and support local activities and the establishment of permanent remembrances of events that occurred during that fateful week in September 1944. The local tourist office assists visitors in viewing sites of interest.

The Arnhem area holds several fine museums that review various aspects of the battle and provide good introductions to the race toward the bridges, defense of the bridges, and the eventual defeat. They present displays and information regarding the participants, their weapons, and inhabitants' struggles in an occupied country. The following museums can be visited before or after the recommended battlefield tours depending upon one's interest and depth of background knowledge.

Airborne at the Bridge
Rijnkade 150, Arnhem
Tel: +31 (0)26 333 7710
Web: https://www.airbornemuseum.nl/en/airborne-at-the-bridge
Open daily from 10:00 to 17:00. Located along the river front just 230 meters west of the famed 'Bridge Too Far.' Public toilets available. Free. (51.976445, 5.909265)
Airborne at the Bridge is an annex of the Airborne Museum 'Hartenstein' and acts as a new reception center for the city of Arnhem presenting information about events in the city and the region. The site offers a phenomenal view of the John Frost Bridge and features audio descriptions of the personal stories of British Lieutenant John Grayburn, German SS-Captain Viktor Gräbner, and Dutch Captain Jacobus

Groenewoud each of whom fought and died during the Battle of Arnhem.

Airborne Museum 'Hartenstein'
Utrechtseweg 232, 6862 AZ Oosterbeek
Tel: +31 (0)26 333 7710
Web: https://www.airbornemuseum.nl/en/home
Open daily from 10:00 to 17:00. Labeling is in Dutch, German and English. Admission fee. Handicap accessible. Located on Utrechtseweg west of central Oosterbeek. (51.987724, 5.832712)

The Hartenstein was constructed in 1864 as a private mansion and became Model's staff headquarters. The building was heavily damaged during the battle but was renovated and reopened as a hotel and later converted to its present function. From 1949 to 1978 the Airborne Museum occupied the Doorwerth castle on the banks of the Nederrijn before moving to the Hartenstein. Current renovations are expected to be completed in spring 2021 when the museum will reopen.

The grounds around the museum are central to the story of the Oosterbeek perimeter fighting and have thus found numerous memorials and relics of the battle. Moving from the parking area accessed from JJ Talsmalaan east of the museum, a visit encounters the following items:

A six-meter bronze sculpture titled **'We'll Meet Again'** stands in the open grass field northeast of the museum. The artwork symbolizes the liberation by paratroopers and their welcome by the civilian population and represents the ongoing battle between freedom and suppression. (51.988137, 5.833185)

Information Panel #1 and **Liberation Route Marker #40**, alongside the driveway east of the museum, recalls without audio the story of two glider pilots who get separated during a crossfire. Their torn armband later reunites the two friends. (51.987920, 5.833288)

The grounds of the museum hold three British 17-pounder antitank guns. A **17-pounder antitank gun** from D Troop once stood immediately north of the Oude Kerk as part of the main defense. The gun, now on the east side of the museum, is in remarkably good condition, never having been used due to a technical problem. (51.987751, 5.833206)

On the west side of the museum a **17-pounder** from X Troop of the 2nd Airlanding Antitank Battery, which defended the Hartenstein along Sonnenberglaan to the northwest, stands beside the **Sherman M4 tank 'Argyll'** that participated in the city's liberation in 1945. (51.987687, 5.832228)

A **17-pounder antitank gun** landed on 17 September in a Hamilcar glider on LZ 'Z' at Wolfheze. The piece was moved to the western perimeter near the intersection of Benedendorpsweg and Ploegseweg where it engaged German tanks to eventually be knocked out by several mortar and artillery shell hits. The gun now stands on the museum grounds behind the Hartenstein along a path to the southeast and its plate and breech display the damage inflicted upon the weapon. (51.986923, 5.833870)

The brick and stone memorial dedicated to the **People of Gelderland** stands near the tourist office entrance at the rear of the museum (51.987566, 5.832356) and is inscribed:

Fifty years ago, British and Polish Airborne soldiers fought here against overwhelming odds to open the way into Germany and bring the war to an early end. Instead we brought death and destruction for which you have never blamed us. This stone marks our admiration for your great courage, remembering especially the women who tended our wounded. In the long winter that followed your families risked death by hiding Allied soldiers and airmen, while members of the Resistance helped many to safety.
You took us then into your homes as fugitives and friends, we took you forever into our hearts. This strong bond will continue long after we are all gone. 1944 – September – 1994.

Numerous other memorials have been placed around the museum terrace including 'The Parachutist' a 80-centimeter or 31-inch bronze mounted upon a concrete column that portrays a landing paratrooper; 'The Guardian' a 200-centimeter or 78-inch winged female guardian angel with arms outstretched. Both works are of noted Dutch sculpture Jits Bakker, who, as a child, witnessed the events of September 1944. An eagle caught in flight mounted upon a polished granite plinth bears a biblical quote from John 15:13 and is dedicated to those members of the **Royal Air Force, Commonwealth, and American Air Forces** that perished during Operation MARKET-GARDEN.
The tourist office is located in the west wing of Airborne Museum Hartenstein and provides entrance into the museum.
VVV Oosterbeek
Utrechtseweg 232, 6862 AZ Oosterbeek
Email: info@VVVoosterbeek.nl
Web: http://www.vvvoosterbeek.nl
Open daily from 10:00 to 17:00.

The **Hartenstein Museum** tour starts on the second floor where a short film featuring veterans recalling their experiences also provides an excellent explanation of the battle. The museum excels in its collection of weapons especially German panzerfausts and bazookas and photos of the town before, during, and after the battle. Numerous displays provide quotations from the recollections of individual soldiers. The first floor focuses upon the history of the hotel, soldiers' medals, and flags. In the first basement indicated as -1 on the elevator, two dioramas depict events. Finally, the '**Airborne Experience**' in the -3 basement presents a battlefield complete with explosions and flashing lights representing the airborne landings and subsequent combat. Cars and cannons, rifles and machine guns are arranged to give the impression that you really walking through the battlefield. Warning: the intensity of the sound and lighting effects may upset sensitive viewers.

Arnhem Oorlogsmuseum 40–45 (Arnhem War Museum 40–45)
Kemperbergerweg 780, 6816 RX Arnhem
Tel: +31 (0)26 442 0958
Web: http://www.arnhemsoorlogsmuseum.com/
Open Tuesday through Sunday from 10:00 to 17:00; closed certain holidays. Handicap accessible; admission fee, no credit cards. Captions are in Dutch, English, and Ger-

man. The museum is located 6 kilometers north of central Arnhem on Kemperberger-weg. (52.026771, 5.871863)

This private museum, housed in an old schoolhouse, holds a collection of artifacts from the battlefields around Arnhem. It does not present history but offers a tremendous collection of rifles, helmets, etc. An unusual collection of communications gear occupies the second floor – some of which appears to be in almost operational condition while others are rusted beyond recognition. The second floor is also dedicated to document displays relating to Dutch life under German occupation and the Dutch resistance. The tour is semi-guided with a guide describing some of the exhibits and its historical significance, but you can also wander on your own. The museum has a collection of vehicles, artillery pieces, and tank remnants scattered around the exterior. A large Russian T34 tank with German markings sits in front of the museum.

Museum Vliegbasis Deelen (Deelen Airbase Museum)
Delenseweg 6877 AE Deelen
Tel: +31 (0)26 370 7138
Web: https://www.museumdeelen.nl/
Open Saturdays and Sundays from 11:00 to 17:00. Admission fee. Partially handicap accessible, see web site. Located 10 kilometers north of central Arnhem on highway N804. (52.061463, 5.897774)

During the Second World War, the Netherlands was the front line of the German air defenses against the large number of Allied bombers based in Great Britain. To protect the Reich from night and day air attacks, the Germans built a chain of defenses that stretched from Denmark south to northern France. Radar stations, search lights, and antiaircraft guns were built on and near the coastline and the airfields where German fighter planes and night fighters were stationed. Command centers, such as the one at the airfield in Deelen, assisted the fighter planes to intercept the Allied bombers.

Deelen was the command center for the 3rd Jagddivision which was housed in a large bunker named *Grossraumgefechtsstand* **Diogenes**. The bunker was built between August 1942 and July 1943 in the Hoge Veluwe National Park and displays impressive dimensions – being 40 meters by 60 meters, over 16 meters high, and wall thickness of three to four meters. The airfield was headquarters for Nachtjagdgeschwader 1, the most successful night fighter wing in the Luftwaffe.

In September 1944, the Luftwaffe radar air control network held a Luftwaffe signals company led by Hauptmann Willi Weber, designated KGr Weber during the Arnhem fighting. The hauptmann assembled ninety poorly armed signalmen to attack LZ 'S' over the Amsterdamseweg Road. After a brief skirmish, Weber withdrew to defensive positions near Deelen Airfield. The action gained time to report the air drop up the Luftwaffe chain of command. The Germans assumed the British landings at Arnhem planned to capture radar technology, so they destroyed everything inside the bunker. Ironically the British purposely avoided the airfield fearing that it would be well-protected with antiaircraft guns. In fact, the Germans had moved all their aircraft and antiaircraft batteries farther east to protect them from the advancing Allied ground forces.

The former air base and German *Gefechtsstand* or Command Post has recently been reopened with a museum in the old NCO mess. The museum focuses on what it labels Night Fight 1940–1945, the air battle above the province of Gelderland. Scale models, original footage, photos, artifacts and military objects including a V-1 buzz bomb replica with original interior show the history of Vliegbasis Deelen during the Second World War. A unique two-by-three-meter map was used by the German Night Fight command to help intercept approaching Allied bomber formations. For more than four years the museum has been trying to put the 4000 pieces of broken glass back together in order to make the map complete again. All objects, photos, uniforms, etc in the museum are original, the bulk of which come from private collectors. The gun in front of the building is a French 75-mm, used by the Germans against the air landings of 17 September.

Diogenes Archiefservice
Koningsweg 13, Arnhem, Netherlands
(52.032809, 5.865619)

Currently, the *Grossraumgefechtsstand* bunker, located 5.7 kilometers to the southwest on the opposite side of the airfield, is used as a depot by the Dutch National Archives. The building is not open to the public; however, the exterior can be viewed, and guided tours can be arranged through the Museum Vliegbasis.

Airborne Posts were erected after the war by officers of the 4th Parachute Brigade. The original wooden posts proved not durable and they were later replaced by the town council with concrete posts. Nine such concrete posts now identify important sites in the battle for the Arnhem bridges. Each carries the Pegasus British Airborne insignia. They are not officially numbered but are identified in the battlefield tour as they are encountered. To assist in identifying these important locations, they are listed below.

1. Dreijenseweg – limit of 156th Battalion's efforts on 19 September
2. Hotel Tafelberg – Generalfeldmarschall Model's headquarters
3. Sint Elisabethshof Hospital – scene of combat and medical treatment during the battle
4. Museum Arnhem on Utrechtseweg – this post has disappeared, but once marked the forward progress of 2nd South Staffordshire Battalion
5. Near the new Nelson Mandela Bridge – nearest point to the highway bridge reached by 1st and 3rd Battalions
6. No 192 Utrechtseweg in the pastor's garden – the forward position held by Lieutenant-Colonel Kenneth Smyth's men from 10th Parachute Battalion for two days
7. Van Limburg Stirum school – Royal Engineers position during highway bridge defense
8. Hallow on Valkenburglaan – Hackett's strongpoint
9. Oude Kerk – final stronghold

> The first site on the tour is the landing zone north of Wolfheze on highway N783. (52.008800, 5.795460)

At 13:00, 134 gliders landed to the north and west of the village as the people of Wolfheze looked on in despair and surprise, still shell-shocked from the bombings earlier that day. Some gliders came down in the trees, others were damaged on landing, often along with the equipment they carried. Most troops set off in the direction of Arnhem as quickly as possible, although the 1st Airlanding Brigade's 2nd South Staffordshire Battalion remained to defend the landing and drop zones for future arrivals.

The Second Lift on 18 September dropped 87 tons of supplies, mostly gun and mortar ammunition, but only a fraction was recovered by British forces with the balance dropped behind German lines. The lost ammunition became painful later in the battle as ammunition shortages limited artillery fire. A few days later, British troops left Wolfheze for Arnhem and Oosterbeek and the Germans took back the village. It was not until April 1945 that the destroyed village was finally liberated.

The **Glider Monument**, in the form of a stylized aircraft aimed at a perilous angle toward the earth, stands across the highway from Landing Zone 'S.' A nearby sign displays a photograph of the burning psychiatric center.

Liberation Route Marker #25 sits beside the glider. In the 'The Bridge to Freedom' audio civilians seek shelter from the Allied bombings then witness the glider landings.

Landing Zone 'L', though not visible, lays to the east on the opposite side of Autoroute A50 and now almost fully subsumed into the Papendal sports complex. The tree line crossing the highway to the north marks the route taken by Colonel Dobie after failing to achieve Amsterdamseweg.

> Proceed south on highway N783. Before crossing the rail line, turn left onto Johannahoeveweg and continue straight to its end. A sometimes muddy track continues parallel to the rail line where, 600 meters ahead, one finds a tunnel under the rail embankment. (52.004111, 5.803194)

On 17 September C Troop, 1st Airborne Reconnaissance Squadron led by Lieutenant Bucknall's jeep approached this point along 'Leopard' route in the opening stages of the battle. At exactly 16:00 slightly farther ahead where the track re-enters the forest, Lieutenant Bucknall was ambushed by heavy machine-gun fire from Krafft's #4 Kompanie on the rail line embankment on their right. Bucknall was killed as were the three occupants of his jeep, one man from the second jeep, and two men from the third jeep.[13] After a 30-minute exchange, the remaining five men – four of whom were

---

13   Lieutenant Peter Lacey Bucknall, aged 23, Trooper Ronald Brumwell, aged 20, Trooper William McKinlay Edmond, aged 27, Trooper Edward James Gorringe, aged 22, Trooper Leslie Percy Goulding, aged 21, and Lance-Sergeant Thomas McGregor, aged 20, are buried in adjoining graves in Arnhem Oosterbeek War Cemetery, Plot 16, Row B, Graves 5 – 10.

wounded – surrendered.[14] The remainder of C Troop (Captain John Hay) was unable to fight through the stronger German force and withdrew. The remaining thirteen jeeps of the Reconnaissance Squadron made no further attempt against the highway bridge.

The pedestrian section of Johannahoeveweg runs around 50 meters north of the rail line which is significantly higher than the path. For most of the distance a ditch runs parallel to and almost immediately adjacent to the rail line. The ditch offered excellent cover and movement opportunities to the German ambush. The path slowly descends into a hollow with burnt brush of a fen on the left, then slowly rises to a forested area ahead, which also held German defenders.

The tunnel under the rail line was used by 4th Parachute Brigade's smaller vehicles on 19 September when they fled the advancing enemy. Captain Lionel Queripel died in the woods to the northwest. These events are related in the next section.

Return to highway N783 and proceed south across the tracks to stop near a memorial opposite the train station. (52.005138, 5.791547)

The **Airborne Memorial** in Wolfheze consists of a circular brick bench emanating from a brick memorial bearing a plaque in memory of those units of the British 1st Airborne Division and the Polish 1st Independent Parachute Brigade which landed in the surrounding landing and drop zones.

Leave Wolfheze west on Parallelweg on the south side of the rail line. Major Gough's Reconnaissance Squadron and 1st Parachute Battalion left DZ 'X' and LZ 'Z' on this street advancing in the opposite direction. The drop zone is shrouded from view by the roadside trees and shrubs but becomes visible upon turning onto Telefoonweg.

Despite the vegetation blocking the views, this is the center of the landing areas. LZ 'S' is to the north across the rail line. Telefoonweg divides DZ 'X' on the west from LZ 'Z' on the east.

Continue south for 2.7 km on Telefoonweg to the monument on the right. (51.98849, 5.74583)

Liberation Route Marker #20 identifies the fields north of Heelsum and Renkum where hundreds of Allied paratroops and gliders landed. The 'Landing of Parachutists and Gliders' audio describes civilians joyously assisting the landing British paratroopers. The two images depict the sky dotted with landing parachutists and gathering soldiers greeted by civilians expecting their liberation to be at hand.

A golf course now occupies Landing Zone 'Z' on the east side of the highway. The 2nd Battalion's rendezvous point was across the golf course in the Fletcher Hotel-

---

14   The Germans left Trooper Richard Minns on the battlefield with serious hip and leg wounds. Minns was rescued the next day, wounded again in the Oosterbeek cauldron, and spent two years in hospitals after the war recovering from his wounds.

Restaurant Klein Zwitserland in the southeastern corner of the drop zone.

If desired, **Major Frost's route to the Arnhem Bridge** can be followed; however, the route offers little of interest besides attractive wooded areas scattered among small suburban communities. From Liberation Route Marker #20 proceed south 230 m to the first roundabout. Take the 3rd exit onto N782 (Bennekomseweg) and proceed 1.6 km southeast to a large roundabout. Take the 2nd exit and continue to follow N782 which becomes Utrechtseweg for 270 m passing under highway A50. Turn right onto Doorwerthsestraat and follow for 200 m. Construction of modern highway N225 forces a deviation from Frost's path which continued east on Doorwerthsestraat. Turn right onto Roggekamp into an upscale residential neighborhood. Follow for 1.2 km as the street passes under highway N225 and then travels beside the highway. Continue straight where Roggekamp becomes WA Scholtenlaan and returns to Frost's route. Follow WA Scholtenlaan for 1.9 km through a beautiful mature forest which ends at the limits of Doorwerth. Continue straight as the name changes to Oude Oosterbeekseweg. The district presents office buildings, apartments and older houses before again becoming forested upon entering Heavadorp. After 1.4 km, turn right at the T junction onto Benedendorpseweg. Continue for 2.9 km to pass the Oude Kerk and under the rail line where the name changes to Klingelbeekseweg. Follow for 1.2 km before bearing right onto Hulkesteinseweg and continue 350 m to the junction with highway N225 (Utrechtseweg). At this point, Frost continued along the riverbank streets (Onderlands, Boterdijk, and Rijnkade) to the bridge, however, construction of the Nelson Mandelabrug and widening of highway N225 has completely altered this area. Turn right onto highway N225 which is also named Onderlangs, then becomes Roermondsplein and carefully follow under the Nelson Mandelabrug ramps noting the left turn onto Roermondsplein after 1.5 km – beware this area is quite complex. Follow Roermondsplein for an additional 160 m where the names become Weerdjesstraat, then Trans, Eusebiusplein, and Oranjewachtstraat. After 950 m, turn right onto Kadestraat, then left in 80 m onto Nieuwe Kade. Pass under the bridge in an additional 60 m

To continue on the recommended tour route, from Liberation Route Marker #20 on Telefoonweg, continue south to the traffic circle. Take the third exit onto highway N782 and continue eastbound for 1.2 km to the memorial on the right. (51.982450, 5.760897)

The **Heelsum Memorial** was constructed in the late 1940s by a local plumber utilizing containers that dropped supplies to the British forces, most of which fell into German hands. A British 6-pounder gun is the focal point. The metal border surrounding the memorial — almost unnoticeable due to the vegetation — consists of the ramps that were used to unload jeeps from gliders. The decorative chains held down the jeeps while the gliders were in flight. Note: the construction of the Autoroute relocated the memorial from its original location.

Follow Utrechtseweg (N782, after 1.2 km the road joins highway N225 with a left turn) east for a total of 3.9 km to the junction with Wolfhezerweg (N783) on the left. (51.988038, 5.813041)

As B Company, 3rd Parachute Battalion approached this 'Tiger' route intersection from the west, Private Frederick Bennett was near the front of the column when a German Citroen staff car approached the intersection from the north rounding a tree-shrouded blind curve. Bennett fired his Sten submachine gun and the car screeched to a halt. The driver tried to reverse and back out of the intersection, but Bennett's second burst riddled the vehicle. The paratroopers cautiously approached to find the driver hanging half out of the door and the body of a senior German officer in the rear seat. Generalmajor Friedrich Kussin, Stadtkommandant Arnhem, was dead. General Kussin was responsible for the military headquarters in the Arnhem area and had just left a conference with Major Krafft at his headquarters in the Hotel Wolfheze one kilometer to the northwest. His death temporarily left the issue of the bridge defense unanswered.

At the next intersection, B Company came under fire from a 37-mm flak gun and troops from Krafft's #9 Kompanie. The initial volley destroyed a jeep towing a 6-pounder. Attempts to flank the German gun were hit by machine-gun or mortar fire. After a brief firefight, the Germans withdrew. At this point Major Lewis's C Company was dispatched north along Bredelaan in a flanking maneuver. A Company, bringing up the rear of the mile-long column again became engaged with enemy troops from #9 Kompanie in a two-hour firefight around Hotel Bilderberg. The battalion, reduced to the sole B Company, continued reaching the Hartenstein in time to enjoy the German Army Group B officers' abandoned cold lunch.

Turn northwest and follow Wolfhezerweg (N783); after 1.2 km pass Hotel Wolfheze, now the remodeled Fletcher Hotel-Restaurant Wolfheze, on the right. The building was Krafft's headquarters on the first day of the battle, but it bears no indication of its wartime use. Continue for an additional 3.1 km. Turn left onto Amsterdamseweg (N224) and continue for 5.6 km to the side road on the left (Wijde Veldweg). Park and proceed on foot west through the treeline to the stone monument on Ginkelse Heide. (52.036918, 5.734587)

Division von Tettau's ill-trained and inexperienced Dutch SS Wachbataillon (Surveillance Battalion) III 'Nordwest' (SS-Major Paul Anton Helle) arrived on Ginkelse Heide piecemeal because of a lack of transport. The battalion band, frequently used to capture downed airmen, made first contact in woods west of Ginkelse Heide at about 17:00 on 17 September when it was ambushed and destroyed by a platoon of the 7th KOSB.

Major Helle committed four companies abreast with one company and his heavy weapons platoon in reserve. KOSB began to run low on ammunition and conducted a fighting withdrawal across the landing zone giving Helle the perception that he was fighting a low-grade unit.

The next day, the sound of the approaching aircraft was the signal for KOSB to counterattack. Helle's #6 Kompanie on the far-right flank was quickly captured

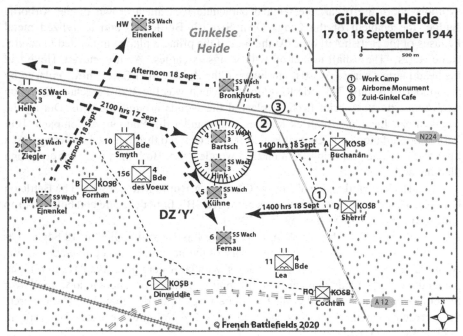

intact. The two center companies, #5 and #3, found themselves fighting the KOSB to the front and British paratroopers descending to their rear. Most of the #5 Kompanie was killed or captured. Its commander (SS-Lieutenant Hermann Kühne) fled the battlefield and was found days later hiding in a house. The #3 and #4 Kompanie formed an all-around hedgehog position but were completely overwhelmed. Helle and his #1 Kompanie fled west. The Heavy Weapons Platoon executed a successful fighting withdrawal to the north holding off the attacking British troops with 20-mm cannon and mortar fire. The 600-man Dutch SS unit suffered more than 200 killed and slightly less than that number fled.[15]

Sicherungs Regiment 26 (Major Wilhelm Knoche) arrived from Ede to replace Helle's defeated companies. Knoche's unit was formidable including two battalions of military police and three French Char tanks which had been converted to mount flamethrowers in place of the usual 75-mm gun. Knoche joined KGr von Tettau attacking east along Amsterdamseweg on 18 September.

The large boulder with an inscription identifies the '**Luchtlanding 17 – 18 September 1944**' despite the fact that no landings took place here during the First Lift.

Ten meters farther west, the 3-meter-high concrete **Airborne Monument** is topped with a copper dove of peace with wings spread as if in full flight. The plinth is shaped like a crystal with the pillar emerging out of it like a prism. Three copper

---

15   Prior to MARKET-GARDEN Wachbataillon III was responsible for guarding camps including at Vught and Sint-Michielsgestel. Immediately after the battle, SS-Major Paul Anton Helle was relieved of his command for inadequate capability. He returned to his command the following month and began a rampage of looting, destruction, and executions that disgraced the unit. Helle was tried in 1949 by a Dutch Court for his wartime abuse of civilians. He was sentenced to fifteen years imprisonment, but was released to German authorities in 1955.

symbols adorn the pillar: the winged parachute wearing a crown of the Airborne Badge, the emblem of the Kings Own Scottish Borderers, and a stylized metal Pegasus of the British Airborne. At the foot of the pillar, a plaque imbedded in natural stone states, 'They shall mount up with wings as eagles.' As it occurred, Helle had his headquarters across Amsterdamseweg in the Zuid Ginkel Café – now replaced by the modern Juffrouw Tok Ede Restaurant – which was the 10th Parachute Battalion rendezvous point. A brief firefight cleared the woods around the café. During the engagement, Lieutenant Patrick Mackey, commander 4th Platoon, A Company, 10th Parachute Battalion and Sergeant Frank Bennett charged through the heather against a Spandau machine gun firing from under a wooden cart. Both men were cut down and died instantly.[16]

Back toward Wijde Veldweg, **Liberation Route Marker #55** 'The Battle on Ginkelse Heide' describes experiences of the KOSB's fight to secure and hold the drop zone. (Approximately 52.036553, 5.735274)

The new **Landmark 'Windows of the Past'** was unveiled on 18 September 2019 to commemorate the 75th Anniversary of the beginning on the liberation of the Netherlands. Six-meter-high steel 'windows' with laser-cut figures display aircraft and parachutists suspended from harnesses dropping to the earth. The windows look over the Ginkelse Heide where the 4th Parachute Brigade landed that day. The concrete base presents panels describing the landing at DZ 'Y' and the Battle of Arnhem. (52.035484, 5.735822)

Return to Verlengde Arnhemseweg (same road as Amsterdamseweg N224) and proceed east 650 m to Heidebloemallee on the left. (52.036288, 5.745817)

After two days of intensive planning, during the night of 29 October 1944, six men of the 501st PIR, armed to the teeth with 'Tommy' submachine guns or M-1 rifles, .45 caliber pistols, pockets full of grenades, and extra ammunition crossed the river at Heteren in two rubber assault boats and spent the night slowly working their way through parties of German patrols or groups digging slit trenches. The black-faced invaders established a hidden observation post in what is now the Planken Wambuis Restaurant along the Arnhem–Ede highway and radioed back information on enemy troop movements and potential artillery targets. The next night, the patrol captured thirty-two enemy troops and took them back across the Nederrijn for interrogation. In the end, only two shots had been fired when an SS captain attempted an unsuccessful escape into the woods.

The action became known as 'The Incredible Patrol'. **Liberation Route Marker #54** on a side road off Verlengde Arnhemseweg (N224), describes the team's adventures. [17]

---

16   Lieutenant Patrick Wallace Mackey, aged 24 from Farnham, Surrey is buried in the Ede General Cemetery, Ede, Netherlands in Row H, Grave 21. Sergeant Frank W Bennett, aged 29, is commemorated on the Groesbeek Memorial in the Groesbeek Canadian War Cemetery.

17   First Lieutenant Hugo S Sims, commander of Company A, 501st PIR was awarded the Distinguished Service Cross for his daring feat. The award was in addition to his Silver and Bronze Stars. He returned home and was elected to the South Carolina state legislature and then became the

Proceed 8.1 km east on Verlengde Arnhemseweg passing the parking bay on the opposite direction. (52.024399, 5.798791)

On 19 September seven jeeps carrying thirty men of C Troop of Major
Gough's Reconnaissance Squadron were performing a reconnaissance along this
stretch of forest-lined highway from Wolfheze toward the by then abandoned drop
zone at Ginkelse Heide. The troop found itself almost completely surrounded by enemy
troops. Heavily outgunned, their only option was to run the gauntlet by speeding down
the highway with their jeep mounted Vickers machine guns firing in all directions.
Only eight men in two jeeps managed to escape. Five men were killed, and seventeen
taken prisoner.

Continue eastbound for 3.7 km to the intersection of Amsterdamseweg (N224) and
Dreijenseweg. Stop at the Total gas station. (52.006887, 5.844223)

Early on 19 September, Brigadier Hackett ordered 10th Battalion (Lieutenant-
Colonel Smyth) to cross LZ 'L' and march toward Arnhem via Amsterdamseweg to
establish a firm flank to the brigade's attack upon high ground north of Oosterbeek
known as Lichtenbeek. By 10:00, the 10th Battalion's D Company moved along the
wooded area south of the highway approximately even with the La Cabine water supply
station on the northern side. The paratroopers came under automatic weapons fire from
unseen positions in the surrounding forests. The prior day KGr von Allwörden with
a strong complement of armored vehicles had arrived to extend *Sperrlinie* Spindler.
        The battalion had no answer to the firepower of the kampfgruppe's armored
vehicles. The paratroopers attempted a flanking movement to the north but engaged
reorganized KGr Krafft[18] in the woods. Close fighting went on for hours. Crossing the
roadway was deadly from fire from German armored vehicles covering the road, while
British mortars kept the armor from advancing.
        Captain Queripel was acting commander of A Company which, in the
confusion and heavy casualties, was a composite from three parachute battalions. At

---

youngest member of the US House of Representatives at age 28. He died in 2004 at age 82 and is
buried in his hometown of Orangeburg, South Carolina.
Master Sergeant Peter Robert Israel Frank, born in Nurnberg, Germany and interpreter on the patrol,
was awarded a Silver Star and a field commission. Frank died in 2003 aged 80.
Corporal William R Canfield of Selman, Oklahoma and Pfc Frederick J Becker of Atlantic, Iowa
received Silver Stars. Canfield died in 1995, aged 73 and is buried in Protection, Kansas.
Private Robert O'Donnell Nicolai of Midlothian, Illinois received a Bronze Star for actions in
Normandy. During Market-Garden he was Colonel Johnson's personal bodyguard. In 1947 he
volunteered to be part of the crew of SS Ben Hecht, a ship loaded with over 700 survivors from Nazi
concentration camps who attempted to force the British blockade to enter Israel. He was arrested by
the British and temporarily held in the notorious Acre Prison. Because of unfavorable publicity in the
United States and after holding the seamen for a month, the British decided they were more trouble
than they were worth and put them on a ship bound for New York.
Private Roland J Wilbur of Lansing, Michigan was designated the unofficial unit sniper for his ability
to hit targets at great distances. He died in 1981, aged 64, and is buried in Eaton Rapids, Michigan.

18   Bataillon 'Krafft' was reconstituted as KGr Krafft and held two companies of Bataillon 'Krafft'
supplemented by companies of marines and military police.

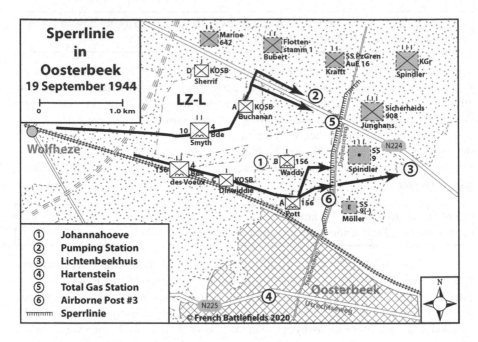

14:00, Queripel's company advanced along the main road towards Arnhem. Continuous machine-gun fire became so heavy that the company became split up on either side of the road and suffered considerable losses. He reorganized his force by crossing and recrossing the road under heavy and accurate fire. Queripel, slightly wounded in the face, carried a wounded sergeant back to the Regimental Aid Post.

Later in the same day, A Company was defending a strip of woodland east of Wolfheze near where the Reconnaissance Squadron had been attacked two days earlier. Queripel, after having received further wounds in both arms, decided that it was impossible to hold the position any longer and ordered his men to withdraw. Despite their protests, he insisted and became cut off with a small party of men in a ditch. Queripel continued to resist all that evening with hand grenades and his pistol until overwhelmed the following morning. He was never seen alive again.[19]

The restaurant across the highway was known as **Leeren Doedel** in 1944 was Spindler's headquarters and essentially marked the northern end of Spindler's *Sperrlinie*. A plaque on the exterior wall recalls the building's destruction on 21 September by RAF Typhoons although the plaque incorrectly states the date as 26 September. The attack struck civilians sheltering in the well-constructed building leaving it full of dead and wounded.

A side road intersects Dreijenseweg a short distance to the south. The woods to the west, especially near this junction, hold remnants of the foxholes and slit

---

19   Captain Lionel Ernest Queripel, aged 24, from a distinguished military family, was born in Winterborne Monkton, Dorset. He served in Northern Ireland during the Troubles before the war, retreated from Dunkerque in 1940 as part of the BEF, fought in North Africa at El Alamein before joining the Parachute Regiment. Captain Queripel was awarded the Victoria Cross posthumously for his outstanding heroism. He is buried in Arnhem Oosterbeek War Cemetery, Plot 5, Row D, Grave 8.

trenches from the desperate fight of the 10th Battalion.

Proceed south on Dreijenseweg for 1 km to Airborne Post #1. (51.998808, 5.844001)

At 08:30 on 19 September, Major John Pott's A Company, 156th Battalion approached this road from the west. KGr Spindler held a long, wooded stretch along Dreijenseweg, with infantry outposts in the woods to the west of the roadway. The bank on the eastern side of the road rose three meters exposing attackers to defensive fire if they rushed across the roadway. German half-tracks mounting MG-42s cruised up and down Dreijenseweg and twin 20-mm antiaircraft guns and 37-mm rapid firing SP guns added their firepower to the defense.

No 4 Platoon advanced before being blocked by machine-gun fire and became pinned down in the shallow roadside ditches. No 5 Platoon attempted flanking to their left. Bren gunners sprayed the trees but could not identify discrete targets. The platoon's commander, Lieutenant David Delacour, although already wounded in the neck by the first German round, stood up and ordered a charge only to be hit a second time. The wounds were serious and he bled to death.[20] A glider pilot platoon was to follow the attack, but it was hit from the flank by a German outpost to the north. Inexperienced when used as infantry, its commander was wounded, second-in-command killed, and their assault went no further as 20-mm exploding rounds ricocheted among the trees.

Major Pott led a dash by No 4 Platoon across the road and into the woods on the opposite side of the road. The platoon commander was killed as was the company second-in-command. Major Pott achieved the objective at Lichtenbeek Woods after six hours of such slaughter, but with only six men and himself twice wounded. The Germans rounded up the survivors.[21]

About 09:00, aware of the difficulties experienced by A Company, Colonel des Voeux sent B Company in an attempt to move around the northern flank of A Company but met the same heavy opposition with fire coming from every direction including even from already passed German outposts. A German half-track ran along the firebreaks firing its 20-mm flak gun into the woods. Company commander, Major John Waddy, was wounded and taken prisoner.[22] The 156th Battalion was finished. It had suffered fifty percent casualties — worse at officer and senior NCO ranks — and was effectively reduced the equivalent of one company.

---

20   Lieutenant Lindsey David Delacour, aged 24, born in Egypt later of Notting Hill, London, is buried in Arnhem Oosterbeek War Cemetery, Plot 25, Row A, Grave 13.

21   Major Robert Laslett John Pott was left on the battlefield by the Germans where he lay for eighteen hours. He was rescued by two Dutchman and carried to the Mill Hill Fathers' House where his wounds were treated before he was eventually taken prisoner. Pott spent the remainder of the war as a PoW.
Born in Khartoum, Sudan to a military family, Pott was first posted to India, then North Africa in 1942, where he was wounded. After joining the Parachute Regiment, he fought in Italy where he was awarded the Military Cross for leading a difficult attack in rugged terrain. After the war, he and his wife performed relief work in Sudan while raising four sons. He died in 2005 at age 85.

22   Colonel John Llewellyn Waddy served in numerous military posts after the war including Palestine, Malaysia, Washington DC and Vietnam. He was a director of Special Air Services (SAS) — precursor to the UK Special Forces. He is now 98 years old and living in Somerset, England.

Airborne Post #1, where the road emerges from the woods before entering Oosterbeek, commemorates the 156th Parachute Battalion's failed attempts to cross the highway north of the marker. The assault upon Arnhem was defeated along this 900-meter stretch of otherwise unremarkable roadway. The roadway and battle ground are little changed from 1944.

Continue south on Dreijenseweg which becomes Stationsweg. After 2.5 km turn left on Benedendorpsweg and park at the entrance to the camping site. (51.978093, 5.840112)

A later tour will return to Oosterbeek to review actions that occurred in the final battle for the Oosterbeek Cauldron.

On Sunday afternoon, Major Frost's 2nd Parachute Battalion, with Major Tatham-Warter's A Company in the lead pressed forward along 'Lion' route until 18:00 when he sighted the railway embankment crossing Benedendorpsweg and the rail bridge over the Nederrijn.

C Company (Major Victor Dover) separated from the main body to follow Polderweg across the meadowland toward the rail bridge. No 9 Platoon (Lieutenant Peter Barry) led with Company HQ following, then No 8 and No 7 platoons. Headquarters took up positions in a brick factory along the bank of the river where a few survivors of a bombing earlier that day offered minimal resistance.

When's No 9 Platoon reached within 300 meters of the bridge, Barry spotted a German soldier race onto the bridge from the opposite end, bend down to fiddle with something, and run back. Barry sensed the soldier was preparing demolitions. He and his platoon raced across the open meadow and reached the bridge embankment where they came under heavy small-arms fire from the south bank. Major Dover's other two platoons presented covering fire from the area around the brickworks. Lieutenant Barry established two sections along the embankment to give close support and climbed the embankment with his third section under cover from smoke grenades.

A demolition party of eleven men was billeted in Dutch houses near the southern end of the bridge. The German soldiers argued among themselves about blowing the railway bridge. Their orders stated that if anything of importance goes on and no officer or no sergeant is available, 'Don't wait for a direct order.' A German lance corporal saw the red berets of The Parachute Regiment coming down the lower road and said to his fellow engineers, 'Look, we will all take the responsibility and I'll give the order. Blow it.'

Dover's firepower momentarily silenced the enemy allowing Barry and his men to start across on the metal plates of the bridge shrouded in more smoke. Wanting to get a better idea of the enemy positions, Barry stopped and gave the order to lie down. Just then a tremendous explosion erupted, and the second span disappeared amid orange-yellow flames. While laying prone, Barry was hit in the leg and his right arm by enemy rifle fire. The section created more smoke and made their way back meeting Major Dover, who had advanced to the embankment. At that point, one man of Barry's section came down the embankment as if to deliver a message to Dover. Before he could say a word, Private Leslie Sadler slumped to the ground dead from a sniper's bullet.[23]

The brickworks no longer exists having been replaced by a camping site known as Oosterbeeks Rijnoever. The bridge was rebuilt postwar and still carries rail traffic across the Nederrijn between Arnhem and Nijmegen . The rail embankments were modified in 2004 by construction of water permeable bridge supports to ease the flow of river water.

> Continue 1.4 km east on Benedendorpsweg to the railway underpass and park in the small turnoff on the right. (51.979259, 5.860119)

Stymied in his attempt to send troops to the south bank of the Nederrijn by the detonation of the rail bridge, Frost continued toward Arnhem, his route passing through a narrow tunnel under the steep railway embankment. An armored car appeared at the curve east of the underpass and fired both its 20-mm gun and its machine gun at the leading scouts, and then withdrew. Almost immediately after passing through the rail line underpass the leading No 1 Platoon (Lieutenant Robert Vlasto)[24] came under indirect fire from high ground, known as Den Brink, 1.3 kilometers on the left.

Frost dispatched his B Company (Major Doug Crawley) to deal with the German fire which dominated his only approach road to the bridge. Lieutenant Peter Cane led B Company's No 6 Platoon through back gardens along Prins Bernhardweg and the deep railroad cut toward the Oosterbeek-Lang train station to circle around Den Brink unobserved.

Nineteen-year-old, acting SS-Corporal Helmut Buttlar had led a small group of men from SS Flak Bataillon 10 across France since their escape from the Falaise Pocket. A dispatch station directed the group toward Arnhem. That morning, the thirteen men were ordered to join SS Bataillon 'Krafft' in Oosterbeek but on the way there, were incorrectly informed by rear-area troops that Oosterbeek was under British control. Without orders or officers, Corporal Buttlar assumed leadership of the small group. When they approached the Oosterbeek-Lang train station from the north, Buttlar observed hundreds of Dutch greeting the marching British paratroopers.

Buttlar worked his way forward along the railroad embankment with three men while the other nine remained by the rail track. Suddenly Dutch civilians near the Oosterbeek-Lang station spotted Buttlar and warned Lieutenant Cane's paratroopers. The Germans and British rushed toward each other, then each ordered the other to surrender. Buttlar stood up in full view and threw a hand grenade, then his group held off the paratroopers until his men ran short of ammunition and the contingent scattered, most of the men joining SS Panzergrenadier Regiment 21 to fight later in

---

23   The body of Private Leslie David Sadler, aged 20 from Balsall Heath, Staffordshire, was never recovered. He is commemorated on the Groesbeek Memorial.

24   Lieutenant Robert Alexander Vlasto, born in Calcutta, India, was captured and held in Oflag 79, Niedersachsen, Germany. After the war he became a successful investment banker and raised three children. He died in Hampshire in 2003 at age 79.

western Arnhem.[25]

After the brief encounter with Buttlar's small group, Cane's platoon resumed movement along the rail cut. The platoon fell victim to a machine-gun team concealed in a workman's shed along the rail line where the cut curved to the east. Scouts Private Tommy Gronert and Private Jack Edwards received wounds that proved to be fatal. Tommy Gronert called out that he had been hit and his twin brother Claude, who was nearby, rushed to help him. While Claude bent over his brother, he was shot in the head. Both brothers died. Lieutenant Cane was wounded but gave the order, 'Charge the Bastards!' before also dying.[26]

Major Crawley's B Company was engaged against Den Brink for most of the next four hours suffering heavy casualties against SS-Captain Möller's 90-man strong SS Panzer Pionier Abt 9. That distraction and the onset of darkness permitted the remainder of 2nd Parachute Battalion to pass.

Crawley eventually disengaged and returned to his original mission of capturing the pontoon bridge. After moving through the darkened streets of Arnhem, he found the central span had been removed. Crawley moved toward the highway bridge the next morning after having received radio instructions from Frost. His No 4 Platoon (Lieutenant Robert Levien)[27] became separated during the fight to penetrate the German perimeter, which had strengthened during the night. Levien's platoon, by then reduced to eleven men, became surrounded, ran out of ammunition, and surrendered. The seventy remaining members of the company entered the bridge perimeter that morning.

Prins Bernhardweg is directly across from the parking area and leads up hill to the north before petering out in a cultivated field. The **Oosterbeek Lang train station** had been closed since 1938 although the building still stands as a private residence. The station is approximately half-way up the road but cannot be seen through the intervening vegetation and embankments. **Den Brink**, now Arnhem Buiten Business Park is identified by the radio and television transmission tower on its summit. The tower is visible from numerous perspectives around Arnhem.

Continue east on Benedendorpsweg which becomes Klingelbeekseweg on the east side of the underpass, then becomes Hulkesteinseweg and merges into Utrecht-seweg (N225). Continue to the next intersection and bear right onto Onderlangs. Park in the area on the left immediately passed the Hotel NH Arnhem Rijnhotel. (51.984124, 5.885957)

---

25   Helmut Buttlar was slightly wounded several days later but survived the battle for Arnhem and was assigned to guard wounded British prisoners as they were transported to medical facilities in Apeldoorn. He returned to Arnhem years later to review the sites of his various exploits.

26   Lieutenant Peter Howard Cane, aged 25 from Reading, Berkshire, was buried with an unidentified Parachute Regiment soldier in a field grave near the Benedendorpsweg railway viaduct. Both soldiers now rest in joint graves in Arnhem Oosterbeek War Cemetery, Plot 18, Row A, Graves 13 – 14. Thomas Gronert, aged 21, a former tin miner from Cornwall, and his brother Claude are buried in Arnhem Oosterbeek War Cemetery, Plot 18, Row A, Graves 17 and 18.

27   Lieutenant Robert Hugh 'Loopy' Levien, from Tonbridge, Kent, was held in Oflag 79. After repatriation he served in several British regiments until leaving the army in 1962. He died in 2004 aged 87.

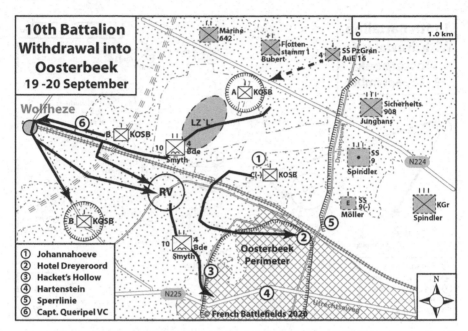

The route just followed formed a surviving section of the 'Lion' route used by Colonel Frost. This intersection is where the 'Lion' and 'Tiger' routes joined and has remained little changed since 1944. Frost took the right fork east along Onderlangs to the Arnhem bridge. The **Rijn Pavilion**, now Hotel NH Arnhem Rijnhotel, ahead on the right, became the overnight headquarters for Colonel Fitch and Colonel Dobie on 18 September when their battalions met heavy opposition approaching Sint Elisabethshof ahead on Utrechtseweg.

Third Lift Disaster, 19 September

During the morning of 18 September, Urquhart and Lathbury remained trapped with the 3rd Battalion near the Rijn Pavilion. The two commanders decided that their return to headquarters was imperative to regain control of the battle. Accompanied by two subordinates, they left the Rijn Pavilion and moved north into the maze of narrow streets west of Sint Elisabethshof where they encountered German troops. Narrowly escaping capture, they abandoned wounded Lathbury and a took shelter in a private home hiding in the attic as the house became surrounded by German troops unaware of their presence. Urquhart was trapped.

Battle

When gliders carrying the Polish Brigade's vehicles and antitank guns approached LZ 'L', the reported approach of German forces from the west forced Hackett to recall his 10th Battalion, then his entire brigade from the deadly encounter with *Sperrlinie* Spindler. The 10th Battalion received orders to disengage from the battle around the pumping station before the glider landings started. Men north of the road crossed under smoke grenades and Smyth's battalion was crossing the open

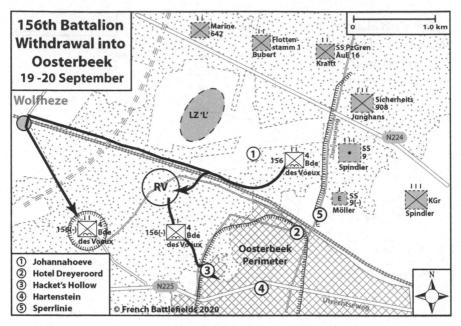

156th Battalion Withdrawal into Oosterbeek 19 -20 September

Wolfheze

LZ 'L'

Marine 642

Flotten- stamm 1
Bubert

SS PzGren AuE 16
Krafft

Sicherheits 908
Junghans

N224

① 156 4. Bde des Voeux

SS 9
Spindler

RV

E SS 9(-)
Möller

KGr
Spindler

⑤

156(-) Bde des Voeux

156(-) 4 Bde des Voeux

②

③

Oosterbeek Perimeter

N225

④

Utrechtseweg

① Johannahoeve
② Hotel Dreyeroord
③ Hacket's Hollow
④ Hartenstein
⑤ Sperrlinie

© French Battlefields 2020

N

ground when the gliders arrived. KGr Krafft followed the battalion from the wood's northern edge and the withdrawal turned into a running gun battle with German units infringing upon the landing areas.

German Bf 109s subjected the gliders to murderous fire during their approach and unloading while the Polish troops struggled to get their vehicles and equipment off the gliders. The Polish, some with little command of English and with different color berets, were mistaken for Germans and shot at by British troops — fire which they returned. Some glider loads were abandoned in the rush to leave the open field. Only a fraction of the equipment was rescued, and some of that arbitrarily commandeered by British officers. Of the 163 scheduled planes, 110 were damaged or shot down.

At 16:00 the 156th Battalion received the withdrawal order from Brigade HQ and executed the action in surprisingly good order. It passed the Johannahoeve Farm but enemy patrols and light armor harassed the withdrawal and in the confusion the battalion split with sections of B and C Companies continuing along the rail line to the Wolfheze level crossing, while the remainder crossed and continued south through the woods.

The rail embankment presented a difficult obstacle for retreating vehicles. Smaller vehicles found safety on the southern side of the rail embankment by passing through the rail underpass near the Bucknall ambush site, but for vehicles it was a more difficult journey. Some slipped through a narrow drainage tunnel, some guns were towed over the tracks where the embankment was less steep, others continued west to the Wolfheze crossing.

The 200-man #9 Kompanie of Krafft's battalion advanced from the cover of the trees near Johannahoeve Farm to fall under the guns of D Company and HQ of KOSB. Survivors retreated back into the woods. However, disasters continued to strike. A Company, KOSB walked into a trap on the northeast corner of LZ 'L' and became surrounded by Krafft's #4 Kompanie. Major Robert Buchanan, felt that he had little alternative and surrendered his 120-man command. The next day B Company became surrounded in the woods near Hotel Wolfheze with almost no ammunition. The 130-man force plus troops from 156th Battalion surrendered.

The 10th and 156th Battalions augmented by Polish soldiers reassembled in the forests to the west to spend an uneasy night. The KOSB now reduced to about 270 men rejoined the 1st Airlanding Brigade in Oosterbeek. Moving with 156th Battalion Brigadier Hackett was able to contact division by radio and agreed to move into the forming Oosterbeek perimeter the next morning. Hackett wanted to strike out through the woods that night, but division recommended waiting until first light — a very bad decision. Before dawn on 20 September, the collection of 4th Parachute Brigade units moved south through the forest then east planning to enter the Oosterbeek perimeter. The 10th Battalion led the way in what became a running gun battle against much stronger German forces.

About sixty men of the 10th Battalion passed inside the perimeter defenses at 13:10 with Lieutenant-Colonel Smyth among the wounded. The remainder of the brigade spent most of the morning avoiding or being attacked by strong German forces. Casualties, especially among officers, mounted. Lieutenant-Colonel des Voeux, badly wounded, ordered his men forward without him while he sat leaning against a tree.[28] Hackett ordered his remaining force into a hollow, where they spent the next eight hours fending off attackers before escaping into the Oosterbeek perimeter.

The mathematics is startling. The 4th Parachute Brigade started with 2,300 men plus about 350 men of the attached 7th KOSB. Within forty-eight hours it was less than 500 with 100 killed, an unknown number of wounded, and the vast majority prisoners.

During the night, the Germans pulled back their defensive line 700 or 800 meters finally liberating Major-General Urquhart from his forced isolation. The relieved commander took a jeep and sped back to division headquarters now at the Hartenstein. He had been out of contact for a total of 39 hours. Urquhart immediately set about rescuing his shattered command. Despite slight hope of completing their mission, he sent Colonel Hilary Barlow forward to assume overall command of the four frontline battalions and produce a coordinated advance toward the bridge. Barlow never got there; his body was never found. After the war, Lieutenant-Colonel Derek McCardie emphasized that he was with Barlow as they ran from a burning building to seek shelter in another building. Going first, McCardie heard the explosion of a mortar round. When he reached a place of safety and looked back, Barlow's body had been completely blown apart. [29]

---

28   Lieutenant-Colonel Sir William Richard des Voeux, aged 32, was killed in action on 20 September fighting in the vicinity of Hackett's Hollow west of Oosterbeek as was the battalion's second-in-command, Major Ernest Vivian Ritson, aged 35. Both officers are buried in the Arnhem Oosterbeek War Cemetery; des Voeux in Plot 6, Row C, Grave 10 and Ritson in Plot 6, Row D, Grave 18.

29   Colonel Hilary Nelson Barlow, aged 38 from Barnsley, Yorkshire, is commemorated on the Groesbeek Memorial.

Chapter Seven
British 1st Airborne Division: Battle for the Arnhem Bridge
17 to 21 September

With Major-General Urquhart and his deputy, Brigadier Lathbury, separated from their commands, decisions fell to Brigadier Hicks. After the 18 September landings, Hicks had three new battalions of paratroopers and he decided to continue with the original MARKET plan. He ordered 1st, 3rd, and 11th Parachute Battalions and the glider-borne 2nd South Staffordshire Battalion to fight through to the bridge. Brigadier Hackett's 10th and 156th battalions were to oppose KGr Spindler's defensive line as described earlier.

British battalion commanders struggled with poor radio communications, lack of an over-all commander, no coordination, and no artillery support. Without reconnaissance and amid narrow streets between stoutly build houses, they attacked along a front only 200 meters wide bordered by the train yards to the north and the Nederrijn to the south. They had no idea what was awaiting them.

Relief Force Stymied, 19 September

At 04:30 on 19 September, the four battalions' advance was shrouded in the early morning river mist. The 2nd Battalion (Lieutenant-Colonel Derek McCardie), South Staffordshire Regiment assaulted along Utrechtseweg. Its D Company (Major John Phillp) led the advance uphill in the early morning darkness followed by B and A Companies with C Company in reserve. Without definitive targets, German machine guns intermittently fired bursts from the higher ground, from the side streets, and along the road. About 05:00, the forward unit met scattered German positions in the vicinity of the hospital, which it quickly overcame, but by then the company had suffered forty percent casualties including its company commander and several of its other officers.

The 1st Parachute Battalion moved on the route along the river supported by the remnants of 3rd Parachute Battalion. The 1st Battalion's route was exposed to Spindler's men in houses on the steep embarkment to the left. The fighting was confused and chaotic. Hand grenades preceded physical assault. Machine guns, mortars, and rifles added their particular sounds to the explosions. Dark and fog initially aided the attack and forward German positions were overrun.

Dawn brought SS Aufklärungs Bataillon 9 an amazing sight from its viewpoint in the brickworks across the river. Dobie's 1st Battalion and Fitch's 3rd Battalion were strung out along Onderlands, the river road, totally unaware of SS cannons aimed at their flanks. The first volley shredded the British paratroopers before they were even aware of the enemy. Bodies disintegrated under bursts of high velocity 20-mm cannon shells. Tracer fire flew flat across the water cutting bodies to pieces. Grenades fell from Spindler's men in the buildings above the roadway.

By 06:30, Dobie's companies had reached the eastern end of the park but most of the officers and NCOs were killed and survivors sheltered in houses or abandoned German trenches. An hour later Colonel Dobie's 1st Battalion with only

17. Paratroopers of the British 1st Airborne Division in a C-47A 'Dakota' aircraft during the flight to Arnhem. (IWM – K7586)

Horsa gliders of the Artillery Regiment are being unloaded on LZ 'Z' while some 1st Battalion paratroopers who should be targeting the adjacent DZ 'X' are coming down among the gliders, 17 September. (IWM – BU1163)

18. The Glider Monument and Liberation Route Marker #25 identify LZ 'S' near Wolfheze where the Pathfinders of 21st Independent Parachute Company were the first to land.

Flood plain crossed by Major Victor Dover's C Company in its attempt to capture the rail bridge over the Nederrijn near Oosterbeek.

19. German SS Polizie in woods prepare to repulse the airborne landings. (IWM – MH3956)

The Ginkelse Heide Airborne Monument stands near the edge of the huge heath visible in the distance, left.

An earlier commemorative stone stood nearby bearing only the words 'Air Landing' and the dates. Despite the inscription, this drop zone was not used on 17 September, below.

20. A German Sd Kfz 250 or light armored half-track from Kampfgruppe Spindler engaged the 156th Parachute Battalion on Dreijenseweg with its MG-42 machine gun. The radio antenna indicates it is a command vehicle despite its damaged right front. Parachutes are visible hanging from the trees. (Bundesarchiv – Bild 101II-M2KBK-771-30 – Höppner)

The Dreijenseweg battle line with Commemorative Post #1. The 156th Battalion's attack was from left to right.

21. Sint Elisabethshof Hospital was occupied by British medical personnel for treatment of the wounded despite the battle raging around its front doors. Commemorative Post #3 is visible to the right.

Zwarteweg #14 where Major General Roy Urquhart hid from German troops is identified by the small plaque hanging next to the window.

The houses on Utrechtseweg where Major Dover's C Company became trapped by German armor and forced to surrender. Airborne House is second from the right.

22. Aerial photograph of the Arnhem bridge showing the tangled wreckage of Kampfgruppe Gräbner. The view is from the northwest putting the river out of view to the right. (IWM – HU2062)

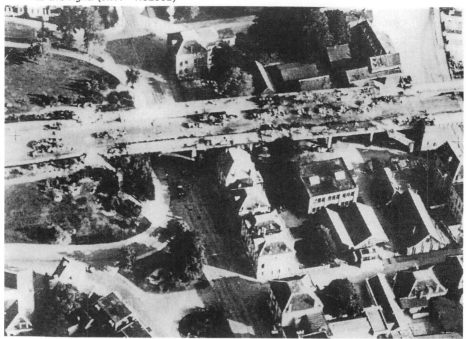

Scene at the north end of the Arnhem Road bridge after the battle. The wreckage of German vehicles can be seen in the foreground. The bridge tower is on the right and the roofless building nearby held No 1 Platoon, A Company, 2nd Parachute Battalion. (IWM – HU2172)

23. A silhouette view of the John Frostbrug as it peacefully appears today.

Steps used to manhandle a 6-pounder antitank gun up to the Arnhem bridge approach road during the initial assault on 17 September. The square form at the top holds the John Frostbrug plaque.

Lieutenant John Grayburn's (inset) battlefield grave was near the grass area on the lower left.

Airborne Monument in Airborneplein and the stone column from the Palace of Justice, below.

24. Major-General Roy Urquhart stands with the Pegasus airborne pennant on the grounds outside his headquarters at Hotel Hartenstein, 22 September. (IWM – BU1136)

A wounded man being carried away by stretcher on the grounds of the Hotel Hartenstein. The wounded soldier's face has been purposely edited.
Note the stocks of ammunition and fuel dump in the background. (IWM – BU1141)

25. The Hotel Hartenstein as it appeared in 1945.
(National Army Museum – 2014-08-16-447)

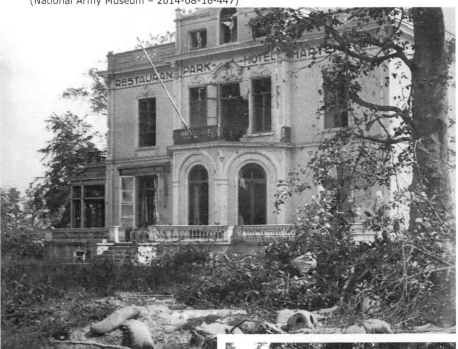

A 17-pounder anti-tank gun stands on the museum grounds behind the Hartenstein where its plate and breech display the damage inflicted during the battle, right.

The monument behind the Airborne Museum 'Hartenstein' thanks the People of Gelderland for their courage, the aid they brought to the wounded, and the hiding of Allied soldiers and airmen, below.

26. Utrechtseweg in front of Hotel Hartenstein immediately after the battle displays the debris from the intense fighting. The destroyed jeep in the foreground was part of the Reconnaissance Squadron. (Bundesarchiv – Bild 101I-590-2330-25A – Erwin)

The 10-meter-high Oosterbeek Airborne Memorial in the center of the park bears images of warfare, below left.
The Memorial Soldier with Flower Girl stands across from the Hartenstein, below right.

27. The Stone of Remembrance and the southern plots of the Arnhem Oosterbeek War Cemetery.

The grave marker of Lieutenant John Grayburn, recipient of the Victoria Cross, left and plot 34 holding Polish soldiers' graves, right.

Three crew members of a Stirling IV heavy bomber from 190 Squadron flew a supply mission to the trapped troops in Oosterbeek on 21 September. The plane was shot down by antiaircraft fire, below.

28. A 6-pounder antitank gun of No 26 Antitank Platoon, 1st Border Regiment, fires against a Flammpanzer tank of Panzer Kompanie 224 in Oosterbeek on 20 September. (IWM – BU1109)

Two British airborne troops dug on the grounds of brigade headquarters in Oosterbeek, 18 September. (IWM – BU1143)

29. The rear of the rebuilt Oude Kerk in Oosterbeek. The heavily damaged building was the final redoubt before the British evacuation.

The Oude Kerk Airborne Memorial, placed at the rear of the church, commemorates the heavy fighting that took place around the church, below.

The Oude Kerk interior including the podium from which Major Richard Lonsdale made his stirring speech on beating the German Army, below.

30. A view of Westerbouwing and its elevation above the Nederrijn as seen from the south bank of the river.

A plaque on the exterior wall of the Westerbouwing Restaurant commemorates the actions of the 1st Battalion, The Border Regiment during the battle, right.

The winding Nederrijn from Westerbouwing towards Arnhem. The rail bridge is prominent, below.

31. A memorial to the crew of a B-25 'Mitchell' bomber from RAF 98 Squadron which was shot down on 25 September and crashed near this spot only yards from the Arnhem bridge.

The Arnhem bridge after its destruction by American bombers on 7 October 1944, right. (Nationaal Archief)

The rail bridge and water pumping station along the Nederrijn where the Germans blew a hole in the dike to flood much of the Betuwe on 2 December, below.

32. The Memorial to the Royal Engineers and the Royal Canadian Engineers near Driel commemorates their evacuation of the airborne troops across the Nederrijn on the night of 25/26 September.

The panel shows the moment when two evacuees are transferred to a boat to across the river, inset.

The memorial to Major General Stanislaw Sosabowski in Driel erected in 2006 by the British Airborne Division to commemorate 'a great Polish hero'.

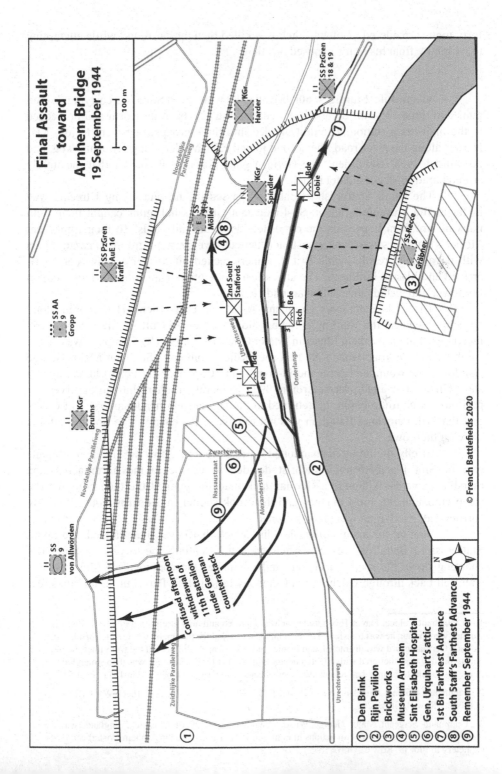

Final Assault
toward
Arnhem Bridge
19 September 1944

0   100 m

Noordelijke Parallelweg

SS PzGren AuE 16
Krafft

KGr Harder

SS PzGren 18 & 19

KGr Spindler

E SS 9(-)
Möller

SS AA 9
Gropp

1 Bde
Dobie

7

8
4

2nd South Staffords

SS Recce 9
Gräbner

3

Utrechtseweg

3 Bde
Fitch

KGr Bruhns

4 Bde
Lea

Onderlangs

11

5

Zwarteweg

6
Nassaustraat

9
Alexanderstraat

SS 9
von Allwörden

Confused afternoon
withdrawal of Battalion
11th German
counterattack
under

© French Battlefields 2020

N

Zuidelijke Parallelweg

Utrechtseweg

1 Den Brink
2 Rijn Pavilion
3 Brickworks
4 Museum Arnhem
5 Sint Elisabeth Hospital
6 Gen. Urquhart's attic
7 1st Bn Farthest Advance
8 South Staff's Farthest Advance
9 Remember September 1944

forty men surrendered.[1] Colonel Fitch was killed by a mortar round while attempting to withdraw from his unit's exposed position.[2]

Meanwhile, Sturmgeschützbrigade 280 with seven StuG IIIs carrying 75-mm guns and three 105-mm SP howitzers entered the city from the north and proceeded to the main train station. The unit divided into three groups: one went to join KGr Harder along the river road, the second joined KGr Möller along Utrechtseweg, and the third to von Allwörden. The German guns provided firepower that the lightly armed paratroopers could not match.

The South Staffordshire Battalion passed the hospital along Utrechtseweg as far as the Museum Arnhem. SS-Lieutenant Gropp's flak guns caught them with flanking fire from houses on the opposite side of the rail yards. To their right front Möller's engineers used panzerfausts and flamethrowers against groups of paratroopers with devastating results while British snipers picked off Möller's men. A StuG III arrived and blasted buildings. The attack lost momentum against the furious German firepower and the advance halted around 10:00.

The 11th Battalion's Company A (Major Dan Gilchrist) sheltered along Utrechtseweg near the Van Linger School, now Montessori College Arnhem only 200 meters west of the Arnhem Museum. Major Gilchrist's small HQ Company was on the south side of the road when a 88-mm shell killed Command Sergeant Major George Ashdown and wounded his second-in-command, (Captain Peter Perse).[3] Lacking HQ staff, Gilchrist awaited orders. Around 09:00 General Urquhart, having observed the perilous attack route before he returned to the Hartenstein headquarters, sent orders that the 11th Parachute Battalion was not to engage the enemy. The South Staffords were on their own.

Briefly sheltering in abandoned German trenches, now the site of apartments east of Sint Elisabethshof, Gilchrist decided to escape to the north across the marshaling yards. Although a German tank machine gunned the men climbing the steep embankment, most made it and then took shelter in a nearby house. Quickly surrounded, every man was taken prisoner.

Waiting for a supporting flanking attack that never materialized, the South Staffordshire Battalion was overwhelmed and essentially destroyed by StuG IIIs charging down the road. Surviving Staffords under the command of Major Robert Cain fell back through Gilchrist's A Company to join 11th Parachute Battalion's rear

---

1   Lieutenant-Colonel David Theodore Dobie was captured and held briefly as a PoW. Because his wounds were minor, he was transferred to the municipal hospital for treatment, where, once bandaged, Dobie's German guard was distracted, and Dobie made his escape. Still behind the front lines, he hid during the day then sheltered with a Dutch doctor until the battle was over. He was then smuggled to Eerde by Dutch Resistance before making his escape across the river. Dobie died in 1971, aged 59.

2   Lieutenant-Colonel John Anthony Fitch, aged 32, is buried in Arnhem Oosterbeek War Cemetery in Plot 20, Row B, Grave 20.

3   Command Sergeant Major George Wilson Ashdown, aged 29 of Chiswick, England, was a recipient of the Military Medal for actions in France in 1940. He is buried in Arnhem Oosterbeek War Cemetery in Plot 19, Row C, Grave 15.

formations. Both forces were without PIATs with which to challenge German armor.

Shortly before 11:00, Division HQ ordered 11th Battalion to turn north and attack over the railway. Lieutenant-Colonel Lea ordered Major Cain to secure the Den Brink high ground which he successfully accomplished despite falling under an intense German mortar bombardment.

The continuing German assault then fell upon the two remaining companies of 11th Parachute Battalion as they withdrew from the maze of houses west of Sint Elisabethshof. The companies moved north from Nassaustraat aiming for bridge over the marshaling yards as ordered. Although what happened next has never been clearly explained, the combination of German tank fire, mortars, snipers, and machine guns decimated the struggling 11th Parachute Battalion. One hundred and fifty survivors drifted back down the hill to Utrechtseweg where they joined the retreat of the other three battalions including Cain's troops toward Oosterbeek.[4]

The 19th of September was the day that all hope of reaching the bridge at Arnhem died. Although only 60 men had been killed, over 1,100 prisoners were taken, and an unrecorded number were wounded. Three parachute battalions had been destroyed.

Battlefield Tour

The tour section begins with a walking tour of sites around Sint Elisabethshof, the route of destruction of the 2nd South Staffords, and defeat of the 4th Parachute Brigade.

> The following sites are best viewed on foot. Total walking distance: approximately 3.4 km, but all but the sites around Sint Elisabethshof are within 1.0 km.
> Ascend the hill from the parking area near the NH Arnhem Rijnhotel to Utrechtseweg and view the narrow gap between houses No 204 and No 206. Do not enter the passageway as it is private property. (51.984275, 5.884654)

Urquhart, Lathbury, and Captain Willy Taylor, the Brigade Intelligence Officer, left Rijn Pavilion through back gardens in an attempt to return to Division HQ. Upon seeing the three men heading in the wrong direction, Lieutenant James Cleminson rushed off to join them.[5] The command group hoped to be hidden by the smoke and fire while German half-tracks and SP guns slowly worked their way through the narrow streets. The men moved north between houses climbing fences and walls to pass into Alexanderstraat.

---

4   Lieutenant-Colonel George Harris Lea, of Franche, Worcestershire was wounded and captured. He spent the remainder of the war in a German PoW camp. After the war, Lea, at various times, commanded the 15th Parachute Battalion, the Royal Marine Commando Brigade, the Special Air Service (SAS), and a NATO unit.

5   Lieutenant James Arthur Cleminson commanded the 5th Platoon, 3rd Battalion. He was wounded later in the battle and taken prisoner. Cleminson was sent to the Prisoner of War hospital in Obermassfeldt where he remained until liberated by US forces. He was awarded the Military Cross for his defense of Oosterbeek from 23 to 26 September. Knighted for his later services to British industry, Sir James Cleminson died in September 2010, aged 89.

Walk a short distance east to Zwarteweg, north to Alexanderstraat, then west along Alexanderstraat to the alleyway beside house No 234. Again, do not enter the private passageway. (51.984813, 5.884400)

The four British officers emerged from a narrow alleyway onto Alexanderstraat, Then, disoriented, instead of veering left to safety, Urquhart and Lathbury turned right toward the oncoming enemy. Cleminson and Taylor, realizing that the two commanders had gone in the wrong direction, gave chase just as Lathbury was hit with a machine-gun burst in the back. The three uninjured officers dragged him into Alexanderstraat No 135. While a Dutch couple tended to Lathbury, a German soldier appeared at the window and Urquhart fired, killing the enemy whose body now lie in the street. Lathbury was temporarily paralyzed and had to be abandoned.

Return to Zwarteweg and proceed north to house No 14 noting the proximity to the Sint Elisabethshof complex. (51.985223, 5.885104)

The three officers entered a maze of back gardens behind houses on Zwarteweg vaulting the fence into the back garden of Anton Derksen. He opened the kitchen door and admitted them into his home at number 14. German soldiers collected around the house unaware that the British commander was sheltering in Derksen's attic. From the attic window, Urquhart saw a German SP gun clank down the street and stop directly in front of the Derksen house. He was trapped.

Continue north and turn left (west) onto Nassaustraat and continue to the memorial on the center median. (51.985570, 5.883967)

Although out of sequence in the battle description, the decisive fighting in west Arnhem which ended British efforts to get a sizable force onto the highway bridge is commemorated with the **Remember September 1944** monument. The 11th Parachute Battalion was destroyed in this area. The pointed stone bears a plaque portraying a dropping parachute, the John Frost Bridge with the 25-pounder gun that continues to guard it, and the ruins of Sint-Eusebius church tower. The telecommunications tower on Den Brink is visible to the west.

From the Nassaustraat monument return to Utrechtseweg and proceed east. (51.984407, 5.885305)

Liberation Route Marker #26 rests at the corner of the Sint Elisabethshof hospital grounds. The plaque and 'Urquhart Presumed Dead' audio present the dilemma of Urquhart and his party that led to their separation from their commands and the presumption of Colonel Urquhart's death.

Continue east on Utrechtseweg to the parking area in front of the hospital. (51.984628, 5.886057)

After the Germans had blown the railway bridge on 17 September, the 2nd

Parachute Battalion's Company C moved toward its second objective, the German headquarters in a building south of the main train station. After the unit passed a section of Sint Elisabethshof, a large number of German soldiers was observed getting off a bus. Major Dover directed No 7 Platoon (Lieutenant David Russell) to open fire. The German contingent was taken by surprise and, as many wounded fell to the pavement moaning, survivors sought shelter in a vehicle. A PIAT round scattered them and some made for the hospital entrance, where they were caught by a second PIAT round. The nine survivors of the quick and well-aimed attack, surrendered.

Also, on 17 September, British 16th (Parachute) Field Ambulance marched directly from the landing zone to **Sint Elisabethshof hospital**, the city's largest hospital, arriving around 22:00. Operating theaters and wards were organized to accept patients. The Germans returned the next morning taking most of the personnel prisoner, although the nineteen-man surgical team was allowed to remain. British surgeons operated for hours while severe fighting took place around the building. Hospital personnel cared for the wounded of both sides even though soldiers at times fought inside or fired from its windows. In total, the surgeons treated over 800 patients and performed 150 operations remaining with their patients until 13 October, when they also entered captivity.

The hospital complex lay near the junction of 'Tiger' and 'Lion' routes where the three battalions began their assault on 19 September. The buildings remain little changed in appearance but are now utilized as a municipal health center housing a variety of medical specialties. The small court in front of the older part of the building holds **Airborne Commemorative Post #3** which recalls the efforts of 16th Parachute Field Ambulance.

Continue up the hill on Utrechtseweg to the Museum Arnhem. (51.985330, 5.892684)

Utrechtseweg and Onderlangs separate east of the hospital and a large park divides the two roadways. The South Staffordshire's B Company temporarily led by Captain Reggie Foote until Major Robert Cain arrived from the landing zone took the lead and the company fought through heavy opposition on the narrow street reaching the western end of Museum Arnhem by 06:00 on 19 September.

Lieutenant-Colonel McCardie sent A Company (Major TB Lane) to swing south of the museum to occupy a wooded hallow behind the museum and reemerge on Utrechtseweg east of the museum. The company's No 10 Platoon with Company HQ occupied the museum building while No 7, 8, and 9 Platoons occupied the three buildings across the street, now renumbered No 82, No 84, and No 88. Slowly advancing down the street, German SP guns fired into the buildings from a distance to avoid British PIAT and Gammon bombs. By 11:30, British antitank PIAT ammunition was exhausted and the German guns closed the range to fire point blank into the buildings. No 8 Platoon in the center building continued small-arms fire even though the roof and one side wall were on fire. The assault guns turned their firepower upon the museum blasting a hole in its wall. German troops assaulted through the breach and the men inside surrendered. The men in the hollow, by now having been joined by Major Cain, were subjected to SP gun fire from vehicles moving along the riverbank and forced to withdraw.

Pause for a moment to view the buildings across Utrechtseweg. (51.985324, 5.893081)

On 17 September, Major Dover's C Company detached from Lieutenant-Colonel Frost's main group intending to seize the German Headquarters building on Nieuwe Plein. The company's nighttime advance was stopped after turning the broad curve in Utrechtsestraat near the museum by German machine guns sited 200 meters ahead firing down the street. The company sheltered in two buildings on the north side on the road – modern No 54 (230 meters ahead) and a second that no longer stands.

The next morning their withdraw along the rear of the 1944 houses was hampered by their high garden walls. German snipers took aim at anyone exposed in open areas and half-tracks followed their progress from the street. When the small group approached Nachtegaalspad, which is now the entrance drive to the office building's parking structure a short distance ahead, they were faced with crossing an area exposed to enemy fire. From a building that stood on the corner immediately east of Nachtegaalspad – where the Alliander Building now stands – Sergeant Campbell threw grenades to distract German attention. The enemy responded by firing 20-mm cannon shells that set the structure on fire. Despite machine-gun fire aimed directly down the open space from the north, Dover brought his survivors across under a cloud from smoke grenades. The unit became pinned down in four houses. While a few men made their escape to the south by braving the machine-gun fire aimed down the street, in the early morning of 18 September, the bulk of the company, approximately 100 men, surrendered.

The 'Airborne House' to the west, now renumbered as No 72, was one of the four houses that held C Company, 2nd Parachute Battalion during their resistance of 18 September. It bears a plaque above the main entrance commemorating thirty members of Major Dover's company who sheltered within. The plaque misidentifies the date.

Continue forward on Utrechtsestraat to the dramatic urban sculpture that extends across the street and the small park opposite. (51.984582, 5.894109

The small park across from the Alliander Building holds the impressionistic stone **Statue to Women in War** and also offers a view down to the Nederrijn River and the Onderlangs route of the relief force advance of 19 September. German StuGs that harbored here attempted to fire upon the 1st and 3rd Parachute Battalions below, but the guns could not sufficiently depress their barrels.

The first building on the right east of the Alliander structure, No 85 Utrechtsestraat and now the ArtEZ Concertzaal, bears a small stone plaque identifying it as the occupation headquarters of the **Sicherheitsdienst**, the intelligence section of the SS and the Nazi Party. (51.984395, 5.894852)

Continue east on Utrechtsestraat for 220 m then turn right on Vijfzinnenstraat and right again on Wolvengang to proceed down the stairs. Onderlangs is difficult to cross, so turn west (right) to the crossing light at Boterdijk pausing briefly at the ramp to the right. (51.983102, 5.896796)

The 1st Parachute Battalion pushed on along the riverfront before becoming the sole focus of German gunners to their front and both flanks. They would be the closest that the relief force would achieve to the Frost contingent 1.3 kilometers ahead.

This marks the approximate **farthest advance** of the 1st Parachute Battalion, although the commemorative post has been placed along the riverfront to the southeast.

Continue east on Boterdijk and then slightly left onto Rijnkade and follow through the park to the commemorative post overlooking the river. (51.981601, 5.898164)

In the confusion of 18 September, Lieutenant MJ Dickson of 3rd Battalion's Machine Gun Platoon led a small party forward along the narrow strip of land between Onderlangs and the river. Finding further advance blocked by the enemy they sheltered in a house. Similarly, Major Tony Deane-Drummond, while attempting to reach Frost's headquarters, took command of three leaderless men and took shelter in a building. These two groups totaling seven men comprised the closest 4th Brigade would get to Frost's perimeter around the highway bridge.[6]

German troops came to occupy the house where Deane-Drummond was hiding in a locked lavatory. After three days, the four men crept out of the house, separated, and swam the Nederrijn. Dickson and his men hid on the roof of their building and also managed an escape.

Airborne Commemorative Post #5 bears a plaque reading, 'On the morning of 19 September 1944 a final attempt by the 1st and 3rd Battalions of the Parachute Regiment to break through to the Nederrijn Bridge failed. After heavy losses the remaining British troops finally withdrew to Oosterbeek.'

The description is, of course, accurate, but postwar reconstruction has altered the street network. The old harbor and the location of the pontoon bridge was 150 meters farther east. The large building on the opposite shore, now a paintball center, occupies the site of the **brickworks** that held German cannon and machine guns. The modern telecommunications tower that locates the high ground of Den Brink is visible to the west.

Return via Onderlangs to retrieve your vehicle.

---

6 Major Anthony John Deane-Drummond was a member of British SAS parachuted into Italy in 1941 to destroy an aqueduct. He was captured, after several foiled escape attempts, he successfully evaded his captors and crossed into Switzerland. For that action, he was awarded a Military Cross. After escaping Arnhem, Deane-Drummond encountered a German defensive line on the south bank, shot a German defender, and was again taken prisoner. While being marched eastward with other PoWs, he slipped away and hid in a cupboard for thirteen days. He established contact with the Dutch Resistance and recrossed the Nederrijn as part of Pegasus I. For his actions in Arnhem, he was awarded a second Military Cross. After the war, Major Deane-Drummond commanded SAS forces in Malaya where he was awarded a Distinguished Service Order. He eventually achieved the rank of major-general.

Defense of the Arnhem Bridge
17 to 21 September

The approach road to the Arnhem bridge first ascends a ramp constructed upon a low earthen embankment. Nearer to the river, the road continues on a raised ramp built upon concrete pillars but left the upper floors of bordering houses and factories overshadowing the roadway. A school building to the east dominated the northern end of the bridge.

At 18:00 on 17 September, thirty armored cars and half-tracks of SS-Captain Viktor Gräbner's SS Aufklärungs Bataillon 9 crossed the Arnhem bridge on their way toward Nijmegen to establish defense positions against advancing XXX Corps. Gräbner would have a difficult day. His reconnaissance battalion reached Elst at 19:00, but he found no enemy troops. The battalion raced to Nijmegen to join with KGr Henke leaving half-tracks with 75-mm antitank guns in Elst. Eventually Gräbner found the defenses at Nijmegen well-organized and returned toward Arnhem intending to reinforce the small detachment guarding its bridge.

Battle
17 September

Lieutenant John 'Jack' Grayburn's leading No 2 Platoon, accompanied by Lieutenant-Colonel Frost, reached the bridge around 20:00 followed by the remainder of A Company and 2nd Battalion's support units, the 1st Parachute Squadron, Royal Engineers (Major Douglas Murray), a RASC platoon with four trailers of valuable ammunition, some military police, and Intelligence Corps men. By this time, B Company had moved on from Den Brink and was at the pontoon bridge. C Company, which had attempted the capture of the rail bridge, was moving toward its alternative objective, the German town headquarters.

Lieutenant-Colonel Frost established his battalion CP in two houses west of the bridge. Brigade Headquarters arrived about forty minutes later and set up in a building adjacent to Frost. No 1 and 3 Platoons cleared the German positions under the bridge and set up defensive positions along the bridge ramp, the embankment and occupied key houses adjacent to the north end of the bridge. From the underpass below the bridge's elevated roadway, Lieutenant Grayburn heard vehicles on the bridge. Preferring not to divulge their presence, he ordered his men patrolling the bridge embankments not to fire on the occasional German traffic still using the bridge.

SS-Lieutenant Karl Ziebrecht had orders to reconnoiter the approaches to the bridge with armored cars from his #1 Kompanie, SS Aufklärungs Bataillon 10. He approached the bridge from the east along Westervoortsedijk at 20:00 as the sun was setting and just as A Company attempted its *coup de main*. Ziebrecht immediately came under fire. Uncertain of the force he was facing in the increasing gloom, he returned fire, withdrew, and made the first report that British paratroopers had reached the bridge.

The first attempt to capture the southern end of the bridge occurred at 20:30 when seven men from Lieutenant McDermont's No 3 Platoon met with heavy gunfire from a 20-mm antiaircraft gun mounted within a wooden pillbox built upon the roof of the western bridge support and an armored car. Frost, keen to control both ends of

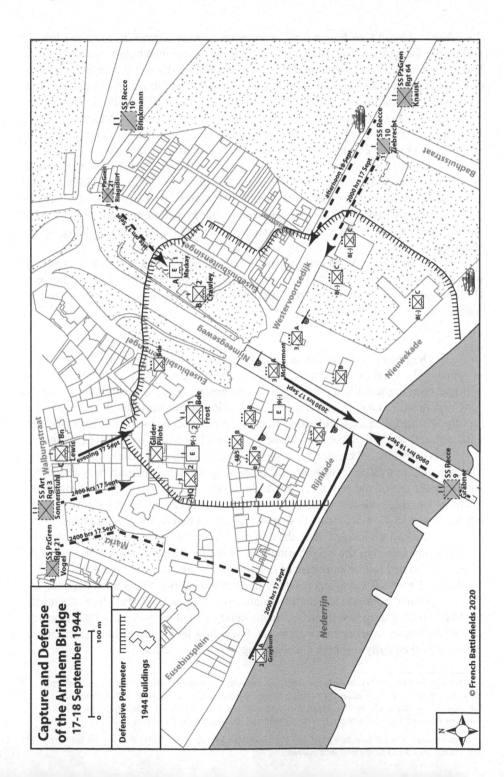

Capture and Defense
of the Arnhem Bridge
17-18 September 1944

Defensive Perimeter

1944 Buildings

100 m

0

© French Battlefields 2020

the bridge, ordered Grayburn's platoon to make another attempt to cross the bridge and secure the southern end. But Grayburn and eight of his men became casualties and had to withdraw. The last attempt that night sent a 6-pounder gun up the embankment onto the approach road to blast the pillbox. A flamethrower in an adjacent house shot its tongue of flame through a hole blasted in the building wall by a PIAT. The flames missed the bunker and instead ignited a gasoline and ammunition storage shed. Heat from the fires was so intense that the bridge's painted surfaces burned. A further assault was now impossible because the whole area lit up as if it were daylight.

At 22:30 a small convoy of four German trucks loaded with troops and ammunition hesitantly drove onto the bridge from the southern end after having received a mistaken report that the bridge had been cleared of British troops. Small-arms fire from Grayburn's platoon stationed on the bridge ramp stopped the trucks and set them ablaze. During the night ammunition blew up in stages adding to the spectacular blaze.

As an alternative to crossing the bridge, Major Murray led a party in search of boats to cross the river, but none could be found. Two platoons of Major Lewis's C Company arrived after their trek through Arnhem and took up positions in the buildings on the southeast perimeter.

The library, indicated as building #27 on the map, was held by the engineers of A Troop, 1st Parachute Squadron, under the command of Captain Eric Mackay. His unit had been in the building for only a few moments before German infantry led by SS-Corporal Alfred Ringsdorf[7] attacked and continued combat through the night with rapidly assembled squads infiltrating from room to room answering British rifle fire with panzerfaust shells. Showers of hand grenades cleared one room after another.

Eventually, Ringsdorf's depleted squad withdrew back up Eusebius-biutensingel. To a passing artillery officer, he suggested that the only way to get the paratroopers out of the buildings was to bring the building down on top of them. 'Believe me, these are real men. They won't give up that bridge until we carry them out feet first.' SS-Colonel Heinz Harmel had already come to the same conclusion.

Mackay concluded that the building was too vulnerable. He therefore withdrew his men into the neighboring Van Limburg Stirum School (building #26), where they joined fellow engineers of B Troop and were later reinforced by elements of 'Pongo' Lewis's C Company resulting in a not too cooperative joint command.

Around midnight a second German counterattack took place from the north. SS-Major Hans-Georg Sonnenstuhl[8] and his lightly armed sixty-eight artillerymen had arrived in Arnhem earlier that evening and marched in file along both sides of the boulevards eventually reaching the beginning of Nijmeegseweg.

---

7   Alfred Ringsdorf, a 21-year-old experienced soldier who had fought in Russia, was in the Arnhem train station awaiting relocation for refitting when his squad was reassigned to #1 Kompanie, I Bataillon, SS Panzergrenadier Regiment 21. Ringsdorf was later wounded in fighting around Elst. After the battle he received a promotion to corporal and the Iron Cross, 2nd Class.

8   Hans-Georg Sonnenstuhl had passed over the Arnhem bridge about 13:00 that day on his way north to his regiment's new camp near Zutphen.

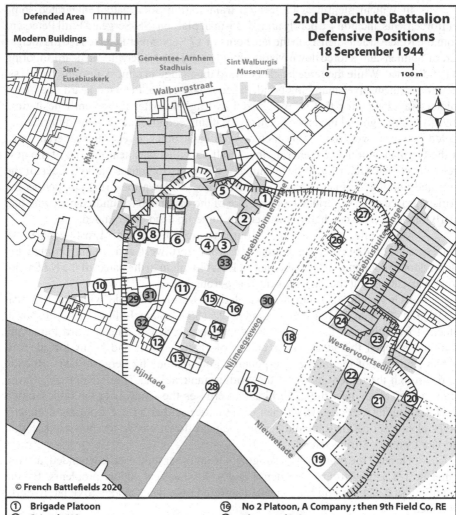

2nd Parachute Battalion Defensive Positions 18 September 1944

Defended Area

Modern Buildings

Gemeentee- Arnhem Stadhuis

Sint-Eusebiuskerk

Sint Walburgis Museum

Walburgstraat

Markt

Eusebiusbinnensingel

Eusebiusbuitensingel

Nijmeegseweg

Rijnkade

Westervoortsedijk

Nieuwekade

© French Battlefields 2020

① Brigade Platoon	⑯ No 2 Platoon, A Company ; then 9th Field Co, RE
② Brigade HQ	⑰ Platoon of B Company
③ 2nd Battalion HQ	⑱ No 3 Platoon, A Company
④ Mortar Platoon	⑲ - ㉒ No 8 Platoon, C Company, 3rd Battalion
⑤ RASC Platoon	㉓ Brigade HQ Platoon
⑥ 9th Field Company, RE	㉔ RAOC & Signals
⑦ Glider Pilots	㉕ HQ Troop RE
⑧ HQ & Support Co.	㉖ A & B Troop RE; C Company HQ
⑨ 1st Airlanding AT Battery HQ	& No 9 Platoon (Van Limberg)
⑩ Mixed Troops	㉗ HQ Troop RE (Sunday night only)
⑪ No 5 & No 6 Platoons, B Company	㉘ Bridge Pillbox
⑫ No 1 Platoon, A Company	**Initial Artillery Positions:**
⑬ No 1 Platoon & MGs, A Company	㉙ 6-pounder gun (Sgt Doig)
⑭ AT Platoon & 9th Field Co, RE	㉚ 6-pounder gun (Sgt Shelswell)
⑮ A Company HQ; B Troop RE	㉛ 6-pounder gun (Sgt Kill)
	㉜ 6-pounder gun (Sgt O'Neill)
	㉝ 6-pounder gun (Sgt Robson)

In Willemsplein near the central train station Sonnenstuhl integrated some reinforcements, including a poorly armed, 35-man platoon (SS-Sergeant Emil Petersen) from the Reichsarbeitsdienst.[9] In the late hours of 17 September Petersen led his men as part of Sonnenstuhl's force down Markt street toward the Nederrijn. He heard shooting in the distance. While the force headed toward the bridge in almost absolute darkness, they found themselves marching beside a secondary force. Petersen heard one of the soldiers say something that he recognized as English. After a moment's hesitation, both forces recognized the other as enemy. Within seconds machine-gun and rifle fire rattled between two groups only meters from each other. Everyone scattered, most of the German contingent sheltering in a small park that was near the site of the new welcome center. Major Lewis's C Company withdrew to houses on both sides of the park and had the Germans trapped in a crossfire. At dawn the firing stopped as the British hurried on to the bridge less fifty-five of the original one hundred men who had nearly made it. Over one half of the German force lie dead or wounded.

Meanwhile, the weak #3 Kompanie (SS-Lieutenant Ernst Vogel), SS Panzergrenadier Regiment 21 approached from northwest and fought through the Markt door to door among the buildings on Eusebiusplein to the banks of the Nederrijn. Frost was cut off, but the encirclement was porous.

KGr Reinhold, a scratch group led by Major Reinhold with the 200-man I Bataillon, SS Panzergrenadier Regiment 22 (SS-Captain Euling) at his disposal, attacked from the east at about 01:00. A platoon from C Company, 3rd Parachute Battalion stopped the attack at the corner of Badhuisstraat and Nieuwe Kade 250 meters southeast of the bridge. A 6-pounder gun manned by Sergeant Cyril Robson fired through the underpass to set the leading tank ablaze. The PzKpfw IV slewed across the roadway near the footbridge that crosses the roadway at the milk factory, blocking trailing vehicles which then came under withering fire from paratroopers. Other elements of KGr Reinhold became bogged down on Westervoortsedijk and at the Van Limburg Stirum school.

Through the night British stragglers from other units, some wounded, arrived at the bridge adding to Frost's defense and to his medical supply problems. By the end of the first day, his 2nd Battalion had suffered nine dead and approximately thirty wounded.

During the night, Major Denis Munford drove back to Royal Artillery HQ in Wolfheze to reset his radio equipment and obtain more batteries. He somehow managed to elude German patrols and returned to the bridge perimeter. His bold exploit produced the only communications that the bridge contingent had during the entire battle because brigade radios remained unable to hear the faintest signal from any division unit despite heroic attempts from the exposed attic of building #2. With contact established on the artillery net, Munford was able to call down artillery fire from the 75-mm howitzers stationed near the Oosterbeek Oude Kerk.

---

9   Reichsarbeitsdienst: Reich Work Service was formed during the depression to put people to work and indoctrinate the Nazi philosophy. During the war its members supported military actions building airstrips, constructing coastal fortifications, and even guarding prisoners. Late in the war, its units became frontline combat troops despite being poorly trained and not equipped for combat.

18 September

By dawn on 18 September, B Company, less its rear guard No 4 Platoon which had become separated, some seventy men in all, arrived in the bridge area as the final addition to the bridge force. Frost's force then numbered approximately 740 men scattered around twenty-seven buildings.

SS-Captain Gräbner watched the flashes of gun fire from the opposite end of the bridge in the growing morning light. At 09:00, the armored vehicles of KGr Gräbner started movement across 600 meters of the rubble-strewn bridge. At first, they were protected by the arc of the roadway, but vehicles became more exposed after they crossed the mid-point. Five Puma wheeled armored cars firing cannon and machine guns raced through the British position and into the town center. The following slower infantry-laden trucks and half-tracks felt the full barrage of British small-arms, antitank, and mortar fire. Grenades were tossed into the open topped vehicles as they attempted to pass the houses bordering the ramp. Flames spread across the streets. The following wave of half-tracks paused in undecided confusion. Two armored personnel carriers attempted to cross, but the intense fire forced the leader to reverse crashing into the follower and both became a tangled mass of metal and flames. Two other vehicles, attempting to maneuver through the wreckage, crashed through the barrier and plummeted onto Rijnkade below. So, it continued to midday when the firing ceased. Of Gräbner's twenty-two vehicles, twelve were flaming wrecks. Fifteen other vehicles from earlier attempts to cross the bridge were strewn about the northern approach ramps. Seventy SS troops were dead including Gräbner.[10]

In the afternoon the German forces were divided into two groups: KGr Knaust[11] (Major Hans-Peter Knaust), consisting of four infantry companies, was assigned to clear the northern ramp from the east and KGr Sonnenstuhl from the north. The west side was not entirely sealed off due to lack of resources. Major Reinhold and his kampfgruppe including Bataillon 'Euling' left for Nijmegen via the ferry at Pannerden to the fate described in Chapter Four.

Late Monday afternoon SS Panzer Aufklärungs Bataillon 10, SS-Major Heinz Brinkmann[12] attacked along Westervoortsedijk from the factory area east of the bridge. A barrage of German artillery and mortar fire was followed by a column of light tanks, armored cars, and half-tracks, which were met by two 6-pounder antitank guns that put two tanks out of commission. Other tanks reached a print shop 220 meters east of the bridge along Nieuwe Kade held by a platoon from C Company. The tanks blasted holes in the brickwork with solid shot followed by high explosive

---

10   SS-Captain Viktor Gräbner received the Knight's Cross only a few hours earlier for personally leading armored counterattacks against British advances in Normandy during the previous July. His body was never found.

11   KGr Knaust: two to three hundred men of Panzer Grenadier AuE Bataillon 64 later joined by Panzer Kompanie 'Mielke' with eight PzKpfw III & IV.

12   KGr Brinkmann was composed of Brinkmann's Aufklärungs Bataillon 10, Knaust's Panzergrenadier AuE Bataillon 64, elements of SS Panzergrenadier Regiment 21, SS Flak Batterie 102, and Panzer Kompanie 'Mielke'.

rounds. SS infantry rushed in and the platoon was captured.[13]

Building #13, occupied by Grayburn's platoon, had became the target of ceaseless mortar and long-range phosphorus shelling from south of the river that set the house on fire. As darkness fell, the platoon evacuated to building #17 near the east side of the bridge ramp. Three tanks attacked from the east destroying building #18 and expelling Lieutenant McDermont's platoon. During the day additional attacks were made against the eastern defenses that finally overran buildings #20 and #21.

Close range fighting continued among the narrow streets. The well-constructed buildings converted every position into a fortress. This hellish combat was not house-to-house but room-to-room. Truckloads of German soldiers attempted to force their way down Rijnkade only to be riddled with small-arms fire from roadside buildings. The survivors were shot down as they searched for cover. On the west side, Vogel's #3 Kompanie, SS Panzergrenadier Regiment 21 maintained the pressure in street fighting among the houses bordering Eusebiusplein.[14]

19 September

By early morning of 19 September, on the west side, the Germans had penetrated as far as the Markt and began setting fire to houses #10 and #11 with 88-mm shells from two Tiger tanks sited in the Markt. On the east side, KGr Knaust had cleared buildings #17, which was later recaptured, and #19 through #25.

Later in the morning, three PzKpfw III tanks began to shell several of the occupied buildings at point blank range causing them to completely collapse. Captain Anthony Frank, second-in-command of A Company, stalked them with a PIAT and successfully knocked out one persuading the other two to withdraw.

SS-Colonel Harmel stood on grassy Eusebiusbuitensingel with his tank and artillery commanders. German attacks then came from the north along two streets on either side of the approach highway where more open ground allowed tank movement. The order was given to shell every floor of every building one-by-one until each building collapsed. Phosphorus shells were occasionally used to set buildings on fire in an attempt to force the defenders to abandon their position. British strongpoints were inexorably reduced to rubble. Buildings, their support walls and beams shattered, collapsed from the roof down. The shelling forced A Company to evacuate and return to a position under the north end bridge road arches and embankment. Frost's force was pressured from three directions by KGr Knaust and KGr Brinkmann. Two 88-mm flak guns flanked the southern approach road and subjected the riverside buildings to their direct fire.

During the evening, German Tiger tanks[15] attached to KGr Brinkmann arrived on the scene. Two Tiger tanks rumbled down Eusebiusbuitensingel firing their 88-mm shells into house-after-house at point blank range. One of the 60-ton monsters was hit

---

13   Building #19 is one of the few original buildings still standing on this part of the battlefield. At last report it held the Van Ginkel Art Supply Store at Nieuwe Kade 2. (51.974381, 5.914872)

14   SS-Lieutenant Ernst Vogel was later killed by machine-gun fire.

15   The two Tiger I tanks were from a detachment of fourteen from schwere Panzer Kompanie 'Hummel' (Hauptmann Hans Hummel).

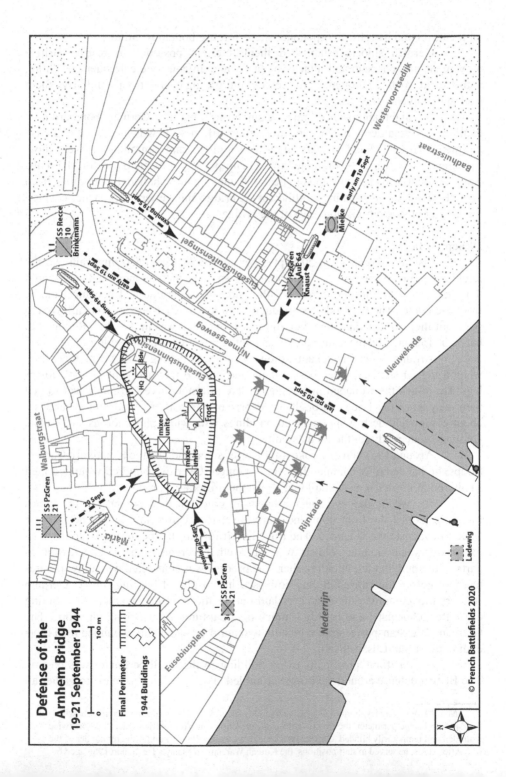

Defense of the
Arnhem Bridge
19-21 September 1944

Final Perimeter

1944 Buildings

© French Battlefields 2020

on the turret and barrel with 6-pounder shells forcing both to withdraw.

German snipers established themselves in positions to restrict British movement and concentrated attacks of tanks and infantry were frequent. Fighting patrols were routinely organized to seek out infiltrating enemy troops and drive them back with bayonet charges.

As night approached, rain began to fall but the German bombardment continued. Casualties mounted and the cellars filled with wounded as the British perimeter shrunk. Food, water, medical supplies, and ammunition were now desperately low; water was rationed to one cup per day. The supply of PIAT bombs was exhausted leaving no weapon to deal with tanks which shelled the buildings from very close range. The 6-pounders still kept the bridge and western approaches covered but could not support positions east of the bridge.

20 September

Dawn on Wednesday, 20 September approached with drizzling rain and the relentless pounding resumed. German snipers and machine-gunners had so covered the entire area that the positions on either side of the bridge had become isolated from each other. The 6-pounders were out of action. Stretcher-bearers were allowed to go about their work unimpeded, but all other movement was impossible. Reduced to between 150 and 200 men, surrender was inevitable and fast approaching.

Around noon, Lieutenant-Colonel Frost was talking with Major Crawley[16] when a mortar shell exploded beside them and blasted fragments into Frost's lower legs. He joined the wounded in a cellar. In late afternoon five German tanks forced their way over the bridge through the debris of the earlier failed attacks and set about completely destroying occupied buildings with white phosphorous shells. The Germans were ready for the final assault.

Around 19:00 Frost awoke after a brief sleep and, unable to actively lead his troops, he handed over command to Major Gough. Over two hundred wounded men sweltered in the cellar as the building above them literally burned.

On Wednesday evening the battalion chief medical officer, Doctor James Logan, unbolted the front door and, carrying a Red Cross flag, left to negotiate a truce to evacuate the wounded. The truce lasted for two hours, during which British paratroopers and German soldiers worked together to remove the wounded even as parts of the building fell into the cellar. The process was completed with only minutes to spare before the entire building collapsed into a pile of burning rubble. German soldiers moved among the stretchers laid out on the river embankment distributing cigarettes, chocolate, and brandy – much of it captured from British air drops. The Germans later transported approximately two hundred and eighty wounded men most ending up at Sint Elisabethshof.

By this time, practically every building in the small perimeter was on fire. The British defense around the bridge crumbled. The decision was made to gather all

---

16   Major Doug Crawley, born in Malta, received his second Military Cross for his actions within the Arnhem bridge perimeter, the first award being for actions in North Africa where he was twice wounded and temporarily blinded. Crawley was held in a German PoW camp for the remainder of the war. Afterwards, he served in staff positions, the Korean War, and in Malaya. He died in 1986 aged 66.

the available men in the large garden area behind 1st Parachute Brigade Headquarters. That night 200 survivors of the bridge defense including Frost, surrendered.[17]

21 September

By 05:00, fifty men located around the west side of the embankment and in trenches in the gardens and amongst the rubble of former buildings still held out. At dawn, a few survivors led by Major Gough emerged from hiding. They scattered hoping to rejoin the division, but it was useless. Gough was captured attempting to hide under a wood pile near the water works.[18]

Told to hold for forty-eight hours until the armored column arrived, Frost had held for eighty-one hours.

Aftermath

Of the 525 officers and men of the 2nd Battalion at takeoff on 17 September, 350 men reached the bridge. Fifty-seven died during the engagement or in German hospitals afterwards. Sixteen were evacuated across the Nederrijn, 272 were captured; and 180 men of the 2nd Battalion were missing; some died in various hospitals or as German PoWs or later escaped through the help of the Dutch Resistance. Of the total 740 defenders of the bridge, 81 were killed or would later die from their wounds.

The bridge was again wired for destruction should the Allies approach from the south, but never detonated. What the German did not do, American bombers accomplished on 7 October when the bridge was bombed and destroyed. It was rebuilt after the war to a nearly identical design.

Major Tatham-Warter, Company A commander who was slightly wounded, was taken prisoner and sent to the Sint Elisabethshof for treatment. With him was Captain Frank, wounded in the ankle by shelling on Wednesday. 20th September. That night the two got out of bed, put on their clothes, climbed down from a first-floor window, crawled through the hospital gardens, and finally reached the railway line a

---

17   Lieutenant-Colonel John Dutton Frost was taken prisoner and held first at Spangenberg, then at the hospital in Obermassfeldt until liberated by General George S Patton's Third Army in March 1945. Frost was born in India to a British Army officer and his wife. He had fought against the Arab revolt in Palestine before joining the Parachute Regiment. He was awarded the Military Cross for his contribution to the Bruneval raid to steal German radar technology, fought through encirclement in North Africa for which he received the Distinguished Service Order. He failed to capture the Ponte di Primosole in Sicily where he was wounded and landed by sea in Italy. Frost received a second Distinguished Service Order for his leadership against an overwhelming enemy at Arnhem. After liberation, Frost participated in the Norway expedition to disarm German soldiers, the Palestinian Emergency, and the Malayan Emergency before returning to duties in England where he commanded the 52nd Division. Major-General Frost died in 1993 aged 80 leaving a son and a daughter. He is buried at Milland, West Sussex.

18   Major Charles Frederick Howard Gough was a member of a highly distinguished military family which sported four Victoria Crosses. By the time of MARKET-GARDEN he was the oldest officer in the division at age 43. Gough had served in the Royal Navy during the First World War and between the wars in the Territorial Army Reserves. Recalled to service, he distinguished himself during the Dunkerque evacuation during the perimeter defense. After transferring to a unit that became the 1st Airborne Reconnaissance Squadron, he fought in North Africa and was awarded a Military Cross in Italy. After the war, Gough remained in various positions being promoted to colonel. In 1971 he was elected to Parliament. Gough died in 1977, aged 76, while on a visit to Italy where he is buried.

mile to the west of the hospital where, quite exhausted, they halted until dawn. The pair fell into the hands of the Dutch Resistance who took them to an isolated farm.

In the weeks after the battle, several hundred airborne personnel collected around the Ede area creating difficulty for the Resistance concealing and administrating the large number. On 22 October, Operation PEGASUS evacuated 138 men across the Nederrijn. Captain Frank was honored by being Mentioned in Dispatches for the part he played in administering this force.[19]

Battlefield Tour

Central Arnhem bears no resemblance to the old city that was shelled and destroyed. It has been rebuilt but not to the same pattern or design as the original. Apartment blocks have been replaced with modern office buildings. The river has been rerouted and the small harbor near the north end of the pontoon bridge is gone.

The tour reviews the most important sites of the entire Operation MARKET-GARDEN effort– the Arnhem bridge and the surrounding sites of Frost's defense and eventual capitulation.

From the Rijn Pavilion area, continue east on Onderlangs (N225) for 1.1 km. Then follow Roermondplein, Weerdjestraat, Trans, Eusebiusplein, and Oranjewachtstraat to Nieuwe Kade. Pass under the John Frost Bridge and turn sharply right to Rijnkade to pass under the bridge again and park along the river front before the Airborne at the Bridge. Note this is not free parking and tickets must be displayed. See Chapter Six for a description of the new visitors' welcome center. (51.976445, 5.909265)

From the **Airborne at the Bridge**, the sites around the bridge are best viewed on foot. Total distance of the walking tour: 1.8 km

Proceed east 130 m to the Airborne memorial in Groenewoud Park (51.976301, 5.911260)

Jacobus Groenewoud was part of Jedburgh Team[20] 'Claude' which was tasked to gain information from the resistance that could help 1st British Airborne Division get to the bridge. The three-man team, which included two Americans,[21]

---

19   As a lieutenant, Anthony Frank was awarded the Military Cross for actions in the airborne drop into Sicily. After the war, he married and raised five sons.

20   Jedburgh Team: small teams of clandestine operatives parachuted into occupied countries to perform sabotage and guerrilla warfare. Members came from the British Special Operations Executive (SOE), the American Office of Strategic Services (OSS), the French Central Bureau of Intelligence and Operations (BCRA), and Dutch and Belgian Armies.

21   Lieutenant Harvey Todd arrived at the Arnhem bridge where Todd became part of the bridge defenses very effectively eliminating a German 20-mm cannon, a machine gun position, and fought fires started by German phosphorus shells. Lieutenant Todd participated in a fighting withdrawal attempting to reach the Nederrijn but became isolated and captured. He escaped a PoW camp and made his way to American lines. Todd was awarded a Distinguished Service Cross for his actions around the bridge. After the war, Todd returned to Marion, Illinois where he died in 1993 at age 77.
Technical Sergeant Carl Scott became separated from the two officers shortly after landing and remained in Oosterbeek. He joined the evacuation across the Nederrijn but was killed in action five weeks later. Scott, aged 21, is buried in Belpre, Ohio.

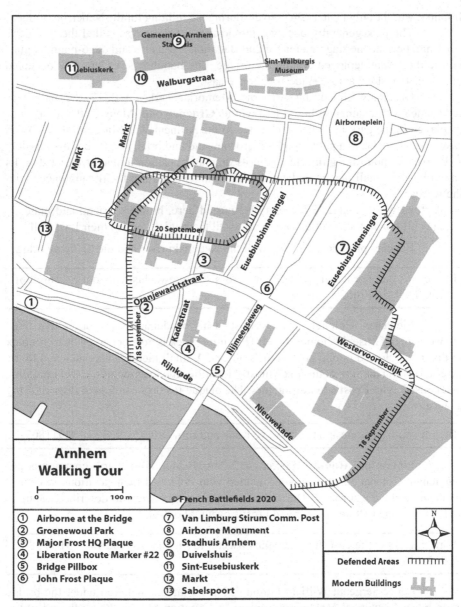

Arnhem Walking Tour

0 — 100 m

© French Battlefields 2020

① Airborne at the Bridge
② Groenewoud Park
③ Major Frost HQ Plaque
④ Liberation Route Marker #22
⑤ Bridge Pillbox
⑥ John Frost Plaque
⑦ Van Limburg Stirum Comm. Post
⑧ Airborne Monument
⑨ Stadhuis Arnhem
⑩ Duivelshuis
⑪ Sint-Eusebiuskerk
⑫ Markt
⑬ Sabelspoort

Defended Areas
Modern Buildings

landed in Drop Zone 'X' around 14:00 on 17 September. Groenewoud started toward the bridge with the headquarters staff of the 1st Parachute Brigade. Along with two British soldiers, they captured documents that contained plans to destroy the harbors in Amsterdam and Rotterdam.

On Monday 18 September, Groenewoud volunteered to leave the bridgehead through German lines to Oosterbeek to deliver orders to the division. After only a couple of hundred meters outside the bridgehead, Groenewoud was shot in the head by a German sniper and died instantly. Jacobus Groenewoud, reserve captain of the

Infantry, was the only Dutch officer to die during the fighting for the Nederrijn bridge.[22]

The park generally occupies the position of what was called the 'builder's yard' and became the staging area for 2nd Battalion's vehicles and the 6-pounder guns before they were deployed around the bridge. The battalion's A Company occupied buildings that stood across Kadestraat to the east.

Originally called the Airborne Memorial Park, in 2017 the park was redesigned and renamed in honor of **Jacobus Groenewoud**. Many of the items once displayed in the park have been relocated to the Arnhem War Museum '40 – '45. A rust-steel plinth bears a photograph of Groenewoud and briefly describes his mission. A **British 25-pounder gun** remains in its dramatic position aimed at the bridge. Its shield bears a small plaque dedicated to the 16th (Parachute) Field Ambulance with the words:

A stone with a badge, a name, a date buried here, brothers, friend and mate they all fought their battles to free us all 'til the bugle sounded their Last Call.

Benches provide a good view of the Nederrijn river and the highway bridge.

Leave to the north on Kadestraat; cross Oranjewachtstraat onto Prinsehof. (51.976909, 5.912062)

Lieutenant-Colonel Frost established his headquarters in houses that lined the west side of Eusebiusbinnensingel. The entire block is now occupied by a complex of tax, housing, and public prosecutor's offices. A small metal plaque attached to the exterior wall of the rear of the Tax Ministry identifies the location of the 1944 building that housed **John Frost's headquarters**. The plaque features a mounted rider carrying a lance.

Return south on Kadestraat to Nieuwe Kade and turn east. (51.975971, 5.911809)

Liberation Route Marker #22, 'A Bridge Too Far,' commemorates Lieutenant-Colonel John Frost and his men who defended their positions in central Arnhem until the last round. The audio uses various characters to describe Gräbner's actions of 17 and 18 September and Frost's eventual defeat.

Forty meters to the east the west stairs ascend to the bridge roadway. (51.975817, 5.912350)

Lance-Sergeant William Fulton of No 3 Platoon sheltered under the bridge ramp when Lieutenant McDermont ordered his section to take the north end of the bridge.[23] Fulton only had seven men, but they climbed the stairs on the west side to

---

22   Reserve Captain Jacob Groenewoud, aged 27, was awarded the Military Order of William 4th Class, the highest Dutch military honor and equivalent to the Medal of Honor or Victoria Cross. Groenewoud is buried in Arnhem Oosterbeek War Cemetery, Plot 20, Row B, Grave 12.

23   Lieutenant Andrew Johnston McDermont, aged 25 from Stirling, Scotland, was seriously wounded on 19 September attacking German troops when he charged up the staircase into the fire of three machine pistols in a house near the bridge. He died three days later. McDermont is buried in Arnhem Oosterbeek War Cemetery, Plot 6, Row D, Grave 7.

the road surface. Fulton halted the group upon hearing German spoken from a troop-carrying truck only 15 meters away. The truck drove off and Fulton led his small force along the right-hand side of the bridge in almost total darkness, becoming the first British soldiers on the Arnhem bridge. A couple prisoners were quietly taken, before Fulton saw a rifle rise to point in his direction. Fulton fired his Sten gun and killed his attacker but was at the same time wounded in his left leg. Fulton ordered his force to draw back and then sheltered behind a steel girder to be later rescued by two medics.[24]

Later that night, Lieutenant John Grayburn was ordered to assault and capture the southern end of the bridge. Moving in two single-files along the iron girders for concealment, their advance was met by fire from an armored car and a pillbox near the northern end. Almost at once, Lieutenant Grayburn was shot through the shoulder, but he continued to press forward until casualties became so heavy that he was ordered to withdraw. He directed the withdrawal from the bridge personally and was the last man to come off the embankment into comparative cover. Grayburn returned to the house occupied by the 2nd Battalion in building #16 for treatment to his shoulder wound that required a blood transfusion before returning to his platoon which had dug slit trenches on the west embankment of the bridge.

At 22:00, Sergeant Ernie Shelswell from Lieutenant Robin Vlasto's No 1 Platoon made a third attempt with a 6-pounder gun jockeyed into position to fire just over the crest of the bridge at the pillbox. The gun fired several Sabot[25] rounds to puncture the pillbox. A flamethrower positioned in a nearby building by Royal Engineers then fired at the pillbox. The arcing tongue of fire missed the pillbox but ignited wooden sheds behind instead. The sheds contained gasoline and 20-mm ammunition and exploded in a shattering roar. The explosion ignited the paint on the bridge surface, which burned throughout the night.

The west stairway tower a short distance ahead held the twin-barreled 20-mm FlaK 38 antiaircraft gun on its roof and became the defensive stronghold for the small bridge guard force until neutralized by PIAT and flamethrower. Inside, a **memorial tablet**, erected by grateful residents of the province, outlines the battle and recognizes the gallant defense and sacrifice of the British forces in their efforts to liberate the Netherlands.

Proceed north 120 m on the bridge approach to a second stairway. (51.976768, 5.913207)

This stairway was used on 17 September to manhandle Sergeant Shelswell's 6-pounder antitank gun up to the bridge ramp. The gun fired the shells that penetrated the pillbox guarding the approach roadway.

---

24   Lance-Sergeant William Fulton spent three days in the cellar of Brigade Headquarters in building #2 before a truce transferred all the wounded to German hospitals for treatment. In November, he was taken to a PoW camp from which he was not liberated until May 1945. William Fulton spent the next two years in hospitals for treatments to his shrunken leg. He died in 2008 and his ashes were spread in the Arnhem Oosterbeek Cemetery — as he wished.

25   Sabot: high impact velocity shells with a tungsten carbide tipped core typically used to penetrate armored vehicles.

The **John Frostbrug** plaque mounted upon the stairway cites a brief poem describing Frost's persistent soldiers and the naming of the bridge after Frost:
This is the bridge for which John D Frost fought
Leading his soldiers persistent and brave
In an advance where freedom was sought
Went a bridge too far which they tried to save
The bridge is now with his name proudly wrought.
(In Dutch and English)

Descend the stairs to the small park. (51.976838, 5.912938)

Throughout the next day and night, the enemy made repeated attacks on building #17 occupied by Grayburn's unit using infantry with mortars, machine guns, tanks, and self-propelled guns. Retention of the house is attributed to Grayburn's display of courage and inspiring leadership. On 19 September, the enemy renewed the attacks, which increased in intensity until eventually the house was set on fire and had to be evacuated.

Grayburn then took command of the remainder of his company and spent the night organizing a defensive position to cover the northern approach to the bridge. On 20 September, he extended his defense by a series of fighting patrols which prevented the enemy from gaining access to houses in the vicinity. The appearance of enemy tanks forced a withdrawal to an area farther north. The German plan was to blow the bridge. Grayburn led a patrol which removed fuses from the demolition charges placed in the archway under the northern-most span. Although again wounded, he refused to be evacuated.

Grayburn, one of about thirty men sheltering from German fire under the bridge, led a party of five or six men attempting to break out of the German ring. Grayburn, who had a bandage around his head, his right arm in a sling, and a bandaged leg, fired his pistol at the enemy with his left hand. The men were picked off one by one until Grayburn and Private Stephen Morgan were on their own; all the other soldiers dead or too wounded to continue. Grayburn patted Morgan on the back and said, 'It's time to go.' They ran in a zigzag pattern firing their weapons until out of ammunition. Morgan reached the cover of the battalion headquarters in building #3 but before Grayburn could join him, a tank to the front fired its machine gun and he fell. Morgan crawled out to pull Grayburn back. The Germans held their fire. Grayburn again said, 'Leave me.' Morgan had no choice.[26] Lieutenant John Grayburn was later buried on the west embankment opposite the 2nd Battalion headquarters. His remains were not discovered until 1948.[27]

Pass under the bridge approach ramp on Oranjewachtstraat and pause for a moment.

---

26   Private Stephen Morgan was later captured. Morgan died on 20 March 2019 aged 93.

27   Lieutenant John Hollington Grayburn, aged 26, who was born in Karachi in what was then British India, was awarded the Victoria Cross. He is buried in the Arnhem Oosterbeek War Cemetery, Plot 13, Row C, Grave 11.

SS-Lieutenant Ziebrecht's troops arrived at this road junction during the night of 17/18 September planning to cross the bridge. They engaged the British troops in heavy fighting around the dairy factory on the opposite corner. On Monday, the first German tanks arrived, albeit old obsolete PzKpfw III training models, they provided a firepower unmatched by the lightly armed paratroopers.

> Continue north on Eusebiusbuitensingel and find the commemorative post 90 meters ahead in the park on the left. (51.976974, 5.914740)

Around 22:30 on 17 September, Captain Mackay's A Troop and Captain TJ Livesey's[28] B Troop, Royal Engineers occupied the Van Limburg Stirum School in building #26 on a narrow strip of land bordering the approach road. The adjacent library in building #27, which was quickly abandoned as being too exposed, lay to the north. The next day, when two of Gräbner's half-tracks attempted to escape British fire by exiting the northern approach ramp, now named Paarden Bleckman, the paratroopers in the upper floor of the Stirum School lobbed grenades into the open-topped vehicles killing the occupants.

That afternoon the Germans began a series of attacks that would continue for much of the day. An hour of concentrated mortar fire was followed by infantry assaults lasting until 19:30. A German flamethrower set the wooden roof of Stirum school on fire. For three hours engineers and troopers fought the flames with the school's fire extinguishers, water buckets filled from a basement toilet, and their parachute smocks.

Around 03:00 on Tuesday morning, a terrific explosion blew off the entire southwest corner of the school building. German troops casually surrounded the building apparently thinking that everyone inside was dead. They were not. The defenders picked their moment and, wishing to save their ammunition, upon a signal from Mackay, lobbed grenades at the intruders, killing approximately twenty while suffering no casualties themselves. Nonetheless, by this time Mackay's force had been reduced from fifty to twenty-one.

In the early afternoon of 20 September, a Tiger tank and SP gun arrived at the street junction to the south and blasted the school building from a range of only 60 meters. Shell after shell fell blowing away the roof and top floor of the school as Mackay's engineers moved from one rubble pile to another amid thickening clouds of smoke and dust. An attempt to evacuate was met with machine-gun fire. Major Lewis, commanding a platoon from his C Company, decided upon surrender. The first soldier sent out with a white towel tied to his rifle was cut down by machine-gun bullets.[29] German infantry assaulted the no longer resisting British and the position was taken.

Down to thirteen unwounded men, Mackay decided upon escape. A mortar barrage reduced the group to only six men, Mackay moved east to seek an escape route. In the next block while making their way through ruined buildings, the small

---

28   Captain Trevor John Livesey, recipient of the Military Cross in Tunisia, was captured and held in Oflag 79 until April 1945. Captain Livesey died in 1959, aged 38.

29   Sapper (Engineer) Norman Butterworth, aged 27, from Werneth, Greater Manchester was wounded in both legs and died five months later in a German hospital. Butterworth is buried among his comrades in Arnhem Oosterbeek War Cemetery, Plot 18, Row C, Grave 9.

party suddenly came face-to-face with two tanks and fifty or sixty German soldiers. The six paratroopers each emptied a magazine into the startled group, cutting them down. Mackay's force dispersed and their leader, exhausted after over sixty hours of combat, settled under a bush for a rest before resuming his escape at night. Shortly later he was woken by a German bayonet poking his pelvis.[30]

The two large school buildings were severely damaged during the fighting and subsequent attempts to bomb the bridge in October 1944. They were not reconstructed and instead the grounds converted to attractive parkway.

Airborne Commemorative Post #7 identifies where the Van Limburg Stirum School was once located. A plaque recognizes that a group of 1st Parachute Squadron Royal Engineers under Captain Mackay held this position near the Nederrijn Bridge from Sunday evening until Wednesday afternoon.

> Continue north along Eusebiusbuitensingel to Vlijtstraat. Enter the sunken round-about through the pedestrian underpass. (51.978415, 5.914894)

SS-Colonel Harmel positioned two 105-mm field cannon in the park north of the bridge. He laid on the ground between two guns and personally selected the targets. The shelling hit directly under the eaves and continued down meter by meter until the building collapsed. The artillery was driven off by a British gun established in a small house on the west side of the bridge ramp. Harmel then left for Nijmegen.

The **Airborne Monument** in Airborneplein is a damaged pillar from the former Palace of Justice. The pillar stands as a memorial to the memories of death but also of victory and life. The text on the pillar simply indicates the date, '17 SEPTEMBER 1944.' There are two reliefs next to the monument, one of the Pegasus Airborne Symbol and the other with the text 'Battle of Arnhem 44, Bridge to the Future 94.'[31]

> Leave Airborneplein to the west on Walburgstraat and continue for 220 m to Raad-huisplein passing the twin-towered Walburgiskerk on the right. The church is the oldest in Arnhem and is now used for concerts and exhibitions. (51.978904, 5.911712)

The plaza in front of the modern Arnhem Stadhuis or town hall presents a metal sculpture of shattered wreckage symbolic of a **Phoenix rising** from the destruction of war. The low wall surrounding the platform bears the inscription, 'This stone sign reports that Arnhem was forcibly damaged and violated, but by citizens regained courage and glory after twenty years.' Nearby the wall shows reliefs of the

---

30   Captain Eric MacLachlan Mackay, born in India, joined the Royal Scots Fusiliers in 1940. After capture, he was transported by truck to Emmerich, Germany, where he and three others again escaped. Moving cross-country, the four men reached the Nederrijn, stole a boat, and paddled back to Allied lines. Mackay remained in military service with duty stations in Indo-China, Java, Malaysia, and Cyprus before becoming Chief Engineer, British Army of the Nederrijn. He retired at the rank of major-general. Mackay died in 1995, aged 73.

31   Bridge to the Future is a non-profit organization which aims to stimulate awareness of war, peace, and freedom, with a major contribution to the Commemoration of the Battle of Arnhem. Sophie Ter Horst, daughter of Kate Ter Horst, is one of the founders of the organization.

church and city hall in three very different time periods, 1900, 1944, and 1968.

> Continue west to the next intersection and view the house on the corner. (51.978967, 5.910934)

Early in the battle, German soldiers gathered at the Duivelshuis and formed into small kampfgruppen. Gefreiter Horst Weber[32] set up a machine gun underneath the large Devil's House balcony. He regularly fired short bursts at near ground level towards Walburgiskerk, the twin-towered church to the east, to prohibit infiltration between the two churches. With other German troops occupying the Markt, those two forces isolated the British troops at the bridge prohibiting reinforcement or resupply.

The so-called **Duivelshuis** (Devil's House) stands across Walburgstraat from the rear of Sint-Eusebiuskerk. The building, so named because of the stone satyrs supporting the oriel window, dates from the 16th century. During the battle, captured British parachutists were held in its cellar. The building was one of the few to survive the battle intact. It now houses ceremonial duties of the mayor of Arnhem. A dramatic stained-glass window portrays Arnhem and its bridge in flames and a phoenix rising above the Devils' House.

> Continue west to the church entrance. (51.979030, 5.909369)

Sint-Eusebius Kerk
Kerkplein 1, 6811 EB Arnhem
Tel: +31 (0)26 443 50 68
Email: info@eusebius.nl
Web: https://eusebius.nl/
Open Monday through Saturday from 10:00 to 17:00; Sundays from 11:00 to 17:00.

Construction of the Gothic-style **Sint-Eusebiuskerk** or **Grote Kerk** started in 1452 upon the site of prior churches, the first of which dated from the 9th century. Wartime damage was extensive with the interior burned out and the weakened tower later collapsing entirely. Its reconstruction took fifteen years. The church is the largest building in Arnhem and an elevator is available to ascend the 73-meter-high spire for dramatic views over the city. The spire presents identification markers for significant locations of the battlefield. In 2018 two glass observation balconies were added for the fearless at elevations of 59 and 62 meters. The tower now is dramatically illuminated at night.

Sint-Eusebiuskerk interior holds several small memorials to the battle for the city including to the Royal Engineers, the city's Liberation by the 49th West Riding Division on 16 April 1945, and to Resistance Fighters of Arnhem. Most memorable are nineteen bronze parachutists suspended from its vaulted ceiling. The carillon bells commemorate the nationalities of the soldiers who participated in the battle. A stained-glass window presents the city in flames from dive-bombing aircraft.

Jonas Daniël Meijerplaats beside the rear of Sint-Eusebiuskerk holds a statue

---

32   Gefreiter Horst Weber was killed on 10 October 1944. He is buried in Ysselsteyn German Military Cemetery in Plot A, Row 7, Grave 155

of a human form that represents the struggle of the ordinary man and commemorates the Battle of Arnhem.

The tour of central Arnhem includes an optional walk into the pedestrian zone. Leave Sint-Eusebiuskerk proceeding north. Continue one street west on Broerenstraat to Bakkerstraat and follow to building No 62. (51.980474, 5.908051) Total additional distance: 460 m.

On the night of 17 September, fourteen British paratroopers of the divisional Intelligence Section, who had become separated from the unit, found their way onto Bakkerstraat suffering casualties in firefights with the still assembling German troops as they moved toward the Arnhem bridge. Meeting a member of the Dutch Resistance, they were taken to a furniture shop at Bakkerstraat No 60 where they spent the remainder of the night. The next morning, they discovered that the shop was next to Wehrmacht Headquarters in Bakkerstraat No 64 and a firefight broke out. The British troopers were surrounded and after 24 hours, forced to surrender when they exhausted their ammunition supplies.

During the nighttime combat of 17 September, Corporal Arthur Maybury was shot in the stomach while crossing Eusebiusplein. Civilians brought him to the cellar of a school building at Rijnkade No 36 where, despite treatment by Doctor Jan Zwolle who was assisted by Jan Mielekamp, Corporal Maybury died early the next morning.[33] Before burying Maybury on the school grounds, the doctor checked Maybury's pockets where he found a list of names of Dutch Nazi collaborators in the Arnhem area who were to be arrested. Zwolle put the list in his pocket. The next day Zwolle was searched by German soldiers investigating the source of rifle fire and the list was discovered. Zwolle and four civilians were taken to Wehrmacht headquarters for interrogation. Soon afterwards, they were shot allegedly for looting and terrorism.

The wartime Wehrmacht Headquarters was demolished in 1984, but a **memorial plaque**, preserved on the left edge of the building's original façade, records the names of the five victims.[34] An investigation to identify the person responsible for the execution proved fruitless.

Return to the riverfront by crossing the old Markt square much of which is now devoted to paid parking especially for the civil servants that work in the many surrounding government offices. The Arnhem food market is held in this square every Friday from 08:30 to 13:00 and Saturday from 08:30 to 17:00. Exit the Markt by passing through Sabelspoort at its southern end. (51.977249, 5.909357)

Medieval Arnhem was entered through one of four gates protecting the walled

---

33   Corporal Arthur Maybury, aged 30, was reburied in Arnhem Oosterbeek War Cemetery, Plot 25, Row A, Grave 4.

34   The victims were Dr Jan Zwolle, a General Practitioner aged 50; Jan Mielekamp, aged 40, a member of the German Air Defense Service which maintained operations in the building and who assisted Dr Zwolle; Cees Veldhuizen, aged 42, concierge of the school; Johan Smit, aged 30, a Dutch Railways electrician; and bookkeeper Henri Smit, aged 23. The Smit brothers had merely sought shelter from the shelling in the school's strong cellar.

town. The only gate to survive is the **Sabelspoort**, built in 1357 to guard trading routes east to Huissen and Cologne. At that time, much of Arnhem lay farther west near the old harbor where the Nederrijn was closer to the city. Over the centuries the Sabelspoort had several names and numerous functions including tollhouse, prison, and insane asylum.

Although badly damaged during the Arnhem fighting, the gate was restored in 1952 as part of the adjacent Gelderland Province House. The inner courtyard of the latter building holds ceremonial displays relating to the battle.

Chapter Eight
British 1st Airborne Division: Oosterbeek Cauldron
19 to 26 September

The tally among Urquhart's units on the evening of 19 September was truly shocking. British 1st Airborne Division units had been badly mauled in western Arnhem attempting to reach the bridge. Dobie's 1st Battalion reported 116 men with its leader captured, Fitch's 3rd Battalion held only 50 men with its commander dead; 11th Battalion had been reduced to 150 men, and the 2nd South Staffordshires to 100. Communications with Frost's 2nd Battalion were still out, so Urquhart had no idea if it even still existed. Frost and his men would have to be abandoned. Disastrous losses in fighting in the woods around Wolfheze had nearly destroyed the 10th Battalion which fielded 250 men and the 156th Battalion fielding only 270.

Urquhart planned to maintain a beachhead on the north side of the Lower Nederrijn within a defensive perimeter around Oosterbeek in hope that Horrocks' tanks would yet arrive. The 3-kilometer-long by 2.5-kilometer-wide pocket started to form during the afternoon of 19 September.

The western side had been well established with Brigadier Hicks commanding the Glider Pilot Regiment, Royal Engineers, 1st Battalion, The Border Regiment, the only complete battalion in the division, and some Poles facing a strengthening KGr Tettau. Lacking the manpower to establish a continuous defense, the Borderers established pockets of resistance and held the length of their defensive zone with patrols. The unit held that line until evacuation on 26 September when it returned to Nijmegen with 250 men from its original complement of 795.

The eastern side was another matter where the 9th SS Panzer Division was determined to force the British even farther away from the Arnhem bridge. Brigadier Hackett commanded the decimated 10th and 156th Battalions, the 1st Airlanding Regiment, and a few glider pilots still struggling through the woods from the northwest. Major Wilson's 21st Independent Parachute Company with Lieutenant-Colonel Robert Payton-Reid's 7th KOSB held the northern edge of the perimeter near the Wolfheze railway.

The division artillery of the Light Regiment under Lieutenant-Colonel WFK Thompson supported by a few glider pilots held the 1.5-kilometer section of the riverfront around the medieval Oude Kerk in Oosterbeek. An artillery forward observer advised Thompson of a column of men retreating along the lower road. Thompson directed Major Robert Cain to gather together what troops he could and provide a defensive screen for his guns. Cain's force gradually grew to 416 men when survivors of the 1st and 3rd Battalions entered his perimeter.

Urquhart had finally discovered the potential of the Driel ferry crossing and he communicated the possibility of transferring troops across the river to British Second Army. But that very day ferryman Pieter Hensen cut the cable on the south side to deny the ferry's use to the Germans. The ferry drifted downstream and sunk near the north bank.

The Germans spent Wednesday, 20 September launching small probing attacks against the newly formed perimeter testing for weaknesses or opportunities to bring mortar or shellfire upon the defenders.

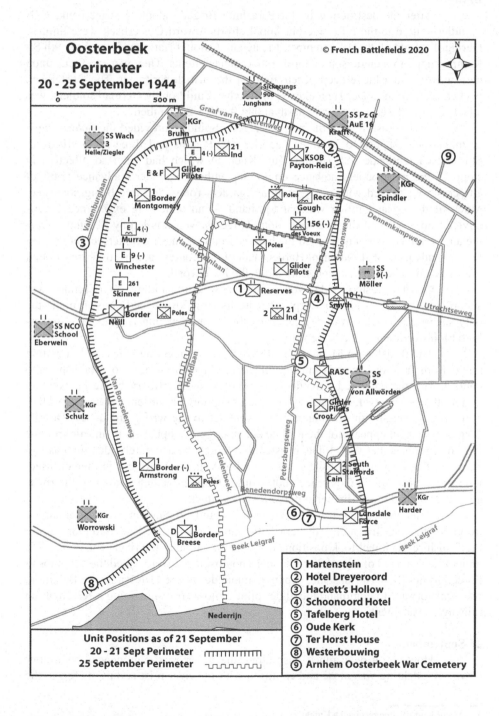

Oosterbeek Perimeter
20 - 25 September 1944

© French Battlefields 2020

N

0   500 m

Sickerungs 908
Junghans

SS Pz Gr AuE 16
Krafft

KGr
Bruhn

Graaf van Re... ...erenweg

SS Wach 3
Helle/Ziegler

E 4 (-)

21 Ind

7 KSOB
Payton-Reid

KGr
Spindler

E & F

Glider Pilots

Pole

Recce
Gough

Dennenkampweg

Valkenburglaan

A 1 Border
Montgomery

156 (-)
des Voeux

E 4 (-)
Murray

Poles

Hartenste...laan

Stationsweg

3

E 9 (-)
Winchester

Glider Pilots

SS 9(-)
Möller

E 261
Skinner

1 Reserves

21 Ind

10 (-)
Smyth

Utrechtseweg

C 1 Border
Neill

Poles

2

SS NCO School
Eberwein

Van Borsselenweg

5

RASC

SS 9
von Allwörden

KGr
Schulz

Hoofdlaan

G Glider Pilots
Croot

B 1 Border (-)
Armstrong

Poles

2 South Staffords
Cain

KGr
Worrowski

Petersbergseweg

Gielenbeek

Benedendorpseweg

6 7 Lonsdale Force

KGr
Harder

D 1 Border
Breese

Beek Leigraf

Beek Leigraf

8

Nederrijn

Unit Positions as of 21 September
20 - 21 Sept Perimeter
25 September Perimeter

① Hartenstein
② Hotel Dreyeroord
③ Hackett's Hollow
④ Schoonoord Hotel
⑤ Tafelberg Hotel
⑥ Oude Kerk
⑦ Ter Horst House
⑧ Westerbouwing
⑨ Arnhem Oosterbeek War Cemetery

Battle

After the destruction of 1st Parachute Brigade along the riverbank, KGr Spindler shifted to the offensive but initial efforts toward Oosterbeek were limited. During the night of 20/21 September, Lieutenant Colonel Harzer reformed the 9th SS Kampfgruppe to include small storm-trooper detachments. They were to focus upon narrow fronts to achieve deep penetrations of the British perimeter. The Oosterbeek pocket, referred to as Der Hexenkessel or Witches Cauldron by German soldiers, was attacked from the east, west, and north at 08:00 on 21 September.

On the east side of the perimeter, KGr Spindler provided the *Schwerpunkt* or main focus supported by three batteries of SP guns and three StuG IIIs from Sturmgeschützbrigade 280 (Major Kurt Kuehne) which had been so effective in stopping the paratroopers advance on 19 September.[1] Spindler's advance north of Utrechtseweg slowed with every building, garden, room, and tree being contested. Much of the urban fighting was hand-to-hand — an unnerving experience for his novice troops. KGr Möller's assault along Utrechtseweg was led by SP guns. When the attack stalled, the guns shelled the houses around Annastraat intersection but still failed to advance. SS-Lieutenant Harder made little progress against defenses around the church despite increased pressure along the lower road.

On the western side, von Tettau, now commanding KGr Tettau, was subordinated to II SS Panzer Corps. Despite its less-experienced units, it made the only successful attack of the day capturing the Westerbouwing Heights, a 30-meter-high bluff overlooking the Nederrijn.

The British 64th Medium Regiment, Royal Artillery had the cauldron within range from positions near Nijmegen and it had also been able to establish radio contact with the encircled defenders. Repeatedly, their artillery broke up German armor attacks, however, desperately needed air support was absent because new UHF radios for ground-to-air communications were set to the wrong frequency. Despite Urquhart's urgent appeals for the RAF to attack targets of opportunity, the air arm just did not do things that way. Pilots insisted that targets be accurately identified as had been so effectively accomplished on the road to Valkenswaard, but in the confused, intermixed positions in Oosterbeek not a single German vehicle crowding the roads and fields around the perimeter suffered from air attack.

After the retreat from Arnhem on 19 and 20 September, the remaining troops of the 1st, 3rd, and 11th Parachute Battalions and the 2nd Battalion, South Staffordshire Regiment took positions from the dike road to the river. The units came under the command of Lieutenant-Colonel Thompson and were called the 'Thompson Force.' Major Richard Lonsdale, deputy commander of the 11th Parachute Battalion, was sent forward to command the glider pilots who were maintaining a screen at the railway embankment.

21 September

However, a determined push along the lower road commenced soon after dawn. The fighting was close and confused with the river mist adding its fog to the

---

1   Major Kurt Kuehne received a Knight's Cross for this action.

dust and smoke of exploding shells. Eventually the glider pilot force was so weakened that Thompson relocated it nearer the church.

In the morning of 21 September, during a visit by Brigadier Hackett to the Colonel Thompson's headquarters, Thompson was injured in a mortar attack. The Light Regiment, Royal Artillery command was transferred to his deputy Major de Gex. The infantry came under the command of Major Lonsdale renamed 'Lonsdale Force.'

Three majors commanded the eastern defense. Remnants of 1st and 3rd Battalions, about 160 men and now commanded by Major Allan Bush, held positions in front of the church. Approximately 100 South Staffords were in the center under B Company's commander, Major Cain with a detachment of thirty men in the fields south of the church. Farther north, 30 glider pilots from G Squadron held the line under Major Robert Croot. The 11th Battalion became a reserve. The units held these positions against all attacks until their evacuation.

During the afternoon of 21 September, four waves of fifty-three Dakota transports and sixty-four Stirling bombers flew resupply missions to revised drop areas in the open fields around the Hartenstein. Six Spitfire squadrons were to provide protection from German fighters, but most fighter planes were grounded in England due to weather around their northern England airfields. The serials came under attack by Messerschmitt BF 109 fighters causing losses to the air fleet. In all sixteen Stirlings and nineteen Dakotas were shot down. As in earlier days, most of the supplies landed in German held territory, the British recovering only four percent of the drop.

In the late afternoon, the 1st Polish Independent Parachute Brigade Group (Major-General Stanislaw Sosabowski) finally left English airfields after two days of delay due to poor weather conditions. However, bad weather continued to plague the delivery of Polish troops. The mission was seriously disrupted after encountering heavy clouds which led to a recall of all planes. Confusion led to approximately one third of the 114 planes responding to the recall order while the others continued to a relocated drop zone. The English weather also limited antiaircraft suppressing air support; German flak was rated as heavy. Nonetheless, 1,003 troops of the planned 1,568 landed southeast of Driel suffering only 41 casualties.

Driel was not the original drop zone; the plan called for the Polish to drop on 19 September in DZ 'K' south of the Arnhem bridge. The weather delay, and subsequent defeat of Frost's force, led to the drop being made opposite the Oosterbeek defense perimeter. Lacking the ferry or boats, Sosabowski could not get his troops across the river. However, the Polish arrival surprised the Germans and forced a reallocation of their forces to protect the Arnhem bridge and the highway to Nijmegen.

The British at Oosterbeek witnessed the air drop but lacked communications with the Poles. Captain Ludwik Zwolanski, the Polish liaison officer with Urquhart, swam the river and informed Sosabowski that rafts would arrive to transport his men across the river. That Thursday night, the Polish general moved his men to the river crossing, but the rafts, constructed from jeep trailers, proved unstable. Polish efforts to find boats on the south bank also failed.

The depleted KOSB held Hotel Dreyeroord on the northern periphery against attack. That night, General Urquhart, recognizing that the northern position held no tactical advantage, ordered the KOSB to fall back in order to shorten his line and provide reserve troops to Brigadier Hackett's eastern side. The positions were now fixed for the remainder of the battle with only slight incursions by German forces.

22 September

Brilliant sunshine opened 22 September illuminating the wreckage and bodies of the previous two days fighting around Oosterbeek. Model regarded the Oosterbeek cauldron as subordinate to defeating XXX Corps' movement up The Corridor. However, with strengthening British forces now on the south bank, Model felt the time had come to end it. General Bittrich determined that he would batter the British into defeat by almost continuous mortar fire and shelling of the Oosterbeek cauldron. The British were to suffer an ongoing stream of casualties while German units recuperated from the engagements of the previous days. Artillerie Regiment 191 with 110 artillery pieces ranging from 12-mm cannon to 150-mm field guns began a systematic raking of the Oosterbeek perimeter. Two batteries of Nebelwerfer rocket launchers arrived to add their terrifying 'screaming meemies' to wear down the defenses.

The defenders became casualties without the opportunity to strike back at the enemy. Mortars hit the reserve ammunition dumps worsening shortages and rationing of return fire. Snipers took their toll by infiltrating the woods facing the western perimeter and hid in trees to fire down upon men in slit trenches. Bursts of Bren-gun fire sheared leaves and branches from trees as those below searched for their enemy with bullets. It was brutal work.

23 September

The skies cleared and a resupply by 123 aircraft arrived in the afternoon. The drops more accurately located the British open ground, but because that ground was now under German observation and fire, only 2.4 percent of the materials were recovered. That night 150 Polish troopers crossed the river to enter the cauldron.

During the night of 23/24 September forty-five King Tiger tanks arrived by railcar from Germany. Seventeen were sent to the Elst area and fourteen to KGr Spindler in Oosterbeek. However, heavy tanks were not ideal weapons for urban combat: their long-barreled gun could not be sufficiently rotated to engage targets and their size and weight made negotiating the narrow streets difficult. The massive King Tigers could, however, destroy a British strongpoint with one 88-mm shell.

24 September

A two-hour cease fire allowed 1,200 wounded British PoWs to be transferred to German hospitals. While the engineers of KGr Möller looked on, a column of wounded was shuttled to Sint Elisabethshof, which was still operated by captured British medical staff. Among the wounded was Brigadier Hackett who had been badly wounded by a mortar explosion at his headquarters.

During the night of 24 September, two companies totaling 400 men of the Dorset Regiment, 43rd Infantry Division paddled boats across the river, but failed to join Urquhart in the cauldron. The Germans responded with a counterattack by 1st Battalion, Sicherungsregiment (Security Regiment) 26 (Oberstleutnant Shennen) from Renkum. The Dorsets were devastated; 140 were taken prisoner, 185 presumably killed or captured.

Broken by eight days of almost constant combat and shortages of food and water, paratroopers started to surrender. German ground commanders culled the inexperienced troops from their ad hoc formations and sent in only skilled combat troops. The eastern perimeter was breached along the river. Tigers moved in along Utrechtseweg. British artillery stopped the advance 500 meters from the Hartenstein headquarters.

General Miles Dempsey, had not met with Horrocks since the offensive began. Now he ordered the XXX Corps commander to meet him at Sint-Oedenrode. Under pressure from Dempsey and Browning, Horrocks agreed that the planned reinforcement of Urquhart was to become instead an evacuation.

25/26 September

At 06:05, Urquhart received the order to withdraw in a movement that was ironically labeled 'Operation BERLIN.' Men shaved and blackened their faces; boots were wrapped in strips of blankets; equipment was secured to prevent rattling. That evening Urquhart thinned his line leaving small groups to maintain fire to deceive the enemy while most of the force slipped south to the river. Artillery positions inside the perimeter fired at will to help disguise movement. At 20:50, XXX Corps artillery batteries south of the river commenced firing heavy concentrations just outside the perimeter. Radio traffic was maintained as a deception.

At 21:00 the perimeter collapse began starting with the northern units. Men set off in the total darkness frequently holding the clothing of the man in front. They moved along one of two routes which passed on either side of the Hartenstein to the departure point near the Oude Kerk led by glider pilots and guided by white tape marking the route to the water's edge. The seriously wounded were left under the care of medical officers and orderlies who remained and were captured.

A steady rain shrouded the noise of their movement from the Germans. Fourteen powered boats manned by Canadian Engineers of the 260 Field Company and assault boats rowed by Royal Engineers began ferrying them across the Nederrijn at 22:00. The Canadians carried the bulk of the men; the British assault boats slowed as the tiring rowers fought the rain swollen river. Some decided swimming was safer than waiting. On the Driel bank, medical staff stood ambulances at the ready for the shift back to Nijmegen. Those who were able marched back.

Men reached the river faster than the boats could transport them across and a queue formed by those waiting their turn. Half the curious fleet of small boats were destroyed creating a backlog of unevacuated men. The line lengthened but was egalitarian — officers waited their turn like the other ranks. Only the walking wounded were given priority, Hundreds anxiously waited to cross. The Germans observed the river activity but assumed that it was another reinforcement attempt. Their mortars and artillery started searching for targets.

As 02:00 approached, the paratroop artillery fired off their final rounds hitting Dutch houses that were once the target of German shells. Artillerymen carried the breech blocks to the river and threw them into the water. By 05:00 the brightening skies and German artillery fire halted the crossings entirely. Three hundred British were left stranded on the north bank to hide or attempt escape.

Despite a brief skirmish with British rear guards, the morning German advance found only weapons and bodies at locations that had been so hotly contested the day before. By 14:00 the last overlooked or stranded patrol had been captured. Quiet returned to Oosterbeek. The battle for Arnhem drew to a close — a pitiful failure.

Aftermath

During that rain and wind-swept night, 1,741 men of 1st British Airborne Division, 422 British glider pilots, 160 men of 1st Polish Independent Parachute Brigade, and 75 men of the Dorset Regiment escaped. They totaled 2,398 of the 10,408 men who had been on the north side of 'the bridge too far.' A total of 1,485 British and Polish troops perished, the remaining 6,525 were taken prisoner.

Official German casualty reports listed 1,100 dead and 2,200 wounded or missing. True figures could have been much higher. German and British medical personal immediately collected 1,700 wounded and began transferring them to the Willem III Barracks in Apeldoorn. The special facility remained open until 26 October when only 20 patients remained. The balance having been transported to PoW camps in Germany.

After Operation MARKET-GARDEN, a static battle followed in which the Germans occupied the high bank of the river at Westerbouwing and crushed every Allied movement in the lowland with their artillery. In the river meadows along the south bank, British infantry troops were dug in, to be replaced later with American Airborne.

During the night of 22/23 October, 138 men led by Brigadier Lathbury successfully escaped from the Apeldoorn area assisted by the Second Army's Escape and Evasion Team and numerous Dutch civilians who organized safe houses, clothes, food, and transport by bicycle and truck. The various groups evaded German searches to rendezvous in the woods near Renkum. American paratroopers from Company E, 506th PIR brought the escapees across the river in assault boats. A second later attempt was foiled when the escapees ran into a German patrol.

Ludwig Spindler received a Knight's Cross for his outstanding leadership of disparate forces in stopping the British. He was killed during the Battle of the Bulge when his staff car was strafed by a fighter-bomber. Hans-Peter Knaust had fought on the Russian Front where he was invalided after losing a leg. He fought the Arnhem battle on a wooden prosthetic. Afterwards, he was awarded the Knight's Cross. Walter Harzer also received the Knight's Cross. After the war Harzer became a consulting engineer and remained active in a lobby group for senior Waffen-SS men. He died in 1982 at age 69. Hans von Tettau had a spotty military career as an inspector rather than a field commander and was considered self-aggrandizing by contemporaries. He received the Knight's Cross of the Iron Cross with Oak Leaves as commander of KGr von Tettau. In the latter months of the war Tettau held several commands on the crumbling Eastern Front. He was captured when the Wehrmacht surrendered and released in 1947. He died in 1956, aged 67. Heinz Harmel received the Knight's Cross of the Iron Cross with Oak Leaves and Swords. After transfer to the Eastern Front, he was removed from command for refusing to obey an order for a doomed attack. He surrendered in Austria while commanding a Waffen mountain division. After the war, he became a manufacturer's representative dying in 2000 at age 94. Kurt Feldt was captured by British troops in May 1945 and was held until 1947. Feldt resettled in Berlin where he died in 1970, aged 82. Josef Krafft returned to his pre-war occupation as a police official. Leutnant Heinz Gropp died in 1990 at age 78.

Conclusions

The German ability to locate and deliver the few armored survivors of Normandy to Arnhem decided the battle. Antiaircraft guns halted the paratrooper attack upon Spindler's line, assault guns drove paratroopers from Utrechtseweg, and artillery and tank fire systematically bludgeoned Frost at the bridge and Urquhart in Oosterbeek. The Polish landings successfully attracted considerable German firepower that, arguably, otherwise would have crushed the British cauldron earlier.

Battlefield Tour
Oosterbeek

The tour reviews sites starting at the eastern perimeter and moving in a generally counterclockwise direction around Oosterbeek. The route reviews central Oosterbeek locations and Airborne Museum Hartenstein before moving toward the final stand around the Oude Kerk and the nighttime evacuation across the Nederrijn.

Two municipal walking tours provide information panels at key sites on the British perimeter around Oosterbeek. The *Informatiepaneel Perimeterroute*, or **Information Perimeter Route Panels** identify eight sites generally south of the Airborne Museum Hartenstein along a 4.0-kilometer route. The first two panels are on the grounds of the museum and make a good starting point for those hiking the suggested route. The *Noordelijke Perimeterroute*, or **Northern Perimeter Route Panels**, also a 4.0-kilometer walk, follows the front line of the British defense in the northern sector. A brochure describing both is available at the VVV tourist information office located in a wing of the museum. The suggested battlefield tour does not follow these routes but indicates the signs as they are encountered.

From central Arnhem, return to Benedendorpsweg and stop at the intersection with Acacialaan 600 m west of the rail underpass. (51.979501, 5.851642)

On 19 September, after their disastrous defeat in western Arnhem, remnants of the 1st, 3rd, and 11th Parachute Battalions and the South Staffords withdrew along the river road in complete disarray. Lieutenant-Colonel Thompson aggressively intercepted the mob of men, reorganized them by battalion, and established a blocking unit named Thompson Force along an intersection to the east (Stennenkruis / Benedendorpsweg) by about 15:00 on 19 September.

German armor cautiously followed the retreating paratroopers but held behind the railway embankment for the night. The next morning the Germans attacked with tanks, SP guns, and infantry but were repulsed. The South Staffords were withdrawn to the ancient church a kilometer farther west; however, their eight 6-pounder antitank guns remained to strengthen the defensive screen being established east of the Oude Kerk. Two of those guns were sited on opposite sides of Benedendorpsweg at this intersection.

Lance-Sergeant John Baskeyfield, 2nd Battalion, South Staffordshires, commanded one of the 6-pounders when attacked by German armor. Baskeyfield's gun crew knocked out two StuG III self-propelled guns and a half-track bearing west on Benedendorpsweg before their gun was destroyed and all its crew killed except the sergeant who was wounded in the leg. He crawled across the road to man a second crewless gun and destroyed a third StuG approaching down Acacialaan before himself being killed by a shellburst from a tank approaching behind the SP gun. His body was never found. German flamethrowers set fire to the houses and Lonsdale ordered a withdrawal back to the church.

A **small metal plaque** in the front garden on the northwest corner identifies a tree planted in Baskeyfield's memory at the location of the second gun that he fired. The plaque, adorned with the badge of the 2nd Staffordshire Battalion, is frequently adorned with poppy rosettes to commemorate heroic Baskeyfield's sacrifice.[2]

Proceed north on Acacialaan; turn right onto the impossibly named Jonkheer Neder-meier van Rosenthalweg and follow for 450 m. Turn left onto Julianaweg and left on Utrechtseweg (N225). Proceed through central Oosterbeek for 1.0 km; turn right onto Stationsweg, then right on Van Limburg Stirumweg immediately after crossing the rail line. Continue to follow the road including a left turn to the cemetery parking area. (51.993113, 5.849760)

Arnhem Oosterbeek War Cemetery
Van Limburg Stirumweg 28, 6861 WL Oosterbeek
Web: https://www.cwgc.org/find-a-cemetery/cemetery/2063800/arnhem%20ooster-beek%20war%20cemetery

The area near the cemetery was a continuation of the battle line along Dreijenseweg from the junction with highway N224 to and including the cemetery.

The Arnhem Oosterbeek War Cemetery is located at the end of a rhododendron-lined, gravel walk path within a beautiful park of mature trees. Near the entrance, the red brick wall to the left bears the Flowers in the Wind plaque, which is headed by a gold Pegasus with the flags of the United Kingdom, the Netherlands, and Poland. The polished stone is dedicated to the 1,765 children who every year pay homage to the men who gave their lives for liberation — one assigned to each grave where, upon a signal, they simultaneously place a flower.

Three information signs immediately to the right of the entrance gate describe the cemetery in Dutch, English, and Polish detailing the cemetery's design and mapping the various burial plots – which surprisingly are not in numerical order as one might expect and as in most other military cemeteries.

Burials total 1,435 known and 245 unidentified. In addition, there are eighty-

---

2   Lance-Sergeant John Baskeyfield, aged 21 from Stoke-on-Trent, Staffordshire, is remembered on the Groesbeek Canadian War Cemetery Memorial. Sergeant Baskeyfield was awarded the Victoria Cross for his actions defending the Oosterbeek perimeter.

two non-Commonwealth foreign nationals comprised of seventy-three Poles, eight Dutch, and one American. Most deaths resulted from the Arnhem fighting or from combat from September 1944 to April 1945 in the Arnhem region. During the initial burial process, the dead from each unit were grouped together; later burials, as bodies were discovered are more random. Numerous exceptions exist such as, brothers from different units buried side-by-side. Discovery of battlefield remains continue to increase the number of graves.

Polish graves are to the right and left immediately upon entering the cemetery. The grave of Robert Tice, an American volunteer, is approximately half-way down on the right among the Polish soldiers with whom he fought – as his parents wished.[3] Although Lieutenant Tice had no Polish heritage, he admired the Polish fighters and respected their country's contribution to the American War of Independence. He joined the Free Polish Army in England and remained after his country entered the war. Tice died of 22 September at Driel when German troops approached his platoon's position speaking English and claiming to be British. Tice was hit with a burst of machine-pistol fire and killed. The grave bears small American and Polish flags to remember a soldier who died in another country's army.

The Stone of Remembrance stands at the entrance and the Cross of Sacrifice at the far rear, with an open area in the middle separating the thirty-four grave plots aligned in a uniform pattern on both sides. The rear section facing the entrance holds over 400 men killed during the later battles south of the Nederrijn. The grave of John Grayburn, whose body was not discovered until 1948, is in the last row near the Cross of Sacrifice.

Many of the gravestones have inscribed epitaphs – some very personal. For example: 'We will always remember when the rest of the world forgets – Sylvia and Micky'. Twin brothers, Claude and Thomas Gronert, members of the Parachute Regiment killed on 17 September when members of Colonel Frost's B Company went against German positions on Den Brink, are buried side-by-side. Their gravestones bear identical epitaphs: 'Winds of heaven blow softly here where lie sleeping those we loved so dear.'

Of the five Victoria crosses awarded for actions during the battle, four were posthumous and three are buried here. They were Lieutenant John Grayburn, of 2nd Parachute Battalion and Captain Lionel Queripel of 10th Battalion, both from the Parachute Regiment and Flight Lieutenant David Lord of 271 Squadron RAF.[4]

The tragedies of war are remembered. Five gravestones closely aligned in Plot 4, Row C record the names of eight members of a Dakota from 48 Squadron which crashed north of Driel on 21 September during a supply mission. The aircraft

---

3   Richard Tice, aged 22, is buried in Plot 34, Row A, Grave 13.

4   Lieutenant David Samuel Anthony Lord, aged 30, from Cork, Ireland, was awarded the Distinguished Flying Cross for flying supply missions over Burma. On 19 September 1944, flying a supply run over the Netherlands in a Dakota III, Lieutenant Lord encountered intense antiaircraft fire and his plane was hit twice. After his run in, he discovered two remaining cannisters. Despite one engine on fire, he made a second run. The plane crashed and the crew was killed except for the navigator. The sole survivor, Flight Lieutenant Harold King was captured, but the events remained unknown until his release in 1945. Lord and his crew of six are buried in adjacent graves in Plot 4, Row B.

was hit by a load dropped from another Dakota.

Continue north on Van Limburg Stirumweg for 200 m to its end. (51.994716, 5.851146)

Air despatchers were members of the Royal Army Service Corps (RASC) with responsibility for materiél transport. Unlike other rear echelon troops, members of the RASC were considered combat personnel. Many of the units' casualties occurred

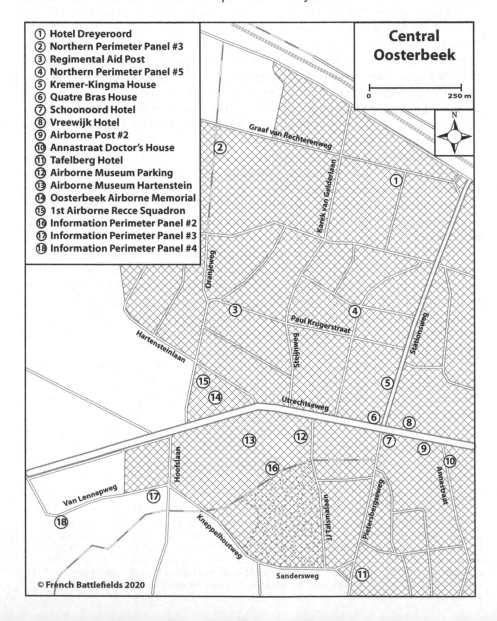

① Hotel Dreyeroord
② Northern Perimeter Panel #3
③ Regimental Aid Post
④ Northern Perimeter Panel #5
⑤ Kremer-Kingma House
⑥ Quatre Bras House
⑦ Schoonoord Hotel
⑧ Vreewijk Hotel
⑨ Airborne Post #2
⑩ Annastraat Doctor's House
⑪ Tafelberg Hotel
⑫ Airborne Museum Parking
⑬ Airborne Museum Hartenstein
⑭ Oosterbeek Airborne Memorial
⑮ 1st Airborne Recce Squadron
⑯ Information Perimeter Panel #2
⑰ Information Perimeter Panel #3
⑱ Information Perimeter Panel #4

Central Oosterbeek

0   250 m

N

© French Battlefields 2020

during the risky dropping of supplies.

The **Air Despatch Memorial** commemorates the air despatchers and aircrews of the Royal Air Force and Royal Canadian Air Force who gave their lives in valiant attempts to resupply the airborne forces during the battle for Arnhem. A white carved sandstone parachute bearing a supply cannister stands upon on a dark brick plinth. The plaques on the sides list the names of eighty members of those units that were killed.

> Reverse direction and return to recross the rail line onto Stationsweg. Immediately turn right onto Nico Bovenweg and shortly left onto Graf van Rechterenweg. Proceed 190 m to the liberation route marker on the left. (51.994068, 5.838493)

Although much depleted after earlier fighting at the Ginkelse Heide and Johannahoeve landing zones, 270 men of the 7th Battalion, The King's Own Scottish Borderers under Lieutenant-Colonel Payton-Reid occupied a hotel and surrounding gardens from the night of Tuesday, 19 September until the evening of Thursday, 21 September against repeated attacks by superior forces. The position marked the northern extreme of the British perimeter and was highly exposed to enemy attack. The hotel was near the only crossing of the Ede–Arnhem rail line suitable for tanks. Because the Scots had trouble pronouncing the name of the hotel-restaurant, **Hotel Dreyeroord**, they called it 'The White House.'

On Thursday, 21 September, the hotel was subjected to heavy mortar fire and Nebelwerfer rockets. In the late afternoon, a company of Panzergrenadiers gained control of the hotel after hand-to-hand fighting and heavy losses to both sides. The Scots, led by Canadian platoon commander Lieutenant James Taylor, succeeded in winning back the hotel with a bayonet charge by his No 12 Platoon.[5] Eventually however, Payton-Reid, having lost one half of his 270 men, decided to abandon the blazing hotel as undefendable and pulled back to positions south of the hotel.

Unfortunately, 'The White House' was demolished in 2018 to make way for a modern structure, but **Liberation Route Marker #41**, 'Hotel Dreyeroord,' records the reminisces of 87-year-old John Crosson, a sniper in No 6 Platoon, B Company and one of the few members of that unit to survive. The image displays the hotel as it appeared after the battle.

Northern Perimeter Route Panel #2 stands along the sidewalk before the building and describes the fighting around Hotel Dreyeroord as recorded above. The plaque bears the image of broken windows on the façade of the hotel.

> Proceed west on Graf von Rechterenweg to the walkpath (Oranijeweg) on the left. Continue on foot 60 m to the information panel. (51.994772, 5.831575)

Northern Perimeter Route Panel #3 stands along a footpath in the forest to the west that once held the Ommerhof estate. That building was destroyed during the battle and never rebuilt. The woods were held by the 21st Independent Parachute

---

5   Lieutenant James Taylor, born in Nottingham, emigrated to Canada with his parents at age five. Taylor was later seriously wounded and taken prisoner at Arnhem. After the war he spent 34 years in the Canadian Army and retired as a lieutenant-colonel.

Company and the 4th Parachute Squadron, Royal Engineers along with seventy glider pilots from 19 to 21 September forming the northern edge of the defense. The units were withdrawn to shorten the perimeter and establish a divisional reserve. Although the sign indicates the presence of remaining slit trenches, heavy vegetation covers most of the area making their identification difficult. The image displays a German half-track which was knocked out on Graaf van Richterenweg.

> Reverse direction and proceed east on Graf van Rechterenweg 270 m to turn right onto Karel van Gelderlaan which becomes Steijnweg. Turn right on Paul Kruger-straat and stop after 130 m. (51.990783, 5.832366)

After the KOSB left the Johannahoeve area on Tuesday, 19th September, the medical team moved the Regimental Aid Station to 'The White House' cellar. Heavy fighting led to its evacuation and the Regimental Aid Station again relocated to the Paul Krugerstraat address where the owners and their lone child sheltered in the cellar while the wounded were treated on the floor above. Medical supplies became scarce as the number of wounded increased, but at least a rain barrel at the rear of the house provided sufficient water.

The morning after the evacuation, a German corporal appeared and distributed cigarettes to those left behind. Later a German officer ordered the walking wounded to be marched away under guard. Days later an ambulance arrived and transported those remaining to a hospital in Almelo.

Northern Perimeter Route Panel #4 identifies the Regimental Aid Post of the 7th KOSB Battalion. The unit occupied this area until the evacuation of 25 September. The wounded, nursing staff, Reverend Captain James Morrison,[6] and medical orderly Sergeant Eric Hyslop remained to be taken prisoner of war. The image, now standing in front of the renumbered No 72, identifies the aid post as being in house No 26 but careful examination shows that the photograph may have been house No 63 across the street.

> Reverse direction and proceed east 300 m on Paul Krugerstraat. (51.990157, 5.836672)

On 23 September, this area was the scene of a duel between a German self-propelled gun and a British PIAT. At a range of twenty meters a member of the 1st Airborne Reconnaissance Squadron fired to eliminate the SP gun. After the battle, local men sheltered in the building at the corner of Mariaweg and Paul Krugerstraat when they were summoned out and ordered by the Germans to bury British corpses.

Northern Perimeter Route Panel #5 stands across the street from the building identified by the accompanying image. The building was almost completely burned out during the fighting.

> Proceed 160 m east on Paul Krugerstraat; then turn right onto Stationsweg and stop

---

6   Captain James Morrison spent the remainder of the war in Oflag VIIB in Eichstätt, Germany. He died in 2008 three days before his 93rd birthday.

after 100 m before house No 8. (51.989035, 5.838389)

Northern Perimeter Route Panel #1 describes the house inhabited by the Kremer-Kingma family in 1944 and defended against enemy troops entrenched in the then undeveloped park-like grounds on the other side of Stationsweg. During the last four days of the battle it was held by the pathfinders of the 21st Independent Parachute Company, glider pilots, and Polish troops (Captain Ignacy Gazurek)[7] that had crossed the river on 22 September. Mrs Kremer-Kingma made a series of photographs that can be seen in the Airborne Museum. The image on the information panel shows bedraggled but still effusive Brits and Poles posing in front of the house.

Continue south on Stationsweg. This street was the front line for five days while the British held the houses on the west side and the Germans fought out of what was then the Dennenkamp woods on the east side. Cross Utrechtseweg and enter the free parking lot on the southwest corner of the intersection. The following sites are best viewed on foot. (51.987817, 5.837630)

The Hotel Schoonoord located opposite the parking area became a Main Dressing Station on the edge of the perimeter. On the morning of 20 September, KGr Möller launched an attack centered upon Utrechtseweg. By 10:00 the medical facilities spread among the buildings surrounding this intersection were overrun. The wounded able to be moved were sent into captivity; the more serious cases remained to be treated. The Germans departed.

On 24 September, the number of wounded British and Germans within the perimeter had grown to 1,200 and were barely being treated because of the lack of surgical facilities, bandages, or morphia. German and British doctors met and together drove to Harzer's headquarters. Bittrich briefly joined the discussion and gave his approval for a cease fire to evacuate the wounded to German hospitals in Arnhem. At 15:00 a two-hour truce began and over 450 troops were carried by convoy to Sint Elisabethshof and other locations to be cared for by German military and Dutch civilian medical staffs. At 17:00 the killing resumed, and more wounded arrived at the Schoonoord.[8]

Both Brigadiers Lathbury and Hackett were among those evacuated; however, to hide their identity, they both adopted the rank of lance-corporal. They later escaped from the hospital with assistance from the Dutch. Lathbury was among

---

7   Captain Ignacy Gazurek, aged 37 from Isteban, Poland, was killed as he arrived at the Kremer house while climbing over the garden wall. He was originally buried in the garden of Stationsweg No 8, later reburied in Arnhem Oosterbeek War Cemetery, Plot XXV, Row B, Grave 5.

8   One incident tarnished the generally humane treatment that the Germans provided for British wounded. Late on 24 September outside Sint Elisabethshof Hospital drunken Karl-Gustav Lerche, a German war correspondent attached to the SS, shot and killed Captain Brian Brownscombe, the South Staffords's Medical Officer. Lerche spent seven years hiding under assumed names until betrayed by his Munich girlfriend who was once married to the nephew of Nazi leader Martin Borman. Lerche was sentenced to ten years in prison but served only five.
Captain Brian Brownscombe, aged 29, is buried in Arnhem Oosterbeek War Cemetery, Plot 15, Row B, Grave 10.

the 138 troopers, medics, and pilots who recrossed to the south bank of the Nederrijn on 22 October during Operation PEGASUS I.[9]

The grand **Hotel Schoonoord**, severely damaged by shellfire, has been replaced by a more modest restaurant/pub, that offers fine refreshments and light meals. Other buildings along Utrechtseweg were also damaged and replaced by more modern structures. (51.987743, 5.838026)

The **Hotel Vreewijk**, on the northeast corner of the intersection, was also used as a temporary medical facility as the need for space for wounded increased. It eventually held one hundred post-operative care patients. The building now houses offices.

Information Perimeter Route Panel #8 is attached to the light post across the street from the new Restaurant Schoonoord. The sign relates the story of the Main Dressing Station in the Hotel Schoonoord and in the Hotel Vreewijk on the opposite side of Utrechtseweg. The panel displays a 1945 image of the hotel ruins. (51.987889, 5.837787)

The **Quatre Bras** building on the northwest corner was defended by the 21st Independent Parachute Company, which manned a Bren-gun position in the garden at that spot. After the pathfinders marked the drop zones and landing fields, they reverted to parachute infantry. The front lawn displays an angular black stone representing the transformation of swords into plowshares. (51.988132, 5.837812)

The inscription reads:

In memory of the 21st Independent Parachute Company, which held this area during the Battle of Arnhem and of the people of Oosterbeek, who sacrificed so much to give their support.

On 19 September, E Troop (Lieutenant Robert Glover), 2nd Airlanding Antitank Battery withdrew its four 6-pounder guns from around Sint Elisabethshof along Utrechtseweg. German tanks and infantry shadowed the unit along parallel streets to the north. While at the intersection with Stationsweg, a German tank cautiously entered Stationsweg 225 meters to the north. Gunner Len Clarke aimed, fired, and hit the tank, which reversed out of sight. Clarke attempted to relocate his gun for a better shot when a second tank appeared along the same line 200 meters distant. Without the time to properly secure the gun's spades on the cobblestone street, Clarke fired three shots scoring a hit on the junction below the turret. A third tank attempted to pass the disabled vehicle and Clarke stopped it with three shots. The feat was more amazing because with each shot the unsecured gun recoiled three meters.[10]

> The next two sites are best visited on foot. Proceed east on Utrechtseweg for 120 m to the front garden of house No 192. (51.987631, 5.839701)

---

9   Born in India in 1906, Brigadier Gerald Lathbury was awarded the Distinguished Service Cross for his actions during and after the battle for Arnhem. After the war, Lathbury resumed command of his old unit, spending a year in Palestine and was promoted to general and later became Governor of Gibraltar. Sir Gerald Lathbury died in 1978, aged 71.

10   Lieutenant Robert Dickson Glover, aged 25, of Lenzie, Lanarkshire, Scotland was killed. He is buried in Arnhem Oosterbeek War Cemetery, Plot 22, Row A, Grave 8. Gunner Len Clarke was wounded shortly later in a mortar barrage eventually losing a leg.

During the night of 20/21 September, Lieutenant-Colonel Smyth led seventy men from his 10th Parachute Battalion to reoccupy buildings along Utrechtseweg east of Hotel Schoonoord. Although in a forward position, they held for two days of close combat against German infantry and StuGs while German guns slowly ground the buildings down while the soldiers continued to fight. Smyth and his second in command, Major Peter Warr, both joined the wounded and twenty Dutch civilians in the cellar of a doctor's home at Annastraat No 2 around the corner to the east. Overcome by shellfire and with the buildings on fire from phosphorous shells and with no battalion officers remaining, thirty survivors surrendered.[11]

Airborne Commemorative Post #6 stands in the front garden of the house on Utrechtseweg to commemorate the stand of those seventy men. The date of withdrawal on the post is one day later than the actual occurrence.

> Continue east on Utrechtseweg to Annastraat. Turn right and continue 60 m to house No 2. (51.987066, 5.840605)

In the **Annastraat house** cellar, Bertje Voskuil grabbed her nine-year-old son, Henri, in fear from the gun shots and scuffling she heard from the floor above. The cellar trap door burst open and a grenade fell among the soldiers and civilians. Private Albert Willingham threw himself on top of the huddling pair and absorbed the explosion. He was killed instantly. Bertje and her son both suffered wounds in their legs so severe that Bertje thought that her son was dead until a German doctor treated the pair.[12] Today, nothing marks the site, but the old house remains.

> Retrieve your vehicle and proceed south on Pietersbergseweg. (51.984735, 5.837023)

In 1939 the municipal council earmarked **Hotel Tafelberg** as a hospital in times of emergency. At the beginning of September 1944, the hotel was commandeered by the headquarters of Heeresgruppe B under the command of the Generalfeldmarschall Model. On 17 September Model was lunching at 14:00 when large, nearby explosions drove him to shelter under the dining table. Taken totally by surprise by the airborne landings, he relocated to General Bittrich's headquarters in Doetinchem.

General practitioners of Oosterbeek equipped the hotel as an emergency hospital, which was then taken over by the British. Dutch and British doctors worked aided by Oosterbeek first responders, Red Cross staff, and community nurses despite the building being hit several times by artillery fire. Operations were carried out on the

---

11   Lieutenant-Colonel Kenneth Bowes Inman Smyth, aged 38, badly injured in the stomach and paralyzed from the waist down, lingered for over one month before dying. He is buried in Arnhem Oosterbeek War Cemetery, Plot 18, Row B, Grave 8.
Major Peter Warr spent the remainder of the war as a PoW.

12   Private Albert Willingham, aged 29, 10th Battalion, Parachute Regiment, was temporarily buried in the rear garden of Annastraat No 4. He now lies in the Arnhem Oosterbeek War Cemetery, Plot 27, Row A, Grave 10.
Young Henri Vokuil lived to adulthood and became a doctor.

hotel's billiard table. Thirty-five British soldiers were temporarily buried in front of the building to be later transferred to the Arnhem Oosterbeek War Cemetery.

Airborne Commemorative Post #2 records the structure's role during the defense of the Oosterbeek perimeter. **Information Perimeter Route Panel #7** stands before the hotel and describes its functions during the battle and bears an image of British troops in their Jeep in front of the hotel entrance.

From De Tafelberg, proceed west on Sandersweg for 620 m which becomes Kneppelhoutweg. Turn right onto Hoofdlaan, then right again onto Utrechtseweg (N255). Pass the front of the Airborne Museum Hartenstein and continue to the next intersection. Turn right and quickly right again to the museum parking area behind the restaurant Klein Hartenstein. (51.987852, 5.835192)

The route passes through the rear areas of the Oosterbeek perimeter.

For a description of the **Airborne Museum 'Hartenstein'** see Chapter Six.

Combat around Oosterbeek was confused. Each side used the other's captured equipment negating a soldier's ability to sense enemy positions by the weapon's sound. Germans were well stocked with British cigarettes, ammunition, even jeeps captured from the misdirected air drops. Positions changed hands in minutes, became surrounded, were relieved in a repeating cycle of death. Meanwhile between six and eight thousand Dutch civilians sheltered in cellars suffering the same lack of food and water as the combatants. German armor roamed the perimeter firing massive shells at any identified British position.

During a pause in a mortar bombardment, Lance-Corporal Sydney Nunn of the KOSB looked over the edge of his slit trench to see a Tiger tank standing nearby. Concealed in nearby brushes stood an antitank gun, its crew dead. Nunn and an unidentified glider pilot began to crawl toward the gun when they were spotted. The tank's main gun's fire brought down trees around the two men. A stream of enemy machine-gun bullets searched them out while they continued to crawl toward the gun. Neither of the men had ever fired such a weapon but to their amazement the gun was aimed directly at the tank. The pilot pulled the trigger and the resultant explosion threw both men onto their backs. The shell penetrated the tank and set its ammunition on fire. The Tiger was a burning wreck.[13]

Information Perimeter Route Panel #2 located on the Hartenstein grounds (at approximately 51.986697, 5.833373) describes the establishment of divisional headquarters in the hotel and the development of the battle. The accompanying image displays British soldiers of the technical services encamped on the hotel grounds. The hotel tennis courts are shown in the background. The fenced courts were used to hold approximately 200 German prisoners during the fighting. (51.986626, 5.833403)

Walk across Utrechtseweg from Airborne Museum Hartenstein or park the side streets around the memorial park (51.988793, 5.831370)

---

13   Lance Corporal Sydney Nunn survived the war to participate in the disarming of German troops in Norway and in the filming of the 1946 motion picture *Theirs is the Glory*, which told the Arnhem story.

A large triangular park holds the **Oosterbeek Airborne Memorial**. The 10-meter-high brick memorial carries engraved stones presenting images of war — paratroopers suspended from their chutes as they drop to earth, Oosterbeek women caring for the wounded, the assistance of the Dutch Resistance, and the heroic last stand. There are larger and smaller inserts, including the Pegasus emblem. The column is surmounted by five figures of soldiers and civilians representing the ideals of freedom, faith, righteousness, hope and love, and finally home with freedom being the highest. The monument was built by the citizens of Oosterbeek in gratitude for the ten-day battle to obtain their freedom. A stainless-steel plaque at the entrance path explains the history and significance of the memorial in four languages.

The **Northern Perimeter Route Panel #6** is almost lost amid the shrubs on the south boundary of the park. It describes the efforts to erect the Airborne Memorial that started almost immediately after the war. The image shows dignitaries including Queen Wilhelmina at the unveiling in 1947. (51.988334, 5.831380)

A stone circle in the northern corner of the park is the children's circle dedicated on the **50th anniversary of Dutch Liberation** on 5 May 1995. (51.989388, 5.830820)

A gray stone obelisk almost lost among the trees north of the Airborne Memorial bears a plaque: (51.989125, 5.830981)

Dedicated to the men of the **1st Airborne Reconnaissance Squadron** also known as the Freddie Gough Squadron that fought so valiantly from 17 September to 25 September 1944 in the Oosterbeek and Arnhem area.

A metal '**Memorial Soldier with Flower Girl**' statue stands near the eastern corner of the park showing the pair walking hand-in-hand. The monument was unveiled on the occasion of the 65th Airborne Walking Tour. (51.988643, 5.832734)

Proceed west on Utrechtseweg past Airborne Museum Hartenstein, then turn left on Hoofdlaan and right onto Van Lennepweg. Stop at the route sign on the left. (51.986467, 5.828923)

C Company (Major William Neill), 1st Borderers, held positions in the woods and back gardens of the houses lining Van Lennepweg defending the Hartenstein headquarters from attack from the west. From their position dug in the edge of the woods, the mortar platoon (Lieutenant Mike Holman) engaged the flame throwing tanks of Panzer Kompanie 224. Major Neill led a counterattack to recapture ground lost to the tanks the previous day despite shrapnel wounds in both arms and a leg.[14]

Information Perimeter Route Panel #3 identifies the shallow depression that sheltered the mortar team with an image of troopers firing a 3-inch mortar.

The following three sites present locations of the 1st Borderer's defense. Proceed 270 m farther west on Van Lennepweg. (51.985776, 5.825116)

---

14   Major William 'Jock' Neill received the Distinguished Service Order for maintaining his command despite severe wounds. After the war, Neill relocated to Tasmania where he died in 1984.

On Tuesday, 19 September, D Company (Captain William Hodgson, acting), 1st Battalion, Border Regiment established a sparse defense of outposts along this roadway on the Oosterbeek western perimeter. That day and the next, the company was subjected to heavy mortar attacks. On Wednesday, tanks attacked from the woods to the west stopped only by the action of a 6-pounder antitank gun. The fighting went on and the company was reduced to about forty active combatants while the neighboring houses harbored their many wounded in its cellars. Hodgson reported to battalion headquarters that his force was surrounded but holding on by using mostly captured German weapons and ammunition. For the next three days the group continued to hold thanks to the support of artillery fire from the guns of XXX Corps.

By Monday, 25 September the company was reduced to nineteen men under Lieutenant Alan Green, Captain Hogdson having been wounded for a second time. Lieutenant Green attempted to establish a cease fire with the Germans in order to evacuate the wounded, but he came under fire and was wounded four times.

Orders for the evacuation failed to get through and, as dawn broke on September 26, the few survivors found relative silence. Airborne engineers arrived with the news that the division crossed the river. Shortly thereafter the Germans arrived and accepted D Company's surrender.[15]

Information Perimeter Route Panel #4 identifies a further 1st Border defensive position. The text states:

The defenders of the western part of the perimeter included men of 1st Battalion, The Border Regiment. To the right you see the road alongside which the British in the photo were dug in. In 1997 the remains of a soldier were found along this road. Earlier, in 1993, the remains of two men were discovered in a garden elsewhere in Van Lennepweg. After identification they were re-interred in the Airborne Cemetery, Oosterbeek.

…The graves of more than 130 soldiers have never been found or registered and approximately 290 Unknown Soldiers lie in the Airborne Cemetery.

The image shows British soldiers along the northern part of Van Lennepweg facing the enemy who had taken up positions a hundred meters to the west.

Follow Van Lennepweg back north toward Utrechtseweg. Unfortunately, access to the highway is not permitted, so turn right on the frontage road back to Hoofdlaan. Achieve Utrechtseweg and proceed west for 550 m. Take the first exit at the traffic circle and continue 400 m to the commemorative post on the left. (51.990333, 5.822237)

By early on 20 September, Brigadier Hackett had already lost one half of his brigade. The 156th Battalion had been reduced to 270 men and 10th Battalion even fewer. At 06:15, the reduced brigade fought a running battle against encircling German

---

15   Captain William Kitching Hodgson, aged 24 from Milthorpe, Westmoreland, died of his wounds and is buried in the Arnhem Oosterbeek War Cemetery, Plot 1, Row B, Grave 1.
Lieutenant Alan Green, from Leicester, was sent to Oflag IXA/Z and in April 1945 as the war approached its conclusion, was marched east before being liberated. After the war, Green taught for fifteen years before becoming a priest. He died in 2005 aged 83.

armor and infantry of SS Bataillon Eberwein from Colonel Lippert's SS NCO School 'Arnhem' which advanced down Wolfhezerweg after clearing Wolfheze. In addition, KGr Krafft was following from the north. Contact was lost with the 10th Battalion, which eventually achieved the perimeter on its own by 13:10 with only 60 men.

What remained of Hackett's Brigade became surrounded roughly 180 meters to the north. Hackett drove out of the encirclement in a jeep carrying wounded Lieutenant-Colonel Derick Heathcoat-Amory as the area was engulfed in flames from a burning second jeep.[16]

Hackett's group, reduced to 150 men along with twenty German prisoners, again became trapped in a wooded hollow behind this marker post. They continued to resist German attacks through the afternoon often in hand-to-hand combat while ammunition and water levels became perilously low. German snipers took their toll. Recognizing that he was about to be wiped out and with only 90 men in fighting shape, at 17:00 Hackett ordered fixed bayonets and led a desperate charge shrouded by smoke grenades across the remaining 350 meters east to the Oosterbeek perimeter. The wounded were left to the Germans. The move surprised the enemy and Hackett arrived at the perimeter of the Border Regiment with few additional casualties.

Airborne Commemorative Post #8 alongside Valkenburglaan identifies 'Hackett's Hollow' where the men were trapped during much of 20 September. A bronze plaque beneath the 1st Airborne's 'Pegasus' insignia identifies the site of the narrow escape in Dutch and English.

Reverse direction and pass through the traffic circle on Utrechtseweg and proceed 950 m to a gravel road on the left. A few meters farther south, follow the path east into the forest to an open area where the next panel stands at the corner of a pasture and overlooks the intersection of Van Borsselenweg and Benedendorpsweg at a distance. (51.979183, 5.828130)

Information Perimeter Route #5 recalls how the Oosterbeek defenses hoped that they would be relieved by XXX Corps advancing from the south. A map presents the various drop zones and routes of march with significant monuments also indicated. The Nederrijn is visible from this point.

Continue south on Van Borsselenweg; turn right onto Benedendorpsweg and proceed 400 m west to the access drive for De Westerbouwing Restaurant. Continue through the forest to the restaurant parking area. (51.975213, 5.82220)

D Company 1st Battalion, Border Regiment (Major Charles Osborne) passed through the undefended Westerbouwing Heights on 17 September but never received orders to hold it. Westerbouwing commands views of much of Oosterbeek and the Nederrijn but neither Urquhart nor von Tettau initially recognized the importance

---

16   Derick Heathcoat-Amory, 1st Viscount Amory, headed the Phantom detachment, a small liaison team which maintained direct radio contact with the War Office in London to provide information on the progress of the operation. After the war he became Chancellor of the Exchequer under Prime Minister Harold Macmillan. He died in 1981, aged 81.

of the dominant position which later played a major role in defeating relief forces attempting to cross the river.

Three platoons from B Company (Major Tom Armstrong), Border Regiment held the Westerbouwing high ground on 21 September when the 600-man Wossowski Battalion of the Herman Göring AuE Regiment (Oberleutnant Artur Wossowski) marched into the surrounding forest seeking to engage their enemy. One of Armstrong's machine guns opened fire on the bicycling grenadiers. Wossowski's men overran the British forward position and its heavy weapons platoon placed its machine guns and opened fire. Charging through the trees, the Germans forced passage into the inn buildings and captured the British inside.

Four French-built Renault Char B1 tanks from Panzer Abt 224 pursued the fleeing survivors into open fields near the Veerweg / Benedendorpsweg crossroads to the northeast where they encountered the reserve platoon. Moving from position to position, Private George Everington knocked out three of the panzers with his PIAT.[17] Major Armstrong rallied his men and attempted to lead an assault back up the hill but was beaten back by heavy fire.[18] B Company had been all but destroyed and its survivors took up positions around a large white house called Dennenoord.

The Wossowski Battalion had also suffered in the engagements. Approximately one half of the battalion were casualties. Wossowski was killed as were all but one of his company commanders.[19]

Major George Breese took command creating the 'Breese Force' when re-enforcements arrived in the form of fragments of platoons from A Company and South Staffords and later some Polish troops. Breese Force held this perimeter for the remainder of the battle and covered the perimeter evacuation on 25/26 September. Breese Force was the last unit to cross the river just as dawn broke that Tuesday morning.

Liberation Route Marker #21 identifies the superior position held by German machine guns that overlooked the river and the paratrooper escape route. The images depict the survivors after they safely recrossed the Nederrijn and paratroopers sorting through weapons. The 'Retreat of the British 1st Airborne Division' audio describes the situation of the men in the Oosterbeek cauldron and their evacuation. (51.975125, 5.822581)

A beautiful slate **The Border Regiment Plaque** attached to the restaurant's exterior wall depicts a landing glider and the Pegasus insignia flanking the unit insignia and commemorates the men and officers of that unit's 1st Battalion that fought and died during the Battle of Arnhem. (51.975108, 5.822180)

---

17   Private George Charles Hugh Everington, aged 20 from Kippax, Yorkshire was killed the next day — four days before the birth of his only son. Everington is buried in the Arnhem Oosterbeek War Cemetery, Plot 18, Row B, Grave 4.

18   Major Tom Armstrong, aged 36, was wounded and taken prisoner and Company Sergeant Major Alfred McGladdery was killed. McGladdery is buried in Utrecht (Soestbergen) General Cemetery, Plot 12D, Row 1, Grave 9.

19   Most sources spell the commander's name as 'Worrowski' but the German War Graves Volksbund records the name as Wossowski. Artur Wossowski, aged 26 from Usedom, Pomerania, is buried in the Ysselsteyn German Military Cemetery Plot TB, Row 1, Grave 5.

The removal of brush on the hillside below the **restaurant terrace** has revealed dramatic panoramic views that sweep from the Grote Kerk in Arnhem on the left, the rail bridge, the ferry crossing below, to the steeples in Driel to the right. The drop down to the highway that travels along the banks of the river and the escape routes can be seen. This is a stunning location from which to view the final escape of the Arnhem survivors.

A stone plaque facing the river on the opposite side of the terrace commemorates the actions of the **4th Battalion of the Dorset Regiment**, which, supported by the 5th Battalion, crossed the river below this restaurant and fought in support of the 1st Airborne Division from 24 to 26 September. A polished stone bearing the unit's insignia is to the left. A sphinx and the word 'Marabout' tops the insignia to commemorate the unit's origins as the 54th Regiment of Foot which captured Fort Marabout Egypt in 1801 and its amalgamation with the 39th Regiment of Foot which besieged Gibraltar Castle between 1779 and 1783. The Motto 'Primus in Indis' translates as 'First in India.'[20] (51.974884, 5.822008)

Hiking trails emanate from the parking lot into the woods and provide scenic overviews of the Nederrijn Valley although most of Arnhem is not visible. Dennenoord no longer exists now replaced by a housing development called Dennenoordpark.

> Return to Benedendorpsweg and proceed east parallel to the river for 1.5 km. Pass the Oude Kerk and turn left onto Zuiderbeekweg then shortly turn right on Ploegseweg and continue 120 m to find convenient parking. (51.979619, 5.840457)

The Lonsdale Force established the Oosterbeek eastern perimeter west of Ploegseweg. The Germans pushed hard against it presumably to cut access to the river and deny the British reinforcements or resupply. The 1st and 3rd Parachute Battalions defended the houses 200 meters east of the church under the command of Major Alan Bush. The survivors of Major Cain's company were cut off from the rest of the battalion, so he positioned his contingent around the houses and gardens around the large Van Hofwegen commercial laundry facility where Cain had established his headquarters. The laundry no longer exists but was between Ploegseweg and Zuiderbeekweg north of Matzer van Blooisplantsoen. (51.979963, 5.839988)

For six days, they were closely engaged with enemy tanks, self-propelled guns, and infantry. On Thursday, 21 September, a StuG III approached the area held by Cain's company by moving south down Ploegseweg. Cain went out to deal with it armed with a PIAT and assisted by glider pilot Sergeant RF Shipley. The German gun immediately halted and turned its cannon on him, shooting away a corner of the house near where the officer was lying. Although wounded by machine gun bullets and falling masonry, Cain continued firing until he had scored several direct hits to immobilize the gun. He then supervised the bringing up of a 75-mm howitzer which destroyed it. Only after the threat was neutralized did he consent to have his wounds treated.

---

20   In 1944, the regiment's official name was The Dorsetshire Regiment. The name was changed to Dorset Regiment in 1951. In 1958, a restructuring of forces formed the Devonshire and Dorset Regiment.

The next morning Cain drove off three tanks with his PIAT, on each occasion leaving cover and taking up positions on open ground with complete disregard for his personal safety. During the following days, Major Cain was everywhere danger threatened, moving amongst his men and encouraging them by his fearless example despite suffering from multiple wounds. During one such engagement, Cain's PIAT shell exploded in the tube. Cain fell backward temporarily blinded and severely wounded. Treated for shrapnel wounds to his head, Cain's sight returned and he returned to the battle. In all Cain repelled or destroyed six tanks, four of which are described as being Tigers, and several SP guns.

On 25 September the enemy made a concerted attack on Major Cain's position, using self-propelled guns, flame throwers, and infantry. By this time the last PIAT had been put out of action and Cain was armed with only a light 2-inch mortar. However, by a skillful use of this weapon and his daring leadership of the few men still under his command, he completely demoralized the enemy who, after an engagement lasting more than three hours, withdrew in disorder.[21]

Reverse direction and return to the Oude Kerk. Parking is not permitted on the grounds but may be found on lower Weverstraat.

In this sector, the Oosterbeek perimeter was held by a section of G Squadron, The Glider Pilot Regiment, led by Lieutenant Michael Dauncey, along a line east of Weverstraat. German tanks frequently approached via Fangmanweg to shell houses held by infantry and the artillery pieces gathered around the church. During a patrol Lieutenant Dauncey and two paratroopers captured eight German soldiers, but the lieutenant received a serious wound in his eye. Taken to the Ter Horst house but left untreated, Dauncey returned to his men the next morning. The ominous squeak of tank tracks warned of another approaching enemy. With a shortage of PIATs, he ran up to a panzer and threw a Gammon grenade resulting in a furious explosion. While the confrontation continued, Dauncey received two more wounds; a bullet went clear through his thigh and a stick grenade broke his jaw inflicting serious flesh wounds as well. Returning again to the Ter Horst house, the over-crowded rooms forced him to be left outside. When it began to rain, Dauncey guiltily removed a blanket from a dead trooper lying beside and covered himself. The evacuation began that night and Dauncey was left to be captured.[22]

Lower Weverstraat was the site of a dramatic confrontation with a PzKpfw VI

---

21   Major Robert Henry Cain, born in Shanghai in 1909, escaped across the river and was awarded the Victoria Cross. Note: the official citation describes the action on the wrong date and identifies the vehicle as a Tiger tank. Cain died in 1974 at age 65 and is buried on the Isle of Man.
Cain's award and that to Lance-Sergeant John Baskeyfield made the 2nd South Staffordshires the only battalion to be awarded two Victoria Crosses in one engagement during the Second World War. The two actions were within one kilometer of each other.

22   Lieutenant Michael Dauncey from Birmingham, England was awarded the Distinguished Service Order for his courage and fearless leadership in attacking enemy positions. After treatment in a special eye hospital in Utrecht, Dauncey eventually made his escape with a seriously wounded senior officer in tow. The pair spent two months in hiding before the Dutch underground organized their return to friendly lines in April 1945. Dauncey retired in 1976 as a brigadier and died in August 2017 aged 97.

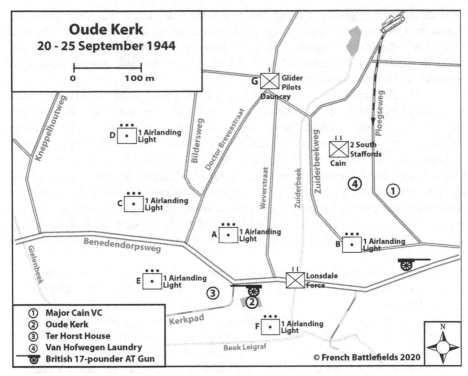

Oude Kerk
20 - 25 September 1944

0   100 m

G   Glider Pilots
Dauncey

Kneppelhoutweg

D   1 Airlanding Light

Bildersweg

Doctor Breveestraat

2 South Staffords
Cain

Zuiderbeekweg

Ploegseweg

④   ①

C   1 Airlanding Light

Weverstraat

Zuiderbeek

A   1 Airlanding Light

B   1 Airlanding Light

Benedendorpsweg

Gielenbeek

E   1 Airlanding Light

Lonsdale Force

③

②

Kerkpad

F   1 Airlanding Light

Beek Leigraf

① Major Cain VC
② Oude Kerk
③ Ter Horst House
④ Van Hofwegen Laundry
⚙ British 17-pounder AT Gun

N

© French Battlefields 2020

on 25 September. The Tiger II approached C Troop of the Light Regiment whose guns were dug in west of Weverstraat. British Artillery officer Lieutenant Adrian Donaldson and Lance-Bombardier James Dickson manhandled a Polish 6-pounder antitank gun into position. Lieutenant Donaldson and Bombardier Dickson put several hits on the panzer without any damage before their gun was destroyed . Donaldson and Dickson returned to their 75-mm howitzer and firing over open sights, hit the panzer six more times before the howitzer jammed. One round hit a track starting a fire. The two British soldiers finally destroyed the Tiger II with two PIAT rounds. This PzKpfw VI was the only one to be destroyed within the Oosterbeek cauldron.

Walk to the old church. (51.978059, 5.837823)

PKN Oude Kerk
Benedendorpsweg 134, 6862 WP Oosterbeek, Netherlands
For information: +31 (0)26 33 42 856
Open to the public 1 May to 1 October on Wednesday, Thursday and Sunday from 14:00 to 17:00.

Twenty-two 75-mm howitzers of the 1st Airlanding Light Regiment, Royal Artillery started arriving around the church on Monday morning with Troops E and F of 3rd Battery taking up positions in the fields south of the church. On Tuesday, Troops A and B of 1st Battery set up in open fields near the laundry west of Ploegseweg. Finally, on Wednesday, Troops C and D of 2nd Battery positioned in an open field north of the Rectory garden. During the worst of the battle from 21–25 September the Regimental Headquarters was on Benedendorpsweg across from the church. The men of the Light Regiment frequently fought as infantry against snipers, as artillerymen firing in support of the surrounding battalion, and as antitank gunners taking on approaching German armor over open sights.

On 20 September, action continued along the river route. The 1st Parachute Battalion came under heavy German fire from the railway embankment and from the north forcing the remnants of the 1st and 3rd Parachute Battalions to retreat to the Oude Kerk. They were given shelter in the old church and the opportunity to wash themselves and clean their weapons. Although wounded several times, Major Lonsdale circulated among his men with bloody bandages on his arm, hand, and one leg. The ancient church's roof was gone, and every new explosion brought down more plaster onto the gathered troopers. Lonsdale climbed up the pulpit steps to rally the men with a stirring speech to defend their piece of the perimeter with everything they had and to hold on until the arrival of XXX Corps by recalling past victories over the German Army:

> You know as well as I do there are a lot of bloody Germans coming at us. Well, all we can do is to stay here and hang on in the hope that somebody catches us up. We must fight for our lives and stick together. We've fought the Germans before — in North Africa, Sicily, and Italy. They weren't good enough for us then and they're bloody well not good enough for us now. They're up against the finest soldiers in the world. An hour from now you will take up defensive positions north of the road outside. Make certain you dig in well and that your weapons and ammo are in good order. We are getting short of ammo, so when you shoot you shoot to kill. Good luck to you all. [23]

The tanks overran 2nd Battery in the rectory garden with only twenty men escaping. Similarly, three Tigers overran A Troop of 1st Battery. Fortunately, the guns' breech blocks and firing pins were destroyed making the guns inoperable for the Germans. The defenders fought back with PIATs, Gammon grenades, direct artillery fire, or supporting fire from across the river forcing the tanks to withdraw.

The church tower had been used as an observation post for the Light Regiment. Suspecting as much, German artillery pounded it with their artillery. On the final day of the battle British gunners watched as the tower crumbled.

The **Oude Kerk**, which may be the oldest church in the Netherlands, stands in a grove of oak trees. The central part of the church is 10th century and various expansions were added over the centuries. The parish gained fame in 1027 when Gisela, wife of Holy Roman Emperor Conrad II, gave birth to a daughter while traveling through the parish. The parish priest was made bishop of Utrecht in thanks for his

---

23   Major Richard Lonsdale, from County Leitrim, Ireland, escaped across the river. He was awarded his second Distinguished Service Order for his actions in Oosterbeek. Temporarily replacing Lieutenant-Colonel Frost who had been injured during the drop, he had earlier received the same award in Sicily for successfully leading the 2nd Parachute Battalion in defense of positions near Primasole Bridge and taking 450 enemy prisoners. In 1937 he had received the Military Cross for actions in India. Lonsdale died in 1988 aged 73 and is buried in the Aldershot Military Cemetery, Aldershot, Hampshire.

assistance. The originally Roman Catholic church was taken over by Protestants after the Reformation.

The church suffered considerable damage during the battle for Arnhem and its dimensions were considerably reduced during its reconstruction. The contrast between the old, darker, rougher stone against the lighter stone indicates the extent of the damage especially on the south, river-facing side where most of the back wall has been reconstructed with bits and pieces of old stone. Bullets and shrapnel marks still scar the walls.

A plaque beside the now seldom used doorway on the north side displays the various additions to the church. The extent of the structure before the battle can be determined from the colored engraving.

The church grounds hold a variety of remembrances. An enormous lime tree surrounded by black iron fence stands near the north side with a small wooden post bearing a bronze plaque that states:

> September 1944 The Battle of Arnhem. In the thick of the fighting, when a patrol of five airborne warriors was standing by this lime tree, a mortar shell hit the place and killed four of them. Only Mark Leaver survived. Staff Sgt. G Squadron Glider Pilot Regiment *20.01.1920 †31.10.2000 (51.978064, 5.837752)

A **long bench** along the northeast corner of the church is dedicated to the memory of the Lonsdale Force and bears wooden plaques displaying the insignia of the various units that comprised the unit. From left to right, they are: 7th Battalion, King's Own Scottish Borderers, Royal Artillery, Glider Pilot Regiment, 1st, 2nd, 3rd, 10th, and 11th Battalions, and 21st Independent Company, The Parachute Regiment, 2nd Battalion, South Staffordshires, 1st Airborne Recce Squadron, Reconnaissance Corps, and 1st Battalion, The Border Regiment. (51.978050, 5.837966)

A medieval leper hole is immediately to the right of the bench. In medieval times the diseased stood outside the church and watched the Mass through the hole since they were not permitted inside.

A **weathered old stone** directly east of the rear of the church bears a polished black plaque with the Pegasus symbol beside the inscription:

> In September 1944 British Airborne soldiers and their Polish comrades, with the support of brave Dutch men and women, fought a grim battle around this ancient church in the struggle to liberate the Netherlands from Nazi tyranny. This stone commemorates all who took part in this action and above all those who died. Not one shall be forgotten (51.978025, 5.838134)

Airborne Commemorative Post #9 slightly to the northeast of the church under an old horse chestnut tree states, 'Around this church various British units fought until the end of the battle in order to make an eventual crossing of the Nederrijn possible.' (51.978202, 5.838195)

Other plaques carry the Airborne Prayer, commemorate the men of the 156th Battalion, The Parachute Regiment, or list names of the fallen from the 1st Airborne Light Regiment, Royal Artillery.

Four benches lining the south side of the church are in memory of men of

1st Airborne Division, who died in combat in September 1944. Unfortunately, only one retains its original plaque, remembering Private William Dodd, 3rd Battalion, The Parachute Regiment. The benches provide viewpoints for the rail bridge across the flat flood plain.

> Continue on foot onto Kerkpad starting at the west end of the church and continue west along the river. Stop briefly after 100 m. (51.978125, 5.836847)

The Light Regiment's medical officer, Captain Randall Martin,[24] established the Regimental Aid Post in the Ter Horst house, a fourteen room, 200-year-old former vicarage on 18 September. By the next day, he started receiving wounded from the various perimeter units, but they received only first aid since Captain Martin had no surgical equipment. By Wednesday the house was on the front lines of the battle. Kate Ter Horst's five children and eleven other civilians sheltered in the 3-meter-by-2-meter cellar while she moved among the wounded ministering as best she could.

British medics used the house for those requiring immediate care leaving the lightly wounded in the garden. Seriously wounded were evacuated to the Schoonoord Hotel until passage through the town became impossible. When a patient inside the house died, the medics just pushed the body out of the window to make room for the next patient. By Sunday over 300 patients filled the entire house.

As the battle progressed, occasional sniper fire was replaced by mortar fire. Then a Tiger tank penetrated the perimeter and entered the rectory garden to fire shells into the upper floor killing many wounded. An enraged medical orderly, Bombardier EC Bolden, grabbed a Red Cross flag – some reports say a white bed sheet – and rushed out of the house and charged the German tank furiously waving the flag and screaming at the tank commander. The tank backed away.

On Tuesday morning, 26 September, the sounds of battle were gone and an uneasy quiet descended upon the Ter Horst home. Kate cautiously rose from her sleep in the cramped cellar to find the British soldiers gone, but the house ringed with German infantry preparing for a final assault. Slowly she opened the front door and approached the nearest German soldier demanding to see his commander. After some hesitation, he complied. Kate told the officer that the British soldiers were gone, and only wounded and medical staff remained in the house. After confirmation that the house held only medical cases, the officer requested German medics who moved forward to tend to the wounded.

Kate returned to her cellar to bring out her family and the civilians that were hiding there. Five-year-old Sophie Ter Horst recalled the experience of leaving the family home. Stepping outside for the first time in days, all she could see were piles of partially naked bodies beneath each window. The family left that afternoon for Apeldoorn.

Kate's husband, Jan, had left a week earlier to scout German positions for the Dutch underground and had been cut-off by the forming of the British perimeter. Jan was allowed to return shortly after his family had been ordered to leave as part of the

---

24   Captain Victor David Randall Martin was a PoW until liberated from Stalag IX-C in April 1945. He returned to medical practice, dying in 2001 aged 82.

civilian evacuation. Ter Horst was spotted by German soldiers who ordered him to dig graves for the dead British who were on the grounds of the house. Ter Horst buried fifty-eight British soldiers in his garden, giving each its own grave. The remains were later reburied in the Arnhem Oosterbeek War Cemetery. A memorial in the small pond in their garden displays the Airborne's Pegasus inscribed upside down so that it can only be recognized by looking at the reflection in the water. [25]

The house is still occupied by the descendants of Kate and Jan Ter Horst. Please respect their privacy.

> Continue west on Kerkpad to the final perimeter sign. (Approximately 51.977573, 5.833683)

During the night of 25/26 September, surviving British troops slowly moved along the Kerkpad passing south of the Ter Horst house to their assigned crossing spots. **Information Perimeter Route Panel #6** describes the withdrawal of British and Polish troops from Oosterbeek adding 'Many soldiers tried to swim the fast-flowing river and some perished in the attempt.' The panel displays an image of scattered war debris on the flood plain as photographed in 1945. (51.977563, 5.833587)

A few meters farther west the men crossed a frail wooden bridge over Gielenbeek before advancing onto the exposed flood plain of the Nederrijn. The occasional vehicle traveling along the Drielse Rijndijk across the river helps to identify the distance to the crossing.

> Retrieve your vehicle and proceed west on Benedendorpsweg. Turn left on Veerweg 800 m west of the church. And follow to the ferry parking area (Generaal Sosab-owskiwaard). (51.973819, 5.823144)

The Driel ferry operated peacefully until 19 September. It appears that British plans took no account of this river crossing despite the ferry appearing in reconnaissance photos. A small bay has been created near the Driel ferry landing where the main river channel once flowed nearer the road below Westerbouwing Heights.

The 43rd Division organized two crossing sites. One was immediately south of the church and the other 850 meters downstream near the ferry crossing at the bend in the river.

The ferry continues to operate carrying only pedestrians and cyclists across the Nederrijn. The Westerbouwing Restaurant and its tower can be seen from the parking area depending upon the season, proving the dominant position of those heights along the river. A 'Slag von Arnhem' information sign describes the operation's failure and the unjust blame heaped upon General Sosabowski.

---

25   In 1947 Kate's son, Pieter Ter Horst, and a friend were killed by the explosion of a wartime antitank mine that had been abandoned in the meadow behind their house. In 1992 an automobile struck down Kate and Jan Ter Horst while they were out for a walk. Kate, aged 85, died and Jan was seriously injured but survived. Jan died in 2003 at age 98.

Chapter Nine
South Bank of the Nederrijn
Polish 1st Independent Parachute Brigade
21 September to 4 October

The Polish 1st Independent Parachute Brigade was created in September 1941 with the intention of dropping into Poland to liberate the country from the Nazis by joining with resistance forces. Under pressure from the British Army, the brigade was transferred to the British 1st Airborne Division. Operation MARKET-GARDEN was its first combat role.

Third Lift, 19 September

The third air lift was intended to deliver Major-General Sosabowski's Polish Airborne Brigade to support Urquhart at Arnhem and reinforce the American airborne units. The equipment gliders enjoyed clear weather at airfields in the south of England and left for the Netherlands. Bad weather at airfields in northern England delayed the departure of troop carriers carrying the second half of the third lift of Sosabowski's Parachute Brigade.

The next day planes rumbled down the English runways at 13:00. Suddenly the planes cut their throttles as jeeps approached the planes. The drop was again postponed for another twenty-four hours. Sosabowski fumed at the delay. His men were ready to go. The Polish general was also concerned about the lack of radio contact with 1st Airborne Division. Who controlled the bridge? More important to him, who controlled the drop zone near the south end of the highway bridge and the landing zone near Johannahoeve farm where his equipment was to land? Sosabowski was right to be worried. The Polish drop zones had been abandoned and were now in enemy hands.

By 20 September, Allied air superiority over the Arnhem battlefield was challenged by the arrival of Oberstleutnant Hubert von Svoboda's flak brigade bringing with it five battalions of 88-mm Flak guns and 20-mm and 37-mm cannon. In addition, 300 fighters from the Luftwaffe's 1st Jagdflieger Division were assigned to cover Arnhem.[1]

Fourth Lift, 21 September

Finally, 114 C-47s flown by the American IX Troop Carrier Command transported Sosabowski's Brigade. Delayed in departing until early afternoon, the flights were further disrupted by heavy clouds closing in over the airfield causing the issue of a recall order. Not all of the planes understood and responded, thus the brigade was further diminished by 41 planes that returned. The others continued on their mission.

Originally planned to drop near the south approach to the supposedly by-then British held bridge, the Poles revised mission was to drop near the village of Driel on the south bank of the Nederrijn near the southern end of the Heveadorp ferry. After nightfall, the paratroopers were to utilize the ferry to strengthen the British perimeter.

---

1   The 1st Jagdflieger Division claimed to have shot down 40 transport and 112 gliders during the remaining days of the battle.

While in flight, General Sosabowski witnessed the chaos along the roadway south of Arnhem as his unit's planes neared the drop zone one kilometer east of Driel. He also saw German vehicles heading south across the Arnhem bridge and realized that the mission was already a failure. The Poles jumped into a hell storm of German antiaircraft fire. Twenty-five Messerschmitts dove from the clouds in attack. The RAF fighter umbrella was absent having been aborted by the English weather conditions. The transport planes were slow, low, defenseless, and easy targets. Polish paratroopers struggled to exit burning aircraft only to fall into strafing machine-gun fire. Artillery and Nebelwerfers fired salvos onto the drop zone. Sosabowski floated down angry that his unit was being sacrificed in what he felt was already a British defeat. Instead of 1,568 men, he was left with only two weak battalions totaling 1,003 men and one quarter of them were scattered across the countryside. The Poles landed and consolidated with surprisingly few casualties — five dead and thirty-six injured — only to find that the German Wossowski Bataillon had occupied the northern ferry landing and the boat had been sunk.

The Allies now had three separate contingents striving to unite on the banks of the Nederrijn: Urquhart's trapped airborne, Sosabowski's Poles in Driel, and Horrocks armored column. The Germans, shifting ad hoc units of inexperienced troops from crisis to crisis, awaited the arrival of two companies of schwere Panzer Abteilung 506 (Major Eberhard Lange) armed with twenty-eight new Tiger IIb tanks.[2]

Final Lifts, 23 September

Weather improved to 'fair' on 23 September and the airlifts resumed. Gavin's often delayed 325th Glider Infantry Regiment with 3,385 troops arrived and so did nearly 3,000 more men for General Taylor's 101st, but nothing for the Poles at Driel. Instead the Polish troops recalled on 21 September were dropped into the 82nd area instead to avoid the possibility of enemy flak over the drop zone and to provide a reserve for the stretched 82nd Airborne Division. Urquhart's men watched their resupply dropped to the Germans. Bad weather over the fighter airfields in England again cancelled or delayed fighter support. Most of the delayed squadrons never caught up with the transports leaving them unprotected from Luftwaffe squadrons of Focke-Wulfs. Thirty-five Allied aircraft fell to flak and fighters.

SS-General Bittrich considered the Polish arrival as a threat to German rear defenses and an action to prevent a counterattack against the Nijmegen bridges. Bittrich considered the 1st Airborne Division finished and could not conceived that Sosabowski's mission was to reinforce the Oosterbeek perimeter. He ordered Major Knaust to rush his kampfgruppe, now strengthen by the arrival the Lange's Tigers, to prevent Horrocks' tanks from joining the Poles.

Battle

At 22:00 on 22 September, the Polish 3rd Battalion (Captain Sobocinski) left

---

2   The Tiger IIb weighed in at 60 tons and mounted the 88-mm gun. They were almost unstoppable. Although many reports indicate forty-five tanks, in fact #1 Kompanie and headquarters was sent to Aachen reducing the number of tanks in MARKET-GARDEN to twenty-eight. Of that number #3 Kompanie was sent to Elst with 14 tanks, leaving only #2 Kompanie in Oosterbeek.

Driel to the riverbank opposite the Oosterbeek church. Royal Engineers had collected six small, two-man reconnaissance boats and an RAF rescue dingy. By tying the boats together and using a cable to pull the boats back and forth across the river, fifteen Polish paratroopers were intended to transfer in each trip. The effort was defeated by the swift river current which suddenly broke the connecting cable. Instead, Polish boatmen paddled the boats across the river, transferring one soldier per trip. At first successful, the operation was spotted, and a magnesium parachute flare illuminated the action for German machine guns and mortars. After a pause, the transit restarted only to halt again under the eerie glow of another flare. The cruel game continued as Polish casualties mounted and all the boats were sunk. After one hour the operation was abandoned. Only fifty-two Polish paratroopers successfully crossed.

Lieutenant-Colonel Taylor's DCLI force carried with it two DUKW[3] amphibious vehicles loaded with supplies and ammunition. At 02:00 Taylor's two-and-one-half ton DUKWs started moving along a muddy road toward the river. But the slippery road and dense ground fog hindered the sixty men manhandling the 9.5-meter-(31-foot)-long vehicles. Both DUKWs slid uncontrollably into a ditch and stuck.

The following night of 23 September saw another attempt to transport Polish soldiers across the river. Fourteen assault boats, survivors of the Waal River crossing, arrived at the bank two-and-a-half hours behind schedule and without crews to man them. The boats had to be dragged 400 meters over fields and over the dike road. The Polish Parachute Engineer Squadron (Captain Piotr Budziszewski) struggled with the unfamiliar equipment under increased German fire. That night only 153 Poles successfully reached 1st Airborne Division perimeter out of the 250 which made the crossing.[4]

Sunday morning, Horrocks met with Sosabowski in Driel to discuss the two options open to them. Either a massive reinforcement with heavy weapons, food, and ammunition or a withdrawal of the survivors back across the river. Horrocks decided to advance 43rd (Wessex) Division across the river.

A tense meeting was held in the Valburg train station later in the day with all the commanders present. The seating arrangement was peculiar with all the British officers, four generals, several brigadiers and their staffs, seated on one side of a long table and two Polish officers on the other. Only Sosabowski had a chair; his translator had to stand. The British plan for two separate crossings was developed without input from the only commander familiar with the ground and, worse, stripped Sosabowski of one of his battalions to be placed under a junior British brigadier (Brigadier BB Walton) of the 130th Infantry Brigade who had not seen the crossing site.

When Sosabowski argued that the force was insufficient to rescue the paratroopers and that it would only result in sacrificing the British and Polish battalions crossing the river, he was summarily ordered to be quiet and threatened with replacement. During a later confrontation between Sosabowski and Browning in

---

3   DUKW nicknamed 'duck': a US Army six-wheeled, amphibious vehicle built upon a truck chassis. The acronym originates with General Motors Corporation's model nomenclature: D - the design year of 1942; U -utility; K - all wheel drive; W - dual tandem rear axles.

4   Despite the failure of the mission, the obstacles were considered so great that Captain Budziszewski who remained in charge despite being wounded was awarded the Military Cross for his efforts.

Nijmegen, the Polish general questioned why an operation that required the crossing of numerous rivers was launched without a supply of boats near the front of the column. Sosabowski's future career in the British Army was over.[5]

Sunday night, as planned at the Valburg train station meeting, the 4th Dorset Battalion (Lieutenant-Colonel Gerald Tilly) repeated the Polish experience of the previous night. At 21:30, Tilly led 420 hand-picked men down to the riverbank. They awaited the arrival of the boats for three hours in a cold rain. When the boats arrived, there were fewer than promised due to the cutting of the Corridor at Koevering. The Dorsets carried nine boats for 600 meters struggling through a swampy marsh and the polder mud. Finally, at 01:00 25 September, the men prepared to launch. The lack of boats forced a cancellation of the Polish part of the crossing.

German mortars and machine guns on Westerbouwing Heights swept the southern bank and were answered by British artillery. The swift current drove the boats outside of the British perimeter. Each of the five waves of Dorsets suffered heavy casualties with only 315 men achieving the north bank. The battalion landed in groups dispersed by the river current and never assembled into a coherent force. Small groups scattered in the forests were surrounded and captured. Of those Dorsets who made the crossing, thirteen died and two hundred were taken prisoner. Only a handful reached Oosterbeek.[6] Sosabowski had been proven correct.

The evacuation of 25/26 September included 160 Poles among the 2,400 men brought back across the river, but unfortunately the Polish 8th Company had not been advised of the withdrawal and 120 of its men were taken prisoner.

Aftermath

Still under fire of German artillery in Driel, the Polish Brigade began a withdrawal by truck to Nijmegen on the morning of 26 September eventually assigned to guarding airfields around Neerloon. On 6 October the unit was relieved and transported back to England. In May 1945, the Polish Brigade became part of the German Occupation Force. Two years later it was dissolved.

101st Airborne Division
4 October to 27 November

General Eisenhower had stipulated that the American Airborne Division should be released from British control as soon as ground forces had passed the positions they had seized. The failure of the mission, and the resulting salient into the front lines changed the calculus of the situation.

Hitler feared further airborne or seaborne landings in the northern parts of the Netherlands. He ordered General Student's First Parachute Army to wipe out the Corridor and committed fresh armored units in the depleted 9th and 116th Panzer

---

5   In his memoirs, Sosabowski was especially critical of Browning for misjudging the key moment in the battle feeling that victory could still be attained with the unopposed landing of the 43rd Division and his brigade farther downstream. Sosabowski argued the troops and equipment were finally up to the river and that only one more effort was necessary to achieve the objective of a Nederrijn beachhead.

6   Lieutenant-Colonel Tilly was captured and held as a PoW for the remainder of the war. Tilly's courageous effort was awarded a Distinguished Service Order.

Divisions, and eventually the restructured but fresh 363rd Volksgrenadier Division to the task. Transport difficulties hampered the appearance of those units onto the battlefield, but local probing continued to improve lines of departure.

On 28 September the 101st Airborne Division became part of British XII Corps. The division's period along the south bank of the Nederrijn was marked by days of boredom, soggy ground that prohibited the deep foxholes that offered the only protection from enemy artillery fire, and a scattering of sharp engagements when the Germans attempted to establish bridgeheads across the river. However, the Germans suffered from similar problems as the Polish relief forces. Too few boats, strong nighttime patrols, and terrain inhospitable to tanks.

Battle of Opheusden
5 to 15 October

On 4 October the 3rd Battalion, 506th PIR took positions along a four-kilometer north-south line from the Nederrijn, through Opheusden south to the Waal River relieving the British 43rd Division. The 2nd Battalion occupied the dike facing the Nederrijn from Randwijk to Opheusden before turning south to the Waal. The

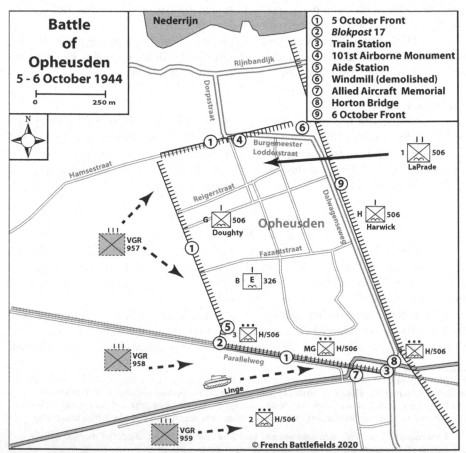

1st Battalion was held in reserve near Zetten. The 10-kilometer line was thinly held. The retiring British troops described the sector as quiet where a live and let live understanding existed with the enemy.

Battle

The next morning, the German Volksgrenadier Regiment 957, 363rd Volksgrenadier Division (Generalleutnant Augustus Dettling) launched a ferocious attack punctuated by a rolling barrage of artillery and Nebelwerfer rockets along the entire line west of Opheusden. Flanking movements against Company H (Captain Robert Harwick) manning a blockhouse of railway ties near the railway station on the southern edge of the town and against Company G (1st Lieutenant Joseph Doughty) in the town proper forced both units back to the eastern edge of Opheusden. The 1st Battalion was committed to the battle while the enemy-held town was pounded by the 75-mm pack howitzers of the 321st GFAB (Lieutenant Colonel Edward Carmichael) causing as much as fifty percent casualty rates among the attacking battalions despite German counterbattery fire. The 1st Battalion assumed responsibility from the rail line to the river while 3rd Battalion re-established a line farther south to Dodewaard. A horrific battle for the town focused upon house-to-house fighting along Dorpsstraat and Dalwagenseweg where platoons from 1st Battalion forced their way back into Opheusden.

The next day the British 5th Battalion, Duke of Cornwall's Light Infantry took over the southern flank in the open fields along the canal while 1st Battalion, 506th PIR continued to focus upon the town. Fearlessly, but foolishly, the DCLI began its assault that afternoon across the field in marching order reminiscent of 18th century infantry attacks. German artillery, mortars, and rockets fired from west and from across the river. The British battalion suffered seventy casualties including nineteen dead. The 501st PIR on the British right made more progress, but with its flank now completely exposed, it was forced to withdraw.

A battalion of 327th GIR formed a second defensive line to the rear allowing the two west-facing battalions to withdraw through the 327th that night. The town was abandoned to permit saturation bombing and strafing by Typhoons.

Repeated German attacks were repulsed for the next seven days with support from 101st and British artillery units. The two 101st Division artillery units[7] poured hundreds of 75-mm shells at the enemy from positions near Hemmen. The 363rd VGD suffered over 1,500 dead in these attacks and on 15 October it drew back two kilometers. Neither side could claim victory and Allied and German forces dug their positions protected by barbed wire and land mines. The front lines stagnated until the Germans flooded the region in December 1944. On 18 April 1945, the Belgian 1st Infantry Brigade (Brigade Piron) liberated the area.

Aftermath

The 101st Division casualties incurred during this defensive phase totaled 1,682 approaching the 2,110 men lost during the airborne phase. The men boarded

---

7 The 321st Glider Field Artillery Battalion was joined by the 377th Parachute Field Artillery Battalion (Lieutenant Colonel Benjamin Weisberg).

their trucks and reversed the course of their advance of two months earlier through Nijmegen, Veghel, Sint-Oedenrode, Son, and Eindhoven. The Dutch population lined the roadways cheering their liberators: 'September 17! September 17!'

Battlefield Tour

The Drielse Rijk runs along a 10-meter-high earthen embankment on the south side of the Nederrijn. The dike is intended to prevent flooding of the lower ground to the south should the river exceed its normal banks during high water periods. The road does not strictly follow the river's contours instead wandering closer or farther from the river. The tour essentially follows the riverfront roadway west from opposite Arnhem to review sites and events on the south banks of the river. It will recross the river at Rhenen to view the first and final acts of the war in the Netherlands.

Cross the John Frostbrug to the south side of the Nederrijn on Nijmeegseweg. Keep to the left after the bridge to turn left onto De Monchyplein which becomes Akel-eistraat. After 130 m, turn left onto Pinksterbloemstraat, right onto Huissensestraat. After 240 m enter a traffic circle and take the 3rd exit onto Groene Weide. Follow for 400 m to Veerpolderstraat which is one way westbound and park in front of the twin, eight-story apartments named Brug Wachter and Dijkgraaf. Cross a footbridge over a water-filled ditch, follow a path to the west, ascend the wooden steps to the dike path, and walk east to a monument on the river side of the apartments. (51.970457, 5.914132)

On 25 September 1944, B-25 'Mitchell' bombers of RAF 98 Squadron and Dutch 320 Squadron bombed German flak positions at Schaarsbergen 7 kilometers north of Arnhem in what became known as the 'Forgotten Bombing.' Unfortunately, German Flak guns positioned near the village church were targets causing civilian casualties. On the return flight twenty German fighters attacked and shot down two Mitchells of 98 Squadron. One crashed in Nijmegen killed three civilians and three crew members. The second plane crashed at this site on the Malburgse Bandijk 500 meters from the Arnhem highway bridge. Three crew members were killed: two Australians, Flying Officer Thomas Lennie and Flight Sergeant Bruce Williams, and British Flight Lieutenant Charles Carter. The fourth crew member, Canadian Frank Browmaster, survived. Bruce Williams at first escaped from the aircraft, but he was shot by a German soldier while descending with his parachute. Dutchman Frits Baars buried Williams in a temporary grave on the side of the embankment.[8]

Two **information boards**, in Dutch only, mark the location along the footpath bordering the river. Both relate the story of the crashed bomber with photographs dominated by that of a Mitchell bomber. Other images on the larger board include the Schaarsbergen village church, four members of the crew, the bombed Nederrijn bridge, and a 2010 commemoration. The spot is within view of the John Frostbrug.

---

8   Thomas Lennie, aged 31, and Bruce Williams, aged 21, are buried in adjacent graves in Arnhem Oosterbeek War Cemetery, Plot 21, Row C, Graves 12 and 13. Charles Carter, aged 25, is commemorated on the Runnymede Memorial, Runnymede, England.

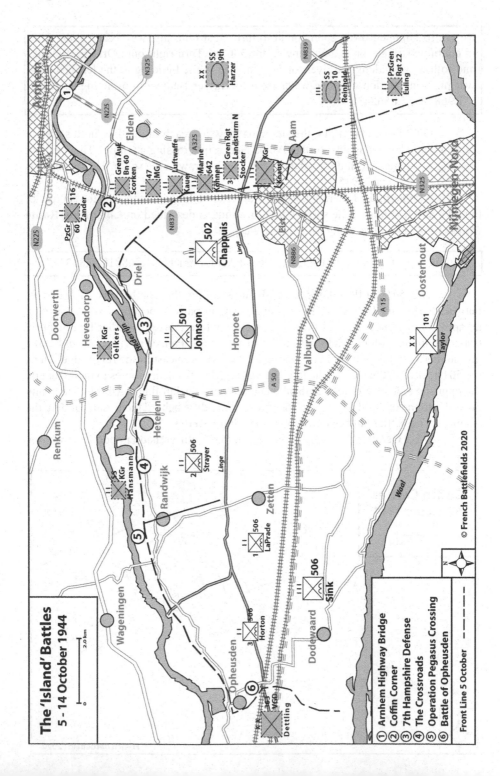

The 'Island' Battles
5 - 14 October 1944

2.0 km

① Arnhem Highway Bridge
② Coffin Corner
③ The Crossroads
④ Operation Pegasus Crossing
⑤ Battle of Opheusden
⑥

Front Line 5 October

© French Battlefields 2020

Return to Nijmeegseweg southbound to turn west onto highway N225. After 700 m continue straight on Batavierenweg for 500 m. Turn right onto Drielse Rijndijk and follow west along the river for 1.6 km. The white building to the left is a pre-war pumping station to move water from the lower Betuwe into the higher river. (51.968481, 5.856843)

On 2 December 1944, the Germans blew a breach in the dike in this area to create a water barrier against further Allied Nederrijn crossing attempts. The resultant flooding was extensive and forced the Allies to withdraw to the south. The breach was not closed until April 1945.

Although, the Liberation Route Marker is no longer at this site, the rupture of the dike and flooding of the surrounding lowlands is described on **Liberation Route Marker #67** audio recording 'Water as a Weapon'.

Continue west for 240 m to the rail bridge at Achterstraat. (51.968818, 5.853377)

The 501st PIR relieved British units along the south bank of the river between Driel and Heteren. Captain Phillips's Company C occupied what was then an apple orchard southeast of this road junction while Panzergrenadier Regiment 60 (Oberstleutnant Colonel Helmut Zander) of the 116th Panzer Division occupied the ground between the dike and the river and the entire area east of the rail bridge. Thus, the 501st, sited to the west of the rail line was faced with enemy forces to their front on the opposite side of the steep embankment and on their left flank. After the company moved into the orchard, German troops crossed the dike behind them, surrounding the troopers. The battlefield became known as **Coffin Corner**.

On 5 October, harassment attacks started with grenadiers coming from the

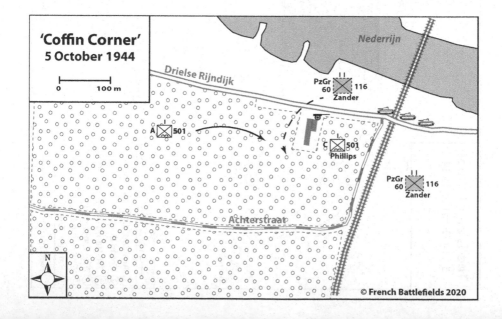

west. German artillery and snipers hidden on the embankment caused casualties and made patrols dangerous. Company A came from Driel to relieve the pressure trapping the German force between two American units. Eventually the Germans broke and attempted to cross the dike to regain their main body north of the roadway. Crossing the open, elevated, road exposed them to merciless machine-gun fire. After taking casualties, seventy-five survivors surrendered. The same evening a StuG IV carrying panzergrenadiers attacked. Machine-gun fire stripped the infantrymen from the gun's deck while the vehicle's machine gun sprayed the defenders. Tech/5 Frank Carpenter of Company C loaded an abandoned British 6-pounder hidden in a hole near the small farm house to the west, bored sighted the gun as the German armor breached the viaduct, and knocked out the SP gun which came to rest at the brick base on the west side of the bridge.[9] The trailing German guns then backed away. The standoff continued. Various units of the 101st Airborne Division held coffin corner until the units moved rearward for rest.

> Continue west for 1.2 km and park on Achterstraat. (51.970640, 5.835779)

During the night of 25/26 September, engineers ferried about 2,400 British and Polish Airborne across the river during Operation BERLIN. The **Royal Canadian Engineers and British Royal Engineers Monument** in Driel was erected by paratroop veterans in gratitude to those almost unseen engineers whom they could not thank that dark night. Two black polished stones are set upon gray stucco and backed by four flags — British, Canadian, Polish, and Dutch. One slab carries the badges of the Royal Engineers and the Royal Canadian Army. The second bears a sketched image of the paratrooper rescue by a Canadian engineer in the driving rain with the words, 'They were just whispers and shadows in the night.' A second sketch illustrates the important buildings across the river and marks the British evacuation from the Arnhem bridgehead. The beautifully executed memorial marks the dramatic conclusion to the battle for Arnhem.

> Continue on the dike road for 700 m to turn right onto Rijnbeekstraat and carefully continue to the ferry crossing.

Drielse Veer
Tel: +31 (0)6 33 31 42 07
Email: info@drielseveer.nl
Web: https://www.drielseveer.nl/vaartijden-en-tarieven/
The ferry operates only during the summer months and carries only pedestrians, scooters, and cyclists for a nominal fee.

The ferry crossing locates the crossing point of the Dorsets on the night of 25 September in their ill-fated attempt to support the Oosterbeek perimeter. The river has been modified for flood control, but the view provides another opportunity to visualize the dominating Westerbouwing Heights across the river.

---

9   Technician Fifth Class Francis J Carpenter was awarded the Silver Star.

Continue on the dike road for 1.3 km and enter Driel on Kerkstraat and follow to the town church. Parking is possible in the town square ahead. (51.961674, 5.814380)

The steeple of the Maria Geboortekerk became a frequent observation post from which British and Polish officers surveyed the river crossing points. The usage attracted German shelling and the church was severely damaged. The modern church has been completely reconstructed.

The left side of the front wall bears a slate plaque commemorating the **5th Battalion, Duke of Cornwall's Light Infantry** 'the Old Comrades' and the unit's dash to Driel on the evening of 22 September in an attempt to relieve the 1st Airborne Division.

The plaque on the right side of the doorway commemorates Johan Kosman, a soldier from Driel who served in the Dutch Army's 8th Regiment of Infantry and died during the Battle of Grebbeberg in May 1940. See: Side Trip Grebbeberg War Cemetery.

Opposite of the church in Driel is Major-General Sosabowskiplein, later renamed Polenplein. (51.961174, 5.813893)

The **National Monument to the Polish 1st Independent Parachute Brigade Group** is in the square in front of the old church in the form of a large stone fronted by a stylized man with hands clasped above his head symbolizing his holding the precious gem of freedom. It bears the slogan 'Arise Poland.' The memorial holds a casket filled with Polish soil and bears the emblem of the Polish Brigade. Flanking columns were added twenty years later. On the left, a black marble plaque lists the names of 94 Polish Parachutists who died in the battle. On the right are the coats of arms of Warsaw and Poland.

The square also holds a Portland stone column bearing a metal inset of the visage of **Major-General Stanislaw Sosabowski**. An adjacent brick wall bears a plaque commemorating the Polish 1st Independent Parachute Brigade and notes General Sosabowski's 'unfair dismissal.' The inscription further notes that the memorial was erected in 2006 by the veterans of the British 1st Airborne Division and The Parachute Regiment 'to record their admiration for an inspiring commander, a fearless fighter for freedom, and a great Polish hero.' The memorial leaves no doubt as to the feelings of the rank and file British paratroopers which stand in stark contrast to the denigration of Sosabowski by British commanders. The record is in English, Dutch, and Polish.

Liberation Route Marker #19 stands in the corner of the square. 'The Polish of Driel' describes the controversial use and misuse of Polish paratroopers in an abandoned Warsaw operation and at Arnhem. The audio continues with a description of his postwar exile and his posthumous recognition. The images present paratroopers fighting behind their machine gun in a dug in position, making radio contact with a portable radio unit and Polish paratroopers prepared to enter battle alongside their transport aircraft. (51.961300, 5.814130)

Return to the dike road and continue west for 1.6 km. (51.957521, 5.795504)

The 7th Battalion, Hampshire Regiment was formed from the Territorial Army in 1939. The unit remained in the United Kingdom until sent to Normandy where it participated in several actions. The battalion entered the fighting on 23 September defending the Nederrijn line west of Elst.

On 1 October, II SS Panzer Corps began its offensive in the Betuwe against XXX Corps' eastern flank utilizing its 9th and 116th Panzer Divisions. KGr Oelkers[10] (SS-Captain Heinrich Oelkers) delivered a feign against the 7th Battalion, Hampshire Regiment during a river crossing to the south bank opposite Kasteel Doorwerth.

Too few boats limited Oelkers's attack force. His dinghy was strafed by machine-gun fire as it approached the south bank sending its five occupants into the water. Planned reinforcements failed to make the river crossing while Oelkers's single company held the Steenfabriek brick factory at the river's edge at the end of a side road 850 meters to the west. The 7th Hampshires attacked the factory for four days, but could not overcome machine-gun positions established within the factory's brick kilns. On 4 October it moved to the German border area near Groesbeek.

An inscribed stone plaque encased in a brick frame forms a memorial to the **7th Battalion, The Hampshire Regiment** and commemorates the unit which was stationed in this area from 23 September to 4 October. The memorial lists the names of forty-two fatalities.

German re-enforcements crossed at 03:00 on 4 October the same day that American paratroopers of 2nd Battalion, 501st PIR relieved the Hampshires. Oelkers's men established foxhole positions dug into the river-side embankment of the dike road. Similarly, American troops dug in on the landward side of the roadway. Neither side could safely shoot at the other and they were too close together for mortar or artillery. A grenade battle ensued with Americans throwing grenades over the roadway in attempts to roll a grenade into an enemy foxhole. The slope of the embankment caused most to roll to the bottom before exploding doing little damage. At dusk on 5 October, the Americans prepared an attack using white phosphorous grenades attached to parachute suspension lines. By adjusting the length of line, the grenades were held against the embankment.

To take advantage of the expected chaos resulting from the shower of grenades, Sergeant Melton 'Tex' McMorries executed a daring plan. When the grenades started to fly, McMorries and Private Hollis Rowland crossed the roadway, shot a German in a foxhole and began firing his light machine gun (LMG) first to the right then to the left along the embankment catching the excited Germans as they attempted to escape the flaming grenades. McMorries suffered a lung wound during his rush across the roadway, but nevertheless stayed most of the night firing at targets of opportunity. Early the next morning, two Germans crept within range and leapt into McMorries foxhole. Tex killed them both. Just before dawn he returned to the south side of the dike with his light machine gun. The Germans had retreated back to the brick factory

---

10   KGr Oeklers consisted of Fliegerhorst Bataillon 3, a company of naval personnel, and troops from the Hermann Göring NCO Training School Arnhem.

in the darkness leaving twenty-six bodies on the slope.[11]

The factory stronghold was protected by German artillery on the heights of the north bank and the defenders resolutely defied Typhoon rocket attacks. Machine guns, snipers, and mortars kept each side at bay during the daylight hours. Movement increased at night, but always threatened to exposure by flares. On 8 October, Company F repulsed an enemy attack. Regimental commander, Colonel Howard Johnson inspected frontline positions when a German artillery shell exploded practically at his feet. Fragments penetrated his arm, neck, and back; the colonel died in the Nijmegen hospital. His last words were, 'Take care of my boys.'[12]

As described, the coordinated panzergrenadier attack failed against the 501st PIR's 1st Battalion at Coffin Corner and the progress of the 363rd Volksgrenadier Division assault on Opheusden (see Battle of Opheusden) eventually halted. Oelkers's men were slowly reduced by days of languid mortar and artillery fire and small-scale attacks. Finally, after ten days and against orders, he abandoned the position leading 35 of the original 120 men back across the Nederrijn.

A side road ahead leads to a private farm which now occupies the location of the brickyard that formed Oelkers's positions. The shell-battered chimney of the **brick factory kiln** is all that remains after much of the ground became part of modern flood defenses. (51.959411, 5.789517)

Continue west on the dike road for 2.1 km and stop immediately east of the A50 bridge over river (51.960682, 5.766640)

A **101st Airborne Monument** stands practically in the shadow of the Heteren Rijn Bridge. The brick monument is inscribed with airborne symbols and the dates October and November 1944. A small plaque below the eagle states, in English and Dutch, 'American of the 101st Airborne Division fought here for our liberty.' The nearby benches are also dedicated to the 101st.

Continue west for 690 m and turn left onto Flessestraat to enter Heteren. After 90 m turn right onto Onze Lieve Vrouwestraat and proceed 230 m to house No 36. (51.960639, 5.753333)

Betuwe War Museum 'The Island' 1944 – 1945
Onze Lieve Vrouwestraat 36, Heteren
Tel: +31 (0)26 472 2285
http://www.betuwsoorlogsmuseum.nl/

---

11   Sergeant Melton Harvell 'Tex' McMorries, from Tarzan, Texas, was nominated for a Distinguished Service Cross, but never received the award. Tex authored the poem '*Geronimo is Dead*' upon the death of the regiment's revered commander. The poem ended by declaring Colonel Howard Johnson as 'King of the parachute crew.' Tex died in his West Texas hometown in 1994 aged 72.
Private Hollis Buster Rowland, from Avondale, Tennessee, died in 2004 at age 92. His is buried in the Chattanooga National Cemetery, Chattanooga, Tennessee.

12   Colonel Howard Ravenscroft Johnson, aged 31 and son of a Maryland shipbuilder, is buried in Arlington National Cemetery, Arlington, Virginia in Section 11.

Open Wednesdays through Sundays from 13:30 to 17:00. A donation is expected.

The smallest war museum in Netherlands is dedicated to combat in the Betuwe area between the Nederrijn and Waal Rivers. The house was used by the 501st PIR as a medical station and was flooded when the Germans blew the dike.

The small display room is packed with weapons and fully outfitted uniforms. Five small dioramas present the fighting in the area. The museum also holds photographs and weapons of the period focusing upon personal histories of each displayed item. Labels are minimal and in Dutch only. Pride of place goes to one of the original British paddles used by the 504th PIR during the Waal River crossing. The owner, Marcel ten Böhmer, claims to have the smallest military museum in the Netherlands, but each item carries its own personal story, which Marcel explains during the guided tour. He pleasantly shares his knowledge of the local Betuwe fighting.

Continue west on Onze Lieve Vrouwestraat. After 300 m turn right onto Bretagnesingel to return to the dike road which changes name several times to become Randwijkse Rijndijk. Continue west 1.8 km to Renkumse Veerweg on the right. (51.958689, 5.731674)

In a diversionary attack from the main German assault against Opheusden, a kampfgruppe[13] crossed the Nederrijn during the night of 4/5 October at a ferry crossing south of Renkum to face Company E, 506th PIR in what became known as the '**101st Crossroads**' battle. That night Company E commander Captain Richard Winters sent a patrol from Randwijk along the dike road to the east to occupy buildings near a riverside factory. The patrol, led by Sergeant Arthur Youman, arrived at this road intersection to find it occupied by a German machine-gun position. The enemy troops threw hand grenades down the dike embankment wounding all five paratroopers and damaging their radio. The five men were able to return to the company CP to warn of the German infiltration.

Captain Winters led a reconnaissance patrol to the crossroads using a ditch on the river side of the roadway for cover. Quietly taking up positions, Winters gave the order and each member of the German seven-man machine gun team was killed in the first volley of shots. A German hidden in a culvert fired a rifle grenade which killed Corporal William Dukeman when fragments pierced his heart. Dukeman became the only American fatality in the engagement.[14]

However, the patrol was trapped in the shallow ditch. An attempt at withdrawal would expose the men the fire from the enemy on the raised dike. The only option was to attack. Winters radioed for a full platoon to come forward and with dawn approaching, he led a bayonet charge scampering to the eastern side of the raised road only to discover over one hundred enemy troops. Winter had unknowingly engaged a company-strength force of SS troops. The paratroopers drove the SS along

---

13   There is some uncertainty as to the composition of this unit, but it was likely a kampfgruppe from SS Panzergrenadier AuE Bataillon 4 under SS-Major Otto Hansmann, a late addition to Division von Tettau.

14   Corporal William H Dukeman Jr, aged 23 from Strasburg, Colorado, is buried in Netherlands American Cemetery, Margraten, Netherlands in Plot G, Row 2, Grave 11.

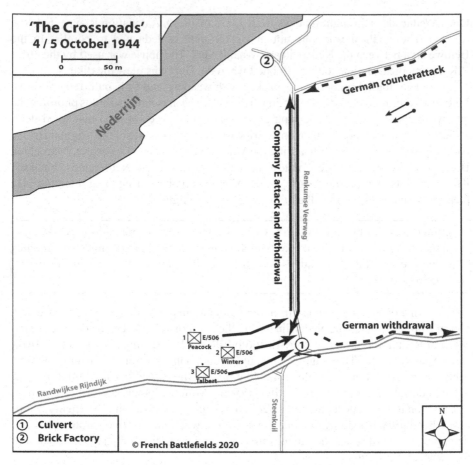

'The Crossroads'
4 / 5 October 1944

0   50 m

Nederrijn

② German counterattack

Company E attack and withdrawal

Renkumse Veerweg

German withdrawal

1 ☒ E/506
Peacock

2 ☒ E/506
Winters

3 ☒ E/506
Talbert

①

Randwijkse Rijndijk

Steenkuil

N

① Culvert
② Brick Factory

© French Battlefields 2020

the lane towards the river to the factory but withdrew after the appearance of a second company of SS troops creating overwhelming odds of about 300 against 35. The Americans suffered twenty-two wounded and one fatality; the Germans fifty killed, eleven captured, and 100 wounded.

Almost nothing has changed since 1944. A fence line on the river side of the dike parallels the drainage ditch used by Winters in his approach. The side road still leads to a riverside brick factory. The culvert from which a German threw a grenade that killed Dukeman passes beneath the roadway to the river and is identified by a roadside warning barrier. The dike rises 7-to-8 meters above the surrounding ground where the German machine gun occupied the highway junction. Only a **small metal sculpture** with a star and helmet outline identifies the location.

Continue west on Randwijk for 2.0 km. Briefly stop at the dirt farm track on the right. (51.955430, 5.704336)

The largest escape of airborne evaders occurred in Operation PEGASUS. Dutch underground workers organized safe houses within the Ede – Apeldoorn area

to shelter what eventually grew to 138 Allied troops who had evaded capture after
MARKET-GARDEN. The group was commanded by Brigadier Lathbury and included
Major Tatham-Warter. With radio communications provided by a four-man SAS team
dropped behind German lines, various small groups rendezvoused in the forest west
of Renkum during the night of 22/23 October. At 21:00, the large group separated
into platoons and proceeded three kilometers to the meadow land on the banks of
the Nederrijn. A red V for Victory signal from their flashlight brought paratroopers
of Company E, 506th PIR, 101st Airborne Division in boats manned by engineers
from British 210th Field Company. The paratroopers protected the perimeter while the
men were transported across the river (embarkation point: 51.963136, 5.702063). The
escapees entered Allied lines near this road stop.[15]

A second escape planned for one month later failed when the escapees
encountered a German patrol. Other groups made successful escapes across the Waal
River in February 1945 including one led by Brigadier John Hackett.

Continue west 700 m to the Liberation Route Marker near a group of benches on the
left. (51.9553333, 5.6942777)

The Germans continued fighting south of the Nederrijn with counter
offensives. The first counterattack took place from 26 to 27 September 1944, when
five companies of German infantry – four Wehrmacht and one SS – crossed the river
unobserved. They managed to get as far as Randwijk before the British noticed what
was occurring. Once the Allies realized that a large contingent of German troops
had managed to cross the river, they dispatched the 7th Somerset Light Infantry
(Lieutenant-Colonel HA Borradaile) to recapture the ferry crossing and wipe out the
new German bridgehead. C Company crossed open ground under enemy fire from
German 88-mm artillery across the river and twenty Messerschmitt fighter planes.
After hours of combat during a torrential rain, 150 German soldiers surrendered.

Liberation Route Marker #30, 'The British Taken by Surprise,' describes
the German offensive to recapture The Island and Nijmegen. German troops discuss
their efforts and expectations of success in renewing the brutal fighting. Unfortunately,
the plaque has been vandalized and the entire site is in disrepair. The road to the north
190 meters ahead, leads to the Wageningen – Randwijk Ferry Crossing.

Continue west on Randwijkse Rijndijk which becomes Rijnbandijk to Opheusden.
Turn left on Dorpsstraat and continue to the park at the intersection of the Burgemeester Lodderstraat and Eikenlaan (51.933408, 5.629337)

The **101st Airborne Monument** stands in front of the Gemeentehuis in
Opheusden to commemorate units of the American 101st Airborne Division and

---

15   The complex action involving phase lines, flare signals, diversionary artillery fire, and registered
artillery support was arranged by Lieutenant-Colonel David Dobie, who was also an escapee and who
had swam across the river days earlier.
The Company E force, led by Lieutenant Frederick Heylinger, was recognized with a Battlefield
Citation for the humanitarian accomplishment.

the Belgian 1st Infantry Brigade. The three brick steles present the 101st Airborne's Screaming Eagle, the plaque of the Brigade Piron which liberated the town, and commemorates the suffering of the local population who died during the war.

> Continue south on Eikenlaan 130 m to Reigerstraat. Turn right, proceed 250 m, and turn left onto Smachtkamp. Continue 400 m to the memorial on the left shortly before the rail line. The memorial is difficult to see when approaching from the north. (51.927675, 5.628566)

A metal 'V' with a simple plaque attached identifies the location of the **101st Airborne aide station** and observation post during the Battle of Opheusden. When enemy pressure increased Battalion Medical Officer Captain Stanley Morgan ordered his men to withdraw but he stood to care for the wounded. Captain Morgan was taken prisoner and marched away. Afterwards the aide station was destroyed by a direct hit from a mortar shell. The plaque lists the names of six soldiers and a 17-year-old Dutch boy who were killed but omits two additional names.[16]

> Continue south across the rail line and turn east on Parallelweg. At the T junction, turn left, onto Pijenkampse Veoldweg and stop at the memorial on the left. (51.925814, 5.635263)

A new **Air War Memorial Neder-Betuwe 1940 - 1945** established on 20 September 2019 remembers the crashes of sixteen Allied aircraft in the Betuwe. A short path ends with a six-meter-high steel pillar bearing a silhouette of a nose-down Douglas C-47A aircraft. The path is lined with similar steel pillars each bearing a stainless-steel information plaque for each of the sixteen incidents noting aircraft type, crash date, crash location, commander and number of occupants. An accompanying map locates each of the crash sites and information on those killed.

> Continue 145 m to the traffic circle. Take the second exit north on Dodewaardsestraat to the small train station parking area south of the bridge over the Linge. Walk to the bridge. (51.926296, 5.637503)

Company H, 506th PIR held their line 500 meters west of the railroad signal station for hours before being forced to withdraw to woods to the south. Major Oliver Horton, 3rd Battalion commander, was fatally wounded by German mortar fire while performing reconnaissance along the rail line.

---

16   The soldiers were: Staff Sergeant Harry A Clawson, aged 24, Pfc Morris L Thomas, aged 19, Sergeant Charles L Easter, aged 28, who is buried in Madisonville, Ohio; Sergeant Garland W Collier, aged 25, Pfc Carl E Pease, aged 26, who is buried in Detroit, Maine; and Corporal Franklin F Stroble, aged 23, who is buried in Muncy, Pennsylvania. The Dutch teenager was Leonardus GM Jeucken. Sergeant Collier, S/Sergeant Clawson, Pfc Pease, and Pfc Thomas are commemorated on the Wall of the Missing in Netherlands American Cemetery. Clawson's and Thomas' remains were discovered in an unmarked grave in tree nursery in 1971. Thomas now rests in Westfield Cemetery in Westfield, New York. S/Sergeant Clawson is now buried in Thatcher, Arizona.

A **small metal plaque** attached to the bridge railing commemorates Major Horton and the soldiers killed in action during the Battle of Opheusden.[17] **Liberation Route Marker #80** stands near the bus stop north of the bridge. The text recognizes the new front line in the Betuwe that formed after the battle for Arnhem. The multiple images display the destruction wrought upon the small town during the struggle over its control. American paratroopers are shown firing a mortar shell and gathering around the train station house. The 'Battle of Opheusden' audio relates the brief friendship of Sergeant Garland Collier of Texas and 17-year-old Leonardus Jeucken. (51.926535, 5.637500)

Side Trip: Grebbeberg War Cemetery

Grebbeberg played an important role in defending the Netherlands from German forces in 1940 as the southern terminus the defensive position known as the Grebbe Line, which ran north to the Ijsselmeer. The line originated in the 18th century but was mostly abandoned after the First World War. Action to reconstitute the line were not complete before the German invasion of May 1940. The Grebbeberg heights were 50 meters high and thus unable to be part of the mostly water barrier. The Germans recognized the weak spot and attacked through it on the second day of the invasion led by the SS *'Der Führer'* Regiment. The three day battle was the fiercest in the war for the Dutch. The Battle of the Grebbeberg cost the lives of 420 Dutch soldiers and about 250 Germans.

> The cemetery is 18.8 km west of Oosterbeek on highway N225; or 10.3 km west and north of Opheusden via highway N233 across the Nederrijn to highway N225, then east on N225 to the cemetery. (51.955251, 5.600511)

Militair Ereveld Grebbeberg (Grebbeberg War Cemetery)

Immediately after the Netherlands surrendered, a cemetery was laid out at the battle site for both Dutch and German military personnel who died during the Battle of the Grebbeberg. Following the war, the remains of German soldiers were relocated to the German War Cemetery in Ysselsteyn. Since 1946, the remains of Dutch war casualties have been reinterred regularly including soldiers who died elsewhere in the Netherlands during the invasion in May 1940 and had originally been buried in family graves. Today, there are over 850 military graves in the cemetery which is in a forested area at the top of the ridge.

Two entrance gates flank the **Lion Monument of the National Army Monument Grebbeberg** which display two stone lions flanking a stone cross. Burial plots are on both sides of a central walkway and the crossing walkway terminates in special memorials to the Dutch 22nd Regiment of Infantry and the Dutch 8th Regiment of Infantry. A granite stone to the rear lists the names of those with no known grave.

There is a permanent exhibition at the cemetery's information center titled 'We have never spoken about it' which affords special attention to three Dutch soldiers, Corporal JA Vermeer and Private DJ Heinen, who both died on 12 May 1940 and are

---

17   Major Oliver Martin Horton, aged 31, from Raleigh, North Carolina is buried in Netherlands American Cemetery, Margraten, Netherlands in Plot G, Row 1, Grave 11.

buried in the cemetery, and Lieutenant NW Lingen, a veteran who survived the battle.

Highway N225 separates the burial plots from the **National Army Memorial** consisting of an open auditorium with a limestone bell tower. The column bears an inscription (in Dutch) by Dutch poet JC Bloem:

Five days – and freedom was lost
Five years – and only then was she reborn
Justice thus triumphs with difficulty
To this realization this ground is dedicated

The Dutch dead are commemorating each 4 May.

A one-half kilometer hiking trail leaves the rear of the cemetery parking area to Heimersteinselaan then west to a **reconstructed trench** of the 1940 Grebbelinie. The rebuilt trench represents only 40 meters of an original that ran for hundreds of meters. Its reinforced wooden sides and floor permit visitors to walk its length. An information panel explains the Grebbelinie and the trench system used to defend the elevated sector of the line. (51.956982, 5.596327)

Intact above ground **casemate GLZ17** can be found in the forest 600 meters east of the trench on Heimersteinselaan. The short entrance trench allows a close-up view of the armored entry door. Built between 1930 and 1940, the concrete structure held a light machine gun but offered three embrasures for a 110-degree arc of fire. The walls are 80 centimeters (31 inches) thick. Access is not permitted. (51.958413, 5.604204)

Side Trip: German Surrender Site
5 May 1945

Wageningen is 13 km west of Oosterbeek on highway N225 or 5.3 km east of the Grebbeberg War Cemetery. In Wageningen turn south on Stationsstraat, then east on Bergstraat to 5 Meiplein, which is in a pedestrian zone. Parking must be found on a surrounding street. (51.967442, 5.667588)

Hotel de Wereld
5 Mei Plein 1, 6703 CD Wageningen
Tel: +31 (0)317 460 444
A virtual tour of the reenactment is available at http://www.capitulatie45.nl/ (Dutch only).

In April 1945 the war came to an end in this sector. On 5 May 1945, the day after Field Marshal Montgomery accepted the German surrender of all forces in the Netherlands, Lieutenant-General Charles Foulkes, commander of the First Canadian Army, decided to draw up a separate surrender document. He summoned Generaloberst Johannes Blaskowitz, commander of German Army Group H, to Hotel de Wereld in Wageningen to sign the capitulation. Initially, Blaskowitz sent his chief of staff, however, he was told that this was not sufficient and that Blaskowitz had to attend personally. At 16:00 that afternoon, Blaskowitz came to the hotel to be handed a detailed document of surrender. Blaskowitz asked for 24 hours to assess the stipulated demands. Blaskowitz returned the next day to sign the official surrender of all German forces in the Netherlands. Prince Bernhard, acting as commander-in-chief of the Dutch

Interior Forces was also present at the meeting.

The surrender room is on the ground floor of the hotel to the right of the foyer. The room is now the hotel lounge, but it is reconverted each 5 May to reenact the surrender events. Visitors are permitted to view the room. A small metal plaque on the exterior of the building identifies the building as the German surrender site.

Side Trip: Loenen Field of Honor

Leave Arnhem north on motorway A50 to exit 23-Loenen. Proceed southeast on highway N786 for 3.2 km. Turn right onto Groenendaalseweg and continue 1.2 km to the cemetery entrance.

Total distance: 25 km north of Arnhem. (52.115045, 5.999862)

Loenen Field of Honor
Groenendaalseweg 64, Loenen
Tel: +31 (0)70 313 1080
Email: info@ogs.nl
Web: https://ereveldvolleven.nl/

In 1947, the Dutch Government decided to return the remains of Dutch people who had been killed in Germany to the Netherlands. These war victims had been laid to rest in foreign soil and many did not get a decent burial. To facilitate this decision, in 1948, the Netherlands War Graves Foundation made plans and on 18 October 1949 HRH Princess Wilhelmina inaugurated **Loenen Field of Honor** as a final resting place for a diverse range of Dutch WWII victims including military personnel who were killed in action, civilians who were members of the resistance, political prisoners, those who escaped the Netherlands to England during the first years of the war to join the Allied forces, and victims of forced labor in Germany. In addition to war victims, since the 1980s, military personnel and civilians who were killed during peacekeeping or security operations have also been buried or reinterred. There are now almost 4,000 Dutch buried in this war cemetery and reinternments still take place regularly.

Loenen Field of Honor was specially designed to inconspicuously scatter the graves over a 17-hectare (42-acre) wooded area in short arcs of graves each marked by a flat stone. Each inscription conveys its own story.

Thatched roof country farmhouses flank the cemetery entrance which is through a gated white brick wall. A chapel of similar construction stands across the initial grass plot at the end of a walk which bisects the cemetery. The chapel houses a shrine for commemorative books, a wooden triptych listing the names of the *Engelandvaarders*,[18] and several urns containing ashes from concentration camps.

---

18   *Engelandvaarders*: a term used to identify individuals who attempted to escape German occupation by crossing the 160 kilometers of the North Sea to England. It is estimated that 90% of these attempts were unsuccessful with the participants disappearing in the sea. Safer, land-based escape routes through Portugal, Switzerland, or Sweden were developed later.

Chapter Ten

Recriminations

The failure of any military operation generates its share of after the fact analysis. Recriminations are part of settling of blame for the loss and suffering of hundreds of brave soldiers and airmen. MARKET-GARDEN is no exception and when elite units like paratroopers are squandered the criticisms are especially severe.

MARKET-GARDEN continues to be analyzed and debated seventy-five years after the event. The issues discussed are numerous befitting an operation that has numerous failures of planning and execution.

Planning failures included:

1. British officers, from Montgomery on down, refused to acknowledge the presence of 9th and 10th SS Panzer Divisions in the Arnhem area as a substantial threat to the operation. Such a realization would not have necessarily meant the cancelling of the operation but would have suggested 1st Airborne Division include more antitank weapons in the early lifts.

2. After the war, Lieutenant-Colonel Frost stated that the lack of interservice cooperation doomed the Arnhem effort even before it began. A lightly armed airborne unit's greatest weapon is surprise. RAF planners insisted that flak defenses near the bridge were too formidable to allow drop zones near the objective. The paratrooper handicap of having to march the 8-to-12 kilometers to the bridge provided response time for German commanders Model and Bittrich.

3. The lack of sufficient aircraft spread the air lift operations over three days, further interrupted by weather conditions in Britain. As a result, the airborne forces – especially at Arnhem – lacked the strength to overcome enemy opposition. Requiring 1st Airlanding Brigade to guard future landing zones further reduced the understrength attack upon the bridge. In addition, a now forewarned enemy inflicted serious losses on later lifts.

4. Generals Browning and Gavin gave priority to capturing the Groesbeek Heights before the Nijmegen bridge which was of paramount importance worth the risk of an undetermined flank attack from the heights and, on 17 September, was completely undefended.

    General Browning also decided to transport his headquarters to the Netherlands, where he made no contribution to the battle, but utilized thirty-eight gliders that could have been better used to deliver artillery and antitank weapons.

5. Resupply and heavy weapons are the Achilles heel of airborne operations. The capture of landing strips would have facilitated both as demonstrated by prior experience in the war. The Germans took the airfield in Eindhoven by parachute in May 1940 and the airport in Crete twelve months later. If the airfield at Deelen had been captured, resupply would have been easy, and the German Luftwaffe radio net disrupted.

6. Why the failure to land an early force near the Arnhem bridge's southern approach? The argument that soft polder south of the Arnhem bridge was unsuitable for an airborne drop is specious. If it was good enough as the designated drop zone for the Polish parachute troops, why not for the British? Conspiracy theories suggesting British efforts to reduce the Polish postwar influence are interesting, but outside the scope of this book.

7. General Sosabowski famously questioned MARKET-GARDEN plans by asking, 'What about the Germans?' The operation was planned and conducted as if the enemy had no input into the result. Planners failed to consider the possibility of a German recovery and resistance to the operation. Only two men, General Sosabowski and Major Brian Urquhart, challenged the optimistic forecasts of an easy victory against old men and boys. Both were summarily dismissed from their positions — clearly a case of 'do not tell me what I do not want to hear.'

8. Fighter-bombers were extremely effective against German armored forces attacking the Corridor, as proven by their performance during the initial advance of XXX Corps on 17 September. Subsequent air lifts necessitated the absence of fighter-bomber support for the ground forces because commanders feared potential collisions between the slow troop carrier aircraft and the swooping fighters.

9. Much has been made about the decision to begin the operation in daytime rather that under the cover of darkness, as was done in Normandy, but these criticisms are without foundation. Factors influencing a daytime drop include the limited experience of many of the aircrew in flying at night and the danger of coordinating massive formations in darkness. Drop accuracy was much improved over scattering of units that was almost guaranteed with a nighttime drop. The threat of German night fighters attacking defenseless transports or gliders was a very real and a terrifying thought; daylight brought Allied fighter superiority. The exposure to German antiaircraft fire was equally as serious in day light or night because German antiaircraft guns were radar controlled.

There were substantial operational failures:

1. General Dempsey's failure to capture the Schelde Estuary contributed to the supply shortage which Montgomery blamed on Eisenhower's broad front strategy. With Antwerp not yet open, supplies and maintenance was tied to a six-hundred-kilometer road back to Channel beachheads.

2. Similarly, Dempsey's failure to capture bridges over the Albert Canal near Antwerp delayed the British advance allowing time for the escape of von Zangen's Fifteenth Army from the Beveland Peninsula. Von Zangen's units strengthened weak German defenses on the western side of the Corridor at a critical moment.

3. During the battle for Arnhem, as word of the events filtered back to England, Major-General Edmund Hakewell-Smith of the 52nd (Lowland)

Division sent a message to General Browning offering to land a brigade near the south end of the Arnhem bridge. Browning refused his request stating that it was not required and that 'the situation was better than you think.' It was most definitely worse than Hakewell-Smith could imagine.

4. The commanding generals of the ground forces, Dempsey of Second Army, Horrocks of XXX Corps, and Adair of Guards Armoured Division failed to communicate a sense of urgency to the units leading the advance to Arnhem.

Despite the need for urgency to support the Arnhem troops, the armored group forces lacked aggressiveness. The British armor refusal to conduct operations at night resulted in overnight delays at Valkenswaard, Eindhoven, where the column was subjected to a devastating Luftwaffe bombing, and Nijmegen. Even the relief column going to Driel was delayed by only two German tanks.

To General Gavin and the troops that hours earlier had risked their lives attacking in flimsy boats exposed to enemy fire on the open waters of the Waal River, there was only one objective: to rescue fellow paratroopers at Arnhem. The failure to push ahead to Arnhem for eighteen hours after the capture of the Nijmegen bridge was inexcusable.

Major-General Sir Ivor Thomas, commander 43rd (Wessex) Division, was subjected to postwar criticism for taking two days to move 125 kilometers (78 miles) from assembly areas near the Belgian border to Nijmegen. On the other hand, Horrocks defended Thomas by recalling the horrendous traffic conditions, German attacks against The Corridor, and confusion in Nijmegen. After the war, Horrocks argued that he was fighting three battles at once. The first was the German efforts to cut the supply line from Eindhoven at the Son bridge; the second were assaults upon the Groesbeek Heights that threatened Nijmegen from the east; and, finally, the effort to reach the Nederrijn at Arnhem.

Horrocks' column suffered shortages of gasoline and ammunition resulting from rupture of his supply line and the resultant massive traffic jams. Horrocks told General Gavin, 'Jim, never try to supply a corps up just one road.'

5. The failure of British VIII and XII Corps to keep pace on the flanks of The Corridor has been blamed for much of the 101st Airborne Division's difficulties in keeping Hell's Highway open. In fact, neither of the British units was ready for combat on 17 September. Again, the blame falls on leadership. Shockingly, General Richard O'Connor, commander of VIII Corps recalled after the war that he had been instructed 'not to press too hard' on his flank.

6. Much has been written about the delays imposed upon the ground column by the failure of American paratroopers to capture the Son bridge intact. While the loss of the bridge did have an enormous impact upon the schedule, it was just the sort of enemy action that should have been anticipated. The criticism belongs to the British commanders who

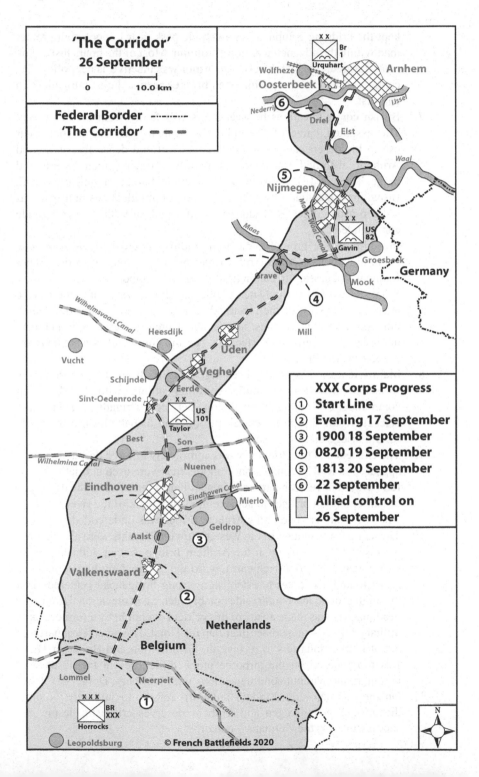

'The Corridor'
26 September

0   10.0 km

Federal Border   ----------
'The Corridor'   = = =

XXX Corps Progress
① Start Line
② Evening 17 September
③ 1900 18 September
④ 0820 19 September
⑤ 1813 20 September
⑥ 22 September
▢ Allied control on
   26 September

© French Battlefields 2020

kept the bridging equipment in a vehicle park near Leopoldsburg rather than within the advancing armored column. Most of the hours lost at Son were during the night when British armor was inactive as per policy. The capture of the Grave and Nijmegen bridges seems almost miraculous in contrast.

7. British communications between units was faulty from the beginning. The assumed range of the radios at Arnhem was based upon their use in the desert campaign, but the wet soil and dense forests around Arnhem absorbed transmissions greatly reducing their operational range. Thus, British 1st Airborne Division had no communications with Browning's headquarters, with a special communications unit that was to keep Montgomery's headquarters informed, or with its own brigade commanders.

    In addition, the ground-to-air VHF radios assigned to the American communications team at Arnhem had not been adjusted to the proper frequency necessary to call in fighter-bomber support.

    What did work was the Dutch public telephone system and the private telephone network of the electrical supply company. Imbedded Dutch officers used the systems to contact Dutch underground members unhindered by German interference, but unit commanders were unaware of their availability.

8. Major-General Urquhart absenting himself from his headquarters worsened the lack of radio communications with his battalion commanders. Command confusion between Brigadiers Hicks and Hackett resulted in a piecemeal introduction of battalions to the battle for the bridge on 19 September.

9. The existence of the Driel ferry was completely ignored despite it clearly appeared in RAF reconnaissance photos that were used at briefings. The ferry would have been a more than adequate alternative to the destroyed rail and pontoon bridges to achieve the south bank of the river at a time when the southern end of the Arnhem bridge was undefended.

10. The tactical advantages of the Westerbouwing Heights were also ignored because of the focus upon the Arnhem bridge. Faced with increasing enemy resistance to movements toward the bridge, Urquhart could have redistributed his forces to establish a strong bridgehead centered upon this high ground in a countryside notably lacking in elevation. Urquhart's headquarters was made aware of this critical oversight by a former Dutch military officer – none other than Jan Ter Horst. However, Urquhart was not at his headquarters to receive the information and Brigadier Hicks was too focused on the airborne units' difficulties in the absence of Urquhart and without communications with Lathbury, Dobie, or Fitch.

11. On the German side, Model's stubborn refusal to immediately blow the bridges in Nijmegen and Arnhem deserves criticism, despite the successful – for the Germans – outcome.

Among the personnel failures were:
1. The notable lack of airborne expertise at the top levels of command negatively impacted the planning stage, especially conceding to the RAF demands that the Arnhem units be delivered too far from their objectives. General Brereton was a tactical air force officer but had never before commanded airborne troops. Similarly, General Browning lacked airborne experience. Brereton's and Browning's inexperience can be contrasted to Lieutenant General Matthew Ridgway, an experienced, aggressive airborne general with an established headquarters staff which had been successful in Normandy.
    Urquhart's appointment to command the 1st Airborne Division without airborne experience led him too willingly accept RAF pressure to land his troops too far from their objectives.
2. The appointment of Brereton over Browning led to disagreements between the two. The launch of a prior airborne operation on short notice led Browning to tender his resignation. Brereton responded by starting a search for a replacement. The operation was cancelled giving Browning an excuse to withdraw his resignation. Browning accepted a similar short schedule for MARKET-GARDEN.
3. Brigadier Lathbury's only combat experience was in Sicily on an enormously different terrain and with considerably different objectives.

The contrast between successful operations led by American and German commanders – Gavin, Taylor, Model, Bittrich, Harmel and Harzer – stands in stark contrast to the failures of the British commanders – Montgomery, Dempsey, Browning, Horrocks, and Urquhart.

In conclusion, Montgomery and Churchill proclaimed a victory, despite that the offensive had not precipitated a German collapse, had not established a bridgehead over the Nederrijn, and the German Fifteenth Army had escaped entrapment. Prince Bernhard of the Netherlands said that his country could not afford the luxury of such 'successes.'

The battlefield soldiers' sacrifice, dedication to duty, courage, and willingness to offer oneself to accomplish the mission remains an inspiration. The 82nd Airborne's crossing of the Waal River in Nijmegen into the teeth of established enemy defenses, one of the greatest acts of unit courage in the war, was motivated by desire to rescue troops at Arnhem that were part of the airborne fraternity. British Airborne troops stubborn refusal to relinquish their hold on the Arnhem bridge and the defense of the Oosterbeek perimeter against larger and well-armored forces is an enduring tribute to their self-sacrifice and dedication to duty. The hubris, unwillingness to accept facts, and desire for recognition by senior commanders is as equally condemnable.

Appendices

Appendix A: Postwar activities of the senior commanders

General Sir Miles Dempsey continued to command British Second Army until the end of the war. He was commander-in-chief of Allied land forces in Southeast Asia (1945-46) and Middle East (1946-57) followed by numerous honorary posts in England. He absolutely refused to write memoirs of his wartime experiences, instead ordering that his diaries be burned. He died in 1969 aged 72.

Lieutenant General Lewis Brereton held several military posts, retired, and wrote his memoirs (*The Brereton Diaries: The War in the Air in the Pacific, Middle East and Europe, 3 October 1941 – 8 May 1945*) which some commentators have accused of being self-serving. He was especially critical of General Douglas McArthur's performance in the Philippines. He died in 1967, aged 77.

Lieutenant-General Frederick Browning left the airborne service a few months later and never received another command. He became chief of staff at South-East Asia Command retiring in 1948 to become treasurer for Princess Elizabeth before she became queen and later for the Duke of Edinburgh. He suffered a nervous breakdown in 1957 and died amid a scandal of drugs and alcohol in 1965, aged 68.

Lieutenant-General Brian Horrocks was invalided out of the service in 1949 due to lingering effects of wounds suffered in 1943. He wrote a memoir (*A Full Life*) and narrated television programs discussing warfare. Horrocks died in 1985 aged 89.

Major-General Allan Adair, 6th Baronet, continued to lead the Guards Armoured Division in the Battle of the Reichswald and until the German surrender. After the war Adair led the 13th Infantry Division during the Greek Civil War and retired in 1947. He held numerous civil and ceremonial posts including at Harrow School, Grenadier Guards, and Freemasons. Adair died in 1988 aged 90.

Major-General Roy Urquhart remained in Army service until 1955, but never achieved higher rank, a reflection of his defeat at Arnhem. Urquhart recorded his story in *Arnhem: Britain's Infamous Airborne Assault of WW II* and served as a military consultant on the motion picture *A Bridge Too Far*. He and his wife raised four children. Urquhart died in 1988, aged 87.

Major General James Gavin worked to racially integrate the US Army and advocated the use of helicopters to transport troops to battlefields. He retired from the army in 1958 at the rank of lieutenant general to write *War and Peace in the Space Age* and later hold several prominent positions as head of a noted consulting firm, ambassador to France, and several corporate boards. He became a visible critic of the Vietnam War and was briefly considered as a presidential candidate in 1968. James Gavin died in 1990 aged 82. He is buried in United States Military Academy Post Cemetery at West Point, New York.

Major General Maxwell Taylor led his division in Normandy and Holland but was not present during the Battle of the Bulge. After the war, Taylor commanded the US Military Academy, allied troops in Berlin, Eighth Army in Korea, and eventually became Chairman of the Joint Chiefs of Staff. It was in this later role that he received criticism for not transmitting military opinions against the Vietnam War to political leaders. Taylor died in 1987, aged 85.

Major-General Stanislaw Sosabowski was relieved of all duties on 9

December 1944 to become a scapegoat for the failings of Montgomery and Browning. The two Polish battalions reacted by going on a hunger strike. The Polish Brigade never reentered the battlefield, but it served as part of the Germany Occupation force for two years before being disbanded. Sosabowski rescued his family from Communist Poland and settled in London where he became a factory laborer. Sosabowski died a relative unknown in 1967, aged 75, and is buried in Powązki Military Cemetery, Warsaw.

Brigadier John Hackett received a second Distinguished Service Order for his actions at Arnhem. He left the airborne service to join the staff of an armored unit in Italy losing one rank. After the war, Hackett served in Palestine and Northern Ireland as commander-in-chief, commanded the British Army on the Rhine occupation force, and a NATO command achieving the rank of general. He was knighted and wrote his memoir *I Was A Stranger*. Hackett died in 1997, aged 86.

Brigadier Gerald Lathbury returned to airborne service after the war as commander of 3rd Parachute Brigade. He was awarded a knighthood and promoted to full general. He was the governor of Gibraltar and aide-de-camp general to the queen in the 1960s. Lathbury died in 1978, aged 71.

After the war the 1st Airborne Division was disbanded with the exception of 1st Parachute Brigade which was transferred to the 6th Airborne Division. The 1st Airlanding Brigade was sent to Norway to disarm the German garrison and upon return to the United Kingdom it was also disbanded with its battalions returning to a conventional infantry role.

Generalfeldmarschall Gerd von Rundstedt, one of Hitler's ablest generals, was relieved of his command for the third time in March 1945. He was captured by American forces in May. After suffering a heart attack while in captivity he was released because of poor health in 1948 and died in 1953, aged 77. Rundstedt is buried in the local cemetery in Hanover, Germany.

Generalfeldmarschall Walter Model was one of the ablest defensive commanders of the war. In spring 1945, he fell out with Hitler by disobeying orders to destroy the Ruhr factories and sacrifice his troops. Instead, Model organized a surrender to save the lives of his men. On 21 April 1945, after being recalled to Berlin, he went into woods near Duisburg and shot himself aged 54. He is buried in the German Military Cemetery, Vossenack, Germany.

SS-Lieutenant General Wilhelm Bittrich was arrested on 8 May 1945. In January 1948, was extradited to France at his own request because of his alleged order to execute seventeen resistance fighters in Nîmes. Although tried, he was not convicted of that crime and had apparently even disciplined the perpetrators. However, as commander he was held accountable for the actions of his men and sentenced to five years, but was soon released because of his long prior detention. Tried again in 1953 for allowing hangings and arson, he was again sentenced to five years, but the conviction was overturned upon appeal. Following his release from prison, Bittrich became active in a revisionist organization of former Waffen-SS members. He died in 1979 aged 85.

Generaloberst Kurt Student was captured by British forces in Schleswig-

Holstein in April 1945 after a brief time on the Eastern Front.

After the successful completion of operations in Crete, Student became acting commander of the island and passed on Göring's order for reprisals against Crete partisans, an act that led to his trial for war crimes in 1947. He was convicted of three of the eight charges of mistreatment and murder of prisoners of war by his men. Sentenced to five years in prison, however he was given a medical discharge the next year. He died in 1978, aged 88.

Appendix B: Comparison of Military Ranks

American	British	German (Wehrmacht)	German (SS)
Private	Private	Soldat / Schütze	SS-Schütze
(no equivalent rank)	(no equivalent rank)	Oberschütze	SS-Oberschütze
Private	Senior Private	Obersoldat	(no equivalent rank)
Private First Class	Lance-Corporal	Gefreiter	SS-Sturmmann
Private First Class	Lance-Corporal	Obergefreiter	SS-Rottenführer
Private First Class	Lance-Corporal	Stabsgefreiter	(no equivalent rank)
Corporal / Specialist	Corporal	Unterofficier	SS-Unterscharführer
(no equivalent rank)	(no equivalent rank)	Stabsunterofficier	(no equivalent rank)
Sergeant	Sergeant	Unterfeldwebel	SS-Scharführer
Staff Sergeant	Staff-Sergeant	Feldwebel	SS-Oberscharführer
(no equivalent rank)	(no equivalent rank)	Hauptfeldwebel	SS-Stabsscharführer
Sgt First Class	Sergeant-Major	Oberfeldwebel	SS-Hauptscharführer
Master Sergeant / First Sergeant	Regimental-Sergeant-Major	Stabsfeldwebel	SS-Sturmscharführer
Sergeant Major	Warrant Officer 1	Oberstabsfeldwebel	(no equivalent rank)

American	British	German (Wehrmacht)	German (SS)
Second Lieutenant	Second Lieutenant	Leutnant	SS-Untersturmführer
First Lieutenant	Lieutenant	Oberleutnant	SS-Obersturmführer
Captain	Captain	Hauptmann / Rittmeister	SS-Hauptsturmführer
Major	Major	Major	SS-Sturmbannführer
Lieutenant Colonel	Lieutenant-Colonel	Oberstleutnant	SS-Obersturmbannführer
Colonel	Colonel	Oberst	SS-Standartenführer
(no equivalent rank)	(no equivalent rank)	(no equivalent rank)	SS-Oberführer
Brigadier General	Brigadier	Generalmajor	SS-Brigadeführer
Major General	Major-General	Generalleutnant	SS-Gruppenführer
Lieutenant General	Lieutenant-General	General der... (Infanterie, Artillerie, Panzertruppen, etc)	SS-Obergruppenführer
General	General	Generaloberst	SS-Oberstgruppenführer
General of the Army	Field Marshal	Generalfeldmarschall	Reichsführer-SS

Appendix C: Glossary of German Military Terms and Abbreviations

	Abbreviation, acronym, nickname or literal translation	Description
Abteilung	Abt	Detachment or section, or battalion-sized unit of armor, artillery of cavalry
Abwehr		Counterespionage service of the German High Command
Allgemeine SS	General SS	Full-time administrative, security, intelligence and police branches of the Schutzstaffel
Armeekorps		Infantry corps
Armeeoberkom-mando	AOK	Field Army Command
Artillerie		Artillery
Aufklärungs Ab-teilung	Aufkl	Reconnaissance unit
Ausbildungs-und-Ersatz	AuE	Training and Replacement (unit)
Bataillon (pl. Bataillone)	Bn or Btl	Battalion
Batterie (pl. Batterien)		Battery
Division	Div	Division
Einsatzkommando		Company-sized execution units which killed Jews, Communists and others on the Eastern Front
Eisernes Kreuz	Iron Cross	Medal awarded for valorous service
Fallschirmjäger	FJ or Fallsch	Paratrooper
Fallschirmjäger Regiment	FJR	Parachute Regiment
Festung	Fs	Fortress
Flakpanzer		Armored self-propelled antiaircraft gun
Flugabwehrkanone	FlaK	Antiaircraft artillery gun
Freya		First operational radar in the Kriegsmarine
Führerhauptquartiere	FHQ	Official headquarters especially constructed for use by the führer
Füsilier		Light infantry
Gebirgsjäger		Mountain troops
Gefallen		Killed in action
Geheime Staatspolizei	Gestapo	Secret State Police
Generalkommando		Headquarters of an army corps
Geschwader		Luftwaffe squadron
Granatwerfer		Mortar
Grenadier	Gren	Infantry soldier or unit
Hakenkreuz	Hooked cross	Swastika used by the Nazi Party

Haubitze		Howitzer
Heeresgruppen-kommando	HGr.Kdo	Army Group Command
Höckerlinie	Dragon's Teeth	Antitank defenses
Jagdbomber	Jabo	Fighter-bomber
Jagdgeschwader	JG	Single-engine fighter wing/group, literally 'hunting squadron'
Jäger	Jg	Hunter
Kampfgeschwader	KG	Bomber wing/group
Kampfgruppe (pl. Kampfgruppen)	KGr	Army battle group usually an ad hoc task force
Kampfwagenkanone	KwK	Turret-mounted main cannon of a battle tank
Kanone		Field gun as opposed to a howitzer
Kaserne		Barracks
Kompanie	Kp	Company
Kübelwagen	Kübel	Open-topped military utility cars
Landesschützen	LS	Militia
Landsturm		Infantry of non-professional soldiers or militia
Landwehr		Territorial Army: a type of militia
Lazarett		Field hospital
Maultier	SdKfz 4	Half-track truck
Nachtjagd-geschwader	NJG	Night-fighter wing/group
National-sozialistische Deutsche Arbeiter-partei	NSDAP	National Socialist German Worker's Party or Nazi Party
Nebelwerfer	Nb W or fog thrower	A family of multi-barrel rocket launchers used for smoke or high-explosive projectiles
Oberbefehlshaber des Heeres	OBdH	Commander-in-Chief of the Army
Oberfehlshaber West	OB West	Commander-in-Chief West
Oberkommando des Heeres	OKH	High Command of the Army
Oberkommando der Luftwaffe	OKL	High Command of the Air Force
Oberkommando der Marine	OKM	High Command of the Navy
Oberkommando der Wehrmacht	OKW	High Command of the Armed Forces
Organisation Todt		Civil and military engineering group named after its founder, Fritz Todt, which built the Autobahns, Westwall (Siegfried Line), Wolfsschanze, and Atlantic Wall; notorious for its use of conscript and slave labor

Panzer-abwehrkanone	PaK	Antitank gun
Panzerfaust	tank fist	Disposable single-use portable antitank weapon
Panzergrenadier	PzGren	Mechanized infantry or a soldier belonging to a mechanized infantry unit
Panzerjäger	PzJg	Tank destroyer or antitank unit fielding a variety of antitank weapons
Panzerkampfwagen	PzKpfw	Armored fighting vehicle (tank)
Panzerschreck	tank terror	Reloadable portable antitank weapon
Pionier (pl. Pioniere)		Combat engineer
Regiment (pl. Regimenter)	Rgt or Regt	Regiment
Reichskanzlei		Office of the German Chancellor (Reichskanzler)
Reichssicherheits-hauptamt	RSHA	Reich Main Security Office or Reich Security Head Office created by Himmler to combine all German security and police departments, including the Gestapo, Kripo and SD
Ritterkreuz des Eisernen Kreuzes	Knight's Cross of the Iron Cross	Highest award for bravery
Sanität		Medical unit or medical personnel
Schützenpanzerwa-gen	SPW	Armored half-track or self propelled weapon
Schutzstaffel	SS	Nazi organization that grew from Hitler's personal body guard into a fourth branch of the Wehrmacht
Sicherheitsdienst der SS	SD	Security service of the SS and Nazi Party, main intelligence and counterespionage section of the RSHA
SS-Totenkopf ver-bände	SS-TV	SS responsible for the concentration camps
Stammlager	Stalag	German prisoner-of-war camp
Sturmabteilung	SA	Storm troopers, originally Hitler's praetorian guard (bodyguard) called Brown Shirts
Sturmgeschütz	StuG	Self-propelled assault gun
Sturz-kampfflugzeug	Stuka	Any dive-bombing aircraft but generally associated with the Ju-87
Tommy		German slang for a British soldier
Unterseeboot	U-boot	Submarine
Vergeltungs-waffen-1	V1	First German vengeance weapon, pilotless, cruise missile powered by a pulse-jet engine
Vergeltungs-waffen-2	V2 or A4	Supersonic long-range rocket

Vergeltungs-waffen-3	V3	Long-range, smooth-bore gun
Volksgrenadier		Honorary title given to mostly low-grade infantry divisions formed late in the war
Volkssturm		People's defense force, composed mostly of boys and old men
Wacht am Rhein	Guard on the Rhine	December 1944 Ardennes Offensive, known by Americans as the Battle of the Bulge
Waffen-SS		Armed military combat branch of the SS
Walküre	Valkyrie	(1) officially a Reserve Army contingency plan in the event of a breakdown in law and order, (2) failed 20 July 1944 plot to assassinate Hitler, arrest SS and Nazi officials, and seize control of the German government
Wannsee Conference		Meeting held on January 20, 1942 near Lake Wannsee in Berlin in which it was made official Nazi policy to totally annihilate European Jews and other ethnic groups
Wehrmacht		Combined three branches of German armed forces
Wolfsschanze	Wolf's Lair	Hitler's Eastern Front military headquarters
Würzburg		German air defense radar
Zu besonderer Ver-wendung	z.b.V.	Literally 'for a special use'; generally a headquarters staff without permanently assigned troops
Zug		Platoon
Zyklon-B		Commercial name for the prussic acid (hydrocyanic acid) gas used in German extermination camps

Appendix D: Order of Battle

Allied Forces:

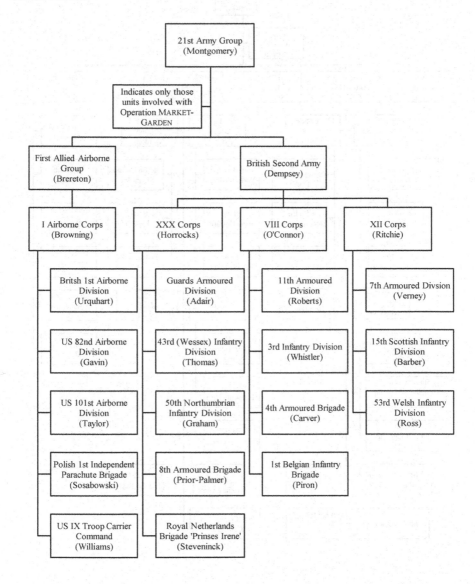

21st Army Group
(Montgomery)

Indicates only those units involved with Operation MARKET-GARDEN

First Allied Airborne Group (Brereton)

British Second Army (Dempsey)

I Airborne Corps (Browning)

XXX Corps (Horrocks)

VIII Corps (O'Connor)

XII Corps (Ritchie)

Britsh 1st Airborne Division (Urquhart)

Guards Armoured Division (Adair)

11th Armoured Division (Roberts)

7th Armoured Divsion (Verney)

US 82nd Airborne Division (Gavin)

43rd (Wessex) Infantry Division (Thomas)

3rd Infantry Division (Whistler)

15th Scottish Infantry Division (Barber)

US 101st Airborne Division (Taylor)

50th Northumbrian Infantry Division (Graham)

4th Armoured Brigade (Carver)

53rd Welsh Infantry Division (Ross)

Polish 1st Independent Parachute Brigade (Sosabowski)

8th Armoured Brigade (Prior-Palmer)

1st Belgian Infantry Brigade (Piron)

US IX Troop Carrier Command (Williams)

Royal Netherlands Brigade 'Prinses Irene' (Steveninck)

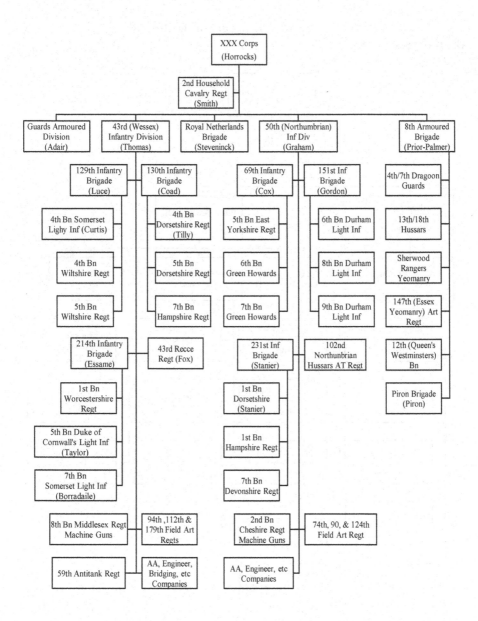

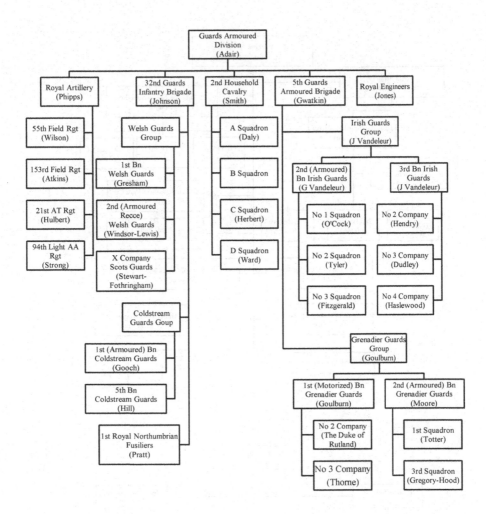

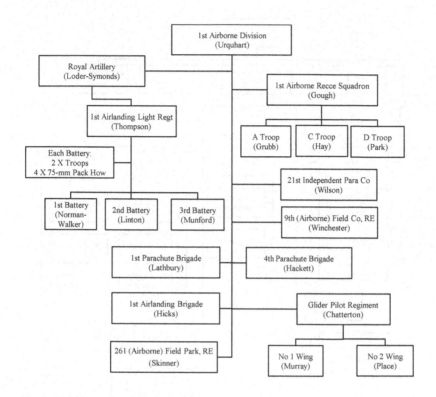

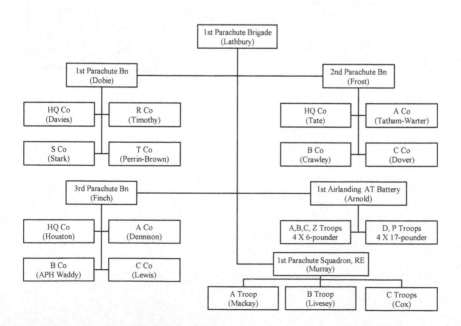

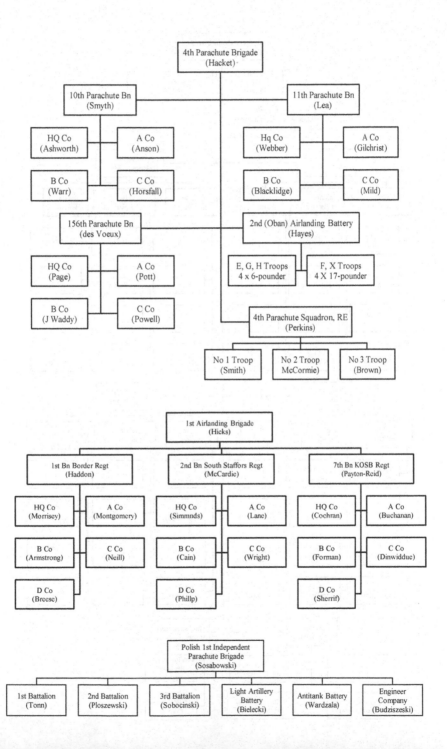

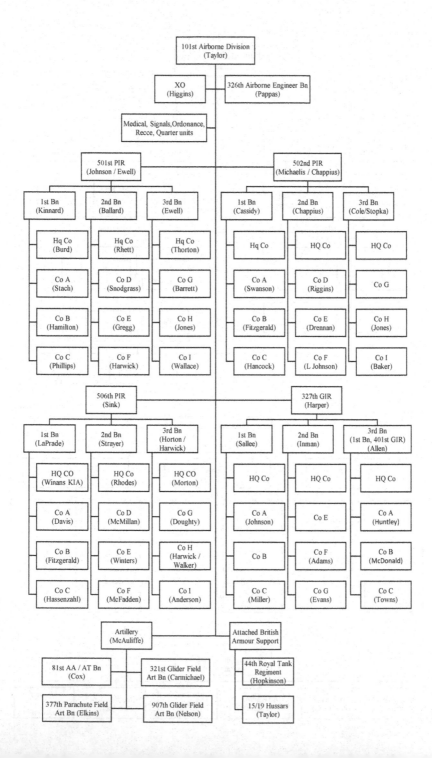

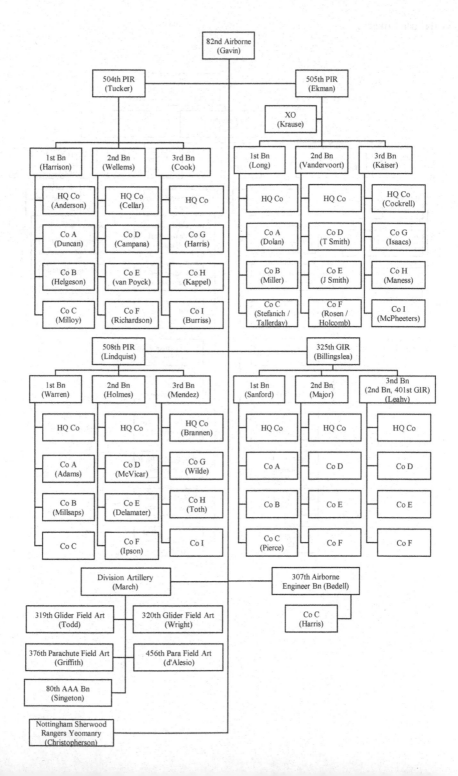

German Forces:

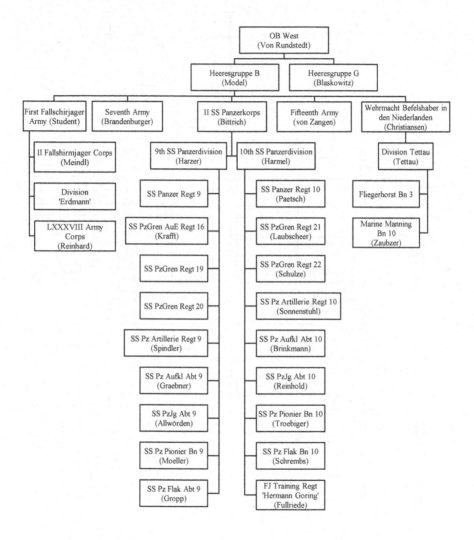

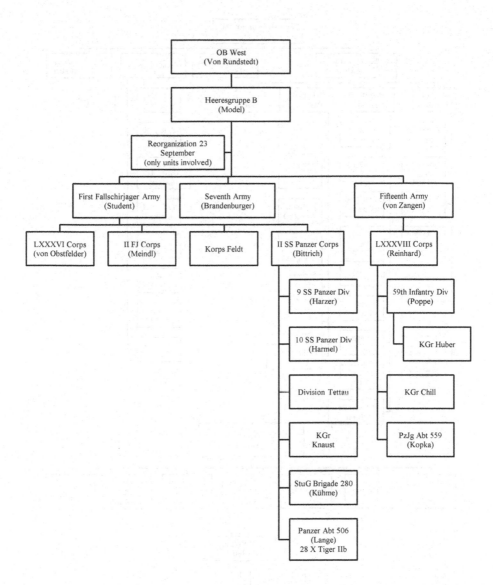

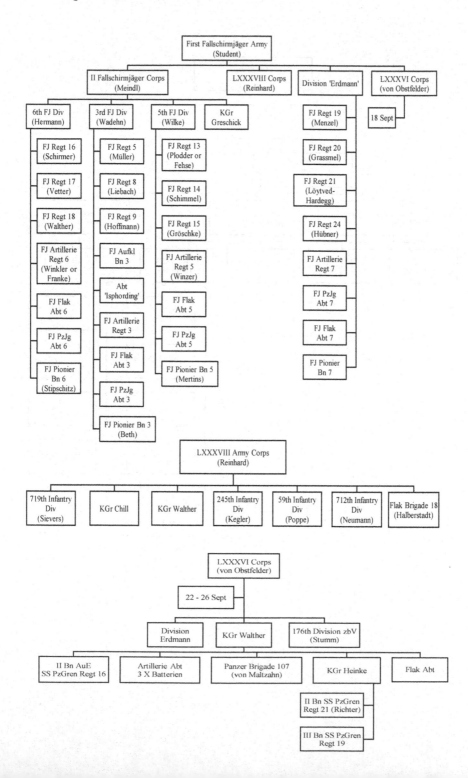

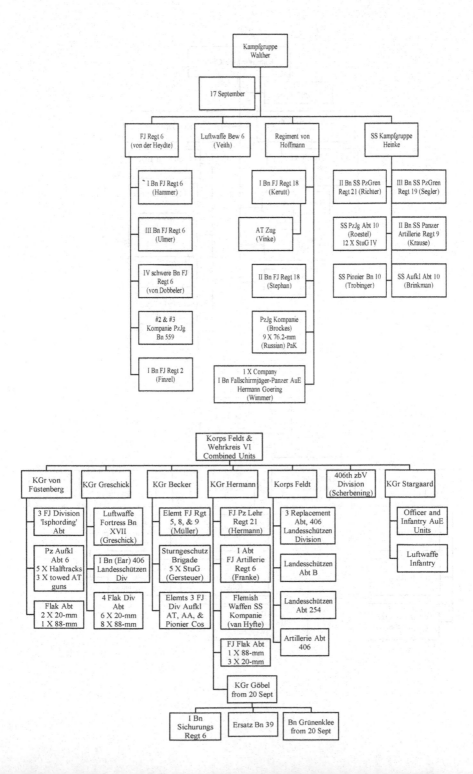

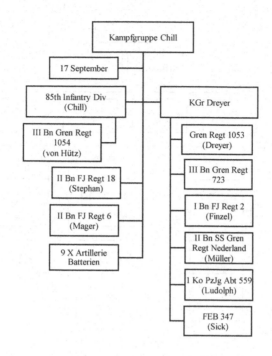

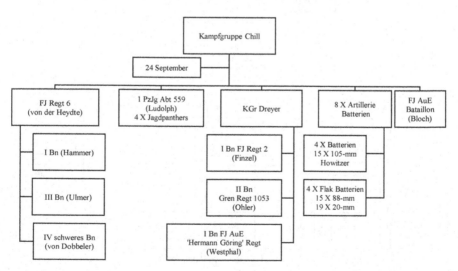

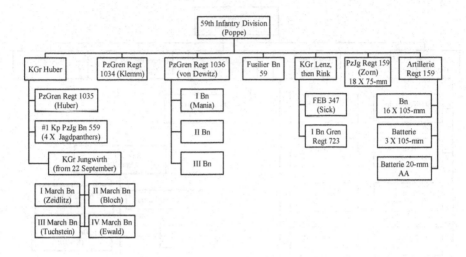

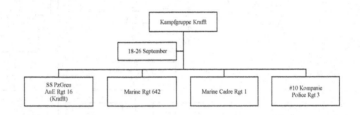

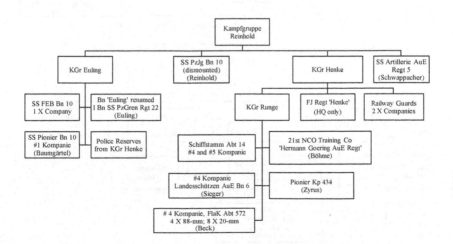

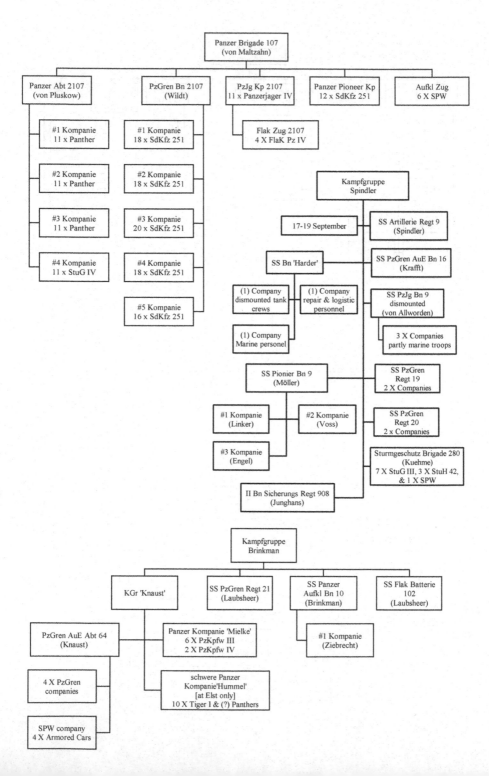

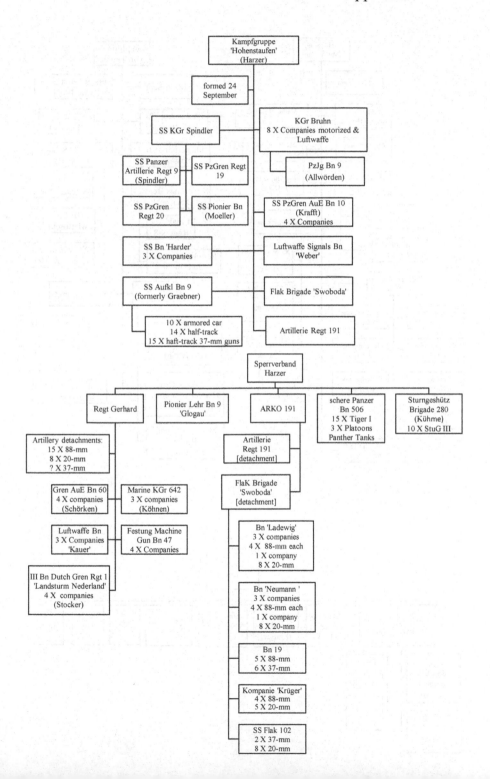

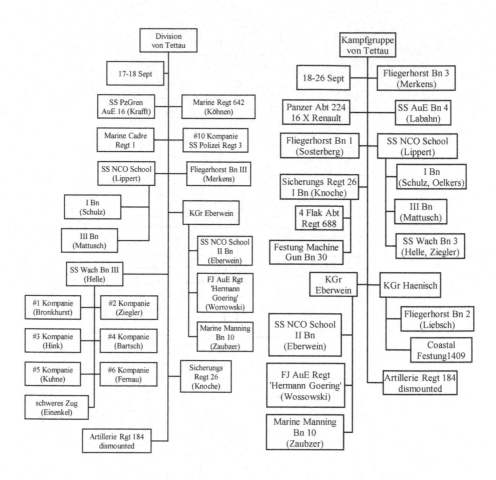

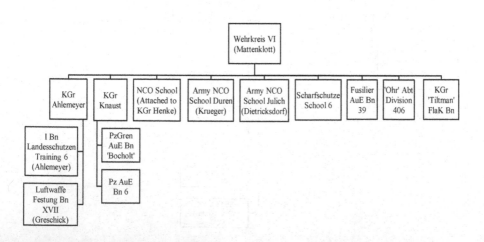

Index

A

Aachen 56, 144, 277
Aalst 21, 31–33, 59
A Bridge Too Far 77, 303
Abwehr 5, 31, 307
Adair, Maj-Gen Allan 4, 17, 298, 303
Adams, Cpt Jonathan E 115, 139–140, 173
Adams, Sgt George 93
Aguerrebere, Private Frank 136
Aircraft
    B-25 'Mitchell' 46
    Spitfire 46
    Waco CG4 166
Alexander, Lt Boyd 135
Andrews, Lt Joseph 40
Antwerp 1, 5, 6–7, 14, 145, 297
Apeldoorn 188, 195, 216, 254, 274, 290
Armstrong, Major Tom 268
Arnhem ix–x, 1, 4–13, 20–22, 28, 30, 43, 50,
    86–88, 99, 107, 113, 115, 120–121,
    132–134, 140, 154–155, 163, 176,
    179, 182–185, 186–194, 195–203,
    207–212, 214–217, 220–247, 248–
    251, 254–256, 261, 265, 276–277,
    282, 285–286, 293, 303
Arnhem–Ede highway 210
Atlantic Wall 7, 308

B

Ballard, Lt Col Robert 75
Barlow, Col Hilary 219
Barry, Lt Peter 214–215
Baskeyfield, Lance-Sgt John 256–257, 270
Battle of
    Arnhem Bridge 201, 220–247, 268, 273
    Best Bridge 63–66, 67–69
    Coffin Corner 284–285
    Crossroads, The 289–290
    Grave Bridge 107–110
    Groesbeek Heights 153–160
    Hechtel 14–15
    Heeswijk-Dinther 79–81
    Heumen Bridge 110–111
    Koevering 86–88
    Mook 155–156
    Nijmegen Bridge 114–128
    Oosterbeek 248–275

Opheusden 280–282
Overloon 43–47
Sand Dunes 85–86
Schijndel 79–81
Veghel 82–84
Battle of the Bulge ix, 17, 51, 55, 69, 74, 77,
    79, 97, 105, 110, 124, 135, 151, 170,
    174, 254, 303
Baumgärtel, SS-Lt Werner 115
Becker, Major Karl-Heinz 158
Beek 105, 154, 156–159, 172–175
Belvedere 116, 127–129, 143
Benko, Sgt Bela 40
Berg en Dal 116, 154, 158–159, 172–174
Bernhard, Prince 294, 301
Bestebreurtje, Capt Arie 134, 162–164
Betuwe 176–185
Billingham, Lance-Sgt Jack 130
Bittrich, SS-GenLt Wilhelm 7, 8, 10, 21, 50,
    152, 181, 190, 252, 261, 263, 277,
    296, 301, 277
Black Friday 181
Blankenship, Lt Robert 148, 150
Blaskowitz, GenObt Johannes 294–295
Böhmer, Marcel ten 289
Böhmer, Oberst d Pol Hans 63
Bokt 51, 56–57
Borradaile, Lt-Col HA 291
Brassesco, 1st Lt Guido 40
Breese, Major George 268
Brereton, Lt Gen Lewis 1–3, 301, 303
Bridges: See also Arnhem
    Arnhem rail bridge 197, 214–215
    Best 10, 50, 67
    De Kamp 108, 111, 154
    De Oversteek 134, 138–140, 152
    Eindhoven 35, 59, 61
    Grave 3, 10, 102, 105, 107–109, 114, 300
    Hatert 108, 111
    Heumen 107–113, 154, 159
    JOE's 16–17, 18, 27
    John Frostbrug ix, 11, 107, 176, 190,
        197–198, 204, 216, 217, 224,
        228–241, 238, 246–247, 251,
        277–278, 194, 133
    Malden 108
    Mook 154, 159
    Nijmegen 10–11, 105–107, 115, 116,
        147–148, 153–154, 158, 176–179,
        133–134

Son 11, 51, 61–63, 298
Valkenswaard 30
Veghel 82, 84, 85, 100
Willem–Hikspoorsbrug 61
Bridge to the Future 244
Brinkmann, SS-Major Heinz 233–234
British Air Units
    Polish Air Force 27
    RAF 12–13, 18, 27, 34, 36, 60–61, 161,
        175, 188, 198, 212, 250, 277, 278,
        282, 300–301
        48 Squadron 257
        49 Squadron 161
        90 Squadron 46
        98 Squadron 282
        271 Squadron 257
        305 Squadron 61
        446th Bombardment Group 146
        Dutch 320 Squadron 282
    Second Tactical Air Force 18
British Army Units: See also Orders of Battle
    - Appendix D
    Armies
        Second 1, 58, 248, 298, 125
    Army Groups
        21st 3
    Battalions
        1st Border 189, 197–198, 248,
            265–269, 273
        1st Northamptonshire Yeomanry 101
        1st Parachute 186, 195–197, 206,
            220, 227, 250, 255, 269,
            272–273
        2nd Glasgow Highlanders 68
        2nd Parachute 188, 195–197, 214,
            216, 224–225, 228–247, 257,
            272, 273
        2nd South Staffords 189, 222–223,
            251, 255
        3rd Parachute 186–187, 192–197,
            208, 220, 226–227, 230–231,
            250, 255, 269, 272–273, 304
        4th Dorset 279
        5th Duke of Cornwall's Light Infantry
            181, 278, 281
        7th Black Watch 101
        7th Hampshire 287
        7th King's Own Scottish Borderer
            186, 189, 197–198, 208,
            208–209, 218–219, 248–250,

        259–260, 264, 273
        7th Seaforth Highlanders 68
        7th Somerset Light Infantry 179, 184,
            291
        10th Parachute 198–199, 210–211,
            213, 220, 248
        11th Parachute 199, 220–224,
            250–251, 255
        156th Parachute 184, 198–199, 204,
            213–214, 218–219, 248, 266,
            273
    Batteries
        1st Airlanding Antitank 189, 192
        2nd Airlanding Antitank 198, 201,
            262
    Brigades
        1st Airlanding 186–197, 200, 205,
            219, 248, 271, 296, 304
        1st Parachute 186–189, 237, 239,
            250, 304
        4th Parachute 184, 186–188, 197–
            200, 204, 206, 219, 223, 260
        5th Guards Armoured 20
        8th Armoured 4, 21
        32nd Guards 181
        129th Infantry 179
        130th Infantry 278
        214th Infantry 179, 181
        231st Infantry 133
        Belgian Piron 21
        Polish 1st Independent Airborne 4,
            11, 113, 186–188, 206, 251,
            254, 276, 286
        Prinses Irene 4, 27, 28, 33, 41
    Companies
        16th (Parachute) Field Ambulance
            189, 225, 240
        21st Independent Parachute 188, 248,
            259–263
        210th Field RE 291
        260 Field 253
    Corps
        I Airborne 3, 5, 50, 107, 165
        Royal Army Service Corps (RASC)
            258
        VIII 12, 25, 43, 62, 77, 85, 298
        XII 12, 43, 68, 77, 176, 280, 298
        XXX ix, 4, 11–13, 17, 22–23, 28, 30,
            33, 36, 56, 62–63, 74, 82, 107,
            111, 116, 176, 228, 252–253,

266–267, 272, 287, 297, 298
Divisions
    1st Airborne 4, 11–12, 120, 154,
        186–219, 237, 248, 260,
        267–269, 273–274, 276–278,
        286, 296, 300–301, 133
    3rd Infantry 18, 44
    6th Airborne 304
    11th Armoured 14, 18, 44
    15th Scottish Infantry 68
    43rd (Wessex) Infantry 4, 70, 85, 87,
        176–182, 252, 275, 279, 280,
        298
    49th Infantry 13
    50th (Northumbrian) Infantry 4, 87
    51st (Highland) Infantry 92, 101
    52nd (Lowland) Infantry 297
    53rd (Welsh) Infantry 168
    Guards Armoured 4, 11, 14–47, 72,
        133–134, 176, 298
Groups
    Coldstream Guards 85
    Irish Guards 16
    Welsh Guards 14, 179
Misc
    4th Parachute Royal Engineers 198
    Breese Force 268
    Lonsdale Force 251, 273
    Thompson Force 250, 255
Regiments
    1/7th Queens Royal 87
    1st Airlanding Light 186, 271, 273
    1st Canadian Armoured Carrier 103
    1st Welsh Guards 179
    2nd Welsh Guards 179
    4th/7th Royal Dragoon Guards 181,
        184
    15th/19th Hussars 18, 62, 66
    44th Royal Tank 62–63, 72, 74, 81,
        84–88, 92–93, 98
    52nd Recce 87
    64th Medium, RA 250
    86th Field RA 18, 62, 85
    123rd Light Antiaircraft 82–83
    165th Heavy Antiaircraft Artillery 84
    Coldstream Guards 14, 44, 156,
        159–160
    Devonshire 18, 269
    Glider Pilot 101, 189, 248, 270, 273
    Grenadier Guards 14, 20, 65, 81, 85–

        87, 111, 116–120, 125–130,
        140–141, 145, 233
    Irish Guards 14–21, 27, 29–31, 72,
        111, 121, 123, 133, 151, 133
    Monmouthshire 41–42
    Nottinghamshire Yeomanry 158, 167
    Royal Norfolk 47
    South Staffordshire 186, 198, 204,
        205, 220, 222, 225, 250, 255,
        261, 273
    The Parachute Regiment 214, 237,
        273–274, 286
    Worcestershire 181, 184, 223
Squadrons
    1st Airborne Reconnaissance 186,
        205, 237, 260
    1st Parachute Field RE 189, 197, 228,
        230, 244
    2nd Household Cavalry 14–16, 18,
        28–29, 31–32, 111, 179, 192
    14th Field, RE 130
    Polish Parachute Engineer 278
    Royal Dragoons 62
Brockes, Hauptmann 17–18, 30
Bronze Star 55, 72, 77, 129, 132, 150, 165,
    211
Browmaster, Frank 282
Browning, Lt-Gen Sir Frederick 3, 5, 48, 50,
    107, 116, 120–121, 125, 165, 253,
    278–279, 296, 296–298, 300–301,
    303–304
Brussels 3, 6, 14, 17, 37, 64
Buchanan-Jardine, Lt Rupert 29
Buchanan, Major Robert 219
Bucknall, Lt Peter 192, 205, 218
Budziszewski, Capt Piotr 278
Bunkers/Pillboxes/Casemates
  Bunker 'Birkenhof' 31
  Casemate 118S 160
  Casemate #534 103
  Casemate #538 103
  Casemate GLZ17 294
  Casemate Nord 108, 112
  Casemate Zuid 108, 112, 153
  Grossraumgefechtsstand Diogenes
    203–204
  Lent B676 153
  Nijmegen Bridge 153
  Nijmegen Rail line 147
  Peel-Raamstelling Line 102–103

Valkhof 127–128, 144
Burd, Capt William 89
Burriss, Capt T Moffatt 121–126, 132, 148
Bush, Major Allan 251
Butterwort, Sapper Norman 243
Buttlar, SS-Cpl Helmut 215–216

C

Cain, Major Robert 222, 223, 225–227, 248,
    251, 269–270
Campana, Capt Victor 109
Campbell, Lt-Col PU 68
Camp Beverlo 23, 24
Canals
    Albert 6, 14
    Bocholt–Herentals: See Meuse–Escaut
    Maas–Waal 4, 10, 105, 107–108, 111, 114,
        116, 153–154, 157
    Meuse–Escaut 4, 10, 14, 17, 21
    Wilhelmina 10, 50–51, 53–56, 63, 66–67,
        154, 265, 295
    Zuid–Willemsvaart 10, 48, 75–77
Cane, Lt Peter 215–216
Carmichael, Lt Col Edward 281
Carnes, Pfc Vernon 129
Carrington, Capt Lord Peter 132
Carter, Flight Lt Charles 282
Case, Norris 147
Cassidy, Lt Col Patrick 70, 75, 81
Casualties
    101st Airborne Division 281
    Arnhem 223, 237
    Arnhem Bridge 233
    Battle for Arnhem 254
    Battle of the Grebbeberg 293
    Civilian
        Eindhoven 34–35
        Hunger Winter 13
        Nijmegen 114, 133, 146
        Operation Oyster 36
        Wolfheze 188
    Dorset Nederijn Crossing 279
    Eindhoven 60
    Groesbeek 107
    Hechtel 15
    Koevering 87
    Market-Garden 12
    Nijmegen Rail Bridge 124
    Oosterbeek 252
    Opheusden 281

Overloon 47
Schijndel 81
Sint Antoniusmolen 94
Sint-Oedenrode 71
The Crossroads 290
Veghel Bridge 84
Waal River Crossing 124, 125
Cemeteries/Walls of the Missing
American
    Abraham Lincoln National 150
    Arlington National 43, 71, 77, 82, 93,
        129, 151, 168, 125
    Beaufort National 116
    Cambridge American 74
    Chattanooga National 288
    Fort Bliss National 93
    Fort Rosecrans National 111
    Fort Sam Houston National 55, 74
    Golden Gate National 63
    Henri-Chapelle American 77
    Heumen Temporary 114
    Massachusetts National 135
    Netherlands American 36, 37, 40, 53,
        57, 58, 63, 69, 74, 79, 89, 94,
        95, 97, 99, 114, 135, 137, 148,
        166, 171, 289, 292, 293
    United States Military Academy Post
        51, 143, 303
    Waterhoef Farm Temporary 53
    Willamette National 135
    Zachary Taylor National 40
Belgian
    Leopoldsburg 24
British
    Aldershot Military 272
    Arnhem Oosterbeek War 101, 205,
        212, 213, 216, 219, 222, 240,
        242, 243, 246, 256–258,
        261–264, 266, 268, 275, 282
    Becklingen War 72
    Groesbeek Canadian War 171, 210,
        256
    Groesbeek Memorial 172, 210, 215,
        219
    Jonkerbos War 119, 128–129, 137,
        175, 179, 184
    Leopoldsburg War 25
    Mierlo War 41–42, 62
    Mook War 160–161
    Overloon War 46

Runnymede Memorial 282
Uden Commonwealth War 74
Valkenswaard War 29
Civil
Ede General 210
Eerde churchyard 94
Eindhoven (Woensel) General 60–61
Mook Communal 160
Nijmegen Graafseweg 114
Sint Servatius Roman Catholic 99
Utrecht (Soestbergen) General 268
Dutch
Grebbeberg War 293–294
Loenen Field of Honor 295
German
IJsselsteyn: *See* Ysselsteyn
Lommel 25–26
Vossenack German Military 304
Ysselsteyn German War 98, 245, 293
Polish
Lommel 26–27
Powązki Military 304
Chappuis, Lt Col Steve 65–66, 82
Chester, Lt Michael 160
Chill, GenLt Kurt 6, 14, 20
Christiansen, Gen d. Flieger Friedrich 7
Chuches
Sint-Antonius Abt Kerk 94
Sint-Eusebiuskerk 224, 245–246
Sint-Joriskerk 34
Churchill, Winston 3, 301
Clarke, Gunner Len 262
'Clay Pigeon' 38
Cleminson, Lt James 223–224
Cole, Lt Col Robert 37, 64, 68–69
Combs, Lt Rex 154
Comparison of Military Ranks 306
Concentration Camps
Buchenwald 21
Vught 101–103
Cook, Major Julian 120–121, 130, 133,
138–139
Corridor, The ix–x, 4, 6, 11–12, 20–21,
48–50, 57–58, 68, 73, 74, 75, 77–79,
82–87, 96–97, 99–100, 111–112, 121,
153, 176, 179, 252, 279, 297–299:
See also Hell's Highway
Covey, Lt Kenneth A 173
Cowan, Lance-Sgt George 28, 31–32
Cox, Lt Col XB 57, 97

Coyle, Lt Jim 140–141
Crawley, Major Doug 215–216, 236
Crerar, Gen Henry 164
Creswell, Lt JN 16
Cronkite, Walter 97
Croot, Major Robert 251

D

Dare, Guardsman Robert 44
Dauncey, Lt Michael 270
Davies, Private Philip 41
Davis, Capt Melvin 54
Dawson, Lt 128
Deane-Drummond, Major Tony 227
Delacour, Lt David 213
Dempsey, Gen Sir Miles 1, 3, 6, 253,
297–298, 301, 125
Den Brink 190, 215–216, 223–224,
227–228, 257
Den Heuvel Woods 168
Dennison, Major Mervyn 194
Derksen, Anton 224
des Voeux, Lt-Col Sir Richard 199, 213, 219
Dettling, GenLt Augustus 281
Dickson, Lance-Bombardier James 271
Dickson, Lt MJ 227
Diel, 2nd Lt James 57
Dikoon, Pvt Walter 135
Diogenes Archiefservice 204
Dobie, Lt-Col David 186, 195, 205, 217,
220–222, 248, 291, 300
Dodd, 1st Lt John 129
Dodewaard 182, 281
Doetinchem 8, 190, 263
Dolan, Capt John J 156–157, 160
Donaldson, Lt Adrian 271
Doughty, 1st Lt Joseph 281
Dover, Major Victor 214, 225–226
Driel 113, 176, 179, 181, 184, 248, 251, 253,
257, 269, 275, 276–279, 284–286,
298–300
Driel ferry 275, 285–286
Driessen, Fritz 70
Drop/Landing Zones
DZ 'A' 48, 53, 98
DZ 'A1' 48
DZ 'B' 50–52
DZ 'C' 50, 70, 75
DZ 'E' 105
DZ 'K' 251

DZ 'N' 105, 153, 156, 161, 166
DZ 'O' 105, 108–109, 111, 113
DZ 'T' 105, 116–117, 153, 156, 168–169
DZ 'X' 189, 206
DZ 'Y' 189, 197–198
LZ 'L' 198, 205, 211, 217–218
LZ 'N' 164–165
LZ 'S' 189–191, 199, 203, 206
LZ 'W' 50
LZ 'X' 198, 206
LZ 'Z' 189, 192, 197, 201, 206–207
Duivelshuis 245–246
Dunavant, Lt Henry 110
Dunning, Sgt Donald B 55
Dustin, Sgt Shelton 111
Dutch Army 107, 112, 160, 286
    26th Regiment of Infantry 113
    Dutch Korps Politietroepen 112
Dutton, Lt Herbert 87

E

Ede 8, 186–189, 192, 209–210, 238, 259, 290
Ede–Arnhem rail line 8, 192, 259
Eerde 48, 75, 81–82, 84–88, 92–94, 222
Eindhoven x, 3, 5, 11, 17, 20–23, 31–35, 41–43, 48–52, 57–62, 77, 282, 296, 298
Eisenhower, Gen Dwight 1, 3, 6, 279, 297
Ekman, Col William 105, 153, 156, 167
Elst 152, 176–185, 228–230, 252, 277, 287
Enigma 5
Erp 82, 97–98
Essame, Brig Hubert 179, 181
Euling, SS-Capt Karl-Heinz 115, 126, 128, 129, 130, 143, 145, 232–233
Everington, Pvt George 268
Ewald, Major Werner 71
Ewell, Lt Col Julian 75, 81

F

Falaise Gap 14, 188
Feldt, Gen d. Kav Kurt 10, 154, 156–158, 168, 174, 255
Fitch, Lt-Col David 186, 192–195, 217, 220–222, 248, 300
Foote, Capt Reggie 225
Fort Beneden Lent: See Fort Hof van Holland
Fort Hof van Holland 151, 152
Foulkes, Lt-Gen Charles 294

Frank, Capt Anthony 234, 237
Frontlijnpad: See Frontline Path
Frontline Path 185
Frost, Lt-Col John 188, 194–197, 207, 214–217, 226–242, 248, 251, 255, 257, 272, 296
Frye, Lt Warren 95
Fulton, Lance-Sgt William 240
Funk, First Sgt Leonard 168
Fuquay, Lt Cecil 93

G

Gavin Brig Gen James 3, 5, 10, 105, 116, 120–121, 133, 153, 156, 159, 161–163, 166–167, 277, 296, 298, 301, 298, 125
Gazurek, Capt Ignacy 261
Gensemer, Lt Harold 155
German Army Units: See also Orders of Battle - Appendix D
    Abteilung
        Flak 428 65
        Panzer 224 268
        Panzer 559 84
        Panzer Aufklarüng 6 158
        Panzerjäger 559 28, 81, 85–86
        SS Panzerjäger 10 82
        SS Panzer Pionier 9 216
        SS Panzer Pionier 10 115, 128, 144
    Armies
        Fifteenth 6, 20, 297, 301
        First Fallschirmjäger 6, 10, 50, 77
        First Parachute Army 279
    Army Forces in the Netherlands 7
    Army Groups
        Group B 7, 190, 208, 263
        Group H 294
    Battalions
        10th SS Artillerie 133
        Bataillon 'Euling': See SS PzGren Regiment 22
        Bataillon 'Ewald' 71
        Bataillon 'Kauer' 176
        Bataillon 'Köhnen' 176
        Bataillon 'Krafft' 190, 211, 215: See also SS PzGren Training and Replacement Battalion 16
        Bataillon 'Schörken' 176
        Bataillon 'Stocker' 176
        Bataillon 'Wossowski' 268

Dutch SS Wachbataillon III 'Nord-
    west' 208
Fallschirmjäger Reserve Training
    'Henke' 115
Feld Ersatz 347 65
Grenadier 1035 87
Machine Gun 47 176
Panzer 2107 98
Panzergrenadier AuE 64 233
Pionier Lehr 'Glogau' 190
schwere Flak 572 115
schwere Panzer 506 190
SS Aufklärungs 9 140, 220, 228
SS Aufklärungs 10 228, 233
SS Flak 9 190
SS Flak 10 215
SS Panzergrenadier AuE 4 289
SS Panzergrenadier AuE 16 190
SS Panzerjäger 9 190
Brigade
    Panzer 107 43, 47, 52, 56, 61–62, 82
    Sturmgeschütz (Assault Gun) 280
        190, 222, 250
Corps
    Feldt 10, 156, 168, 174
    II SS 7–8, 250, 287
    LXXXVIII 8, 17
Divisions
    3rd Fallschirmjäger 158
    4th Flak 156–157
    9th Panzer 279, 287
    9th SS Panzer 5, 7, 10, 20, 115, 188,
        190, 248, 296
    10th SS Panzer 5, 7–8, 10, 29, 82,
        107, 156, 188, 190, 296
    12th SS Panzer 191
    59th Infantry 10, 50, 64
    85th Infantry 6, 14
    116th Panzer 279, 284, 287
    363rd Volksgrenadier 280–281, 288
    406th zbV 115, 154
    719th Infantry 6, 14
    Von Tettau 10, 191, 198, 208, 289
Kampfgruppe
    Becker 157–158, 170, 173
    Göbel 154–155
    Goltzsch 47
    Gräbner 190, 233
    Greschick 154, 157–158, 168
    Harder 194

Henke 228
Hermann 155–156, 159–160
Huber 79–80, 87
Jungwirth 76–81, 86–88, 95–96
Knaust 176–179, 181–182, 233–235,
    254, 277
Köppel 59
Krafft 195, 211, 218, 267
Möller 190, 222, 250, 252, 261
Rink 64
Runge 117, 125, 126, 136–137
Sonnenstuhl 233
Spindler 190–191, 195, 197, 199,
    211–213, 217, 220–222, 252,
    254–255
Stargaard 154
Tettau 248, 250
Von Allwörden 190, 195, 211
Von Fürstenberg 157–158, 174
Walther 21–24, 28, 98
Weber 203
Misc Units
    Marine Einsatzkommando (MEK)
        145
    Panzer Kompanie 'Hummel' 176,
        181, 234
    Panzer Kompanie 'Mielke' 178,
        233–235
    Reichsarbeitsdienst 194, 232
    SS NCO School 'Arnhem' 198, 267
OB West 6, 10, 308
Regiments
    Armored Artillerie 9 190
    Fallschirmjäger 2 71
    Fallschirmjäger 6 17–18, 69, 85–87
    Fallschirmjäger 18 17–18
    Fallschirmjäger 20 14–15
    Fallschirmjäger 21 56
    Fallschirmjäger Artillerie 5 155
    Fallschirmjäger Artillerie 6 155
    Fallschirmjäger Ausbildungs 21 155
    Fallschirmjäger-Panzer AuE Hermann
        Göring 14, 51, 53, 73, 115,
        141, 287
    Fallschirmjäger von Hoffmann 17
    Flak Regiment 53 51
    Flieger 93 70, 71
    Grenadier 723 64
    Grenadier 1034 65
    Grenadier 1036 65, 81

Panzergrenadier 60 284
Panzergrenadier 1035 79, 81
Sicherungs 26 209, 252
SS Artillerie Ausbildungs 5 115
SS Panzer 9 194
SS Panzer 10 115
SS Panzergrenadier 19 190
SS Panzergrenadier 20 190
SS Panzergrenadier 21 82, 115, 215,
    230–231, 233, 234
SS Panzergrenadier 22 115, 232
SS Police 3 63
Volksgrenadier 957 281
Wehrkreis IV 155
German Luftwaffe Units 6–9, 12, 17–18, 21,
    27, 60, 70, 133, 146, 154, 157, 176,
    195, 203, 276–277
1st Jagdflieger Division
    276
German Military Terms 307–309
German Surrender 294–295
Gibbs, Capt Vicary 128–129
Gilchrist, Major Dan 222
Ginkel Heath 184, 259
Ginkelse Heide 188, 197–198, 208–210
Gleim, Lt Edward 169
Glover, Lt Robert 262
Göbel, Oberlt Günther 155
Goltzsch, Oberst Rudolf 47
Gough, Major CFH 186, 189, 192, 206, 211,
    236–237, 265
Goulburn, Lt-Col Edward 116, 130
Gräbner, SS-Capt Victor 140, 200, 228,
    233–234, 240, 243
Grassmel, Major Franz 14–15
Grave Bridge: See Bridges, Grave
Grayburn, Lt John 197, 200, 228–230, 234,
    241–243, 257
Greenall, Lt Peter 127–128
Green, Lt Alan 266
Greenwalt, Lt Howard 116
Gregg, Lt Frank 75, 76, 77
Gregory-Hood, Major Alec 119
Griffin, Sgt Frank 60
Groenewoud, Jacobus 201, 238–240
Groesbeek 3, 8, 10, 37, 94, 105, 107, 114,
    116, 121, 153–154, 156–172, 210,
    219, 256, 287, 296, 298
Groesbeek Heights 3, 10, 105, 107, 153,
    156–159, 168, 296, 298

Gronert, Pvt Claude 216
Gronert, Pvt Tommy 216
Groote Barrier 14, 16
Gropp, SS-Lt Heinz 190, 222
Groups: See Regiments
Grünewald, SS-Major Adam 102
Gueymard, Capt Adolph 97
Gullixon, S/Sgt Roger 98
Gwatkin, Brig Norman 20, 178

H

Hackett, Brig John 188, 198, 204, 211,
    217–218, 220–224, 261, 266–267,
    291, 300, 304
Hakewell-Smith, Maj-Gen Edmund 297
Hall, Pvt John 125
Hamilton, Lt Ian 81
Hankey, Lt-Col JBA 87
Hansmann, SS-Major Otto 289
Harder, SS-Lt A 194, 250
Harmel, SS-Col Heinz 8–10, 107, 125,
    152–153, 230, 234, 244–245, 254,
    301
Harmisch, Oberstlt Siegfried 155
Harper, Col Joseph 57
Harper, Cpl John 25
Harper, Fl-Sgt James 41
Harris, Air Chief Marshal Arthur 175
Harris, Capt Wesley 139, 150
Harrison, Lt-Col Willard 107–108, 151
Harwick, Capt Robert 281
Harzer, SS-Lt-Col Walter 7, 176, 250, 254,
    261, 301
Hatert 108, 111, 154–155
Haus Robert Janssen 128, 143
Hay, Capt John 206
Heathcoat-Amory, Lt-Col Derick 267
Heathcote, Lt Keith 18
Hechtel 14–17, 25
Heelsum 186, 192, 198, 206–207
Heeswijk Castle 50, 89–92
Helgeson, Capt Thomas 110
Helle, SS-Major Paul 208–210
Hell's Highway x, 77–101, 298: See
    also Corridor, The
Henderson, S/Sgt Alvin 140–141
Henke, Oberst Fritz 115, 120
Hereford, Gerald Page 147
Hermann, Oberstlt Harry 155–156, 159–160
Heteren 210, 284, 288–289

Heumen 114, 155
Heylinger, Lt Frederick 291
Hicks, Brig Philip 186, 189, 220, 248,
        300–301
Hikspoors, Willem 61
Hills
    Duivelsberg 158, 172–174
    Kiekberg 155, 158
    Sint Jansberg 155
Holcomb, Lt Joseph 129
Holmes, Pvt Eric 161
Hooper, Lt Wallace 92
Hopkins, Lt Harry 179
Horrocks, Lt-Gen Brian 4–5, 14, 18, 22–23,
        36, 85, 120–121, 133–134, 171, 181,
        248, 253, 277–278, 301, 303
Horton, Major Oliver 37, 59, 96, 292, 293
Hotel Bilderberg 208
Hotel de Wereld 294–295
Hotel Dreyeroord 251, 259–260
Hotel Schoonoord 261–263
Hotel Sionshof 116, 134
Hotel Tafelberg 204, 263
Hotel Vreewijk 262
Hotel Wolfheze 191, 208, 219
Howard, Lt Harry 94
Hummel, Hptmn Hans 234
Hunnerpark 115–119, 125–129, 134, 136,
        141–144
Hunt, Lt-Col P 68
Hyslop, Sgt Eric 260

I

Incredible Patrol 210
Information boards
    Forgotten Bombing 282–283
    Slag von Arnhem 275
Information Northern Perimeter Route 255
    Panel #1 261
    Panel #2 259
    Panel #3 259
    Panel #4 260
    Panel #5 260
    Panel #6 265
Information Perimeter Route 255
    Panel #1 201
    Panel #2 264
    Panel #3 265
    Panel #4 266
    Panel #5 267

Panel #6 275
Panel #7 264
Panel #8 262
Ion, Pvt James 41
Iron Cross 6, 10, 82, 155, 230, 254, 307

J

Jedburgh Team 238
Jedlicka, Pvt Joseph 148
JOE's Bridge: See Bridges, JOE's Bridge
Johannahoeve Farm 198, 218–219, 259–260,
        276
Johnson, Col Howard 48, 79, 81, 85, 92,
        96–97, 211, 288
Johnson, Guardsman Leslie 131
Jones, Capt Robert 63–64
Jones, Lt AGC 130–131, 152
Jungwirth, Major Hans 76–77, 81, 86–88,
        95–96

K

Kaiser, Major James L 164
Kampschmidt, 2nd Lt Omar 98
Kappel, Capt Carl 121–125, 138–139
Kasteel Henkenshage 75
Keizer Karelplein 115, 126, 134–136, 139,
        156
Keizer Lodewijkplein 115–119, 126–127,
        140–141
Keizer Traianusplein: See Keizer Lodewijk-
        plein
Kerutt, Major Helmut 17–18, 31–32
Kiley, Capt John 58
Kingston, Capt David 89
Kinnard, Lt Col Harry 75–81, 85–86, 89–91
Kleve 7, 172
Knight, Lance-Sgt 131
Knight's Cross 6, 10, 33, 82, 129, 155, 233,
        250, 254
Knoche, Major Wilhelm 209
Koevering grain mill 95
Kopka, Oberlt Franz 84–88, 95
Krafft, SS-Major Josef 190–193, 195, 197,
        205, 208, 211, 218–219, 255
Krause, Lt Col Edward 167
Kronenburgerpark 126–127, 136–137
Krueger, SS-Capt 128
Krzeczkowski, Trooper Mieczysław 161
Kuehl, Capt Delbert 150
Kuehne, Major Kurt 250

Kühne, SS-Lt Hermann 209
Kussin, Genmaj Friedrich 208

L

Lamm, Lt George 135, 139
Lampard, Lt Duncan 16, 18
Landing Zones: *See* Drop/Landing Zones
Lane, Major TB 225
Langton, Capt Roland , 133, 133
LaPrade, Lt Col James 51, 54–55, 95–96
LaRiviere, Lt Richard 124–125, 152
Lathbury, Brig Gerald 186, 192–195,
        217, 220, 223–224, 254, 261–262,
        300–301, 304
Layman, Lt Fred 135
Lea, Lt-Col George 199, 223
Legacie, Pvt James 138–139
Lennie, Flying Officer Thomas 282
Lent 115, 125, 128, 130–132, 148, 151–153,
        176–178, 182
Leopard Route 186, 192, 205
Leopoldsburg 5–6, 17, 21–25, 36, 300
Levien, Lt Robert 216
Lewis, Major RPC 192, 194, 208, 230–231,
        243
Liberation Route
    Marker #2 113
    Marker #4 161
    Marker #9 166
    Marker #14 137
    Marker #15 146
    Marker #16 145
    Marker #17 139
    Marker #19 286
    Marker #20 206
    Marker #21 268
    Marker #22 240
    Marker #25 205
    Marker #26 224
    Marker #30 291
    Marker #31 185
    Marker #35 113
    Marker #40 201
    Marker #41 259
    Marker #48 134
    Marker #54 210
    Marker #55 210
    Marker #67 284
    Marker #80 293
    Marker #100 27

    Marker #101 28
    Marker #104 29
    Marker #105 30
    Marker #108 35
    Marker #109 34
    Marker #110 58
    Marker #112 61
    Marker #113 52
    Marker #114 56
    Marker #115 69
    Marker #116 95
    Marker #117 47
    Marker #120 99
    Marker #121 91
    Marker #123 112
    Marker #128 94
    Marker #129 96
    Marker #130 68
    Marker #203 43
Lifts
    Final Lifts 277
    First Lift 52, 188, 197, 209
    Fourth Lift 276–277
    Second Lift 51, 65, 156, 165, 168, 188,
        197–198, 205
    Third Lift 217–219, 276
Lindemans, Christiaan 5
Lindquist, Col Roy 105, 115, 154, 156
Lindsey, Pvt Thomas 55
Lion Route 188, 194, 197, 200, 214, 217,
        225
Lippert, SS-Col Hans 198, 267
Livesey, Capt TJ 243
Logan, Dr James 236
Logtenburg Woods 87, 96
Lonsdale, Major Richard 250, 251, 256, 269,
        272–273
Lord, Flight Lt David 257
Luce, Brig GHL 179
Luijkx, Adri 35

M

Maastricht 6, 36, 42
Mackay, Capt Eric 230, 243–244
Mackey, Lt Patrick 210
Malden 108, 111
Mandle, 1st Lt William 139
Manners, Charles John: *See* Rutland, Duke of
Mann, Pfc Joseph 67–68, 69
Marcus, Lt Maurice 110

Mariaplein 116, 140
Martin, Capt Randall 274
Matthews, Trooper Stanley 74
Maybury, Cpl Arthur 246
McAuliffe, Brig Gen Anthony 77, 97
McCardie, Lt-Col Derek 219, 220, 225
McDermont, Lt Andrew 197, 228, 234, 240
McGraw, Pvt Robert 108
McGregor, Lt Joseph 76
McMorries, Sgt Melton 287–288
McRory, Lance-Sgt James 72
Medals / Awards
  Distinguished Conduct Medal 132, 181
  Distinguished Flying Cross 99, 257
  Distinguished Flying Medal 99
  Distinguished Service Cross 43, 69, 82,
      87, 91, 97, 110, 111, 116, 135, 137,
      140, 148, 150, 151, 160, 165, 168,
      170, 210, 238, 262, 288
  Distinguished Service Order 227, 237,
      265, 270, 272, 279
  Medal of Honor 37, 67, 69, 137, 151, 168,
      179, 240
  Militarie Willemsorde: See Military Order
      of the Knights of Willem
  Military Cross 17, 29, 131, 179, 195, 213,
      223, 227, 236, 237, 238, 243, 272,
      132
  Military Medal 72, 119, 132
  Military Order of the Knights of Willem
      147, 150
  Presidential Unit Citation 132, 147
  Victoria Cross 25, 132, 212, 240, 242,
      256, 270
Megellas, Lt James 151, 170–171
Meiklejohn, Flying Officer Robert Bruce 38
Melchers, Anton 163
Meyers, Lt James 126, 136–137
Michaelis, Col John 50, 63, 65, 72–73, 81,
      82
Michelman, Lt Isaac 136–137
Middleton, Lt Martin 109
Mielekamp, Jan 246–247
Mier, Lt Harry 93
Millar, 2nd Lt John 41
Miller, Capt Walter 57
Miller, Lt Harold 155
Millsaps, Capt Woodrow 136
Model, GenFM Walter 7, 10–11, 21, 50, 77,
      107, 152, 154, 156–157, 190, 201,
      204, 252, 263, 300, 301, 304
Molenhoek 105, 154, 159
Moller, Lt John A 119
Moller, Lt John C 116
Möller, SS-Capt Hans 190, 216
Montgomery, FM Bernard Law 1–6, 10, 43,
      50, 294, 296–297, 300–301, 304
Monuments/Memorials
  1st Airborne Recce Squadron 265
  4th Battalion of the Dorset Regiment 269
  5th Battalion, Duke of Cornwall's Light
      Infantry 286
  7th Armored Division 47
  7th Battalion, Hampshire Regiment 287
  15th Scottish Infantry Div 68
  19 September Bombing of Eindhoven 35
  26th Regiment of Infantry Pieta 113
  44th Royal Tank Regiment 74
  50-mm PaK 38 antitank gun 143
  50th Anniversary of Dutch Liberation 265
  50th Anniversary of the Grenadier Guards
      145
  51st Highland Division 92
  82nd Airborne Division 113, 166
  101st Airborne Aide Station 292
  101st Airborne Division 58, 182, 288, 291
  501st PIR Geronimo 94
  508th PIR 169
  Airborne Commemorative Posts 204
    Post #1 214
    Post #2 264
    Post #3 225
    Post #5 227
    Post #6 263
    Post #7 244
    Post #8 267
    Post #9 273
  Airborne House (2nd Para Bn) 226
  Airborne Memorial (1st AB) 206
  Airborne Memorial (506th PIR) 63
  Airborne Memorial Park (1st AB) 240
  Airborne Monument (1st AB) 244
  Airborne Monument Ginkel Heath 209
  Airborne Plaque Sionshof 134
  Air Despatch 259–260
  Arnhem Bombing 244
  Arnhem Executions 246
  Baskeyfield Plaque 256
  Battle of Anhem Bridge Tablet 241
  Belgian Prisoners of War 146

Bergeijk Gate of Liberation 27
Betuwe Crashes 292
Border Regiment 268
Browning Landing Site 165
C-47 Memorial 99
Children Remembrance Wall 146
Cole, Lt Col Robert 69
Company A, 506th PIR 55
Company B, 502nd PIR 74
Crossroads, The 290
Deelen Airbase 203
De Schommel 146
De Vleugel 185
Elst Executed Hostages 185
First Canadian Army 166
Fusilladeplaats 102
Gavin, Gen James 166
Glider LZ 'S' 205
Grave Bridge 111
Groenewoud Park 238–239
Groesbeek Evacuating Civilians 163
Groesbeek signboards 163–164, 167
Heelsum Airborne 207
Heeswijk Airborne 91
Horrocks, Gen Brian 36
Horton, Major Oliver 293
Irish Guards 27
IX Troop Carrier Command 53
Joe Mann Cross 67
Joe Mann Memorial 69
John Frostbrug 242
John Frost Headquarters 240
Leopoldsburg 23
Liberation Monument
    Eindhoven 35
    Hoek 29
    Nuenen 62
    Zetten 184
Lion Monument of the National Army 293
Mierlo-Hout 42
Mission Accomplished 166
Monument to the Dutch 73
National Army Memorial 294
Nijmegen Bombing Victims 114
Nijmegen RR Plaques 151
Oosterbeek Airborne 265
Operation Oyster 36
Oude Kerk 273
Overloon Recovered Dead 47
People of Gelderland 201

Philips Employees 36
Polish 1st Independent Parachute Brigade
    286
Remember September 1944 224
Royal Air Force, Commonwealth, and
    American Air Forces 202
Royal Canadian Engineers and British
    Royal Engineers 285
Sint-Michielsgestel Executions 100
Soldier with Flower Girl 265
Son - 50th anniversary 56
Sosabowski, Maj-Gen Stanislaw 286
Statue to Women in War 226
Taylor, Gen Maxwell 36, 96
'The Guardian' 202
'The Parachutist' 202
Valkov Rulers 145
van Hoof, Jan 137, 143, 147
Waal Crossing 147–148
Mook 8, 107, 114, 154–161
Morgan, Capt Stanley 292
Morgan, Pvt Stephen 242
Morrison, Capt James 260
Morrow, Edward R 153
Müller, Hauptmann Willi 14, 15
Munford, Major Denis 232
Muri, Pfc Leo 125, 150
Murray, Major Douglas 228, 230
Museums
    Airborne Museum 'Hartenstein' 200–202,
        264
    Arnhem Museum 222
    Betuwe War Museum 'The Island' 1944 –
        1945 288
    Beverlo Military Camp 23
    Freedom Museum 167–168
    Graafs Kazematten 112
    K-Block 23, 24
    National Liberation Museum 1944-1945:
        See Freedom Museum
    'No Man's Land' Museum 182
    Overloon War Museum 46
    War Museum 40–45 Arnhem 202
    Wings of Liberation Museum 69–70
Muszynski, Pfc Walter 148

N

Nau, Cpl Charles 110
Nederrijn: See Rivers, Nederiijn
Neerpelt 17, 82

Neill, Major William 265
Nelson, Lt Col Clarence 87
Neville, Capt John 116–117, 124–125,
    136–137
Nickrent, S/Sgt Roy 72
Nijmegen ix–x, 4, 8–11, 21–22, 77, 85,
    97, 99, 105–108, 113, 114–154,
    156–162, 168, 171–175, 176–179,
    185, 190, 215, 228, 233, 244, 248,
    250–251, 253, 277, 279, 282, 288,
    291, 298–301
Nijmegen Post Office 139
Nijnsel 70
Normandy ix, x, 1, 3, 7, 10, 14, 17, 18, 20,
    28, 48, 55, 57, 62, 68, 69, 72, 82, 89,
    91, 95, 105, 146, 154, 165, 171, 174,
    176, 186, 188, 190, 211, 233, 255,
    287, 301, 303
North German Plain 7
Nuenen 62–63
Nunn, Lance-Cpl Sydney 264

O

O'Brien, Pvt John 72
O'Cock, Capt Michael 18
O'Connor, Gen Richard 298
Oelkers, SS-Capt Heinrich 287–288
Olland 72, 74
Oosterbeek ix, 11, 12, 85, 89, 101, 107, 161,
    179, 181, 190, 194–197, 198–201,
    205–206, 211, 214–216, 219, 223,
    227, 232, 238–239, 248–275, 285,
    293–294, 277–279
Oosterbeek-Lang train station 215–216
Oosterhout 120, 175, 178–179, 184
Operations
  Aintree 43
  Argument 146
  Berlin 253
  Bruno 63, 145
  Comet 3, 186
  Englandspiel 31
  Goodwood 14, 17, 82
  Greif 26
  Market-Garden ix, xi, 1, 4, 5, 10–13,
      21, 26, 34, 36–37, 42–43, 48, 63,
      66, 70, 76–77, 89, 99, 105, 107,
      110–111, 114–115, 133, 163–164,
      176, 182, 184–185, 186, 200, 202,
      209, 237–238, 254, 277, 291,
  296–297, 301
  Overlord 48
  Oyster 36
  Pegasus 165, 204, 210, 227, 238, 244,
      262, 265, 268, 290
  Veritable 168, 169, 171
Opheusden 37, 288–289, 291–292
Order of Battle
  Allied Forces 311–317
    1st Airborne Division 314
    1st Airlanding Brigade 315
    1st Parachute Brigade 314
    4th Parachute Brigade 315
    21st Army Group 311
    82nd Airborne Division 317
    101st Airborne Division 316
    Guards Armoured Division 313
    Polish 1st Independent Parachute
        Brigade 315
    XXX Corps 312
  German Forces 318–326
    59th Infantry Division 323
    Division von Tettau 326
    First Fallschirmjäger Army 320
    Kampfgruppe Chill 322
    Kampfgruppe Hohenstaufen 325
    Kampfgruppe Krafft 323
    Kampfgruppe Spindler 324
    Kampfgruppe von Tettau 326
    Kampfgruppe Walther 321
    Korps Feldt 323
    LXXXVI Corps 321
    OB West 318–319
    Panzer Brigade 107 324
    Sperrverband Harzer 325
    Wehrkreis VI 323, 326
Osborne, Major Charles 267
Oude Kerk 201, 204, 207, 232, 248, 253,
    255, 256, 269–274
Overasselt 108–109, 113

P

Pacey, Sgt Cyril 130
Palmer, Lt Michael 33
Pannerden 107, 115, 133, 133
Parker, Major Harry 181
Partizanen Actie Nederland 35
Patton, George S Jr 1, 237
Paulushof 52, 53
Payton-Reid, Lt-Col Robert 248, 259

Peel, Major David 16–17
Petersen, SS-Sgt Emil 232
Philips Electronics 34, 101
Phillips, Capt Robert 92, 284
Phillp, Major John 220
Philp, Sgt-Maj Reg 181
'Piccadilly Filly' 38
Piron, Bvt Lt-Col Jean-Baptiste 21, 281, 292
Plasmolen 155, 165
Polish Army Units
    10th Polish Dragoons 161
Poppe, Gen Lt Walter 10, 50, 65
Pott, Major John 213
PoW Camps
    Oflag 79 215, 216, 243
    Oflag VIIB 195, 260
Powierz, Flight Lt Tadeusz 27
Prager, S/Sgt Clarence 164–165
Prescott, Lt Peter 126
Presnell, Lt George 160
Prinzhor, Oberlt Hans-Friedrich 145
Puhalski, Lt Henry 79
Purple Heart 55, 77, 110, 124, 129, 132, 150,
    151, 154, 165

Q

Quatre Bras 262
Queripel, Capt Lionel 206, 211, 212, 257

R

Recriminations 296–302
Redwood, Flying Officer Charles 38
Reichswald Forest 105–107, 133, 154,
    156–158, 164–165, 168, 172
Reinhard, Gen d. Inf Hans 17
Reinhold, SS-Major Leo 115, 176, 232–233
Reithorst 105, 155, 156
Rendezvous with Destiny 97
Renkum 186, 190, 198, 206, 253, 254, 289,
    291
Rhine: See Rivers, Nederrijn
Richards, Capt David 181
Richardson, Capt Beverly 109
Richter, SS-Capt Friedrich 82
Rider, Tech/5 Jack 98
Ridgway, Lt Gen Matthew 3, 105, 301
Riethorst 155
Rijn Pavilion 192–195, 200, 217, 223, 192
Ringsdorf, SS-Cpl Alfred 230
Rivers

Aa 10, 48, 75, 79, 92, 98
Dommel 3, 10, 29–30, 35, 50, 57, 61, 70,
    71, 73, 74
Linge 13, 182
Maas 3–4, 10, 41, 43, 46, 92, 105–109,
    111–112, 114, 116, 153–155, 157,
    160, 171–172
Meuse: See Maas
Nederrijn 3–4, 11, 13, 186, 190, 194–196,
    200, 214–215, 220–222, 253,
    267–268, 275, 276–277, 279–284,
    287–291, 298
Tongelreep 21, 31–33, 59
Waal ix, 7, 10, 105–107, 114, 120–125,
    134, 137–139, 147–153, 156–159,
    170, 175, 176, 182, 278, 289, 291,
    298, 301
Roberts, Maj-Gen George 44
Robinson, Sgt Peter 130–132, 152
Robson, Sgt Cyril 232
Roestel, SS-Capt Franz 29, 32, 82
Rosen, Capt Robert 119, 143–145
Rowland, Pvt Hollis 287
Ruhr ix, 1, 3, 7, 41, 304
Russel, 1st Lt Whitney 139
Russell, Lt David 225
Rutland, Capt the Duke of 119

S

Sabelspoort 247
Sampson, Father Francis 89
Savell, Lt William 129
Schaeffer, Lt John 109
Schelde estuary 1, 50, 172, 297
Scherbening, GenLt Gerd 154
Schijndel 72–73, 79–80, 84–86, 89–90, 95,
    100
Schmitz, 1st Lt Raymond 97
Schwappacher, SS-Capt Oskar 115–116,
    120, 123, 128
Seaton, Lance-Cpl Joseph 29
Shelswell, Sgt Ernie 241
's-Hertogenbosch 50
Sherwood, Pvt Robert 60
Shipley, Sgt RF 269
Shulman, 2nd Lt Herbert 98
Sicherheitsdienst 226
Siebert, Flight Lt John 60
Siegfried Line 3, 308
Sievers, GenLt Karl 6, 14

Silver Star 32, 37, 43, 71, 72, 77, 79, 108,
110, 124, 129, 132, 135, 148, 150,
151, 154, 165, 170, 210, 211, 285
Silvester, Maj Gen Lindsay 43
Simonds, Lt-Gen Guy 103
Sims, 1st Lt Hugo 210
Sims, Lt Edward 124–125, 152
Sink, Col Robert 50–51, 53, 55, 59, 62, 84,
87
Sint-Elisabethshof 190, 195–197, 199,
204, 217, 222–225, 236–237, 252,
261–262
Sint-Eusebius Kerk 245
Sint Lidwina Hospital 92
Sint-Michielsgestel 100–101
Sint Nicolaaskapel 144
Sint-Oedenrode 10, 48, 50, 56, 63, 70–75,
84, 85, 87, 95, 253, 282
Slob, Lt Adriaan 128
Smith, 1st Lt James 119, 129
Smith, Capt Taylor 116
Smith, Lt Gen Walter Bedell 6
Smith, Pvt Homer 60
Smit, Lt Morton 71
Smyth, Lt-Col Kenneth 198, 204, 211,
217–218, 263
Snodgrass, Lt Richard 76
Sobocinski, Capt W 277
Son 3, 10–11, 48–56, 58, 61–63, 66–67, 73,
75, 85, 282, 298, 300
Sonnenstuhl, SS-Major Hans-Georg 230
Sosabowski, Maj-Gen Stanislaw 4–5, 188,
275, 276–279, 286, 297, 303
Soviet Army Units
Red Army 21
Sperrlinie Spindler 198–199, 211–213, 217
Spindler, SS-Lt-Col Ludwig 190, 195, 197,
199, 211–213, 217, 220, 250, 252,
254–255
Stach, Capt Stanfield 81
Stackhouse, Pvt Wendell 73
Stanley-Clarke, Lt John 16
Stanley, Major HF 126
Stefanich, Capt Anthony 165
Stoner, Pvt Benjamin 98
Strayer, Major Robert 59
Strong, Kenneth 6
Student, Gen Oberst Kurt 304, 305
Student, GenObt Kurt 6, 10, 43, 50, 77, 82,
101, 198, 279

Sunsetmarch 139
Swales, Major Edwin 25

T

Tabor, Lt David 31, 33
Tanks (on display)
Churchill 46
Cromwell 46
Crusader 46
Panther 46
Sherman 46
Sherman M4A2 25
Sherman M4A4 'Firefly' 22
Sherman M4 tank 'Argyll' 201
T34 46
Tatham-Warter, Major Digby 197, 214, 237,
291
Taylor, Capt Willy 223
Taylor, Lt-Col George 181, 278
Taylor, Lt James 259
Taylor, Maj Gen Maxwell 3, 36, 48, 51, 57,
65–66, 77, 85, 87, 96, 277, 301, 303
Taylor, S/Sgt John 60
Ter Horst house 270, 274–275
Ter Horst, Jan 274, 300
Ter Horst, Kate 244, 274–275, 300
Ter Horst, Sophie 244, 274
Thomas, Maj-Gen Sir Gwilym Ivor 179, 298
Thompson, Lt-Col WFK 248, 250, 251, 255
Thompson, Lt John 108–110, 112
Thorne, Major George 117–119
Thorogood, Trooper John 74
Tidd, Sgt Roy 108
Tiger Route 188, 192–194, 208, 217, 225
Tilly, Lt-Col Gerald 279
Timothy, Major 'Tim' 195
Toman, Sgt John 148
Tourist Offices
Airborne at the Bridge 200, 238
Information Center WW2 Nijmegen 134
VVV Berg en Dal 159
VVV Eindhoven 34
VVV Nijmegen 134
VVV Oosterbeek 202
VVV Sint-Oedenrode 73
Towle, Private John 178–179
Trenches
Reconstructed trench 294
Trotter, Major John 130
Tucker, Col Reuben 105, 108, 113, 120–122,

125, 133, 139
Turner, Lt Billy 79

U

Uden 48, 74, 77, 82–83, 95–97, 99–100, 103
Urquhart, Brig Robert 4–5, 11, 181, 186,
    192–195, 217, 219, 220–224, 248–
    253, 267, 276–277, 300–301, 303
Urquhart, Major Brian 5, 297
US Army Units: *See also* Orders of Battle -
    Appendix D
  Air Corps
    53rd Troop Carrier Wing 52
    82nd Troop Carrier Squadron 40
    83rd Troop Carrier Squadron 40
    86th Troop Carrier Squadron 40
    314th Troop Carrier Group 182
    315th Troop Carrier Group 113, 182
    316th Troop Carrier Group 113
    442nd Troop Carrier Group 98
    IX Troop Carrier Command 53, 276
  Battalions
    80th Airborne Antiaircraft 124, 156
    81st Airborne Antiaircraft 57, 82, 97
    307th Airborne Engineer 139, 156
    319th Glider Field Artillery 156, 170
    320th Glider Field Artillery 156
    321st Glider Field Artillery 281
    326th Airborne Engineers 48, 56, 63,
        75, 77, 98
    376th Parachute Field Artillery 121,
        139, 163, 169
    377th Parachute Field Artillery 281
    907th Glider Field Artillery 87, 93,
        94
  Corps
    XVIII Airborne 3
  Divisions
    7th Armored 43, 47, 87
    82nd Airborne 3, 10, 12, 105–175,
        277, 301
    101st Airborne 3, 10, 12, 17, 18,
        21, 33, 35–36, 40, 48–104,
        109–111, 279–293, 280, 285,
        288, 291, 292, 298
  Regiments
    325th Glider Infantry 113, 158, 173,
        277
    327th Glider Infantry 51, 57, 66, 84,
        85, 97, 281

501st PIR 48–50, 75, 81–82, 85–86,
    94, 96–98, 210, 281, 284,
    287–289
502nd PIR 50–52, 66, 68, 70–72,
    74–75, 81–82, 87
504th PIR 105, 107–108, 120, 133,
    147, 168–169, 175, 178, 289
505th PIR 105, 116–119, 126,
    153–159, 164–165, 167
506th PIR 50–53, 55, 58–59, 63–64,
    77, 85–87, 95, 97, 99, 254,
    280, 281, 291, 292
508th PIR 105, 111, 115–116, 134,
    153–154, 156–159, 167–170,
    172–174
SHAEF 6

V

Valkenswaard 17–21, 29–33, 38–39, 250,
    298
Valkhof 114, 126–129, 134, 141–145
Valkof Citadel: *See* Bunker, Valkof
Vandeleur, Lt-Col Giles 17, 121, 178
Vandeleur, Lt-Col John 16–17, 20, 177
van der Poll, Herman 116, 136
Vandervoort, Lt Col Benjamin 116, 119,
    120, 129–130, 140–141, 153
van Hees, Geert 115, 119, 135
van Hoof, Jan 137, 143, 147
van Poyck, Capt Walter 108–109
Veghel 3, 10, 48–50, 52, 58, 74–91, 95–101,
    109, 282
Venray 43, 47
Vietnam War 89, 303
Villa Belvoir 129, 140–141
Vlasto, Lt Robert 215, 241
Vlokhoven Tower 58
Vogel, SS-Lt Ernst 232, 234
von Allwörden, SS-Capt Klaus 190, 195,
    211
von der Heydte, Oberstlt Friedrich Freiherr
    17, 21, 28, 69, 85, 93
von Hoffmann, Oberst Helmut 17, 31
von Maltzahn, Major Berndt-Joachim Frei-
    herr 52, 56–57, 62, 75, 97, 99
von Obstfelder, Gen d. Inf Hans 82
von Plüskow, Major Hans-Albrecht 98
von Rundstedt, GenFM Gerd 6, 10, 50, 56,
    304
von Svoboda, Oberst Hubert 276

von Tettau, GenLt Hans 10, 250, 254, 267
von Zangen, Gen d. Inf Gustav-Adolf 6, 14,
    297
Vught 50, 101–102, 209
VVV: *See* Tourist Offices

W

Waalbrug: *See* Bridges, Waal; *See also* Ni-
    jmegen Road Bridge
Waddy, Major Peter 192, 213
Walcheren 6, 20
Walther, Oberst Erich 21, 85–86
Walton, Brig BB 278
Wandam, Hptmn Siegfried 38
Warren, Lt Col Shields 116–117, 134–135,
    154, 168
Warr, Major Peter 263
Watkins, Capt Bill 87
Weapons: *See also* Tanks (on display)
    17-pounder antitank 201–202
    50-mm PaK 38 antitank gun 143
    Armored troop carrier 104
    British 25-pounder 240
    V-1 flying bomb 47
Weatherby, Capt Christopher 62
Weber, Gefreiter Horst 245
Weber, Hptmn Willi 203
Wehrmacht-befehlshaber in den Niederlande:
    See Army Forces in the Netherlands
Weinberg, Lt Stanley 155
Weller, 2nd Lt Millford 55
Westerbouwing Heights 250, 267, 275, 279,
    285
West Wall 3, 7, 10
Whistler, Maj-Gen Lashmer 44
Wierzbowski, 2nd Lt Edward 64–67
Wignall, Major FEB 31
Wilde, Capt Russel 116
Williams, Flight Sgt Bruce 282
Windmills
    Groesbeek Zuid Molen 164
    Sint Antoniusmolen 93
Wingard, Sgt Jacob 94–95
Winters, Capt Richard 62, 289–290
Wolfheze 113, 186–189, 191–192, 195, 198–
        199, 201, 205–206, 208, 211–212,
        218–219, 232, 248, 267
Wolfswinkel 53, 96, 99
Worrowski: *See* Wossowski
Wossowski, Oberlt Artur 268

Wray, Lt Waverly 136–137
Wrottesley, Capt Lord Richard 179
Wurst, Sgt Spencer 129
Wyler 154, 156–159, 167, 169–171, 172

Y

Young, Lt Arthur 179
Young, Major Sidney 179

Z

Zander, Lt Col Helmut 284
Zetten 184, 281
Ziebrecht, SS-Lt Karl 228, 243
Zipf, Tech/Sgt Ralph 98
Zutphen 7, 188, 230
Zwolanski, Capt Ludwik 251
Zwolle, Dr Jan 246